To Mother Saint Luke
with every good wish and
a cordial "God bless you"

Father Kearney

22 August, 1950

THE EXEMPTION OF RELIGIOUS IN CHURCH LAW

THE
EXEMPTION OF RELIGIOUS
IN CHURCH LAW

By JOSEPH D. O'BRIEN, S.J., S.T.D., J.C.D.

BY
1935
O37

THE BRUCE PUBLISHING COMPANY
MILWAUKEE

Imprimi potest: Franciscus J. Seeliger, S.J., Praepositus Provinciae Californiae
Nihil obstat: H. B. Ries, Censor librorum
Imprimatur: ✠ Moyses E. Kiley, Archiepiscopus Milwaukiensis

Die 18 Augusti, 1942

PREFACE

The Fathers of the Third Plenary Council of Baltimore rejoiced at the peaceful relationship existing between the secular clergy and the religious Orders, and to guarantee its continuance thought it opportune to have extended to this country the Constitution *Romanos Pontifices* of Leo XIII, which defined the status of exempt religious with respect to local Ordinaries.[1]

In order to maintain this spirit of unity and to work with effectiveness for the salvation of souls, both religious and Ordinaries have at the present time the same need of an accurate knowledge of the laws of the Code which determine their mutual relationship.

The present treatise, it is hoped, will help to advance that knowledge, for it purposes to explain the canonical provisions regulating the exemption of Regulars and of other religious who enjoy a like privilege.

Special consideration is paid to several elements which, on account of their bearing on practically all matters pertaining to exemption, seem to demand particular attention. Thus, Part II of this work contains a rather lengthy discussion of the nature, kinds, and extent of jurisdictional power possessed by local and religious Ordinaries; and Part IV offers an analysis of the norm regulating limitations of exemption and an explanation of its application to the general exemption and to the special exemptive rights enjoyed by particular religious institutes. Throughout the treatise the passive exemption possessed by religious is carefully distinguished from active exemption, and general exemption from special exemptive rights. Greater precision in determining the extension and limitations of exemption seems to result from close adherence to these distinctions.

The third part of the treatise, which deals with the extension of exemption, explains the amplitude of this privilege relative to persons, whether physical or moral, to places and to things. As the greatest number of cases of exemption pertain to things, it has been thought expedient to treat of them in accordance with the divisions and sequence employed in the Third Book of the Code.

It is hoped that this work may aid in furthering the knowledge of the matter under discussion, for a better understanding of Church law promotes its observance and consequently the well-being of subjects, which is the very purpose of law.

[1] Cf. Conc. Pl. Balt. III, 86.

v

BIBLIOGRAPHY

SOURCES

Acta Apostolicae Sedis, Romae, 1909.
Acta et Decreta Concilii Plenarii Baltimorensis Tertii, Baltimorae, 1896.
Acta Sanctae Sedis, 41 vols., Romae, 1865–1908.
Bullarium Romanum, 24 vols., Editio Taurinensis, 1857–1872.
Codex Juris Canonici Pii X Pontificis Maximi Jussu Digestus Benedicti Papae XV Auctoritate Promulgatus, Romae, 1917.
Codex Juris Canonici Fontes (Gasparri-Serédi), 9 vols., Romae, 1923–1939.
Collectanea in Usum Secretariae Sacrae Congregationis Episcoporum et Regularium (Cura A. Bizzarri), Romae, 1885.
Collectanea S. Congregationis de Propaganda Fide, 2 vols., Romae, 1907.
Collectio Declarationum Sacrae Congregationis Cardinalium Sacri Concilii Tridentini Interpretum (Zamboni), 4 vols., Atrebati, 1860.
Corpus Juris Canonici, 2 vols., Lipsiae, 1922.
Decreta Authentica Congregationis Sacrorum Rituum, 5 vols., Romae, 1898; Appendix I, Romae, 1912; Appendix II, Romae, 1927.
Institutum Societatis Jesu, 3 vols., Florentiae, 1892.
Sacrorum Conciliorum Nova et Amplissima Collectio (Mansi), 59 vols., Parisiis, 1901–1927.
Synopsis Actorum S. Sedis in Causa Societatis Jesu, Vol. I, Florentiae, 1887; Vol. II, Lovanii, 1895.

AUTHORS

Alphonsus, S., *Theologia Moralis* (cura Gaudé), Romae, 1905-1912.
Augustine, O.S.B., *A Commentary on the New Code of Canon Law,* 8 vols., St. Louis, Mo., 1918–1922.
—— *Rights and Duties of Ordinaries,* St. Louis, Mo., 1924.
—— *The Canonical and Civil Status of Parishes in the U. S.,* St. Louis, Mo., 1926.
—— *Liturgical Law,* St. Louis, Mo., 1931.
Ayrinhac, S. S., *Administrative Legislation,* New York, 1930.
—— *Constitution of the Church,* New York, 1929.
—— *General Legislation,* New York, 1930.
—— *Legislation on the Sacraments,* New York, 1928.
—— *Marriage Legislation,* New York, 1934.
—— *Penal Legislation,* New York, 1936.
Bakalarczyk, Congr. Marian, *De Novitiatu, Dissertatio,* Washington, D. C., 1927.

Balmès, O.M.I., *Les Religieux à Voeux Simples d'Après Le Code*, 2 ed., Lyon, 1921.

Barbosa, A., *Opera Omnia*, Lugduni, 1645.

Bastien, O.S.B., *Directoire Canonique à L'Usage Des Congrégations à Voeux Simples*, 4 ed., Bruges, 1933.

Battandier, *Guide Canonique Pour Les Constitutions Des Instituts à Voeux Simples*, 6 ed., Paris, 1923.

Benedictus XIV, *De Synodo Dioecesana*, Venetiis, 1792.

——— *De Sacrosancto Missae Sacrificio*, Romae, 1748.

——— *Institutiones Ecclesiasticae*, Romae, 1750.

——— *Opera Omnia*, Prati, 1839.

Beringer-Steinen, S.J., *Les Indulgences*, 2 vols., 4 ed., Paris.

Berutti, O.P., *Institutiones Juris Canonici*, Vol. III, *De Religiosis*, Taurini, 1936.

Besson, J., "*Erection et Exemption Des Maisons Religieuses*," N.R.T., 1908, pp. 587–592.

Biederlack-Führich, S.J., *De Religiosis*, Oeniponte, 1919.

Blat, O.P., *Commentarium Textus Codicis Juris Canonici*, Romae, 1921.

Bondini, O.F.M.Conv., *De Privilegio Exemptionis*, Romae, 1919.

Borkowski, O.F.M., *De Confraternitatibus Ecclesiasticis* (Dissertatio), Washington, D. C., 1918.

Boudinhon, *La Nouvelle Législation de L'Index*, 2 ed., Paris, 1924.

Bouix, *De Jure Regularium*, 2 vols., Paris, 1883.

Bouscaren, S.J., *The Canon Law Digest*, Vol. I, 1934; Vol. II, 1937; Supplement, Milwaukee, 1941.

Cappello, S.J., *De Visitatione SS. Liminum et Dioceseon*, 2 vols., Romae, 1912.

——— *Summa Juris Canonici*, 3 vols., 2 ed., Romae, 1932.

——— *Summa Juris Publici Ecclesiastici*, 3 ed., Romae, 1932.

——— *Tractatus Canonico — Moralis de Censuris Juxta Codicem*, J.C., Romae, 2 ed., 1933.

——— *Tractatus Canonico — Moralis de Sacramentis*, 3 vols., Romae, 1928–1933.

Castropalao, S.J., *Opus Morale*, Lugduni, 1631.

Cavagnis (Card.), *Institutiones Juris Publici Ecclesiastici*, 4 ed., Romae.

Cespedes, Cler. Reg., *Tractatus de Exemptione Regularium*, Venetiis, 1697.

Chelodi-Bertagnolli, *Jus de Personis*, 2 ed., Trento, 1926.

Chelodi-Dalpiaz, *Jus Poenale*, 4 ed., Trento, 1935.

Chokier, *Tractatus de Jurisdictione Ordinarii in Exemptos*, Coloniae Agrip., 1620.

Choupin, S.J., *Nature et Obligations de L'État Religieux*, 6 ed., Paris, 1928.

Cicognani, A., *Canon Law*, Philadelphia, 1935.

Ciravegna, S.J., *De Societatis Jesu Paupertate, Quaestiones Variae*, Prati, 1892.

Claeys Bouuaert-Simenon, *Manuale Juris Canonici*, 4 ed., Gandae, 1934.

Cocchi, *Commentarium in Codicem J.C.*, 4 ed., Taurinorum Augustae, 1931.

Conte a Coronata, O.F.M.Cap., *De Locis et Temporibus Sacris*, Taurinorum Augustae, 1922.

—— *Institutiones Juris Canonici*, 5 vols., Taurini, 1928.

Creusen, S.J., *Religious Men and Women in the Code*, 3 ed., Milwaukee, 1940.

—— *Epitome Juris Canonici* (Vermeersch-Creusen), 5 ed.

d'Angelo, *La Esenzione dei Religiosi*, Torino, 1929.

D'Annibale, *Summula Theologiae Moralis*, 3 ed., 3 vols., Romae.

Davis, S.J., *Moral and Pastoral Theology*, 4 vols., London, 1936.

De Buck, S.J., *De Exemptione Regularium*, Bruxellis, 1869.

—— *Examen Historicum et Canonicum Libri* R. D. Mariani Verhoeven, Bruxellis, 1847 (De Buck-Tinnebroeck).

De Franchis, *Controversiae Inter Episcopos et Regulares*, Romae, 1656.

Delbene, C. R., *De Immunitate et Jurisdictione Ecclesiastica*, 2 vols., Avenione, 1659.

De Luccia, O.F.M.Cap., *De Jure PP. Minorum S. Francisci Capuccinorum Deciso*, Romae, 1737.

De Meester, *Juris Canonici et Juris Canonico-Civilis Compendium*, Brugis, 1923.

De Peyrinis, Minim., *Opero Omnia*, Lugduni, 1668.

Devoti, *Jus Canonicum Universum Publicum et Privatum*, Romae, 1837.

Donatus, O.P., *Rerum Regularium Praxis Resolutoria*, Coloniae Agrippinae, 1691.

Fagnanus, *Commentaria in Quinque Libros Decretales*, Venetiis, 1752.

Falco, *Introduzione Allo Studio Del "Codex Juris Canonici,"* Torino, 1925.

Fanfani, O.P., *De Jure Parochorum*, 2 ed., Romae, 1936.

—— *De Jure Religiosorum*, 2 ed., Romae, 1935.

Feldhaus, *Oratories, Dissertation*, Washington, D. C., 1927.

Ferrari, Barnab., *De Statu Religioso Commentarium*, 2 ed., Romae, 1899.

Ferraris, O.F.M., *Bibliotheca Canonica Juridica Moralis Theologica (cum additionibus Bucceroni)*, Romae, 1885–1899.

Ferreres, S.J., *Institutiones Canonicae*, 2 ed., 2 vols., Barcinone, 1920.

Fine, S.J., *Juris Regularis Tum Communis Tum Particularis Quo Regitur Societas Jesu Declaratio*, Prati, 1909.

Gardelini, *Decreta Authentica Congregationis Sacrorum Rituum Ex Actis Ejusdem Collecta*, 8 vols., Romae, 1856–1858.

Gasparri, *Tractatus Canonicus de Sacra Ordinatione*, 2 vols., Paris, 1893.

—— *Tractatus Canonicus de Sanctissima Eucharistia*, 2 vols., 1897.

—— *Codicis Juris Canonici Fontes*, 9 vols., Romae, 1926.

Gatticus, Can. Lat., *De Oratoriis et de Usu Altaris Portatilis*, Romae, 1775.

Genicot-Salsmans, S.J., *Institutiones Theologiae Moralis*, 2 vols., ed. 13, Bruxellis, 1936.

Gillet, *La Personnalité Juridique en Droit Ecclésiastique*, Dissertation, Malines, 1927.

Giraldi, *Expositio Juris Pontificii*, Romae, 1839.

Goyeneche, C.M.F., *De Religiosis*, Romae, 1938.

Jansen, *Canonical Provisions for Catechetical Instruction*, Dissertation, Washington, D. C., 1937.

Kahl (alias Calvinus), *Magnum Lexicon Juridicum*, 2 vols., Coloniae Allobrogum, 1759.

Kilker, *Extreme Unction*, St. Louis, Mo., 1927.

Laymann, S.J., *Theologia Moralis*, Monachi, 1630.

Lehmkuhl, S.J., *Theologia Moralis*, Friburgi Brisg., 1910.

Leurenius, S.J., *Forum Ecclesiasticum Seu Jus Canonicum Universum*, Venetiis, 1729.

——— *Forum Beneficiale*, Coloniae, 1742.

Lezana (De), O. C., *Summa Quaestionum Regularium*, 3 Tom., Lugduni, 1678.

Lucidi, *De Visitatione SS. Liminum*, 3 ed., Romae, 1883.

Maire, *Histoire Des Instituts Religieux et Missionnaires*, Paris, 1930.

Many, *Praelectiones De Locis Sacris*, Paris, 1904.

——— *Praelectiones De Missa*, Paris, 1903.

——— *Praelectiones De Sacra Ordinatione*, Paris, 1905.

Maroto, C.M.F., *Institutiones Juris Canonici*, 3 ed., Romae, 1921.

Mayr, O.F.M., *Trismegistus Juris Pontificii Universi*, Augustae Vindelicorum, 1742.

McManus, C.SS.R., *The Administration of Temporal Goods in Religious Institutes*, Dissertation, Washington, D. C., 1937.

Melo, O.F.M., *De Exemptione Regularium Dissertatio*, Washington, D. C., 1921.

Michiels, O.F.M.Cap., *Normae Generales Juris Canonici*, Lublin, 1929.

Miller, *Founded Masses*, Dissertation, Washington, D. C., 1926.

Miranda, O.S.F., *Manuale Praelatorum Regularium*, Coloniae Agrippinae, 1617.

Molitor, O.S.B., *Religiosi Juris Capita Selecta*, Ratisbonae, 1909.

Mullan, S.J., *The Sodality of Our Lady in the Documents*, New York, 1912.

Nervegna, *De Jure Practico Regularium*, Romae, 1900.

Nilles, S.J., *Selectae Disputationes Academicae Juris Ecclesiastici*, Oeniponte, 1886.

Noldin-Schmitt, S.J., *Summa Theologiae Moralis*, 3 vols., Oeniponte, 1935.

Novarius, *Lucerna Regularium*, Neapoli, 1638.

Ojetti, S.J., *Commentarium in Codicem J.C.*, Romae, 1927.

——— *Synopsis Rerum Moralium et Juris Pontificii*, 4 vols., 3 ed., Romae, 1909.

Orth, O.M.C., *The Approbation of Religious Institutes*, Dissertation, Washington, D. C., 1931.

Pallotini, *Collectio Omnium Conclusionum et Resolutionum S.C. Concilii ab Anno 1564 ad Annum 1860*, 17 vols., Romae, 1867–1893.

Palmieri, S.J., *Tractatus de Romano Pontifice*, Prati, 1902.

Papi, S.J., *Religious in Church Law*, New York, 1924.

——— *Religious Profession*, New York, 1918.

——— *The Government of Religious Communities*, New York, 1919.

Pasqualigo, C. R., *De Sacrificio Novae Legis*, Venetiis, 1707.
Pejska, C.SS.R., *Jus Canonicum Religiosorum*, 3 ed., Friburgi, 1927.
Pellizzarius, S.J., *Manuale Regularium*, 2 Tom., Lugduni, 1653 (Index).
—— *Tractatio de Monialibus*, Venetiis, 1680 (Index).
Petra (Card.), *Commentaria ad Constitutiones Apostolicas*, 5 vols., Venetiis, 1741.
Piat, O.F.M. Cap., *Praelectiones Juris Regularis*, 2 vols., 2 ed., Paris, 1898.
Pignatelli, *Consultationes Canonicae*, 11 vols., Coloniae Allobrogum, 1700.
—— *Novissimae Consultationes*, 2 vols., Cosmopoli, 1740.
Piontek, O.F.M., *De Indulto Exclaustrationis Necnon Saecularizationis Dissertatio*, Washington, D. C., 1925.
Pirhing, S.J., *Jus Canonicum*, Venetiis, 1759.
Prümmer, O.P., *Manuale Juris Canonici*, 5 ed., Friburgi Brisg., 1927.
Reiffenstuel, O.S.F., *Jus Canonicum Universum*, Paris, 1864.
Reilly, C.SS.R., *The Visitation of Religious*, Dissertation, Washington, D. C., 1938.
Riposta *per parte dei Regolari ai Dubbi proposti dai RR. Vescovi d'Inghilterra alla S.C. della Propaganda*, Romae, 1881.
Rodericus, O.S.F., *Quaestiones Regulares et Canonicae*, Venetiis, 1616.
Rotarius, Barnab., *Theologia Moralis Regularium*, Bononiae, 1720–1722.
Salmeron, S.J., *Doctrina de Jurisdictionis Episcopalis Origine et Ratione*, Moguntiae, 1871.
Santi-Leitner, *Praelectiones Juris Canonici, 6 vols.*, Ratisbonae, 1898–1901.
Schäfer, O.F.M.,Cap., *Compendium de Religiosis*, Münster, 1931.
Schmalzgrueber, S.J., *Jus Canonicum Universum*, Romae, 1843.
Sole, *De Delictis et Poenis*, Romae, 1920.
Steiger, S.J., *De Jure Ordines et Instituta Nunc Regente (pro manuscripto)*, Angiae, 1908.
Suarez, S.J., *Opera Omnia*, Vives ed., Paris, 1859.
—— *Tractatus De Legibus ac Deo Legislatore*, Neapoli, 1872.
—— *De Censuris*, Lugduni, 1604.
Tamburini, C.V.U.O.S.B., *De Jure Abbatum et Aliorum Praelatorum*, 3 vols., Lugduni, 1640.
—— *De Jure Abbatissarum et Monialium*, Romae, 1638.
Tarquini, S.J., *Juris Ecclesiastici Publici Institutiones*, Romae, 1890.
Thesaurus, S.J., *De Poenis Ecclesiasticis*, Romae, 1831.
Thomassinus, Orat., *Vetus et Nova Ecclesiae Disciplina*, Venetiis, 1752.
Toso, *Ad Codicem Juris Canonici . . . Commentaria Minora*, 2 ed., Romae, 1921.
Van Hove, *Commentarium Lovaniense in Codicem Juris Canonici*, Vol. I, 5 Tom., Mechliniae, 1928.
Vermeersch, S.J., *De Religiosis Institutis et Personis*, 2 ed., Vol. I, 1907, Vol. II, 1909, Brugis.
—— *De Prohibitione et Censura Librorum*, 4 ed., Romae, 1906.
Vermeersch-Creusen, S.J., *Epitome Juris Canonici*, Vol. I, 6 ed., Vols. II, III, 5 ed.

Vidal, S.J., see Wernz-Vidal.
Villada, S.J., *De Confessariis Nostris,* Vallisoleti, 1892.
Vromant, C.I.C.M., *Jus Missionariorum,* 7 vols., Louvain, 1934.
Wernz, S.J., *Jus Decretalium,* 6 Tom., 3 ed., Prati, 1913.
Wernz-Vidal, S.J., *Jus Canonicum,* 7 vols., Romae, 1927–1938.
Wilmers, S.J., *De Christi Ecclesia,* Ratisbonae, 1897.
Woywod, O.F.M., *A Practical Commentary on the Code of Canon Law,* 3 ed., 2 vols., 1929.

PERIODICALS

American Ecclesiastical Review, Philadelphia, 1889–
Commentarium Pro Religiosis, Romae, 1920–
Il Monitore Ecclesiastico, Romae, 1897–
Jus Pontificium, Romae, 1921–
Nouvelle Revue Théologique, Tournai, 1869–
Periodica de Re Morali, Canonica, Liturgica, Brugis, 1905–
Revue des Communautés Religieuses, Louvain-Paris, 1925–
The Clergy Review, London, 1931.

LIST OF ABBREVIATIONS

AAS	*Acta Apostolicae Sedis*
An. J. P.	*Analecta Juris Pontificii*
ASS	*Acta Sanctae Sedis*
Bied.-Führ.	*De Religiosis*, Biederlach-Führich
Biz.	*Collectanea in usum Secretariae Sacre Congregationis Episcoporum et Regularium*, cura A. Bizzarri
Cancell.	The Apostolic Chancery
Cesp.	*Tractatus De Exemptione Regularium*, Cespedes
Cod. Com.	The Pontifical Commission for the Authentic Interpretation of the Code
Coll. P. F.	*Collectanea Sacrae Congregationis de Propaganda Fide* (1907, Romae: 2 vol.).
C.p.R.	*Commentarium pro Religiosis*
Datar.	The Apostolic Datary
Decr. Auth.	*Decreta Authentica S.R.C.*
Epit.	*Epitome Juris Canonici*, Vermeersch-Creusen
E.R.	*The American Ecclesiastical Review*
Fagn.	*Commentaria in Quinque Libros Decretales*, Fagnanus
Fontes	*Codicis Juris Canonici Fontes*, Gasparri-Serédi
Inst. S.J.	*Institutum Societatis Jesu*
J.P.	*Jus Pontificium*
Monit.	*Il Monitore Ecclesiastico*
N.R.T.	*Nouvelle Revue Théologique*
Pell.	*Manuale Regularium*, Pellizzarius
Per.	*Periodica de Re Morali, Canonica, Liturgica*
Peyr.	*De Privilegiis Regularium*, Peyrinis
R.C.R.	*Revue des Communautés Religieuses*
Reiff.	*Jus Canonicum Universum*, Reiffenstuel
Rit. Rom.	*Rituale Romanum* (Romae, 1938: Desclée)
Rod.	*Quaestiones Regulares et Canonicae*, Emm. Rodericus
Rota	The Sacred Roman Rota
S. C. Caer.	S. Congregatio Caeremonialis
S.C.C.	S. Congregatio Concilii
S. C. Consist.	S. Congregatio Consistorialis
S.C.EE.RR.	S. Congregatio Episcoporum Et Regularium
Schmalz.	*Jus Canonicum Universum*, Schmalzgrueber
S. C. Indul.	S. Congregatio Indulgentiarum

S. C. Neg. Eccl. Ext.   S. Congregatio Pro Negotiis Extraordinariis
S. C. Or.   . . . .   S. Congregatio Pro Ecclesia Orientali
S.C.P.F.   . . . . .   S. Congregatio de Propaganda Fide
S. C. Rel.   . . . .   S. Congregatio De Religiosis
S. C. Sacr.   . . . .   S. Congregatio De Disciplina Sacramentorum
S. C. Sem.   . . . .   S. Congregatio De Seminariis Et Universitatibus
Sec. Stat.   . . . .   Secretaria Status
Signatura   . . . .   Signatura Apostolica
S. Off.   . . . . . .   S. Congregatio S. Officii
S. Poen.   . . . . .   Sacra Poenitentiaria Apostolica
S.R.C. .   . . . . .   S. Congregatio Rituum
Tamb.   . . . . .   *De Jure Abbatum Et Aliorum Praelatorum Episcopis Inferiorum*, A. Tamburini
W.-V.   . . . . . .   *Jus Canonicum*, Wernz-Vidal

CONTENTS

PART IV

THE LIMITATIONS OF EXEMPTION

PART I

Preliminary Notions

CHAPTER I

THE MEANING OF TERMS

Exemption, generally speaking, denotes a privilege whereby persons, places, or things are withdrawn from the jurisdiction of a superior to whom they would otherwise be subject.[1]

In canon law exemption implies two things: *withdrawal* from the jurisdictional power of one superior, and *subjection* to some other authority. Thus, Bishops sometimes withdraw certain convents and other pious places from the care of the parish priest and place them under special supervision (cf. can. 464); so also the Holy See removes some persons, such as soldiers, from the charge of local authorities and puts them under the control of military Ordinaries (cf. cc. 216, § 4; 451, § 3).

The chief case of exemption met with in ecclesiastical law is that of religious institutes. By reason of this provision, certain religious organizations are withdrawn from the jurisdiction of local Ordinaries and placed under the immediate authority of the Roman Pontiff alone. The latter ordinarily governs them by means of superiors legitimately chosen from their own numbers. Bishops have no power over them except in the instances expressly specified by law.

Regulars, together with their houses and churches (can. 615), and other religious, such as the Passionists and Redemptorists (cf. can. 500)[2] enjoy the exemption just described. As will be seen, this is likewise true of nuns who by their rules and constitutions are subject to Regular superiors (can. 615).

This treatise is primarily concerned with the exemption of Regulars, yet in the course of its development it deals with many questions involving the exemptive rights and obligations of other religious endowed with special privileges.

Kinds of Exemption

1. Authors distinguish three types of exemption: personal, local, and mixed.[3] Personal exemption is the privilege of immunity attached to an individual and adhering to him wheresoever he may be. Cardinals have this

---

[1] Cf. Chokier, p. 1; Ojetti, *Synopsis Rerum Moralium*, V. *"Exemptio"*; Melo, p. 1.
[2] Biz., p. 742.
[3] Cf. Vermeersch, *De Rel.*, I, 362; Bondini, p. 6; Melo, p. 2.

exemption (cf. cc. 239, 2227). Local exemption is that which is attached to a place, such as an oratory, church, monastery, territory, or the like. Persons indirectly benefit by this privilege, for so long as they remain in exempt places they are immune from the authority of outside superiors. Thus, for example, a local Ordinary cannot exercise jurisdiction over religious in an exempt church or monastery. Mixed exemption comprises the privileges of the two types explained, for by it persons, places, and things are withdrawn from the jurisdiction of the local Ordinary and are placed under the authority of their own prelates.[4] This last named is the exemption enjoyed by Regulars.[5]

2. Considered from another point of view, exemption is said to be either *active* or *passive*. Active exemption denotes the fullest immunity from external superiors. Persons possessing the privilege have their own appropriate and distinct territory, so that they are neither *in* nor *of* the diocese of any Bishop. The superior ruling such a territory has jurisdiction not only over the Regulars who are subject to him, but also over the secular clergy and the faithful.[6] Superiors of this kind are called abbots or prelates "nullius," that is, of no diocese. They have the same jurisdiction, obligations, and independence as a residential Bishop in his diocese (can. 323, § 1). Passive exemption denotes immunity from outside superiors in the government of one's own religious subjects. Those enjoying this privilege govern no particular territory; they and their monasteries or religious houses are in a diocese but do not pertain to it; in other words, though they are within diocesan territory they are not under the jurisdictional authority of the local Ordinary.[7]

Regulars possess this passive exemption and are thereby withdrawn, by a legal fiction, as Leo XII expressed it, from the diocese.[8] Hence, a local Ordinary who should attempt to exercise jurisdiction over Regulars, outside the cases expressed in law (can. 615), would be in the same juridical condition as a Bishop endeavoring to govern persons and places in another diocese. In such cases, a Bishop is not competent, and any attempted legal action on his part is null and void. Therefore, though a Bishop has jurisdiction in every part of his territory or diocese, he has in general no authority over exempt persons or places within the confines of the same.

On the other hand, prelates of institutes or houses having passive exemption, though ecclesiastical superiors in the strict sense and endowed with

---

[4] Cf. Melo, p. 2; Bondini, p. 6; Creusen, 308.

[5] Cf. Vermeersch, *De Rel.*, I, 362; Melo, p. 2.

[6] Cf. Conc. Trid., sess. XXIII, c. 10, *de reform.*, sess. XXIV, c. 9, *de reform.*; c. 19, X, *de praesc.* II, 26; Leurenius, *Jus. Can. Univ.*, L. I, tit. 31, q. 877, Resp. 3; Tamb., *De Jure Abb.* II, Disp. I, q. 5, nn. 1 ff.; W.-V., III, 395.

[7] Cf. Conc. Trid., sess. XXV, c. 20 *de regul.*; Bened. XIV, *De Syn. Dioec.* L. II, cap. 2, n. 2 ff.; AAS II, 345 and III, 84; Bied.-Führ., 35; W.-V., III, 395, and II, 563; see below, Section II.

[8] Leo XII, const., *Romanos Pontifices*, par. 7; see Vermeersch, *De Rel.*, II, Suppl. VII, par. III, 2; W.-V., III, 395.

jurisdiction over their own religious, have no authority over other clerical or secular persons.[9]

3. Exemption is said to be either *total* or *partial*, depending upon whether the withdrawal from the jurisdiction of local Ordinaries is entire or not. The many restrictions placed on the exemption of Regulars, especially since the time of Boniface VIII[10] make it clear that these religious enjoy only partial exemption (cf. can. 615, "Regulares . . . exempti sunt, *praeterquam in casibus a jure expressis*"). The cases in which Regulars are subject to the jurisdiction of local Ordinaries will be discussed later in this work.[11]

4. The term "exemption" is used in a *strict* and in a *broad* sense. Exemption in the strict acceptation of the word is that which is possessed by Regulars; in the broad acceptation, that had by all religious institutes of pontifical right; that is, by institutes which have received at least the "decretum laudis" from the Holy See (cf. can. 488, § 3). This latter type is very restricted in nature, for by it religious are withdrawn from the jurisdiction of local Ordinaries in but a few matters, such as the administration of the organization and its religious discipline.[12]

There are four grades of exempt institutes, in the strict acceptation of the term: exempt clerical orders, exempt clerical congregations, exempt orders of laymen, and exempt nuns.[13] Exemptive rights are more extensive in clerical than in lay institutes.

The following terms used throughout this discussion are accepted in the sense defined by the code:

a) *Regulars* are religious who have made profession of vows in an order (can. 488, 7°); that is, in any institute in which, according to the Rules or Constitutions, solemn vows are taken by at least some of the members (can. 488, 2°).[14] Therefore all professed religious of such institutes — whether they be professed with solemn or simple vows, and whether the latter be temporary or perpetual — are Regulars properly so called.[15] Included under the term "Regulars" are monks[16] or religious who belong to either monastic congregations or independent abbeys or monasteries, provided, of course,

---

[9] Cf. Pirh, L. I, Tit. 31, M. 126; Tamb., *De Jure Abb.*, II, Dist. I, q. 5, nn. 6, 8; Leurenius, *Jus can. univ.*, L. I, tit. 31, q. 877, resp. 3; Melo, p. 3; Bondini, p. 7; Schäfer, 419.

[10] Cf. Wernz, III, 701–702; Woywod, I, 531.

[11] The terms total and partial exemption are sometimes employed in another sense: total, to signify that both persons and places enjoy an equal, full exemption, so that even strangers are exempt when in such places; partial, to signify a local exemption which favors only the persons for whom it was granted. Cf. *Epit.* I, 716.

[12] Cf. Schäfer, 419; Prümmer, p. 314, q. 239.

[13] Cf. Schäfer, 419.

[14] Cf. Berutti, III, cap. I, 4.

[15] Cf. Schäfer, 46.

[16] Monks are members of ancient religious orders which are given over to the contemplative and solitary life, v.g., the Benedictines. In the congregation of Beuron monks are the religious professed with solemn vows; lay brothers and those professed with simple vows are not monks, though they are Regulars. Cf. Schäfer, 46.

that solemn professions of vows are made in these institutes. This is in conformity with the definition of the term "Order" given in canon 488, 2°.[17] The term "Regular" is applied to both men and women who are members of religious Orders (cf. can. 615).

b) *Nuns* are religious women with solemn vows or, unless it appears otherwise from the nature of the case or from the context, religious women whose vows are normally solemn, but which, by a disposition of the Holy See, are simple in certain regions (can. 488, § 7). Regions where their vows are simple are: France, with the exception of Nice and Savoy; Belgium,[18] the United States, with the exception of the five monasteries of the Visitation in Georgetown, Baltimore, Mobile, St. Louis,[19] and Springfield, Missouri.

By reason of the decree of the Congregation of Religious, June 23, 1923,[20] nuns in France and Belgium may hereafter ask the Holy See for the restoration of their right to pronounce solemn vows. The following provisions are contained in the Decree:

I. "In France and Belgium, monastic nuns in monasteries which profess the rule of a Regular Order, or where the vows taken are according to their institute solemn, although in fact they profess only simple vows, are true monastic nuns of pontifical law in the sense of canon 488, § 7, just as are other monastic nuns in the universal church."

II. "Those monasteries, however, in the absence of a peculiar privilege, are not subject to Regular superiors, and hence have not the privilege of exemption under canon 615; but are subject to the jurisdiction of the Ordinaries of places in those matters in which the code gives Bishops jurisdiction over monastic nuns."

III. "If any monastery asks for it, there is at present nothing to prevent the nuns of that monastery from pronouncing solemn vows and keeping the papal cloister, provided they obtain that right from the Holy See."[21]

It is clear that this Decree makes provision for religious women pertaining to monasteries which follow the Rules of Regular Orders, and for those also belonging to institutes which by rule or constitution permit the solemn profession of some of their members.

Both these classes of religious women are nuns properly so called and are consequently religious of pontifical right, for there exists no such thing as an institute of nuns of diocesan right.

Since all nuns pertain to an Order (can. 488), they are Regulars in the strict sense of the word.[22] However, when they are not subject to superiors

---

[17] Cf. Melo, p. 5.
[18] Cf. Biz., pp. 86, 454 ff., 739.
[19] Cf. S. C. Rel., May 22, 1919, AAS, XI, 240; Biz., pp. 487, 723 ff.; Creusen, 15.
[20] AAS, XV, 358.
[21] Cf. Bouscaren, I, can. 500; *Per.*, XII, pp. 76–81, and XIII, pp. 63–68, and XV, p. 230; Creusen, 15.
[22] Cf. Schäfer, 47.

of Regulars they remain under the jurisdiction of local Ordinaries (cc. 500, 615). Yet even this latter class is not entirely under the control of local Ordinaries. Thus these Ordinaries cannot dispense the nuns from their vows; they cannot grant them indults of exclaustration or secularization; they cannot dispense them from obligations connected with the law on the dowry; they cannot permit them to leave the cloister except in accordance with the provisions of canon 601, etc.[23]

Among the nuns whose rule includes solemn vows are "the Benedictines, the Poor Clares, certain canonesses of St. Augustine, the Carmelites, the Dominicans (of the second order), the Ursulines (who belong to the Roman Union), Visitandines, etc. The great number of women religious who are called tertiaries of St. Francis or of St. Dominic, are not nuns, neither are the members of those congregations which have adopted in part some ancient rule, for instance, the Franciscans of the Holy Family, of the Sacred Heart; the Dominicans of the Sacred Heart; the Ursulines who belong to diocesan congregations, etc." (Creusen, 15.)

It is a general canonical principle that institutes with simple vows do not enjoy the privilege of exemption unless it has been specially conceded to them (can. 618, § 1), as is the case with the Redemptorists, the Passionists and, in a special form, the Daughters of Charity of St. Vincent de Paul.[24]

---

[23] Cf. Schäfer, 47; *Per.*, XII, p. 80.

[24] Cf. Creusen, 313; Bastien, p. 403. Nevertheless pontifical congregations are far less dependent on local Ordinaries than are diocesan institutes. This is clear from the prescriptions of the Code which render it unlawful for Ordinaries: to make any changes in their constitutions or to enquire into the administration of their temporal affairs, save in the cases provided for in canons 533–535 (can. 618, § 2, 1°); to interfere in their internal government and discipline, except in the cases expressed by law (can. 618, § 2, 2°); to suppress any of their houses (can. 498); to extend the canonical visitation beyond the limits defined in canons 512, § 2, 2°, 3° and 618, § 2, 2°.

CHAPTER II

THE JURIDICAL NATURE OF EXEMPTION

The "juridical nature" of exemption is taken here to signify its legal force, acquisition, acceptance, use, interpretation, and cessation.

ARTICLE I. THE LEGAL FORCE OF EXEMPTION

Exemption of Regulars has the force of a papal privilege, and of a universal law of the Church.

I. EXEMPTION IS A PRIVILEGE OF REGULARS

Before the promulgation of the Code the concession of this privilege to religious orders was manifest from papal documents. For examples of such grants consult the following: (*a*) the constitution *"Regimini Universalis Ecclesiae,"* par. 9, of Sixtus IV,[1] and the constitution *"Ratio Pastoralis Officii"* of Clement VIII (Dec. 20, 1597),[2] in favor of the Friars Minor; (*b*) the constitution of Sixtus IV (Aug. 31, 1494) in favor of the Dominicans;[3] (*c*) the constitution *"Dum fructus uberes,"* par. 42, of Sixtus IV (Feb. 23, 1474) in favor of the Hermits of St. Augustine;[4] (*d*) the constitution *"Dum attenta,"* par. 60, of Sixtus IV (Dec. 2, 1476) in favor of the Carmelites;[5] (*e*) the constitution *"Licet,"* par. 13, of Paul III (Nov. 17, 1549), the Brief *"Dolemus"* of Leo XIII (July 13, 1886) in favor of the Society of Jesus,[6] etc.

Furthermore, the Code itself speaks of exemption as a privilege, and consequently it may be classified as a privilege "contained in the Code." The following reasons bear out this statement:

1. Exemption of Regulars (can. 615) is placed in the chapter treating of the privileges enjoyed by religious.[7]

2. Canons 500, § 1, 616, and 618 explicitly refer to the law enunciated in canon 615, as the privilege of exemption.

3. The Code admits the existence of this type of privilege (cf. cc. 71, 72, § 4), and the provision of canon 615 seems identical in nature with those privileges which prior to the new legislation were called "privilegia in corpore juris contenta."

---

[1] Cf. B.R., III, III, 141.
[2] Ferraris, v, *Privilegium,* Art. I, 26.
[3] Cf. B.R., III, III, 144.
[4] Cf. Lezana, Tom. III, pars I, pp. 91–100.
[5] Cf. Lezana, Tom. III, pars II, pp. 134–164.
[6] ASS, XIX, 49.
[7] Cf. Code, Book II, Part II, tit. XIII, chap. II.

What is the nature of such a privilege?

A privilege contained in the Code (or in the law) is a common ecclesiastical law made up of a prescription which is beyond or contrary to the scope of a more general law, and which favors a particular class of persons or things, v.g., Bishops, religious, religious institutes or churches.

Any ordinance of the Code affecting a class of persons or things can be either simply a common law, or at one and the same time a law and a privilege. If such an ordinance is a provision necessary for the common good, or if it does not contain elements which are beyond or opposed to the common law, it is simply a law. On the other hand, a favorable ordinance is simultaneously a common law and a privilege in two instances: first, if it exempts the recipient from a more general law to which he would otherwise be subject; second, if it accords him favors or rights not had by virtue of common law. Thus the incapacity of minors to exercise their legal rights is a common law (can. 89), while the juridical action "restitutio in integrum" which a judge may accord them, is at one and the same time a common law and a privilege (cf. cc. 1687–1689). The subjection of the faithful in a diocese to the authority of the local Ordinary is a common law (cf. cc. 329, § 1; 334, § 1; 335); the exemption of Regulars (can. 615) from this same authority is a common law and a privilege.[8]

Privileges contained in the Code must be looked upon as laws constituting part of the general law of the Church. In a certain sense they may be said to form exceptions to common laws, but exceptions which were taken into account and definitely decreed when the general law was formulated and unified in the present Code. Hence, in the strict sense, they are not exceptions to the general law of the Code, but are a part of it.[9] It is true that exemption is a special law, inasmuch as it derogates the common law that prescribes subjection to the jurisdiction of local Ordinaries, yet, as it is a provision of the common law, it is really a general limitation of one of the common laws.

It is to be remarked that, since the promulgation of the Code, authors of note, such as Ojetti,[10] Maroto,[11] Melo,[12] Cicognani,[13] have maintained that the exemption of Regulars is a *privilege contained in the Code.*

Even though a person may deny that exemption is this kind of privilege, he is forced to concede that, aside from canon 615 of the Code, special privileges of exemption have been granted to all religious orders. These particular grants have not been revoked, but, on the contrary, are confirmed by the legislation now in force. This is a direct consequence of canon 4, which asserts that acquired rights, privileges, and indults which up to the present time have been granted by the Apostolic See to either physical or

---

[8] Cf. Van Hove, *De la Notion du Privilège,* N.R.T., Tom. 49 (1922), p. 76, note (5).
[9] Cf. Van Hove, N.R.T., *loc. cit.,* p. 76.
[10] *Com. in Cod.,* can. 72, 4 (p. 302).
[11] Maroto, 291, B.
[12] Melo, pp. 32, 34.
[13] Cicognani (1935), p. 781.

moral persons and are still in use and not revoked, remain in their entirety, unless they are expressly revoked by the Code itself. Therefore, the privileges of exemption possessed by Regulars prior to the promulgation of the Code unquestionably retain their legal force.[14] Further, when expressly treating of the privileges possessed by religious institutes (can. 613), the legislator states that each institute enjoys those privileges which are contained in the Code, and those which have been directly granted to it by the Apostolic See. Paragraph 2 of the same canon declares that privileges of a Regular institute belong also to the nuns of that Order, in so far as they are capable of sharing them.

Considered as a privilege, exemption is a private law which primarily and directly benefits Regulars and ultimately the whole Church.[15] Since it favors a category of persons, and generally juridic persons, such as institutes, churches, and religious houses, it is called a *common* privilege to distinguish it from a private privilege, which benefits only individuals (cf. cc. 69, 72).

Exemption of Regulars is spoken of as a *remunerative* privilege, for frequently it has been granted to them by the Holy See in token of gratitude and as a reward for their labors and activities in the Kingdom of Christ.[16] N.B. Obviously this is neither the sole nor the most important reason for these concessions.[17]

II. THE EXEMPTION OF REGULARS IS A LAW OF THE CHURCH

Though prior to the Code many authors held that the exemption of Regulars was a privilege embodied in the Law of the Church and consequently was itself a common law, yet this remained a disputed point. Exemption is now a common law, for canon 615 states: Regulars both men and women, including novices, except those nuns who are not subject to Regular superiors, are exempt, together with their houses and churches, from the jurisdiction of the local Ordinary, except in the cases provided for by law. Hence it has the juridical force with which all law is vested, and is governed according to the legal principles enunciated in the First Book of the Code.

Conclusion

Since the exemption of Regulars is both a law and a privilege it is regulated by the general norms for laws and by the general norms for privileges. Wherefore, these two sets of norms or principles should be applied to matters of exemption, when, of course, they are not opposed to one another;

---

[14] Cf. AAS, XXV, 245; *Per.,* XXII, 98 ff.; Melo, p. 36.
[15] Cf. Van Hove, *De la Notion du Privilège.* N.R.T., Tom. 49, pp. 5–18.
[16] Cf. AAS, XXV, 245; *Per.,* XXII, 98–101.
[17] Cf. Leo XIII, *Romanos Pontifices,* 2, 7; De Buck, p. 127; Vermeersch, *De Rel.,* I, 364; Bondini, pp. 10, 11; Melo, pp. 26–31.

that is to say, when their simultaneous observance is possible. Should a conflict preclude the application of the two sets of principles, then a choice must be made between them.

It would seem that such a choice should be made as will prove more favorable to the exemptive rights of Regulars. This follows from the very nature of exemption, as will be shown presently in the article on interpretation. Hence, if a norm for privileges is more favorable to Regulars than a norm for laws, it should be applied rather than the latter.

A good exemplification of this may be drawn from the case involving the cessation of an exemptive right, considered in Article IV of this Chapter.

ARTICLE II. THE ACQUISITION, ACCEPTANCE, AND USE OF EXEMPTION

Acquisition. In the past, most exemptive privileges have been acquired either by *direct grant* from the Apostolic See, or by *communication*. The latter method entitled certain persons, places, and institutes to share in the favors which were conferred on others.[18] Communication of the privilege of a principal beneficiary is effected in two ways: in a form equally principal, or in an accessory form (cf. cc. 64, 65). "In the first case the enjoyment of the privilege communicated becomes independent of the grant made to the principal beneficiary; in the second case, it shares in all the vicissitudes of the grant made to the principal beneficiary."[19]

Mendicants generally enjoyed a full and perfect communication of privileges in a form equally principal. This was true both of the privileges acquired by all such orders and of those acquired by other Regular institutes and congregations. The congregations of the Passionists and Redemptorists likewise enjoyed a mutual interchange of privileges. Except in special instances, Tertiaries participated neither in the privilege of other Tertiaries nor in those of the first order to which they pertained. Confraternities participated in an accessory manner in privileges of archconfraternities to which they were affiliated.[20]

The extension to nuns of the privileges accorded to the first order (can. 613, § 2) is not to be considered a communication properly so called. Nevertheless, since the privileges are directly granted to the first order, any alterations or modifications affecting concessions made to the Regular order of men immediately affect the second order, i.e., the nuns.[21]

Besides the methods of acquisition just mentioned, some exemptive privileges were also obtained by way of custom and by prescriptive right.

Exemptive and other privileges, no matter how obtained, which have not been revoked, continue in force after the promulgation of the Code,

---

[18] Cf. Vermeersch, *De Rel.,* I, 351.
[19] Creusen, 304.
[20] Cf. Vermeersch, *De Rel.,* I, 351; Creusen, 304.
[21] Cf. Creusen, 304.

unless the Code itself has made an express revocation of the same (can. 4).

Interpreters have been divided concerning the meaning of canon 613, § 1. Some maintained that all privileges formerly acquired by communication were suppressed;[22] others claimed that only future acquisitions by communication were affected by this law. [23] The Code Commission has settled the controversy in favor of the latter solution by declaring that all privileges already acquired by communication which have not been expressly revoked by the Code continue in force.[24]

Acceptance. Exemption being a papal law produces its legal effect independently of the wish of Regulars. Whether they are unwilling or should even refuse to accept their exemptive rights and status accorded them by the Code, is of no juridical consequence; the law, and consequently their exemption, depends entirely upon the will of the Sovereign Pontiff. Like all other laws, that of exemption became obligatory when promulgated (cf. can. 8).[25]

Use. Regulars are obliged to use their exemption. It is not within their power to change their status, which has been determined by the Holy See. This obligation to use exemptive rights is based on the nature of their privilege and particularly on the fact that their exemption is now a common law. Canonists commonly agree that this privilege of religious Orders procures the common good of these institutes and the well-being of religion in general, and, therefore, it must be used by those possessing it.[26] Moreover failure to use exemption would do injury to the rights of the Holy See, which has exclusive authority over Regulars. As has been intimated, a more stringent obligation arises from the fact that exemption is now a common law. Of their very nature, all ecclesiastical laws promote the welfare of the Church, and the violation of any of them produces the opposite result.

It follows as a juridical corollary that others may not hinder Regulars in the use of their exemptive rights. Local Ordinaries, therefore, cannot issue orders nor take any actions which would interfere with the freedom of these religious. In the event of an infringement of this nature, Regulars are in nowise bound to submit to the Ordinary, for the latter's action would be legally null and void.[27] Because of the scandal often arising from such controversies, it is frequently advisable to notify the Holy See of the difficulties.

---

[22] Cf. Blat, C.p.R., II, 601; Bondini, p. 15; Bied.-Führ. 145.

[23] Cf. Augustine, III, can. 613; Choupin, *Nature et obligations de l'état religieux*, p. 489; Fanfani, 277; Coronata, I, p. 312; Larraona, C.p.R., III, pp. 205–214; Melo, pp. 39–41; Schäfer, 387; Creusen, 304.

[24] Cf. Cod. Com., Dec. 30, 1937, AAS, XXX, p. 73.

[25] Cf. Suarez, *De Legibus*, L. IV, c. XVI.

[26] Cf. c. 12, X, *de foro*, II, 2; Suarez, *De Legibus*, L. VIII, c. 23, m. 8; Pell., VIII, I, 84; Schmalz., V, XXXIII, 97; Reiff., V, XXXIII, 190 ff.

[27] Cf. Melo, p. 34.

Superiors of Regulars may not tolerate encroachments, for they have an obligation to the Church, to their institute, and to their subjects, to rule in accordance with the norms set down in law, and to suffer no illegal interference with their office. Submission on their part to a local Ordinary in cases in which they are exempt would be illicit and invalid. This would be so even though the superior yielded in order that he might avoid greater harm or inconvenience.[28]

ARTICLE III. THE INTERPRETATION OF EXEMPTION

To interpret is to explain the meaning of a law.[29] This comprises an exposition of law in conformity with the mind and will of the legislator; that is, according to the meaning which the legislator intended when he enacted the law, and which he really embodied in the legal terms employed.[30] Since it is an explanation, interpretation presupposes some obscurity or ambiguity.

According to its diverse authorship, interpretation is classified as: authentic, or doctrinal, or usual (i.e., interpretation from usage). All three are employed in explaining exemptive rights, though authentic is the most important.

Authentic interpretation of exemption in general is the authoritative explanation given by the lawmaker or his successor, or those whom he has delegated to interpret his law. When it is given in the form of law, or its equivalent, it has the force of law and binds all subjects; when given by way of judicial sentence, or rescript, it binds those persons only to whom it was directed and merely in the matters affected by the terms of the sentence or rescript (cf. can. 17).

Before the promulgation of the Code, authentic interpretation of exemption was a subject of controversy amongst canonists. Some held that Bishops had the right to interpret authoritatively doubtful or obscure cases. This opinion, however, was questionable, for it directly opposed the provision of Innocent III.[31] Another opinion, equally questionable, maintained that individual grants of exemption contained faculties entitling the superiors of Regulars authoritatively to interpret controverted cases. The more reasonable, and the common doctrine, taught that disputes between Bishops and Regulars concerning the exemption of the latter, should be referred to the Holy See, for they involved a papal law which the legislator alone could authoritatively interpret.[32]

---

[28] Cf. c. 5, X, *de excessibus praelat.*, V, 31; Suarez, *De Legibus*, VIII, c. 23, nn. 8, 9.
[29] Cf. *Epit.*, I, 120; Cicognani, can. 17; Maroto, I, 235.
[30] Cf. Maroto, *loc. cit.*, 235.
[31] Cf. c. 12, X, *de judiciis*, II, 1.
[32] Cf. c. 31, X, *de sent. excom.*, V, 39; c. 8, *de concessione praebendae*, III, 7, in VI; Clem. X, Const., *Superna*, June 21, 1670.

Leo XIII[33] declared that in any dispute concerning their exemptive rights, Regulars were empowered to make a suspensive appeal to the Holy See. Hence, pending the authoritative reply, the religious enjoy the full exercise of the exemptive matter under dispute (cf. can. 1889).

Finally, reason itself demands that controversies concerning the exemption of Regulars be settled by the Holy See, for the rights under dispute are papal in character and cannot be subjected to the judgment of any inferior authority.[34]

Since the issuance of the Code, there is no possibility of further controversy on this point. Because exemption is a papal right and now a law, the Holy See, or its delegate, must settle any disputed cases; no one else can give an authentic interpretation of law (can. 17).

The only body possessing this delegated authority is the special Commission for the authentic interpretation of the Code established by Benedict XV.[35] Because this Commission has the power to interpret only and not to legislate,[36] it is not competent to issue restrictive or extensive interpretations, for these latter constitute legislative enactments.[37]

The competency of the Commission is limited to the laws of the Code. Cases, therefore, involving exemptive privileges of an institute, which are not provided for in the Code, are not subject to the jurisdiction of this body. In such matters the Congregation of Religious possesses exclusive jurisdiction, for it has been expressly declared that all questions involving rights, privileges, etc., of religious individuals or communities, belong exclusively to this Sacred Congregation, with the exception of matters pertaining to the Holy Office (as the Eucharistic fast for religious priests, matters of faith, censure of objectionable books, etc.).[38]

Doctrinal and Usual Interpretation. These two kinds of interpretations also have their place in the exposition of exemptive rights. The former, which consists in the explanation of a law given by those skilled in legal affairs, of itself (i.e., per se) obliges no one; its binding force is commensurate with the reasons adduced by the interpreter; the latter, which draws the explanation of a law from the customary observance of the greater part of a community, can and normally does impose an obligation on those subject to the law, for custom being the best interpreter of law (can. 29) constitutes the best and safest rule of action.

However, the legitimate use of these two methods of interpretation in matters of exemption demands that the rule of broad interpretation be

---

[33] Cf. Const., *Romanos Pontifices*, 13.
[34] Cf. Melo, p. 33.
[35] Cf. Bened. XV, *Motu Proprio, Cum juris,* Sept. 15, 1917, AAS, IX, 483, f.
[36] Cf. Bened., *Motu Proprio,* just cited.
[37] Cf. Maroto, C.p.R., Annot. X, XI.
[38] Cf. Instr., Mar. 24, 1919, AAS, XI, 251; see canon 251.

followed in every case (cf. cc. 19, 68, 50). As presently will be seen, in doubtful cases there exists a legal presumption which always favors Regulars.

The exemption of Regulars is subject to *broad* interpretation. Strict and broad interpretation should be carefully distinguished from restrictive and extensive. The two former employ the proper meaning of the terms of a law, but in either a narrow or wide sense, while the two latter use the terms in a sense which is narrower or wider than their proper meaning.

Prior to the Code it was the common opinion of authors that the exemption enjoyed by religious orders was subject to broad interpretation.

Many reasons were alleged in support of this contention. For example, it was claimed that exemption was a privilege favoring religion and the common good; that it was a remunerative privilege; that it was a papal right and enhanced the authority of the Holy See.[39] In treating of this matter, Castropalao[40] states that privileges which favor religion must be broadly interpreted even though they be derogatory to common law, because it is of the highest moment for the common welfare of the Church to favor persons consecrated to God in the religious state. He further adds that these privileges must be interpreted broadly because they are conferred on religious in perpetuity, and consequently must be regarded as grants incorporated in the law itself.[41]

Further, when a doubt or controversy arose concerning the existence of some exemptive right, the presumption always favored the Regulars, for their exemption was considered a notorious or patent privilege. The burden of proof, therefore, rested with those contesting the right. For example, a local Ordinary who claimed jurisdictional power over Regulars was obliged to prove that the law expressly justified his contention.[42]

The new Code has not made any alteration in the norms for interpreting the exemption of Regulars. Favorable rights or faculties, whether granted by privilege or law, are subject to broad interpretation. (Favorabilia sunt amplianda, odiosa restringenda. Cf. Reg. 15, R.J., in VI.)

The scope of exemptive *privileges* must be discerned from the wording of the document, and must not be extended or restricted (can. 67).

If a doubt arises as to the meaning of terms contained in a *privilege,* the norm of interpretation set down in canon 50 is to be followed; in every case interpretation must be of such a nature as to admit the acquisition of some favorable concession (can. 68). Canon 50 states that the following must be strictly interpreted: privileges which refer to ecclesiastical trials,

---

[39] Cf. Suarez, *De Legibus*, L. VIII, c. 27; St. Alph., *Theol. Mor.*, Appendix, *De Privilegiis*, 8; D'Annibale, *Summa* I, 220; Vermeersch, *De Prohibitione et Censura Librorum*, 64.

[40] Cf. *Opus Mor.*, tr. III, Disp. IV, punct. 10, nn. 5, 6.

[41] Cf. also Sanchez, L. 8, Disp. I, 13; Bonacina, Disp. I, q. 3, punct. 7, par. 1, nn. 6, 7; Rotarius, *Theol. Mor. Regularium* (Venetii, 1735), L. III, c. 5, n. 15.

[42] Cf. Mayr, V, XXXIII, 189; Piat II, q. 5; Vermeersch, *De Rel.*, I, 365, c, and II, Suppl. VII.

or which infringe on the rights of a third party, or grant exemption from the law in favor of private individuals, or deal with the acquisition of a benefice. All others, such as the exemption of religious, are to be broadly interpreted.

Viewed as a *law,* exemption of Regulars is to receive the same broad interpretation. According to the Code, those laws are subject to strict interpretation which decree a penalty, or restrict the free exercise of one's rights, or form an exception to the general law (can. 19). Since exemption does not belong to any of the classes enumerated, it is to be interpreted in the broad sense.

At first sight it might be thought that exemption should be classified as an exception to the general law. However, this is not so. There are two opinions concerning the signification of the exceptions to the general law spoken of in canon 19, and neither of them would classify exemption as such an exception.

One opinion, that of Vermeersch and others, declares that no law of the Code can, properly speaking, be called an exception to the law; all provisions contained in the Code are modes of the law. The promulgation of the Code is the promulgation of *one* law. Wherefore the rule of strict interpretation for exceptions to the law cannot be applied to any law, such as that of exemption, contained in the Code.[43] Van Hove, on the other hand, admits that the exceptions mentioned in canon 19 may occur in the Code itself, v.g., canon 236. Yet, according to his theory, the exemption of Regulars would not fall under this classification. For the legislator enacted this law because of its necessity and utility. These reasons moved him to recede from the norm of common law which subjects religious to local Ordinaries, and to establish the singular law favoring Regulars. Canon 615, therefore, must, in view of these reasons, be interpreted in a broad sense.[44]

Another reason postulating broad interpretation can be drawn from the principle contained in canon 29, namely: *custom is the best interpreter of law.* This affords us a clear norm, for both before and after the promulgation of the new Code, there has prevailed an invariable custom in cases of doubt to interpret the exemption of Regulars in such a manner as to favor the recipients of the privilege. Verification of this may be deduced from declarations of Roman Pontiffs[45] and the testimony of the theologians.[46]

---

[43] Cf. *Epit.,* I, 60 and 126; Ojetti, can. 19; Chelodi, *Jus de Personis,* 67; Cappello, *Summa J.C.,* I, 87; *Per.,* XI, (13)–(15).

[44] Cf. Van Hove, I, Tom. II, 306–310.

[45] Cf. Sixtus IV, Const., *Regimini,* par. 9, Aug. 31, 1474; Paul III, Const., *Licet debitum,* par. 13, Nov. 17, 1549, etc.

[46] Suarez states: ". . . privilegium exemptionis . . . religiosorum . . . etiamsi deroget juri communi, ampliatur in favorem religionis," *De Legibus,* VIII, c. 27, n. 7; see also, Reiff., L. I, III, 138; Schmalz., L. V, IV, X, 126; Castropalao, L. III, IV, X, 6; S. Alph., *Priv.,* I, 8; Vermeersch, *De Rel.,* I, 357, and II Suppl. VII; Melo, p. 34; *Epit.,* I, 774; Schäfer, 419.

N.B. The manner of interpreting the exceptions to exemption which are expressly mentioned in law, will be treated in the last two chapters of this work.

ARTICLE IV. THE CESSATION OF EXEMPTION

Though laws, and privileges which do not contain a provision to the contrary (can. 70), are perpetual in character, nevertheless it is possible for them to lose their juridical force. The purpose of the present article is to consider the cases involving the cessation of exemptive rights. Cessation of rights in general can be effected either by an intrinsic or by an extrinsic cause. We shall, therefore, divide our exposition as follows: (I) Cessation of exemption effected by an intrinsic cause; (II) Cessation of exemption effected by an extrinsic cause.

I. CESSATION OF EXEMPTION EFFECTED BY AN INTRINSIC CAUSE

Such a cause can bring about the termination of the *law* and the *privilege* of exemption. We consider each separately.

A. *Cessation of Law*

The law of exemption or any particular right contained therein will cease if the subject matter of the law has undergone a complete, general, and permanent change,[47] or, if the purpose of the lawmaker can no longer be accomplished by means of his legal enactment.

The cessation spoken of must be strictly interpreted; when it is doubtful, a presumption exists which favors the continuance of the exemptive right.

B. *Cessation of Privilege*

Exemptive privileges cease only by reason of a *contrary* transformation, that is, when they become injurious or their use illicit (can. 77). Therefore a mere negative change, namely, the cessation of the reason which moved the Holy See to grant the privilege, does not cause its termination.[48] Worthy of note is the fact that the judgment of the superior, in our case the Holy See, and not the opinion of Regulars or local Ordinaries, determines when cessation has occurred by reason of a contrary intrinsic change (can. 77).

---

[47] A change in the matter (that is, in the intrinsic end of the law) or in the purpose of the law (that is, in the extrinsic end of the law) may be either a *contrary* or a *negative* change. When an intrinsic transformation is negative, the execution of the law is rendered useless, because there no longer remains a reason for its existence; when contrary, the execution is positively harmful. Cf. Suarez, *De Legibus,* L. VI, c. 9, nn. 2 ff.; Van Hove, I, Tom. II, cap. VII, art. I; Ojetti, I, can. 21; Cicognani, can. 21.

[48] Cf. Suarez, *De Legibus,* L. VIII, c. 30, nn. 6, 7.

II. CESSATION EFFECTED BY AN EXTRINSIC CAUSE

Exemptive rights have been principally lost through revocation. This constitutes the chief extrinsic cause of the termination of such concessions, and is defined canonically as the partial or total annulment of a law or privilege by the authority of a competent superior.[49]

The only superior competent to revoke exemptive rights is the Holy See.[50] Neither local Ordinaries nor Regular superiors or Chapters have any repressive jurisdiction over such matters.[1]

A. *Revocation of the Law of Exemption*

The law of exemption (can. 615) can be revoked only through a new law enacted by the Sovereign Pontiff, which would expressly abrogate the former, or contain a contrary prescription, namely, one subjecting Regulars to local Ordinaries, or readjust the entire matter of exemption (cf. can. 22).

Since the revocation of laws or legal rights in general is odious, it is subject to strict interpretation. Hence, canon 23 decrees that in cases of doubt, the revocation of an already existing law is not to be assumed, but new laws should, as far as possible, be aligned and made to harmonize with former ones. It is clear, therefore, that in a case of doubt concerning the revocation of exemptive rights, there exists a legal presumption which favors their continuance.[2]

B. *Revocation of the Privilege of Exemption*

Since the privilege of exemption is possessed by religious Orders, through special concession or by communication, independently of the Code, its revocation is governed by canon 60.

This law states that concessions of the type in question which are revoked by a special act of the superior are valid until the one who obtained them is notified of the revocation. They are not revoked by a contrary law, unless an express revocatory provision is contained in the law itself.

Hence, there are two ways of revoking particular exemptive privileges enjoyed by religious Orders or congregations, namely, by a special act of

---

[49] Different terms are often employed to designate the various ways in which a right can be lost. Thus, revocation is called abrogation, when the entire law or privilege is revoked; derogation, when a right is only partially revoked; subrogation, when a right is altered by the addition of some new element; abrogation, when a right is changed through the substitution of a law or privilege containing a provision contrary to the one previously in force. Ecclesiastical legislators do not always use these terms according to their technical meaning, v.g., the term "abrogation," found in canon 22, has two significations. In the first place, it denotes revocation in the general sense of the term; in the second, the enactment of a law contrary to a former one. Cf. Cicognani, can. 22.

[50] Cf. *Regula juris*, 1, *in Decret. Greg.*, IX.

[1] Cf. Melo, p. 35; Maroto, II, p. 516.   [2] Cf. Suarez, *De Legibus*, L. VI, c. 27, n. 4.

the Roman Pontiff, or by a special provision inserted in a contrary law of the Holy See.

Abrogation, therefore, of the privilege of exemption can only be effected by a special act of the Holy See, which is manifested to the privileged party. The necessity of notifying the possessor of the privilege precludes the possibility of tacit revocation.

Paragraph 2 of canon 60 requires that revocation made by contrary laws be provided for in the laws themselves. Unlike the case mentioned in canon 22, incompatibility of a law with exemptive rights derived from privileges, in no way affects or revokes the privileged rights. Hence, such revocation is verified only when the law contains express abrogatory clauses.

Very probably privileges of *Regulars* are not annulled by the *general* revocatory expressions employed in papal documents, whether these be *common* formulae, as, "all privileges to the contrary notwithstanding" (non obstantibus quibuscumque privilegiis), or *extraordinary* formulae, as "notwithstanding all privileges to the contrary, expressed under any form whatsoever, even if a word for word mention of them be demanded" (non obstantibus privilegiis quibuscumque sub quacumque verborum forma conceptis, etiamsi eorum mentio de verbo ad verbum fieri deberet). It is claimed that the revocation of such privileges must be made expressly, that is, by a *special* formula which specifically refers to the privilege possessed by the Regulars.

Nevertheless, when it is *otherwise* clear that the Sovereign Pontiff wishes also to include a privilege of Regulars under a general revocatory formula, unquestionably this privilege is abolished: for the words of the lawmaker should be interpreted according to his expressed intention.[3] For this reason, the privileges in question will certainly be revoked, even when no special clause is used, if the revocatory decree be issued under the form "motu proprio et ex certa scientia," or "ex plenitudine potestatis," for these expressions signify that the Roman Pontiff has the knowledge of existing privileges and consequently the intention of annulling them.[4]

C. *Renunciation of the Privilege of Exemption*

Renunciation is the voluntary abdication or surrender of an existing right. At the outset it is obvious that there can be no question of Regulars renouncing the law of exemption. It is absurd to think of subjects renouncing a law. Canon 615 is in nowise dependent upon the acceptance or renouncement by Regulars either individually or collectively, but draws its juridical force exclusively from the will of the Sovereign Pontiff. He is the supreme legislator and source of this law and he alone is competent to

---

[3] Cf. Chokier, p. 247; Melo, pp. 36, 37.
[4] Cf. Melo, p. 37.

repudiate it.[5] For this reason the Code declares that neither a community nor any group is at liberty to renounce a privilege which was granted in the form of law (can. 72, § 4).

Prior to the promulgation of the Code, all authors admitted that Regulars could not renounce their privilege of exemption without permission of the Holy See.[6]

"The privilege of exemption," says Schmalzgrueber,[7] "was introduced in favor not so much of the exempt as of the Apostolic See and the Pope." It is apparent, and has been often affirmed by the Holy See, that the flourishing condition of religious Orders furthers the spiritual work and supernatural end of the universal Church and of each particular diocese.[8] Hence, the renunciation of exemption would be a violation of the authority of the Roman Pontiff who has withdrawn Regulars from the jurisdiction of local Ordinaries and placed them under his immediate control, and would prove harmful to the Church itself.[9]

Furthermore, this renunciation would be prejudicial to Regular institutes, for their exemption is of grave importance to them. It forms the bond of unity which promotes the perfection of the Order and which greatly facilitates the organization and success of its ministries.[10] By reason of it, dangers from outside interference are greatly diminished, thereby guaranteeing a tranquil and peaceful rule by the superiors who are familiar with the principles of the religious life peculiar to each institute.[11]

Likewise, the Code declares that neither a community nor any other group is at liberty to renounce a privilege if such a renunciation would be prejudicial to the Church or to other persons (can. 72, § 4). This is true for exemption in general, and for each individual exemptive right. Thus, for example, a Regular superior cannot allow a local Ordinary to make a canonical visitation of his religious house.[12]

Because exemption can be abolished only by the authority of the Holy See, it is clear that neither a contrary custom nor nonuse can annul this privilege (can. 76). Even though a local Ordinary seems to be in possession of a right abolishing exemption, he has not in reality acquired such jurisdiction, for this would be equivalent to tacit renunciation by Regulars, which is forbidden.[13]

---

[5] Cf. Suarez, De Legibus, L. IV, c. 16.
[6] Cf. Melo, p. 31.
[7] Cf. De Privilegiis, V, 33, n. 265.
[8] Cf. Vermeersch, De Rel., I, 364.
[9] C. 5, X, de arbitr., I, 43; c. 14, de privilegiis, V, 23; see also Pell., VIII, VI, 85; Fagn., C., Quod supra his, 9, De major. et obed., 14 ff.; Donatus, XIII, q. 10; Navarrus, V, "exemptio," 33; Piat, II, q. 8.
[10] Cf. Leo XIII, Const., Romanos Pontifices; see also Vermeersch, De Rel., I, 364.
[11] Cf. Chokier, p. 4; Bouix, De Jure Regul., II, p. 114; Creusen, 309.
[12] Cf. Creusen, 305.
[13] Cf. Melo, p. 32.

PART II

Jurisdiction Over Exempt Religious

INTRODUCTORY REMARK

The jurisdictional power exercised over exempt religious bears an essential relation to exemption itself.[1] The nature of this jurisdiction definitely determines the nature of exemption; the jurisdictional authority possessed by exempt institutes specifies in a positive manner the character and the amount of power which has been withdrawn from local Ordinaries and vested in religious prelates.

From canons 500 and 615 it is clear that Regulars and other religious are exempt from the *jurisdiction* of local Ordinaries. To explain the full import of this declaration, we shall endeavor, in this part of our work, to define: the exact meaning of the jurisdiction under consideration; the efficient cause of its withdrawal from local Ordinaries and its bestowal on religious superiors; special characteristics of this jurisdiction; and, finally, its diverse functions, namely its legislative, judicial, and coactive powers.

---

[1] Cf. Suarez, tr. VIII, L. 2, c. 1, n. 6; Tamb., *De Jure Abb.*, II, Disp. 1, q. 2.

CHAPTER III

JURISDICTION IN CANON 615

ARTICLE I. THE MEANING OF JURISDICTION

Ecclesiastical jurisdiction is the public power of government communicated by Christ to His Church.[2] It confers on the hierarchy the right and duty to regulate, restrain, supervise, and control the faithful in matters pertaining to the end for which the Church was established. Destined as it is for the direct and immediate spiritual government of subjects, this power is employed to guide their mind and will, to control efficaciously their manner of living, and thus to enable them to secure their sanctification.[3]

In canon law the term *jurisdiction,* when used in its unrestricted sense, comprises the entire governmental authority of ecclesiastical superiors, namely, their legislative, judicial, and coactive powers.[4] It will be seen in Chapters IV, V, and VI that this is the meaning of the jurisdiction which forms an essential element of canon 615.

There are two distinct species of ecclesiastical jurisdiction: first, the *teaching authority* which rules over matters or objects of belief (credenda) — jurisdictio magisterii; and second, the *governing authority* which regulates the other objects or acts to be undertaken or omitted by the faithful (agenda) — jurisdictio regiminis. This distinction is expressly referred to in the Vatican Council.[5] It is worthy of remark that, in their exercise, both the teaching and the governing authority demand the obedient submission of the faithful.

The teaching office constitutes one of the principal functions of ecclesiastical jurisdiction.[6] By reason of this power the Church has her mission not only to preach to all men, but also to employ whatever means are necessary and helpful to increase, preserve, and defend the faith of her subjects.

Chief among these means are her infallible definitions proclaiming re-

---

[2] Cf. Suarez, XV, tr. 7, L. 2, c. 18, n. 5; Cappello, *Summa Juris Publici,* 25.

[3] Cf. Suarez, XV, tr. 7, L. 2, c. 18, n. 5; Cappello, *Summa Juris Publici,* 187, 190.

[4] Cf. Suarez, *De Censuris,* Disp. 14, sect. 1, n. 12; and Disp. 26, sect. 4, n. 19; Pihring, L. I, tit. 31, n. 1; Reiff., L. I, tit. 29, nn. 1 ff.; Cappello, *Summa Juris Publici,* 187.

[5] Cf. Conc. Vatic., sess. 4, cc. 1, 4; see also Bouix, *De Principiis J.C.,* pp. 499 ff.; Tarquini, 4; W.-V., II, 48; Cappello, *Summa Juris Publici,* 190.

[6] Cf. Leo XIII, Encycl., *Praeclara,* June 20, 1894; see W.-V., Tom. IV, Vol. II, 614.

vealed truth and proscribing error.[7] The Church also teaches by means of preaching, schools, seminaries, etc. Both the oral and written word are utilized and regulated in the exercise of this authority. Thus, books, pamphlets, the press, radio, sermons, catechetical instructions, etc., are used as aids in propagating, furthering, and defending the faith; just as the profession of faith by teachers, etc., and the prohibition of books, are employed as helps in safeguarding against dangers to the same.[8] We shall see presently that the two species of authority just described are contained in the jurisdiction spoken of in canon 615.

ARTICLE II. THE ROMAN PONTIFF WITHDRAWS JURISDICTION FROM LOCAL ORDINARIES AND BESTOWS IT ON RELIGIOUS PRELATES

I. WITHDRAWAL OF RELIGIOUS FROM THE JURISDICTION OF LOCAL ORDINARIES

In the case of exemption, it is the Roman Pontiff who withdraws religious from the authority of local Ordinaries and places them under that of their own superiors. In other words, he is the efficient cause of exemption.

By reason of the primacy he has full, supreme, and immediate jurisdiction over the universal Church, both in matters of faith and morals, and in those which pertain to the discipline of the Church throughout the world.[9] He is the Roman Pontiff, and Bishop and Pastor of all churches, all Bishops, and the entire faithful (can. 218, § 2).[10] He enjoys, by divine right, the plenitude of supreme jurisdictional authority (can. 219).

Hence, it is the Sovereign Pontiff who restricts or amplifies the jurisdiction of Bishops with respect to the persons, things, and territory over which they rule.[11] No legislator or group of legislators can validly enact laws that would be prejudicial to papal provisions, for the subordinate superior cannot invade the sphere of Christ's supreme Vicar.[12]

Bishops possess ordinary jurisdiction, but always within the limits prescribed by the Roman Pontiff. Their authority extends to their own subjects alone, and in accordance with restrictions fixed by pontifical law (can. 329). Therefore, they have no authority, generally speaking, over persons, places, or objects which have been withdrawn or exempted from their jurisdiction. Whatever the Holy See has established for the whole Church, or for a group of persons, or for an individual cannot be interfered with, diversified, or annulled by another legislator. Since, therefore, the exemption of religious is

---

[7] Cf. Conc. Vatic., sess. III, Const., *de fide cath.,* in prooem., et in fine; Leo XIII, Epist. ad Archiep. Baltimor., Jan. 22, 1899; Palmieri, pp. 163 ff.; Wilmers, pp. 53 ff. and 371 ff.; W.-V., Tom. IV, Vol. II, 614.

[8] Cf. W.-V., Tom. IV, Vol. II, 614.

[9] Cf. Conc. Vatic., sess. 4, c. 1; Palmieri, Theses I, IV; Wilmers, L. II, cc. I-III.

[10] Conc. Vatic., sess. 4, c. 1.

[11] Cf. Bouix, *De Principiis J.C.,* pp. 505-508.

[12] Cf. Conc. Vatic., sess. 4, c. 3.

a pontifical law (can. 615), it is inviolable and cannot be modified by any authority inferior to the Holy See.

This immunity of exempt religious as will be shown in Chapter IV, excludes the possibility of jurisdictional interference from both individual local Ordinaries and groups of the same, such as Plenary or Provincial Councils.[13]

II. SUBJECTION OF EXEMPT RELIGIOUS TO THEIR OWN SUPERIORS

By membership in the Church and in a particular institute religious are subject to a double hierarchy of power; one, the exterior hierarchy, is external to the religious institute, as such, and is composed of persons who are superiors in the Church; the other, the interior, is made up of religious superiors.[14]

N.B. When treating of the government of exempt religious one will avoid much confusion by bearing in mind the difference between jurisdictional and dominative authority. The former consists of the public power of governing in the Church, which includes the right to enact laws, to hold judicial trials, and to use coaction against those who violate the laws. The latter, that is, dominative power, is private in character, as that of a father over the household. The authoritative right of superiors endowed with dominative power arises from the agreement or pact whereby a person freely places himself under the rule of a religious institute and thus assumes the obligations incumbent upon a member thereof.[15] Thus, in the case of nuns: the superioress exercises only dominative power; the local Ordinary, only jurisdictional (in cases expressed in law), not dominative power. Whether religious of pontifical law be exempt or not, their interior government is in the hands of their own religious superiors, and this, independently of local Ordinaries, save in the cases expressly stated in law, as for example in canons 506 and 512.[16]

By reason of exemption, religious are freed from dependence upon all external superiors, with the exception of the Roman Pontiff. It is obvious that this latter cannot personally govern and direct all the religious institutes, places, and persons which have been withdrawn from the jurisdiction of local Ordinaries. He has, therefore, vested superiors of exempt clerical institutes with ecclesiastical jurisdiction (can. 501, § 1), so that major superiors are the properly constituted Ordinaries of their religious (can. 198) and hold the hierarchical position that would otherwise be occupied by the local Ordinaries.[17]

---

[13] Cf. Bened. XIV, *De Syn. Dioec.*, L. 7, 8, 9, c. 15; Suarez, *De Legibus*, L. IV, c. 20, n. 5.
[14] Cf. Creusen, 49.
[15] Cf. Suarez, XV, tr. 7, L. 2, c. 18, n. 5; Tamb., *De Jure Abb.*, II, Disp. I, q. 2; Cappello, *Summa Juris Publici*, 28; Schäfer, 105; *Epit.*, I, 619.
[16] Cf. cc. 501, § 1; 618, § 2, 2°; see also W.-V., III, 88; Creusen, 53.
[17] Cf. Suarez, XVI, tr. 8, L. 2, c. 1, nn. 6, 16; W.-V., III, 94.

ARTICLE III. NATURE OF THE JURISDICTION EXERCISED BY
SUPERIORS OF CLERICAL EXEMPT INSTITUTES

The jurisdiction possessed by religious Orders, and exercised by their superiors and chapters, comprises both teaching and governing authority. This is readily deduced from the declaration of the Holy See and the common teaching, prior to the promulgation of the Code, and from the laws of the Code.

I. PRIOR TO THE CODE

Declarations of Roman Pontiffs

Various Pontiffs have stated that full and inviolable power of governing the temporal and spiritual affairs of Regular institutes, houses, and persons is possessed by their own proper superiors ("Plena et libera potestas regendi et gubernandi in temporalibus et spiritualibus").[18]

1. Sixtus IV declared that jurisdiction in the Dominican Order was ". . . magisterii officium plane et libere in omnibus . . ."[19] The jurisdiction exercised in clerical exempt Orders he describes as, ". . . omnimodam jurisdictionem ordinariam in spiritualibus et temporalibus congregationis hujusmodi personarum."

2. Paul III stated that Regular superiors have unrestricted power and authority and faculties with respect to each and every subject.[20]

3. Paul V describes the governing power in Regular Orders as "supreme jurisdiction in spiritual and temporal matters," and states "capitulum . . . haberet . . . jus supremum."[21]

This same extensive scope of the jurisdiction of Regulars, and hence of their immunity from authorities external to their institutes, was often asserted by Roman Pontiffs in declaring that Regular superiors possessed that jurisdiction in their Orders which Bishops have in their dioceses. Thus, Pius V speaks of Regular prelates: "Ipsi per seipsos omnino possunt in fratres et moniales . . . sibi subditos, quod possunt episcopi in clericos et laicos sibi subditos, tam quoad absolvendi et dispensandi hujusmodi, quam alias quascumque, facultates, eadem facultate et tenore, etiam perpetuo concedimus, et indulgemus ac etiam declaramus."[22]

To specify the jurisdiction of Regular superiors over their subjects, Roman

---

[18] The force of this formula is found in the Decretals, cf. c. 24, I, 6, in VI; see Molitor, 184.

[19] Sixtus IV, *Regimini universalis*, par. 1, Aug. 31, 1474; Greg. XI, *Virtute conspicuos*, par. 2, Mar. 6, 1374.

[20] Cf. Const., *Exponi nobis*, par. 5, Aug. 25, 1535.

[21] *Ad immarcescibilem*, pars. 3, 5, Feb. 13, 1567; cf. also Molitor, 159, 184; Cappello, *De Visit. SS. Lim.*, II, pp. 405 ff.

[22] *Romani Pontificis*, par. 3, July 21, 1571; cf. also Sixtus IV, *Sedes Apostolica*, par. 5, May 27, 1474; Alex. IV, ap. c. 3, V, 7, in VI; and Molitor, 181, 182; Suarez, Tom. 16, tr. 8, L. II; Reiff., L. 5, t. 7, p. 9, n. 417 ff.; Piat, I, p. 752; Vermeersch, *De Rel.*, I, 415.

Pontiffs stated that they had "the care of the souls" of their subjects.[23] Because of this office, they were called *pastors* in the strict sense of the term.[24]

Statements of Authors

Authors called the jurisdiction of Regulars quasi-episcopal power, for it was considered similar in nature to that of Bishops.[25]

"Generally after religious institutes of men became exempt and immediately subject to the Roman Pontiff, their superiors, and particularly General Chapters, from a definite moral necessity, acquired besides dominative power, a real, ordinary and quasi-episcopal jurisdiction over their religious" (Wernz, III, 687).

"Authors commonly teach that the power of Regular superiors is quasi-episcopal; that is, it is the same as the authority which Bishops possess with respect to their subjects" (Piat, *op. cit.,* I, pars 4, C. 2, a. 2, quaest. 4).[26]

"Regulars withdrawn from the care and custody of Bishops cannot be immediately directed in all the affairs of daily life by the Roman Pontiff as sole *pastor*. It follows, therefore, that this noble portion of the Lord's flock is either wholly deprived of a pastor and pastoral care, and thus is in a more miserable state than the rest of the faithful; or their Regular superiors must be said to exercise the pastoral office" (Molitor, 184).[27]

From the statements of Sovereign Pontiffs and approved authors it is seen that Regular superiors possess a plenitude of spiritual jurisdiction over their subjects. This power involves the care of souls, and so is called pastoral. It is termed quasi-episcopal because similar in nature to that exercised by Bishops. As a consequence, it contains the rights and faculties which are necessary for the increase, preservation, and defense of the faith. These characteristics show that jurisdiction in religious orders is made up of both governing and teaching authority.

II. THE DISCIPLINE OF THE CODE

In every exempt clerical institute, the superiors and Chapters, conformably to the constitutions and to the universal law, have ecclesiastical jurisdiction in both the internal and external forum (can. 501, § 1). This power extends over all the male members of such institutes and over those nuns who by their constitutions are subject to Regulars (cc. 500, 501, 615).[28] Only

---

[23] Cf. Gregory XI, *Virtute conspicuos,* par. 2, Mar. 6, 1374; Eug. IV, *Romani Pontificis,* Aug. 13, 1437; Clem. VI, *Solicitudinis,* par. 1, Aug. 31, 1474.
[24] Cf. Urban II, *Cum universis,* par. 8, Apr. 6, 1090; Eug. III, *Sacrosancta,* par. 6, Aug. 1, 1152; Bonif. VIII, *In dispositione,* par. 11, May 18, 1297; Martin V, *Cum generale,* cap. 8, June 21, 1430.
[25] Cf. c. 3, *de privil.,* V, 7, in VI; Suarez, Tom. 16, tr. 8, L. II, c. 2, nn. 9–14; Pirhing, L. 1, t. 31, par. 10; Chokier, q. 17, n. 25; St. Alphon., L. 1, tr. 2, Append. 2, *De Privil.,* c. 4.
[26] Cf. Vermeersch, *De Relig.,* I, 415; Bouix, *De Jure Regul.,* II, Append. q. 2.
[27] Cf. Wernz, III, 683; Fagn., in c. 24, X, III, 31.
[28] Cf. Berutti, III, 26, scholion II.

in exceptional cases have local Ordinaries jurisdiction over these religious (cc. 500, 615).

Hence, by virtue of ecclesiastical law superiors and Chapters of exempt clerical institutes participate in the public government of the Church. They govern all the persons and affairs of their religious organization. Religious institutes, provinces, and houses are constituted independent moral bodies or corporations (cc. 531; 36, § 1), and are ruled by their respective superiors in much the same way as a diocese by the resident Bishop.[29]

It follows that exempt clerical institutes and their units are not to be looked upon as establishments separated from the normal and general hierarchical organization of the Church; they form, like dioceses and ecclesiastical provinces, a constituent element in the hierarchical order, for they are governed by the Sovereign Pontiff, and by their proper Ordinaries endowed with the public power of the Church.[30]

The legislation of the new Code clearly shows that the jurisdiction possessed by exempt institutes includes teaching and governing authority. This is the proper meaning of the phrase *jurisdiction in the external forum* (can. 501, § 1), and since the law adds no restrictions, it should be accepted in this sense.[31] Further, there is no reason to assume that the legislator intended to modify the discipline in force prior to the Code, which granted Regular superiors this twofold power.

Besides the argument just given, many provisions of the Code make manifest the fact that superiors of exempt clerical institutes have teaching authority with respect to their own subjects, and therefore the right and duty to adopt all means necessary for the preservation, furtherance, and defense of their faith.[32]

Thus, such superiors have authority and control over the faculties for the confessions of their subjects (can. 875, § 1), and for sermons to members of their communities (can. 1338, § 1); catechetical instructions (cc. 509, 565); the internal schools, as novitiates and schools for the philosophical and theological studies of their religious (cc. 542–571, 587–591, 1383); the previous censorship of books destined for the exclusive use of their subjects,[33] and the prohibition of dangerous books (can. 1395, § 3; see also can. 1402, § 1). Canonical visitation which aims to preserve, advance, and protect the faith and piety of subjects (can. 343, § 1), is to be made at stated times by those major superiors designated in the constitutions (can. 511). Except in the cases expressed by law, exempt religious are immune from episcopal visita-

---

[29] Cf. Bied.-Führ., 35; Schäfer, 110, and p. 190, n. 6.
[30] Cf. Larraona, C.p.R., IV, pp. 107–109, and VII, pp. 34 ff.
[31] Cf. Melo, p. 51.
[32] Cf. W.-V., Tom. IV, Vol. II, 646.
[33] Cf. W.-V., III, 142.

tion.[34] In general, *the care of the souls* of the religious is entrusted to their own prelates, not to others.[35]

ARTICLE IV. OTHER CHARACTERISTICS OF THE JURISDICTION HAD IN EXEMPT CLERICAL INSTITUTES

The jurisdiction enjoyed by prelates of exempt clerical institutes is *ordinary* (can. 197, § 1), and as a consequence is in nowise affected by the restrictions placed on delegated power (can. 199).[36]

In its amplitude, this jurisdiction is complete, extending to the internal and external forum (can. 501);[37] in its exercise, it is not subordinate to any authority outside the institute, save the Holy See.

This governing power is shared differently by different superiors. Superiors-General have jurisdiction over all provinces, houses, and members, but must exercise it in accordance with the provisions of the constitutions; others such as provincials and local superiors, have authority within the limits of their charge (can. 502).

Canon 501, § 1, states that *superiors* of clerical exempt institutes are endowed with jurisdictional power in accordance with their constitutions and the universal law. The Code supposes all such superiors to be capable of acquiring jurisdiction in the external forum, and even seems actually to concede them faculties which postulate authority of this kind (cc. 202, § 3; 501, § 1; 875, § 1; 1245, § 3; 1313, 2°; 1320; 1338, § 1).[38]

If minor local superiors have ordinary jurisdiction in the external forum, they are undoubtedly *prelates* in the true sense of the term (can. 110). In the constitutions of many of the institutes in question, these superiors are expressly acknowledged to be prelates, or are accorded faculties that suppose them to be endowed with jurisdiction.[39] Before the promulgation of the Code it was admitted that local superiors of Regulars were prelates.[40] The Code itself makes no express provision altering this commonly admitted doctrine, but appears rather to confirm it (cc. 10 and 501, § 1).[41]

It is clear from canon 198 that only major superiors (can. 488, 8°) of clerical exempt institutes are religious Ordinaries.[42]

---

[34] Cf. Conc. Trid., sess. 25, c. 20; see W.-V., III, 146.

[35] Cf. W.-V., III, 142.

[36] Cf. Piat, I, Pars IV, c. 2, a. 3; Larraona, C.p.R., VII, p. 35; Maroto, I, 700 ff.

[37] Cf. Maroto, I, 717 ff.

[38] Cf. Larraona, C.p.R., IV, p. 76 and notes; II, p. 114.

[39] Cf. *Per.*, 17, pp. 229*–231*; for instances from different constitutions see Larraona, C.p.R., IV, p. 76, nota (337).

[40] Cf. c. 3 *de privilegiis*, V, 7 in VI; Pius V, const. *Romani Pontificis*, July 21, 1571; Suarez, Tom. 16, *de Relig.*, tr. 8, c. 2, n. 10; Tamb., *De jure abb.*, II, Disp. 1, q. 2, n. 2; Pell., tr. IX, c. 3, n. 15; Ferrari, 78; Piat, I, pp. 492 ff.; Ojetti, *Per.* 17, pp. 230*–231*; Larraona, C.p.R. IV, *loc. cit.*

[41] Cf. Schäfer, 105; Larraona, *loc. cit.*

[42] Cf. Larraona, C.p.R., IV, pp. 39 ff.

The jurisdiction of religious Prelates is *personal* in character, and so it affects subjects irrespective of their dwelling place, i.e., whether outside the house or beyond the confines of the province.[43]

Abbots Primate and superiors of monastic congregations have not the full jurisdiction that the universal law confers on major superiors. Their authority and jurisdictional powers are defined by their respective constitutions and by particular decrees of the Holy See, without prejudice, of course, to the prescriptions of canons 655 and 1594, § 4 (can. 501, § 3).[44]

ARTICLE V. JURISDICTION OF LOCAL ORDINARIES OVER EXEMPT RELIGIOUS

1. Local Ordinaries have very restricted powers over exempt religious institutions. The general principle of this: local Ordinaries have authority over exempt religious in those cases only which are expressly mentioned in law (cc. 500, 615). Special attention will be given these cases throughout the remainder of this work.

2. Lay religious Orders, and institutes of nuns not subject to Regular superiors do not generally enjoy exemptive rights. Normally, the superiors of such religious are not endowed with ecclesiastical jurisdiction (can. 118) and consequently they depend for their jurisdictional government on superiors external to their institute, as, for example, local Ordinaries.[45]

The jurisdiction of local Ordinaries over nuns and other lay Regulars subject to them, is not entirely unrestricted. Since such religious belong to institutes approved by the Holy See, the local Ordinary may not: (*a*) make any change in the constitutions, or inquire into the temporal administration, saving the dispositions of canons 533–535; (*b*) interfere in the internal government and discipline, except in the cases expressed by law (can. 618).

Nevertheless, in regard to lay institutes, the local Ordinary can and must inquire: whether the discipline is maintained conformably to the constitutions; whether sound doctrine and good morals have suffered in any way; whether there have been breaches of the law of enclosure; whether the reception of the sacraments is regular and frequent. And if superiors having been warned of the existence of grave abuses have failed to duly remedy them, the Ordinary himself shall provide; if, however, something of greater importance, which will not suffer delay, occur, the Ordinary shall decide immediately; but he must report his decision to the Holy See (can. 618).

Further, the local Ordinary has the right to preside over assemblies for the election of a superioress in a monastery of nuns (can. 506, § 2); he can dismiss nuns with temporary vows in accordance with the terms of canon

---

[43] Cf. Schäfer, 105.

[44] Cf. Leo XIII, const., *Summum semper,* nn. I, II, IV, V, July 12, 1893; Decr., S.C.EE.RR. Sept. 16, 1893 (ap. ASS, 26, p. 371); W.-V., III, 98.

[45] Cf. Melo, p. 51; Larraona, C.p.R., VI, pp. 291, 292.

647; he approves their confessors (can. 525); he determines the limits of the cloister of nuns and can modify them for lawful reasons (can. 597, § 3), and is charged with the custody of their enclosure (can. 603). His previous consent must be obtained by the superioress of nuns: in the investment of money (can. 533) and of the dowries of nuns (can. 549); for any alteration in the disposition of property treated of in canon 569, § 2 (can. 580, § 3); for the alienation of temporal goods (can. 534). He must be furnished annually, or even oftener if the constitutions so prescribe, with an account of the superioress' administration of the monastery (can. 535); he must be informed by the superioress, at least two months in advance, of approaching admissions to the novitiate, and to the profession both of temporary and perpetual, or of solemn or simple vows (can. 552); he must make the canonical visitation prescribed by law (can. 512).

Apostates from lay religious institutes incur excommunication reserved to the Ordinary of the place in which they reside and are deprived of all the privileges of their Order (Can. 2385).

Several limitations of the authority of local Ordinaries arise from the fact that the matters involved are of the greatest consequence to institutes of pontifical law, so that their government practically necessitates papal care and protection. Thus it is decreed that the local Ordinary has no authority to dismiss religious professed of perpetual vows (can. 650), nor to grant them indults of exclaustration or secularization (can. 638). He cannot issue even a partial condonation of the prescribed dowry to be provided by postulants (can. 547). It is not within his power to permit nuns to leave the cloister, except in case of imminent danger of death or other very serious evils (can. 601).

The permission of the local Ordinary does not suffice for the canonical establishment of a monastery pertaining to the institutes in question (can. 497). He is not competent to prolong the three-year period of temporary profession (can. 574), nor to dismiss a religious who has made profession of perpetual vows either in a nonexempt clerical institute or in a lay institute approved by the Holy See (cc. 650, 651, 652, §§ 2 and 3).

In conclusion, it is to be noted that the jurisdiction of Regular superiors over nuns subject to them is: *internal,* that is to say, it is the jurisdictional power which religious superiors exercise over their own proper subjects; and in a sense *external,* that is, it is true ecclesiastical jurisdiction in the external forum.[46] This is different from the jurisdiction exercised over nuns by local Ordinaries. Their authority over religious does not constitute local Ordinaries religious superiors, but external ecclesiastical superiors with jurisdiction over the religious.[47] Therefore, they have no jurisdiction in the in-

---

[46] Cf. Larraona, C.p.R., VI, p. 185, nota (86).
[47] Cf. Larraona, C.p.R., VI, p. 186.

ternal government of the religious institute, save in the cases expressly mentioned in law (can. 618).[48]

Nuns, though subject to the jurisdiction of local Ordinaries, remain religious of pontifical law in the sense of canon 488, 7°, just as other monastic nuns in the universal Church,[49] and where no legal exception is in force, they must be treated as such.[50]

The jurisdiction granted to religious Orders includes, as has been said before, legislative, judicial, and coactive power. These functions will be studied separately in the three following chapters.

---

[48] Cf. Coronata, I, 330.
[49] Cf. S. C. Rel., Decree, June 23, 1923, ap. AAS, XV, 357; Bouscaren I, can. 500.
[50] Cf. Larraona, C.p.R., VI, p. 186.

CHAPTER IV

LEGISLATIVE POWER

Legislative authority empowers superiors to prescribe, or, in other words, to propose in an obligatory manner, whatever is necessary and useful for the well-being of a religious institute.[1] The precise amplitude of this function is determined by common law and particular rights and constitutions.

Therefore, the appropriate exercise of legislative power is the enactment of laws,[2] and the issuance of decrees which regulate the means necessary and useful to the end of a particular institute. Naturally flowing from this function are the rights: to interpret authentically and dispense from laws and decrees, and to exercise all administrative acts necessary for the good government of a community.[3]

Our present discussion is confined to the enactment of laws, for authentic interpretation has already been explained (Chap. II, Art. III), and administrative functions are sufficiently treated later on in the section dealing with the extension of exemption (Part III).

THE ENACTMENT OF LAWS

I. AUTHORITY VESTED IN EXEMPT CLERICAL INSTITUTES

The Code declares the following principle: conformably with the constitutions and the universal law of the Church, superiors and Chapters of clerical exempt institutes possess the faculty to enact laws for the government of their own religious subjects (can. 501). Regular superiors of male orders have the same power with respect to the nuns subject to them.[4] This legislation is in full agreement with that which was in force prior to the promulgation of the present law.[5] In the distribution of legislative authority

---

[1] Cf. Cappello, *Summa Juris Publici*, 70.
[2] Cf. Suarez, *De Legibus*, L. 4, c. 6, n. 12.
[3] Cf. Cappello, *Summa Juris Publici*, 73, 201.
[4] Cf. Noldin, I, 132.
[5] Cf. Urban VII, *Plantata*, Apr. 25, 1634; Greg. XV, Const., *Pastoralis*, par. 7, Feb. 12, 1621; Alex. VII, Const., *Sacrosancti*, par. 2, Nov. 5, 1659; Innoc. XII, Const., *Pastoralis Officii*, par. 3, June 21, 1695; Clem. XII, Const., *Inter religiosorum*, Aug. 2, 1738; see also Suarez, XVI, tr. 8, L. 2, c. 8, n. 2; Pell., tr. IX, c. III, n. 18; Bouix, *De Jure Regul.*, II, p. 6, c. 3, par. 2; Piat, I, p. 4; Wernz, III, 690; Vermeersch, *De Rel.*, I, 423; Molitor, 163.

within an institute, the power to enact laws is ordinarily reserved to general Chapters, and not, therefore, granted to individual superiors.[6]

II. AUTHORITY VESTED IN LOCAL ORDINARIES

By reason of their exemption the religious in question together with their houses and churches have been withdrawn from the jurisdiction of local Ordinaries, save in cases of express exception (can. 615). Hence, generally speaking, neither individual local Ordinaries nor groups of the same can legislate for exempt religious. According to Suarez, Regulars ". . . sunt simpliciter exempti a jurisdictione tam episcoporum quam synodorum episcoporum, ergo maxime sunt exempti a primo actu jurisdictionis, qui est legem ferre."[7] As a consequence, neither Plenary or Provincial Councils, nor diocesan Synods can enact laws or statutes which are in any way prejudicial to the exemptive rights or privileges of religious institutes.[8]

Both past and present legislation show that Regulars enjoy this exemption. Gregory IX ordered prelates and others to desist from forcing Regulars to obey synodal decrees (c. 17, X, *de excess, prael.,* V, 31).[9] Benedict XIV explains in detail this exemption and the corresponding incompetency of local Ordinaries (*De Syn. Dioec.,* L. IX, c. 15). Councils and Synods had jurisdiction over Regulars in those cases only which were expressly defined by law.[10] From canons 500 and 615 of the Code, it is clear, too, that exemption comprises this immunity from enactments of local Ordinaries whether these latter legislate singly or collectively.[11]

Decrees of Plenary and Provincial Councils and of diocesan Synods purpose to regulate opportunely and according to the needs of a definite territory, whatever pertains to the progress of faith, the preservation of morals, the correction of abuses, the settling of controversies, and the introduction and maintenance of uniformity of discipline (cc. 290, 356). The persons primarily envisaged are secular clerics and the faithful. Certainly no attempt should be made to establish uniform discipline for secular clerics and exempt religious, because the Holy See, by her law and concession of privileges, sanctions and approves diversity in their juridical status. Furthermore, legislative intervention on the part of local Ordinaries is generally uncalled for. Prescriptions of canon law, rules and constitutions combined with jurisdiction, and care of their proper prelates, adequately provide for the government and well-being of exempt religious, the fulfillment of their obligations as

---

[6] Cf. Wernz, III, 690; Piat, I, p. 4; Bied.-Führ., 37; W.-V., III, 127.

[7] Cf. Suarez, *De Legibus,* L. IV, c. 20, n. 8.

[8] Cf. Bened. XIV, *De Syn. Dioec.,* L. 7, 8, 9, c. 15; Ferraris, v., *Regulares,* art. II, n. 109; Melo, p. 68.

[9] Cf. Suarez, *De Legibus,* L. IV, c. 20, n. 5; Fagn., in Lib. V, Decr., c. 17.

[10] Cf. c. 1, *de priv.,* V, 7, in VI, Bened. XIV, *loc. cit.;* Fagn., *loc. cit.;* Suarez, *loc. cit.;* Leo XIII, Const., *Romanos Pontifices.*

[11] Cf. W.-V., II, 629; Melo, pp. 68, 69.

priests and religious, and the advancement of their apostolic works. On their part, however, these religious are bound to observe laws of councils and synods when this is necessary in order to avoid scandal. Nevertheless, in such instances, the obligation arises not from the positive laws enacted by local Ordinaries, but from the natural law.[12]

The law expressly states the cases in which local Ordinaries can bind exempt religious by legislative acts.

1. Exempt religious must abide by synodal decrees defining the amount which constitutes the stipend for manual Masses (can. 831, § 3). A stipend more generous than the one prescribed may be accepted when it has been spontaneously offered; likewise a smaller one, unless this has been forbidden.[13]

2. Local Ordinaries can form laws governing the celebration of Mass by visiting priests, and the exaction of fees for the use of utensils, vestments, etc., from the same. Particular provisions of this kind must, however, be in conformity with general laws.

Courtesy and clerical hospitality demand that priests who are strangers in a place be received with reverence and charity by the secular and religious clergy. On the other hand, the visiting priest who desires to offer up the Holy Sacrifice of the Mass, should have commendatory letters (a *celebret*) vouching for his good standing.[14]

The local Ordinary may permit a tax for the use of vestments, etc., only when the church in question is poor.[15] Vermeersch states that since the general term "Ordinary" is employed in canon 1303, § 2, the provision can be interpreted to mean that the religious Ordinary may allow such a tax, independently of the diocesan legislation.[16] This was held by authors prior to the Code.[17] If the Bishop in the diocesan Synod or otherwise, has fixed the fee that may be exacted, no one, not even exempt religious, may demand more (can. 1303, §§ 3 and 4).[18]

3. Matters of divine worship: Local Ordinaries can enact laws concerning the matters of divine worship provided for in canon 1261. It is their duty to take the measures necessary to protect the faithful against superstitious practices, and to defend them from anything which is discordant with faith and Catholic tradition, or which savors of sordid money-making. The law expressly states that exempt religious are obliged to comply with

---

[12] Cf. Suarez, *De Legibus,* L. IV, c. 20, n. 6.

[13] Cf. W.-V., IV, Vol. II, 81; Ayrinhac, *Legislation on the Sacraments,* 122; *Epit.,* II, 105; Melo, p. 73.

[14] Concerning the *celebret,* consult below, Chap. XII, Art. III.

[15] Cf. Gasparri, *De Sanctissima Eucharistia,* II, 672.

[16] Cf. *Epit.,* II, 631.

[17] Cf. Lehmkuhl, II, 274.

[18] Cf. Coronata, II, 884; Augustine, IV, can. 804; Ayrinhac, *Legis. on the Sacr.,* 69; Bondini, pp. 81, 82.

the diocesan statutes regulating such matters, and that local Ordinaries may visit their churches and public oratories to see that their orders are obeyed (can. 1261). This legislation of the Code is similar to that which was formerly in force.[19] It will be seen, in Part III in the Chapter on Divine Cult, that this legislative authority of local Ordinaries is definitely restricted in character as is their right of visitation[20] in relation to such enactments.

4. Pastors and vicars belonging to exempt institutes: By divine law, diocesan Bishops are placed over individual churches which they govern with ordinary jurisdiction under the authority of the Roman Pontiff (can. 329). They are the ordinary and immediate pastors in the dioceses entrusted to them (can. 334), and consequently exercise legislative power in the government of the spiritual and temporal affairs of their dioceses, conformably with the rule of the sacred canons (can. 335).

When promulgated, episcopal laws bind all persons subject to them (cc. 335, § 2; 362). Hence, since religious pastors and vicars, as such, are subject to local Ordinaries, they must obey all diocesan laws and statutes regulating matters pertaining to their office (can. 631). Such religious, even though exempt, are subject, as secular pastors, to the visitation, correction, and immediate authority of the local Ordinary in everything connected with their pastoral care.

---

[19] Cf. Conc. Trid., sess. 25, *de invocatione*.
[20] Cf. Reply of Cardinal Gasparri, Apr. 8, 1924; Coronata, II, 834; Goyeneche, C.p.R., VI, pp. 357–360; Marcellus a P. Jesu, C.p.R., IX, pp. 235–244; Kraemer, C.p.R., IX, pp. 245–248.

CHAPTER V

JUDICIAL POWER

I. JUDICIAL POWER IN EXEMPT INSTITUTES

Such institutes are exempt from the judicial power of local Ordinaries and subject to that of their own superiors (cc. 501, 615). Those cases only are excepted which are expressly specified by law, v.g., canon 616. The judicial power in question is effective in both the internal and external forum (can. 501).

A. *In the Internal Forum*

Jurisdiction in the internal forum operates primarily and directly for the private good of the individual religious and is chiefly exercised in sacramental confession for the remission of sins.

JURISDICTION TO HEAR CONFESSIONS

By common law, superiors in clerical exempt institutes have ordinary jurisdiction to hear the confessions of their own professed religious, of their novices, and of the persons enumerated in canon 514. Because this power is ordinary, it may be delegated, and, according to canon 875, § 1, even to priests who belong to other institutes or to the secular clergy.

In an exempt lay institute the superior proposes the confessor, who, however, must receive jurisdiction from the Ordinary of the place in which the religious house is situated (can. 875, § 2).

Canon 876 makes provision for the confessions of religious women and novices of their institutes. "Every contrary particular law or privilege being revoked, all priests, whether secular or Regular, no matter what may be their dignity or office, must have special jurisdiction to hear validly and licitly the confessions of religious women and novices, safeguarding, however, the prescriptions of canons 239, § 1, n. 1; 522, 523."

"This jurisdiction is conferred by the Ordinary of the place in which the house is located, according to the norm of canon 525." Therefore, Regular priests of the same Order as the penitent, and those who have jurisdiction in the external forum over nuns, depend entirely on the local Ordinary for these faculties.[1]

---

[1] Cf. Creusen, 109; cf. below, Chap. XII, Art. IV.

B. *In the External Forum*

Prelates of exempt institutes have judicial power in the external forum over their own religious subjects.[2] Since this authority is vested only in religious superiors of clerical exempt institutes (cc. 501, 1575), it is not shared by lay superiors. Hence, nuns subject to Regulars are under their jurisdiction in judicial matters.[3]

Major Superiors in clerical exempt institutes are the prelates ordinarily endowed with this judicial power.[4] Superiors of monastic congregations, though not possessing the full jurisdiction accorded by law to superiors of religious Orders (can. 501, § 3), are nevertheless vested with some judicial power. This is clear from canons 655; 1579, §§ 1 and 2; 1594, § 4. The abbot primate of the confederation of the so-called "Black Benedictines" has no jurisdiction over the single congregations or abbeys, or over the various abbots or members. He exercises ordinary jurisdiction over the College of St. Anselm, in Rome, whose abbot he is, but is accorded no jurisdictional powers by the Apostolic brief *"Summum Semper,"* July 12, 1893, creating him primate of the fraternal confederation.[5]

Unless otherwise determined in the common law and constitutions, the prelate competent to take cognizance of the prosecution of a suit at its inception (i.e., the judge of the first instance) is the Provincial superior, and in an independent monastery, the local abbot.[6] The judge of the second instance in all cases that have been tried before the court of the Provincial, is the supreme moderator of the institute, in cases tried before the local abbot, the supreme moderator of the monastic congregation (can. 1594, § 4). The court of last instance is the Rota (cc. 1598–1601).

II. LIMITATIONS OF JUDICIAL POWER

Though all religious, men and women, subject to superiors of exempt clerical institutes, are under their judicial power, yet they depend upon that of local Ordinaries in the cases expressly defined by law. Further lack of authority, and hence judiciary dependence is had in cases which the Holy See has reserved to its own tribunals. The following are the important cases that limit the judicial authority of exempt institutes.

A. *Cases Pertaining to the Holy See*[7]

Only the tribunals of the Apostolic See have the right to judge cases

---

[2] Cf. Suarez, XVI, tr. 8, L. 2, c. 9; Lega, *De Jud. Eccl.,* IV, 500; W.-V., VI, 57.
[3] Cf. Suarez, XVI, tr. 9, L. 1, c. 12; Pell., *De Mon., C.,* X, sect. 1, subj. II; Lega, *loc. cit.;* W.-V., *loc. cit.;* Bied-Führ., 42, 4; Melo, p. 52.
[4] Cf. can. 1579, Bied.-Führ., 42, 4.
[5] Cf. Aug., III, p. 112; Melo, p. 52.
[6] Cf. Bied.Führ., 42, 4; Cappello, *Summa J.C.,* III, 98.
[7] Cases under A are limitations of *judicial* power, not of exemption.

involving exempt religious institutes and monastic congregations (can. 1557, § 2, 2°). Other courts, being absolutely incompetent, are unable to take cognizance of or pass judgment on the same (can. 1558).

Canon 501, § 2, strictly forbids superiors to interfere in cases pertaining to the Holy Office. Any such reserved matters coming to the notice of Regular prelates must be referred to the said tribunal.[8] Therefore, Regular Superiors cannot take judicial action against a religious guilty of a reserved crime, v.g., they cannot issue canonical warnings, nor attempt to dismiss the offender from the institute because of his delinquency.[9]

Chief among these cases are the following:

1. Causes referring to matters of faith and morals: These embrace heresy, schism, apostasy (can. 2314, par. 2), other crimes which render one juridically suspect of heresy (cc. 2316; 2319, § 2; 2320; 2332; 2340, § 1; 2371), and those connected with heresy (cc. 2317, 2318). Clerics and religious who have themselves enrolled in Masonic or similar associations, should be denounced to the Holy Office (can. 2336, § 2).

Regulars who are suspect or guilty of heresy are subject to the judicial power of local Ordinaries and not that of their proper superiors (can. 1555).[10] This is clear from the following declaration of the Holy See: "Uti pluries a Summis Pontificibus sancitum est in rebus ad S. Officium spectantibus nullo modo ad Superiores Regulares pertinere subditorum suorum causas agnoscere, nulloque proinde titulo aut praetextu posse vel debere, nisi de expresso S. Congregationis mandato, de his inquirere, denunciationes recipere, testes interrogare, reos excutere, judicium instituere, sententiam ferre, aut alia quavis ratione vel modo in eis sese immiscere vel manus apponere; sed quos Religiosi Viri ex suis subditis vel confratribus vel etiam superioribus hujusmodi criminum (praesertim quod ad abusum Sacramentalis Confessionis spectat), reos vel suspectos, noverint, strictim teneri absque ulla cum aliis quibuscumque communicatione, nulla petita venia, nullaque fraterna correptione aut monitione praemissa, eos S. Officio aut locorum Ordinariis incunctanter denuntiare. Ne vero sanctissimas has leges ex ignorantia (quod Deus avertat) negligi aut infringi contingat, Superioribus grave onus incumbere eas, quo opportuniori putarint modo, ad subditorum suorum certam et distinctam identidem deferre notitiam earumque ab eis plenam observantiam urgere." (S.R. et U. Inquisitio, May 15, 1901.)[11]

2. Grave cases involving an abuse of sacraments: Among such are in-

---

[8] Cf. Larraona, C.p.R., VII, p. 95.

[9] Cf. Larraona, loc. cit.

[10] Cf. c. 9, X, de heret., V., 7; c. 17, de heret., V, 2, in VI; Trid. sess. V, c. 2, de Ref.; Paul V, Const., Romanus Pontifex, Sept. 1, 1606; Variae regulae in curia Romana servandae, Sept. 29, 1908, ap. AAS, I, 36–108; also W.-V., II, 488, nota (37); Melo, pp. 54–56; Bondini, pp. 57, 58; Epit., I, 775; Schäfer, 106; Larraona, C.p.R., VII, pp. 93–98.

[11] ASS, 34 (1901–1902), p. 383. This is a fortiori true of delinquents who are members of exempt clerical congregations.

cluded: solicitation in the act, on the occasion or under the pretext of hearing confession (cc. 904, 2368); violations of the sacramental seal (cc. 889, 890, 2369); simulations of celebrating Mass or hearing confession by those not promoted to the priesthood (can. 2322, 1°).

Local Ordinaries have judicial power over cases of solicitation which have been denounced to them, even though the accused party be an exempt religious (can. 904).[12] Religious superiors are here incompetent. The same must be said of simulation of Mass and sacramental confession, for these would render a religious suspect of heresy,[13] and hence subject to the local Ordinary.[14]

3. Cases impugning the validity of ordinations because of a substantial defect in the sacred rites: The competent tribunal is the court of the diocese in which the ordination was performed (can. 1993), when, of course, the Holy Office refers the case to the same.

4. All questions concerning the Eucharistic fast for priests in the celebration of Mass belong to the Holy Office exclusively (can. 247, § 5).

5. Until the Apostolic See rules otherwise, cases involving violations of the oath against Modernism and refusal to subscribe to the oath, are reserved to the Holy Office.[15]

6. Cases of dismissal from an institute are handled by the Sacred Congregation of Religious: The Code outlines the procedure to be followed in the case of religious belonging to clerical exempt institutes. Dismissal of other religious is effected by administrative, not judicial action.[16]

Religious of clerical exempt institutes are immune in this matter from any judicial intervention on the part of local Ordinaries. When there is question of the dismissal of such a religious professed of final vows, whether solemn or simple, the canonical process must be instituted by his proper superior (cc. 654-668). Every privilege exempting from this process is revoked (can. 654). The few exceptional cases not demanding judiciary action are specified in canons 646 and 668.

Though endowed with some jurisdiction, religious superiors of exempt institutes are not accorded complete independence in cases of dismissal, for a sentence cannot be carried into effect unless it be confirmed by the Sacred Congregation of Religious. Hence, the president of the religious court must, as soon as possible, transmit all the proceedings of the trial to this Congregation (can. 666). After ratification, the sentence should be

---

[12] *Epit.*, II, 191; Melo, pp. 55, 56.
[13] Cf. Greg. XIII, Const., *Officii nostri*, Aug. 6, 1574, ap. Gasparri *Fontes*, I, n. 145; Coronata, IV, 1890.
[14] Cf. *supra*, n. 1; also Melo, *loc. cit.*
[15] Cf. Resp. S. Off., Mar. 22, 1918, ap. AAS, X, 136.
[16] Cf. cc. 649-643; and Schäfer, 582.

executed by superiors, according to the prescriptions of the aforesaid Congregation.[17]

The Code does authorize superiors to effect the immediate dismissal of subjects in cases of grave scandal or of very serious imminent danger to the community. This is clear from canon 668 which states: in the case provided for in canon 653, the religious can be dismissed immediately by the higher superior, or if there be danger in delay and the time does not admit of recourse to the higher superior, by the local superior with the consent of the Council; the religious must immediately put off the religious habit. After dismissal the trial must be held at once, according to the procedure indicated in the foregoing canons.

7. Cases concerning the nullity of religious profession: Prior to the promulgation of the Code, the judicial process was required in cases contesting the validity of a religious profession.[18] The Council of Trent designated religious superiors and local Ordinaries judges in the matter.

The Code omits mention of court trial. Controversies of this kind are left to the decision of the Sacred Congregation of Religious (can. 586). It is probable that settlements will be made in an administrative rather than judicial manner.[19] In the event that judiciary action is taken, the norms which regulate trials against the validity of sacred orders (cc. 1993–1998) may be employed[20]

B. *Cases Pertaining to the Local Ordinary*

Besides those mentioned under n. I, the Code specifies certain definite controversies concerning exempt religious which must be submitted to the court of the local Ordinary. Such disputes are (can. 1579, § 3):

1. Those between physical or moral persons of different religious institutes;
2. Those between religious of the same lay institute, even though exempt;[21]
3. And, lastly, those between a religious (whether Regular or not) and a secular cleric or layman.[22]

Local Ordinaries have the right to settle controversies, even among exempt religious, regarding the cases of precedence referred to in canon 106, 6°. This is similar to the ruling of the Council of Trent (Trid. sess. 25, c. 13).[23]

Only the cases concerning precedence which are mentioned expressly in law fall under the jurisdiction of the local Ordinary (cc. 500, § 1; 615). In law these are actually limited to disputes concerning the *collegiate* precedence

---

[17] Cf. Michalicka, *Judicial Procedure in Dismissal of Clerical Exempt Religious* (Dissert. C. U., 1923), p. 99.

[18] Cf. Trid., sess. 25, c. 19, *de Reg.;* Bened. XIV, Const., *Si datum,* Mar. 4, 1748, ap. B. B., II, 393.

[19] Cf. Bied.-Führ., 165; Melo, p. 54; Schäfer, 541.

[20] Cf. Schäfer, *loc. cit.*

[21] Cf. Cappello, *Summa J.C.,* III, 98; W.-V., VI, 93; Melo, p. 56.

[22] Melo, p. 56.

[23] Cf. Piat, II, p. 42, q. 5; Vermeersch, *De Rel.,* I, 527; Bondini, pp. 15–17.

of one group over another (can. 106, 6°). Furthermore, the Code restricts his jurisdiction to the more urgent cases, for the purpose of the prescription is to preclude the possibility of public disputes,[24] when circumstances prevent recourse to the ordinary authorities in such matters. In normal cases, *administrative* settlements are made by the Congregation of Religious (cc. 250, § 3; 251, § 1).[25] *Judicial* settlements of such controversies can be made by the Ordinary of the place (can. 1579, §3),[26] appeal can be made to the S. R. Rota.

From the Ordinary's decision, an appeal "in devolutivo" only is allowed (can. 106, 6°). Hence, pending the reply of the Holy See, exempt religious must obey his orders. As is manifest, the local Ordinary cannot make a settlement that is prejudicial to the rights of either contestant. Hence, he must observe the provisions of canon 491, and any particular decrees issued by the Holy See.[27]

---

[24] Cf. Ayrinhac, *Gen. Legis.,* 231.

[25] Cf. Chelodi, 103; Coronata, I, 162.

[26] Cf. Chelodi, *loc. cit.;* Coronata, *loc. cit.;* Ojetti, *Com. in Cod.,* II, pp. 208, 7.

[27] According to canon 491, religious take precedence over the laity; clerical institutes over lay institutes; Canons Regular over monks; monks over other Regulars; Regulars over religious congregations; religious congregations approved by the Holy See over diocesan congregations. For those in the same kind of institute, the disposition of canon 106, n. 5, is to be observed. But the secular clergy precede the laity and the religious outside their own churchs and, in the case of a lay institute, even in their own churches; the cathedral or collegiate chapter, however, precedes them everywhere.

CHAPTER VI

COACTIVE POWER

Article I. The Coactive Power of Religious Superiors

Coactive power is that function of jurisdictional authority whereby ecclesiastical superiors are enabled efficaciously to enforce the observance of law and good order. Those, therefore, having this power are authorized, within the limits of their jurisdiction, to impose and remit penalties in both the internal and external forums.

The present article treats chiefly of the coactive power enjoyed by religious superiors with respect to exempt religious. Because, nevertheless, in certain cases simple confessors and priests have been accorded definite powers to remit penalties, we think it useful to call attention to these faculties in the course of our discussion.

I. POWER TO IMPOSE PENALTIES

Canon 501, § 1 states the general principle, namely: in a clerical exempt institute superiors and Chapters have ecclesiastical jurisdiction, in accordance with the norms of their constitutions and common law, both for the internal and for the external forum. In its proper sense the expression "ecclesiastical jurisdiction" signifies legislative, judicial, and coactive power. Therefore, unless particular constitutions or common law determine otherwise, superiors and Chapters of clerical exempt institutes possess this threefold power.[1]

Common law (can. 501, § 1) by employing the general term "superiors" does not restrict the jurisdiction in question to religious Ordinaries. Cappello maintains that the Code refers here to major superiors, and that, unless constitutions expressly state the contrary, coactive power is not granted to other superiors.[2] However, it seems preferable to accept the term "superiors," as the Code uses it, in an unmodified sense. Reason itself appears to war-

---

[1] Cf. above, Chap. III, Art. III. Before the Code ample proof of the existence of this power was had from express declarations of the Holy See and from the statements of authors; see, v.g.: Innoc. III, Const., *Omnipotenti Deo,* § 8, July 25, 1208; Boniface VIII, Const., *Ad augmentum,* § 1, May 10, 1296; Sixtus IV, Const., *Dum attenta,* §§ 29, 31, Nov. 28, 1476; Paul III, Const., *Exponi nobis,* § 4, Aug. 25, 1536; Pius V, Const., *Etsi mendicantium,* § 2, May 16, 1567; consult Bouix, II, P. 6, sect. 2, c. 1, 2; Wernz, III, 692; Molitor, 170 ff.; Vermeersch, *De Rel.,* I, 380.

[2] Cf. Cappello, *De Censuris,* 11, and footnote 8.

rant this interpretation. Authority to impose penalties is a natural consequence of legislative authority, for the latter would prove ineffective and
useless without the former. But it is generally admitted that even local
superiors may possess legislative power. Therefore all superiors authorized
to issue laws or jurisdictional precepts, i.e., all who have jurisdiction in the
external forum, possess coactive power (can. 2220).[3] Such a conclusion is
entirely in conformity with canon 2220, just cited, and with other norms,
v.g., canon 603, § 2, which permits Regular superiors having custody over
the cloister of nuns to inflict penalties on any persons violating the laws of
cloister.

Only by reason of special privilege do superiors of nonclerical exempt institutes possess coactive power.

Superiors and Chapters endowed with legislative power can, within the
limits of their authority, impose appropriate penalties not only for violations
of their own laws and precepts, but, should circumstances warrant it, for
infractions of divine laws and of ecclesiastical laws and precepts issued by
higher superiors (can. 2221). It is, however, to be noted that superiors cannot reserve to themselves censures which are already reserved to the Apostolic See (can. 2247, § 1).

By virtue of canon 2222 superiors have authority to impose a just penalty
for the violation of a law which has no sanction attached to it, if scandal
has been given or the peculiar gravity of the transgression demands such
punishment.

In general it can be said that superiors of clerical exempt institutes have
coactive power over their subjects in much the same way as Bishops over
the faithful of their dioceses.[4] There is, however, this characteristic difference, the authority of religious superiors is not territorial in nature, unless
they rule over a definite territory, as a province of their institute.[5] As a consequence superiors can generally impose personal but not local interdicts.[6]

It has been seen in Chapter V that religious superiors are incompetent in
those matters of faith and morals which have been reserved to the Holy
Office (can. 247, § 1), hence they cannot impose penalties on subjects guilty
of delinquencies in such cases (can. 501, § 2).[7]

In practice particular penal laws and precepts binding members of a religious institute are for the most part enactments of General Chapters or
Congregations. Individual superiors endowed with coactive power are sel-
dom forced to exercise it, for their administrative measures usually produce
the desired results.

---

[3] Cf. W.-V., VII, 165; Cerato, *Censurae Vigentes,* 2 ed., 7.
[4] Tamb., *De Jure Abb.,* II, Disp. 14, q. 1, n. 5; W.-V., III, 199; Bied.-Führ., 43.
[5] Cappello, *De Censuris,* 40.
[6] Cappello, *De Censuris,* 468.
[7] Pejska, pp. 243 ff.

II. POWER TO REMIT PENALTIES

In the case of exempt religious the power to absolve from censures and to dispense from vindicative penalties is governed by the following norms.[8]

A. *Concerning Penalties in General*

The Code lays down the following rules for penalties in general.

1. Absolution from censures and dispensation from vindicative penalties can only be granted by the person who imposed the penalties, or by his competent superior, or successor, or one to whom such power has been committed (can. 2236, § 1).

Ordinaries who can exempt from a law can remit penalties attached to the law (can. 2236, § 2). Hence they can remit penalties attached to laws over which they have been explicitly or implicitly conceded such power. Furthermore, even when no positive concession has been made to Ordinaries, the Code empowers them, under stated conditions, to grant dispensations from all purely ecclesiastical laws, and as a consequence from all penalties. Canon 81 determines the conditions which must be verified simultaneously in each case, namely; recourse to the Holy See must be difficult, there must exist grave danger of harm in any delay, and the case must be of the type for which the Holy See usually accords a dispensation.

2. In public cases, Ordinaries can remit "latae sententiae" penalties established by common law, with the exception of those falling under any one of the classifications given in canon 2237, § 1.

In occult cases, however, Ordinaries can personally or through others remit all "latae sententiae" penalties, whether medicinal or vindicative, excepting those reserved in a special way or very special manner to the Apostolic See, without prejudice to the power accorded by canons 2254 and 2290 (can. 2237, § 2).

B. *Concerning Specific Penalties*

Besides the general norms just stated the Code contains special laws governing the remission of both medicinal and vindicative penalties. The jurisdiction enjoyed by exempt religious and their immunity from the authority of local Ordinaries in these matters will be seen from the statement of the laws themselves.

1. Medicinal Penalties

The power of absolving depends to a large extent upon whether or not a censure has been reserved; for nonreserved censures can be remitted by applying the general norms which have just been seen.

Special norms governing the absolution of censures are divided into three

---

[8] Bied.-Führ., 44.

groups: those referring to cases of danger of death, to ordinary cases, and to more urgent cases.

(A) Danger of Death

All priests, even those not approved for confessions, can validly and licitly absolve exempt religious in danger of death, from all sins and censures howsoever reserved, though they be notorious, and in spite of the fact that a priest approved for confessions is present, without prejudice to the provisions of canons 884 and 2252 (can. 882).

It is to be remarked that a religious in danger of death who has incurred the excommunication mentioned in canon 2388, § 1, which under the circumstances specified in the Decree *"Lex sacri coelibatus"*[9] is now reserved exclusively to the Sacred Penitentiary, may, in virtue of canon 2252, be absolved by any priest.[10]

(B) Ordinary Cases

Outside cases of danger of death any priest approved for confessions can grant absolution in the sacramental forum from nonreserved censures, except in instances already brought to the contentious forum (cf. can. 2237).[11] Only priests who have jurisdiction over the delinquent in the external forum can grant him absolution outside of confession (can. 2253, 1°). It is clear that those who have jurisdiction in the external have it also in the internal forum (can. 202, § 1).

Censures which have been reserved *"ab homine"* can be absolved by him to whom they have been reserved, according to the norm given in canon 2245, § 1, and this holds true for cases in which the penitent has transferred his domicile or quasi-domicile[12] (can. 2253, 2°).

In view of this rule, therefore, superiors and confessors of exempt institutes cannot absolve a member of their institute from censures which, v.g., as provided for in canon 619, the local Ordinary has reserved to himself.

It must be remembered that, according to the norm given in canon 519, any confessor approved by the local Ordinary has the power to absolve a religious from all sins or censures reserved in his religious institute.

A censure reserved either by common or particular law, v.g., by rules or constitutions, can be absolved by the one who established it or by him to whom it has been reserved, and by the competent superiors, successors, or delegates of these persons (can. 2253, 3°).

---

[9] S. Poen., Apr. 18, 1936, AAS, XXVIII, 242, Bouscaren, II, can. 2388.

[10] S. Poen., May 4, 1937, AAS, XXIX, 283, Bouscaren, Supplement — 1941, can. 2288.

[11] Cf. Cappello, *De Censuris*, 119.

[12] In practice it is more reasonable, in view of the dispute on this matter, to maintain that *"ab homine latae sententiae"* penalties are not reserved unless expressly so declared in the precept of a superior (cf. can. 2245).

Hence, major superiors of exempt clerical institutes, i.e., religious Ordinaries, can absolve personally or through others, censures which are reserved by common law to Ordinaries. The superiors mentioned have such power with respect to their own subjects, not to the faithful in general, for, as Cappello states, they enjoy this power as Ordinaries, but they are Ordinaries of their subjects only, i.e., of the religious under their jurisdiction and of the persons mentioned in canon 514, § 1.[13]

It should be recalled that Regular prelates have been deprived of faculties which, in virtue of privileges especially that of St. Pius V,[14] formerly enabled them to absolve from cases reserved in a special or very special manner to the Holy See.[15]

However, at present, by reason of privileges still in force, some exempt institutes enjoy faculties which are more extensive than those granted by common law.[16]

(C) More Urgent Cases

In more urgent cases, if, for example, a "latae sententiae" censure cannot be observed without grave danger of scandal or loss of reputation, or if it be difficult for the penitent to remain in the state of mortal sin until the competent superior grants absolution, any confessor can in the sacramental forum absolve from any censure, no matter how it has been reserved. He must, however, impose upon the penitent the obligation of having recourse within a month, either personally or through the confessor, if this can be done without grave inconvenience, to the Sacred Penitentiary, or Bishop, or other superior endowed with faculties, and he must further impose the obligation of abiding by the mandates issued in the case. The name of the penitent is not to be mentioned in the recourse made to the superior (can. 2254, § 1).

Even after having received absolution and after having had recourse to a superior the penitent is not forbidden to go to another confessor endowed with faculties, and having again confessed at least the delict to which the censure is attached, to receive absolution. After he has received absolution and has been given the mandates he is not bound to abide by other mandates issued by the superior to whom he had formerly had recourse (can. 2254, § 2).

If in some extraordinary case, excluding that provided for in canon 2367, this recourse is morally impossible, the confessor may absolve the penitent without imposing the obligation of recourse; but he must enjoin whatever

---

[13] Cf. Cappello, *De Censuris*, 123.
[14] Pius V, Const., *Romani Pontificis*, July 21, 1571.
[15] Cf. S. Poen., Dec. 5, 1873; S. Off., Mar. 22, 1881; see Cappello, *De Censuris*, 123, nota 27.
[16] Cf. Cappello, *De Censuris*, 123.

is required by law, and must oblige the penitent to perform an appropriate penance and to make satisfaction for the censure, in such wise that if the penitent neglects within the time specified by the confessor to perform the penance and satisfaction he will fall back into the censure (can. 2254, § 3).

If the circumstances described by the Decree *"Lex sacri coelibatus"* (S. Poenit., April 18, 1936) concerning the delict mentioned in canon 2388, § 1 are verified, then the censure incurred is so reserved to the Sacred Penitentiary that no one, unless in a case of danger of death (cf. above, II, B, 1, [A]), can ever absolve from it, notwithstanding any faculty granted either by canon 2254, § 1, or by privilege, or finally by any other law whatsoever; cf. S. Poenit., *Declaratio,* May 4, 1941; ap. AAS, 29, 283, and ap. Bouscaren, *The Canon Law Digest,* Supplement, 1941, can. 2388.

2. Vindicative Penalties

Provisions are set down in the Code for the remission of vindicative penalties in ordinary and more urgent cases.

(A) *Ordinary Cases*

Vindicative penalties cease by expiation or by dispensation granted by one endowed with the proper powers, in accordance with the norm contained in canon 2236 (can. 2289).

(B) *More Urgent Cases*

In more urgent occult cases, if by observing a vindicative "latae sententiae" penalty the delinquent should betray himself with loss of reputation or scandal, any confessor may in the sacramental forum suspend the obligation of observing the penalty; but he must bind the penitent to have recourse within a month, either personally or through a confessor, if this can be done without grave inconvenience, to the Sacred Pententiary, or Bishop, or superior endowed with faculties, and to abide by the mandates issued. The identity of the delinquent should not be disclosed (can. 2290, § 1).

If in some extraordinary case this recourse is impossible, then the confessor himself may grant the dispensation according to the norm given in canon 2254, § 3 (can. 2290, § 2).[17]

ARTICLE II. THE COACTIVE POWER OF LOCAL ORDINARIES

The exemption of religious pertaining to exempt institutes renders them immune from the coactive jurisdiction of local Ordinaries, except in the cases expressly mentioned in law (can. 615). When express subjection is

---

[17] For an explanation of this faculty, consult: Coronata, IV, 1823; Rainer, *Suspension of Clerics* (Dissert. C.U., 1937), p. 231; Woywod, II, 2131; *Epit.,* III, 491; DeMeester, III, 1787, 3.

specified, the jurisdictional authority of local Ordinaries enables them to coerce exempt religious, even by penalties (can. 619).[18]

Melo maintains that the phrase "even by penalties" (*etiam poenis*), employed in canon 619, should be understood in its strict meaning; and that in this acceptation it empowers the Ordinary to impose *vindicative* but not medicinal penalties on Regulars.[19] On the contrary, Coronata holds that Regulars not endowed with a special privilege, are bound by episcopal censures in the cases in which they are explicitly subjected to the jurisdiction of Ordinaries. He adds, however, that even in these instances, Regulars are not bound by the penalties unless the local Ordinary has made an express declaration to this effect.[20]

Canon 619 contains no revocatory clause abolishing privileges that are contrary to its provisions. Therefore, even in the instance of subjection, expressed in law, v.g., canon 603, § 1, religious may, by special privilege, enjoy exemption from episcopal coercion (can. 4).[21] Thus, Mendicants and others to whom their privileges have been communicated are immune from episcopal censures except in three cases, namely: (*a*) if they *presume* to preach in their own or any other church without the Bishop's approval;[22] (*b*) if they *presume*, without episcopal approbation, to hear the confessions of seculars;[23] (*c*) if they expose for public veneration images that are unusual or that have been depicted in a scandalous manner.[24]

Penalties, other than censures, can be inflicted on Mendicants and those possessing their privileges for delinquencies in matters in which exempt religious are expressly placed under the jurisdiction of local Ordinaries.[25] Hence, unless specially privileged, they are bound to observe local interdicts (can. 2269, § 2). Furthermore, interdicts placed on a city affect even exempt places situated therein (can. 2273).[26]

As a general rule local Ordinaries should refrain from imposing penalties on exempt religious unless it be manifest that they have authority to do

---

[18] Cf. Vermeersch, *De Rel.*, I, 380; Chelodi, *Jus Poenali*, p. 28; Melo, p. 172.

[19] Cf. Melo, *loc. cit.* The same should hold for other exempt religious.

[20] Cf. Coronata, I, 626; Claeys Bouuaert-Simenon, 676.

[21] Cf. Schäfer, 425; Ferreres, I, 906, III; Melo, p. 174.

[22] Cf. Greg. XV, Const., *Inscrutabile*, par. 6, Feb. 5, 1622.

[23] Cf. Innoc. X, Const., *Cum sicut accepimus*, May 14, 1653; see also S. Alph., VII, 241; Fagn., L. IV, in c. Quanto, *de priv.*, n. 9.

[24] Cf. Urb. VIII, Const., *Sacrosancta Tridentina*, Mar. 15, 1643; Ball.-Palm. VII, 67 ff.; Bucceroni, *Inst. theol. mor.*, II, 1194, quaer. 6. Concerning these exceptions, consult: Cappello, *De Censuris*, 21; "Societas Jesu (*Const. Paul III*, 'Licet debitum,' Oct. 18, 1549), et generatim omnes Mendicantes, qui etiam si delinquent in iis, in quibus Episcopo subjiciantur, nequerunt *ex speciali prevligio*, censuris plecti, exceptis tantum tribus casibus . . ."; see also Ferrari, *op. cit.*, 91; Vermeersch, *De Rel.* I, 380; Piat, II, q. 13; Ojetti, *Syn.*, 957 ff.; Ball.-Palm., *Opus theol.*, tr. II, *De Cens.*, 81–86; W.-V., III, 404, and VII, 228, nota 44; *Epit.*, I, 775 and III, 416; Coronata, I, 626; Schäfer, 282.

[25] Cf. Melo, pp. 175 ff.

[26] Cf. Melo, p. 164 ff.

so; for, in doubtful cases, as has been seen, there is a legal presumption that they lack jurisdiction.[27]

The basic principles underlying ecclesiastical government, especially if it be punitive in character, are Christian charity and mercy. Moderation and kindness must be shown even in inflicting penalties (can. 2214). An Ordinary would violate this norm if his penal measures against exempt religious were more drastic than those he employs in other cases. When forced to punish, local Ordinaries must abide by the equitable norms prescribed in law (can. 2218 ff.). Of special importance is canon 2223, § 3, which obliges a Bishop to abstain from inflicting penalties when the delinquent is wholly penitent and has repaired the scandal and harm done, or when he will be sufficiently punished by civil authority (or by his own religious superior). Though this canon does not make the express statement, it does contain the clear implication that coercive measures taken by one superior should deter other superiors from further action in the case.[28] In instances involving censures, punishment by the religious Ordinary should certainly be deemed sufficient; for, owing to his intimate knowledge of his subjects, he is the one best able to apply adequate medicinal penalties. The following is a treatment of the principal cases in which Regulars are subject to the coactive power of local Ordinaries.

I. REGULARS ABSENT FROM THEIR HOUSE

Regulars unlawfully dwelling outside their house, even under pretext of having recourse to their superiors, do not enjoy the privilege of exemption (can. 616, § 1).

A Regular who absents himself for a notable period, which Coronata states to be two or three months,[29] is considered *living* outside his house, according to the terms of the canon.

Absence from the house is unlawful if protracted contrary to either the wish of the superior or the prescriptions of law (cc. 601, 606, 607). Only this type deprives a Regular of his exemptive rights. Fugitives and apostates from religion are obviously unlawfully absent from their convent or monastery (cc. 644, § 3; 684, §§ 1 and 2).[30] Religious who have been forced to dwell outside their house, e.g., in time of persecution, are not unlawfully absent.[31] They, therefore, enjoy full exemption. Persecution or expulsion should not diminish but rather increase the protection of their rights.[32]

The second paragraph of canon 616 provides for a case in which Regulars may be coerced by local Ordinaries. It decrees that Regulars who have com-

---

[27] Cf. Pejska, pp. 42, 207.
[28] Cf. Melo, p. 176.
[29] Cf. Coronata, I, 624.
[30] Cf. Cappello, *Summa J.C.*, 631.
[31] Cf. AAS, II, 492; III, 432; S.R.R. decisions, III, 312 ff.; Schäfer, 421.
[32] Cf. W.-V., III, 400; *Epit.*, 776; Schäfer, *loc. cit.*

mitted a crime outside their house and are not punished by their superior after he has been warned of the fact, can be punished by the local Ordinary, even though they may have lawfully left their house and have returned to it.

It is manifest that the jurisdiction here accorded a local Ordinary is conditional. He cannot adjudge or punish the delinquent unless the latter's superior, when admonished, takes no punitive measures.[33] After being warned of a subject's offense, the superior should not inflict a penalty until he is juridically certain of the fact. Notification of the imposed punishment should be given the local Ordinary.[34] According to some authors, a religious who has committed a delinquency in a parish united to his monastery is not embraced by this law.[35] Melo claims a like exception for offenses committed in the Church or monastery of an Order, even though these may have caused scandal to the faithful.[36]

II. EXEMPT RELIGIOUS WITHIN THEIR MONASTERIES

Local Ordinaries have no coactive authority over these religious. Yet they have certain responsibilities. The Code declares: if abuses have crept into the houses and churches of Regulars, or of other exempt religious, and the superior having been warned of the fact neglects to provide a remedy, the local Ordinary is bound to refer the matter immediately to the Apostolic See (can. 617, § 1).

The obligation of vigilance does not give the local Ordinary any right to obtrude upon the religious or the affairs of a formal house or church, but merely to admonish the superior of existing abuses; and, in case the superior does not correct them, it imposes upon the local Ordinary the duty of informing the Holy See. This is the extent of his relation to such matters. Once he has fulfilled his office, he ceases to have further authority.[37]

The canon under consideration treats only of *abuses that have crept into* churches and houses of exempt religious. It refers, therefore, to *grave* and *habitual* violations of ecclesiastical laws, not to single offenses.[38] Further, it is not necessary that the abuses cause scandal to people, for the Code employs the term "abuse" without qualification.[39] An example of such an abuse in a monastery is the failure to keep proper custody of enclosure; abuses in a Regular church are: nonobservance of the laws governing the celebration of Mass, sacred music, the confessional screen, custody of the Blessed Eucharist, and the like.[40]

Canon 617, § 1, does not grant the Ordinary of the place leave to make a visitation.[41]

---

[33] Cf. Bied.-Führ., 15.
[34] Cf. Coronata, I, 624.
[35] Cf. Ferraris, v. *Regulares,* art. II, 37–38; Melo, p. 178.
[36] Cf. Melo, *loc. cit.*

[37] Cf. Coronata, I, 624.
[38] Cf. Bondini, p. 66.
[39] Cf. Schäfer, 421; Coronata, *loc. cit.*
[40] Cf. Bondini, *loc. cit.*
[41] Cf. W.-V., III, 402; Coronata, I, 624.

The local Ordinary has fuller care of nonformal houses[42] for canon 617, § 2, states that every nonformal house remains under his special vigilance; and, that he can himself provisionally deal with abuses arising in such places, which are a source of scandal to the faithful.

Though nonformal houses remain exempt, they are subject to episcopal vigilance to the extent herein defined.[43] This care does not permit the infliction of canonical penalties.[44]

Intervention of the local Ordinary is limited to: (a) cases of *abuse*, that is, not to single, but to protracted offenses;[45] (b) cases which are a cause of scandal to the faithful.

Unlike the prescription of canon 617, § 1, the present rule does not oblige the local Ordinary to warn the religious superior, or to refer the matter to the Holy See. As protector and promoter of the common good, he is entitled immediately to guard his flock against the harm arising from scandal. Nevertheless, since the remedy he may apply is not absolute, but merely *provisional*, it is implied that he must have recourse to someone else for definite adjustment. The circumstances of such abuses, religious courtesy, and reasons drawn by analogy from the first paragraph of canon 617, seem to indicate that the religious superior should be the one first asked to deal with the case.

The canon appears to suppose that the superior is not in a position, e.g., because living at a distance, opportunely to meet the situation, and consequently permits the Ordinary of the place to apply temporary remedies. Neither the provision itself nor norms of good government indicate that the corrective measures to be taken should follow a procedure different from that outlined in canon 617, § 1, viz., first the religious superior should be notified; in the event of neglect on his part, the Holy See.[46]

III. RELIGIOUS PASTORS OR VICARS

If a religious pastor or vicar neglects the duties of his office, the local Ordinary may issue opportune orders and inflict merited penalties. These faculties are not exclusively his, for the religious superior, together with the local Ordinary, has cumulative rights in the matter; in such a way, however, that the decrees of the latter must prevail in a conflict of decisions (can. 631, § 2).

This is a limitation of the immunity of exempt religious from the coactive authority of diocesan Ordinaries (cc. 631, § 1; 1425, § 2); but not, strictly

---

[42] Cf. can. 488, 5°.
[43] Cf. W.-V., III, 401; Coronata, *loc. cit.*; Larraona, C.p.R., III, pp. 50 ff., nota 188; Bondini, p. 68.
[44] Cf. Schäfer, 421; Coronata, *loc. cit.*
[45] Cf. Schäfer, *loc. cit.*; Coronata, *loc. cit.*
[46] Cf. Bondini, p. 69.

speaking of their exemption,[47] for the religious in question may be punished only on account of offenses which are violations of their pastoral obligations.

In law, the rights and duties of parish priests and parochial vicars are equivalent (can. 451).

A parochial vicar is a priest who exercises the actual care of souls in a parish united "pleno jure" to a religious house, capitular church, or other moral person. Such a one has exclusively the entire care of souls, and all the rights and obligations of a parish priest, in accordance with the norms of common law, approved diocesan statutes, and praiseworthy customs (can. 471).

Which matters belong to the pastor's office can be determined from the law, from documents of the Holy See, and from the common opinion of authors.

The pastor's chief duties generally include: administration of the sacraments (can. 467, § 1); spiritual care of the sick (can. 468, § 1); catechetical instructions to the people (cc. 1329, 1332), and to children in preparation for reception of the sacraments (cc. 1330, 1331); preaching to the people on Sundays and holydays of obligation (can. 1344); proper care and custody of the church (can. 1178); custody and care of the Holy Eucharist (cc. 1265–1272); custody of the holy oils (cc. 735, 946).

The Ordinary should proceed against a pastor guilty of grave neglect of duty, in accordance with the norms set down in canons 2182–2185 (can. 2382). At the outset he should warn the offender, reminding him of his strict obligations and of the punishments to which he has exposed himself. Should this prove ineffective, the Bishop, after taking the counsel of two examiners who have investigated the case, and after allowing the accused opportunity to defend himself, should correct the guilty party and inflict punishment proportionate to the gravity of the offense. If corrections and punishment are without result, the Ordinary may at once deprive of his parish any pastor who is not irremovable. Upon an irremovable pastor, he may inflict total or partial privation of the fruits of his benefice. When it has been proven that this latter persists in his evil, he may be removed from his parish in accordance with the norm set down in can. 1576, § 1, 1°.

Grave negligence in registering matters in the parish books (cc. 470, 776–778, 1103, 1238, 1988), and insufficient custody of these books, may be punished at the discretion of the Ordinary in proportion to the gravity of the offense (can. 2383).[48] In all such matters offenses of the pastor or vicar can be punished by the local Ordinary or by the religious superior.[49]

This cumulative right seems to permit them to punish separately or con-

---

[47] Cf. Passive exemption, Chap. I.
[48] Cf. W.-V., VII, 517; Fanfani, *De jure parochorum*, 52, 425.
[49] Cf. Berutti, III, 143.

jointly. Yet both should not apply punitive measures simultaneously against the same delinquency, for, ordinarily, this would lead to excesses. However, if one superior judges that the other has been too lenient, he can add to the already inflicted penalties, and even remove the delinquent from his parochial office. In the case of removal, he should notify the other superior of his decision (can. 454, § 5).[50]

The religious superior alone possesses coercive authority over matters relating to religious discipline.[1]

Bishops may apply penal measures to compel the exempt religious pastors designated in canon 358, § 1, 6°, to attend diocesan synods, and they may punish those who have unlawfully absented themselves therefrom (can. 359).

IV. MORAL AND LITURGICAL CONFERENCES

Exempt religious exercising the care of souls must attend the moral and liturgical conferences held at the times designated by the Ordinary of the place (can. 131, §§ 1 and 3, cf. below, Chap. XIX, C, 18), and it is left to the prudence of the latter to punish anyone who should contumaciously violate this prescription (can. 2377).

If like conferences are not had in their religious houses (can. 591), other religious who have faculties for hearing confessions from the local Ordinary must be present at the diocesan ones (can. 131, § 3). Suspension from hearing the confessions of the faithful is to be inflicted on those who are delinquent in this respect (can. 2377).

V. EXEMPT MISSIONARIES

Exempt religious engaged in the sacred ministry in mission territories are governed for the most part by laws similar to those regulating the relationship of Regular pastors and local Ordinaries.[2] Instead of a diocesan Bishop, the Vicar or Prefect Apostolic has coactive authority in matters pertaining to the government of the mission, the care of souls, the administration of the sacraments, the direction of schools, the care of gifts made in favor of the mission, and the execution of pious legacies made in behalf of the same (cc. 295, 296).[3] Vicars and Prefects Apostolic possess this power cumulatively with the religious superior, but the authority of the former is to prevail in the case of conflicting decisions.

The schools mentioned in canon 296 are the elementary (parish) institutions conducted by the religious — not other schools or colleges. In mission territories, secondary and higher schools under the direction of Regulars

---

[50] Cf. Coronata, I, 635; Melo, pp. 85 ff.; Bondini, pp. 35 ff.
[1] Cf. Fanfani, *op. cit.,* 426; Melo, p. 85.
[2] Cf. Melo, p. 92.
[3] Cf. Bened. XIV, Const., *Firmandis,* par. 10, Nov. 6, 1744; cf. Vromant, *De Personis,* 85.

are exempt from all visits of local Ordinaries, by virtue of the privilege which Leo XIII granted in his constitution *"Romanos Pontifices,"* n. 20.[4] In many places, outside mission territories, "where the general laws of the Church are in force, this privilege has been acquired by legitimate custom or by prescription."[5] However, such a prescriptive right could be acquired only by schools which are subject to the jurisdiction and visitation of religious prelates (can. 1509, 7°).

It should be remarked that recourse against the decision of Vicars or Prefects does not free one from the duty of submitting to them, for this recourse is devolutive, not suspensive (can. 513, § 2).[6] Their authority over religious, however, does not permit Vicars or Prefects Apostolic to issue decrees which would be prejudicial to the missionary statutes approved by the Holy See for particular institutes, v.g., for the Society of Jesus.[7]

By reason of canon 297, Vicars and Prefects Apostolic have, in certain circumstances, special jurisdictional authority over religious residing in their territories. In case there is not a sufficient number of secular priests in the missions, they may, after having heard the religious superior, compel even exempt religious who are attached to the vicariate or prefecture to undertake the care of souls. However, as stated in the Constitution *"Speculatores,"* of Clement IX, Sept. 13, 1669, Vicars and Prefects Apostolic should not transgress particular statutes which have been approved by the Holy See (cf. Chap. XIV, Art. I).[8] Concerning the parochial functions proper to missionaries, consult Vromant, *op. cit., De Personis,* 282 ff.

In single cases, and only for a grave reason, may Vicars or Prefects Apostolic deny religious missionaries permission to exercise the sacred ministries (can. 295, § 2).

VI. THE CLOISTER OF NUNS

The enclosure of nuns, even those subject to Regulars, is under the vigilance of the local Ordinary, who can correct and coerce, even with penalties and censures, the delinquents, not excepting male Regulars (can. 603, § 1).

By reason of this provision, local Ordinaries are obliged to exercise vigilance over the cloister of nuns, even when these latter are under the jurisdiction of male Regulars. In addition, a local Ordinary can inflict penalties and censures on delinquents, whether they be nuns or others. Hence, though the enclosure of nuns is not subject to his jurisdiction, nevertheless "by

---

[4] Cf. Vermeersch, *De Rel.,* II, 589; also Augustine, II, can. 296; Creusen, *N.R.T.,* 1929, pp. 43-56; and *Rel. Men and Women,* etc., 94.
[5] Cf. Creusen, *Religious Men and Women, loc. cit.*
[6] Cf. Melo, p. 93.
[7] Cf. Augustine, II, can. 296.
[8] Cf. Augustine, II, can. 297; Melo, p. 93.

reason of an offense on this point any lay person and any religious become subject to the Ordinary of the place where the sin is committed (cc. 201, § 1; 1566)."[9]

The custody of the enclosure of nuns subject to Regulars is confided also to the Regular superior who can likewise inflict punishment on the nuns or his other subjects, if in this matter they be found guilty (can. 603, § 2).[10]

According to the Instruction of the Congregation of Religious, Feb. 6, 1924,[11] the superioress may, in virtue of the authority granted her by the Holy See, allow ingress to all persons whose services are required within the monastery; but she should obtain beforehand from the Ordinary of the place at least his habitual approbation. If in some extraordinary case it is urgently necessary that someone enter the monastery, and there is no time to ask the Ordinary for his approval, this approval is presumed by law, that is, the law itself confirms the presumption thereof. The superioress is enjoined in all cases to employ the required safeguards.[12]

VII. THE DOWRY OF NUNS: ADMISSION TO THE NOVITIATE AND TO PROFESSION

In the cases defined in canon 2412, local Ordinaries should punish superioresses even of exempt religious women, according to the gravity of their fault, including, if necessary, deposition from office.

1. Dowry of Nuns (cc. 547–551; 2412, 1°)

The dowry of nuns is absolutely inalienable.[13] After the first profession of a religious, the superioress with her Council, and with the consent of the local Ordinary and of the Regular superior, if the house be dependent on Regulars, must place the dowry in a safe, lawful, and productive investment; but it is strictly forbidden that, before the death of the religious, the dowry be expended for any purpose, even for the building of a house or the liquidation of debts (can. 549).

If a superioress, contrary to this prescription, has presumed to spend, in whatever manner, the dowries of the young girls received into the institute, she becomes subject to the coercive authority of the local Ordinary (can. 2212, 1°).

The dowry is irrevocably acquired by the monastery or the institute only on the death of the religious (can. 548), and hence cannot in justice be alienated beforehand.[14] The law does not expressly determine the proprietorship of the dowry during the lifetime of the religious, but it definitely implies that the monastery or institute has at most a conditional dominion over such goods.[15]

---

[9] Cf. Creusen, 290.
[10] Cf. Pejska, p. 159.
[11] Cf. AAS, 16, 96 ff.
[12] Cf. Bouscaren, I, can. 600; Per. 13, p. 58.
[13] Cf. Creusen, 186.
[14] Cf. Coronata, IV, 2232.
[15] Cf. Epit., I, 555; Coronata, I, 577.

The law governing this matter (can. 2412, 1°) requires presumption on the part of the delinquent.

Canon 2412, 1°, safeguards the rights and obligations treated of in canon 551. Hence, if from whatever cause a professed religious, either with solemn or simple vows, leaves the institute, her dowry must be returned to her intact, but not the interest already derived therefrom. If, however, by virtue of an apostolic indult, the professed religious joins another institute, the interest on her dowry during her new novitiate, without prejudice to the prescription of canon 570, § 1, and, after the new profession, the dowry itself must be given to the latter institute; if the religious passes to another monastery of the same Order, the dowry is due to it from the day the change takes place (can. 551).

2. Admission to the Novitiate and to Profession

The superioress, even of exempt religious, must inform the local Ordinary, at least two months in advance, of the approaching admission to the novitiate and to the profession both of temporary and perpetual, of solemn or simple vows. The local Ordinary, or if he is absent or otherwise impeded, a priest delegated by him, must, at least thirty days before admission to the novitiate and to profession, carefully examine the dispositions of the aspirant, and this gratuitously, without, however, entering the enclosure; he must inform himself as to whether she has been constrained or beguiled, and whether she understands the import of the step she is about to take; and, if he is fully satisfied regarding her pious intention and freedom of action, then the aspirant may be admitted to the novitiate, or, if already a novice, to profession (can. 552).

If, contrary to the prescription of this canon, the superioress has omitted to inform the local Ordinary concerning the approaching admission of a subject to the novitiate or to profession, she is guilty of a delinquency and is punishable to the degree specified in canon 2412, 2°.

The purpose of this examination is solely to make certain that persons entering a novitiate or pronouncing their vows are acting with full knowledge and liberty. Therefore, the questions of the local Ordinary should concern this twofold end alone. It would be a usurpation of authority should the local Ordinary or his delegate conduct this investigation either to test the individual's vocation or to approve of her admission.[16] Suitableness of the candidate is a matter left to the judgment of the religious superiors.

The local Ordinary must abide by the definite provisions of the Code, and hence may not delay this investigation beyond the time prescribed by canon 552. Should he do so, the Regular superior, after the *thirty-day* limit has passed, may, without consulting the Ordinary of the place, proceed

[16] Cf. Creusen, 190; Melo, p. 117.

with the reception or profession. Such was the decision rendered by Pius V, in his Constitution, *Etsi Mendicantium,* 1567,[17] which by virtue of canon 6, 2°, 3°, constitutes at present a legitimate norm of interpretation.[18]

It should be noted that failure to notify the local Ordinary would not invalidate the reception or profession.[19]

Exaction of any fees for the canonical examination is strictly forbidden, nor can any custom to the contrary be any longer tolerated, even where it has existed for more than one hundred years.[20] It is permitted to accept traveling expenses.[21]

Conclusion

The Church decrees in clear, definite language the manner which ecclesiastical superiors should adopt in the exercise of coactive authority. The following teaching of the Council of Trent contained in canon 2214, § 2 of the Code of Canon Law is an admirable example of this.

An Ordinary, whether local or religious, must show himself a pastor rather than a chastiser of his flock. All domineering manifestations of authority are to be avoided. His government should be characterized by that Christlike charity which will induce him to look upon subjects as his children and brethren, and will cause him to exert every effort to prevent them from sinning. He must endeavor by exhortation and admonition to deter them from unlawful acts, and thus remove, as far as possible, any need of invoking his coercive powers. His actions must, above all, be free from vindictiveness. When, through human frailty, persons have fallen into sin, he should, following the precept of the Apostle, reason with them, implore them and warn them in all kindness and patience; since those in need of correction are generally more efficaciously moved by benevolence than by austerity, by exhortation rather than by threats, by charity rather than by authority. If, nevertheless, the gravity of the delinquency necessitates the use of coercion, force must be tempered with mildness, justice with mercy, and severity with gentleness. Thus the maintaining of salutary and necessary discipline will be effected without harshness, and those corrected will make amendment, or, if they remain recalcitrant, others, seeing their deplorable condition, will be deterred from sin.

---

[17] Ap. Ferraris, v, *Monialis,* Art. I, 69, 95.
[18] Melo, p. 118.
[19] Cf. Fagn., L. I, c. 8; Bouix, I, p. 653; Ferreres, *Theol. Mor.,* II, 191, resp. 4; Melo, *loc. cit.*
[20] Cf. Response of the S. C. Rel., Mar. 20, 1922, ap. AAS, 14, 352; N.R.T. (1922), 101; *Per.,* XI, 79.
[21] Cf. Creusen, 190.

PART III
The Extension of Exemption

INTRODUCTORY REMARK

It has already been seen (Chap. I) that the exemption of Regulars is mixed and passive in nature;[1] mixed, because it is both personal and local; passive, because it actually accords no jurisdictional authority over non-exempt clergy or laity, but merely renders religious immune from the jurisdiction of local Ordinaries.

In the present Part of this work we shall endeavor to point out the *extent* of the exemptive rights enjoyed by Regulars and other privileged religious. The Code (can. 615) proclaims that Regulars, together with their houses and churches, are exempt from the jurisdiction of the local Ordinary; in other words, that *persons, places,* and *things* pertaining to religious Orders do not fall under the authority of local Ordinaries.[2] The same norm applies to exempt congregations (can. 500, § 1).

---

[1] Cf. Bened. XIV, *De Syn. Dioec.*, L. II, c. XI, 2.
[2] Cf. d'Angelo, *La Esenzoine Dei Religiosi*, Capo IV.

The Exemption of Persons

We shall consider here the extension of that exemption possessed by the *persons* pertaining to exempt religious institutes. This exposition of personal exemption comprises two chapters. The first, Chapter VII, is devoted to the extension of the exemption possessed by physical persons, namely by the members of clerical and lay institutes. The second, Chapter VIII, explains the extent of exemptive rights enjoyed by the juridical or moral persons pertaining to exempt religious.

EXEMPTION OF PHYSICAL PERSONS

Exemption frees religious from the jurisdiction of local Ordinaries, and, as a result, subjects them to their own proper superiors. This immunity is a right of the exempt religious wheresoever he resides, and hence is wider in scope than that which is derived from mere local exemption. Immunity in the latter sense does not extend beyond the boundaries of the exempted territory.[1]

ARTICLE I. PERSONS ENDOWED WITH EXEMPTIVE RIGHTS

It is important to determine with precision which persons are embraced by exemption. The better to accomplish this we shall review the discipline in force prior to the promulgation of the Code, and then explain the existing law.

A) Previous legislation

The persons formerly considered immune from the jurisdiction of the local Ordinary were not so clearly determined as they are at present. The following brief statement exposes the respective exemptive status of the persons generally connected with a community of Regulars:

1. *Professed religious* and *novices* of orders and independent monasteries certainly possessed exemption. Explicit declarations found in the particular privileges conferred on different institutes testify to this fact.[2]

Because of the notoriety which such grants gradually acquired, the existence of the exemptive rights contained in them was accepted as a presumption of law, so that the legitimacy of any episcopal claim to authority over Regulars had to be proven. The declaration of Leo XIII, "Haud immerito RR. PP. . . . clerum regularem Episcoporum jurisdictione exemptum esse statuerunt,"[3] is an evidence of this accepted status of Regulars.[4]

2. Nuns, in general, were considered exempt. All classes of nuns did not,

---

[1] Cf. Piat, II, p. 6, q. 7.
[2] Cf., v.g., Concessions to the Dominicans: Greg. XI, Const., *Virtute*, Mar. 6, 1374; Eugen. IV, Const., *Romanus Pontifex*, Apr. 11, 1440; Sixtus IV, Const., *Regimini*, Aug. 31, 1474; to the Franciscans, Sixtus IV, Const., *Regimini*, Aug. 31, 1474; to the Canons of the Lateran, Sixtus IV, Const., *Dum ad*, Aug. 23, 1476, etc. See also St. Alph., *op. cit.*, *De Priv.*, 74; Wernz, II, 638; Piat, I, Pars. IV, sect. 2, c. 2; Vermeersch, *De Rel.*, I, 363.
[3] Cf. Const., *Romanos Pontifices*.
[4] Cf. Bened. XIV, Bull, *Apostolicum ministerium*, May 30, 1753; Ojetti, Syn. v, *Exemptio*.

however, enjoy the same immunity from episcopal jurisdiction. Those subject to the care and jurisdiction of Regulars were subject to local Ordinaries only in exceptional cases; those immediately under the Holy See alone were subject to the jurisdictional authority of Bishops acting as papal delegates.[5]

3. Persons attached to the community (de familia) of Regulars shared the exemption of the religious.[6] In this category were included: postulants, boarding students, guests, the infirm residing with Regulars, and domestic servants. Not all those in the service of the religious were included in the last-named class, but only persons who worked for and habitually boarded with the community.[7]

B) Present legislation

The general relation of religious to the authority of local Ordinaries is expressed in canons 500 and 615.

Canon 500 declares that religious are subject to the local Ordinary, except those who have obtained from the Apostolic See the privilege of exemption, without prejudice to the power which the law accords, even over these latter, to the local Ordinaries. Nuns who are placed by their constitution under the jurisdiction of Regular superiors are subject to the local Ordinary only in the cases provided for by law.

This canon is directly concerned with the subjection of religious men and women to the jurisdiction of local Ordinaries, but, in order that confusion and error be avoided, it declares that some religious enjoy exemption from this same authority.[8]

The general norm of subjection is this: persons, places, and things in a diocese are governed by the Ordinary of the place (cc. 334, 335), and are subject to his visitation (can. 344), unless by privilege they have been declared exempt.

A privilege of this type is possessed by all Regulars and by religious of several congregations, such as the Passionists,[9] and the Redemptorists.[10] Religious thus privileged are subject to the authority of the local Ordinary in those cases alone which are expressly defined by law.

---

[5] Cf. Conc. Trid., sess. 25, c. 9, *de regul;* S.C.EE.RR., Sept. 8, 1725, and Feb. 27, 1863, ap. Biz., pp. 353 ff., and pp. 169 ff.; see also Ferrari, pp. 202, 206; Piat, p. 4, q. 6; W.-V., III, 400, nota (28).

[6] Cf. Conc. Trid., sess. 25, *de regul.,* C. 11; see also Vermeersch, *De Rel.,* I, 365; Piat, II, pp. 177, 178.

[7] Cf. Julius II, Const., *Dudum,* July 28, 1506; Paul III, Const., *Licet debitum,* Oct. 18, 1549; Leo X, Const., *Dum intra,* par. 7, Dec. 19, 1516; Clem. X, Const., *Superna,* par. 4, June 21, 1670; see Vermersch, *De Rel.,* I, 518.

[8] Cf. Larraona, C.p.R., VI, p. 181.

[9] Given by Clem. XIV, Sept. 21, 1771.

[10] Given by Pius VI, Const. *Sacrosanctum,* Aug. 21, 1789; see also ASS, I, pp. 91–98; Biz. (Edit. 1), p. 796 ff.; Maire, pp. 246–256; Vermeersch, *De Rel.,* I, 367.

Besides this exemption derived from particular concessions, all Regulars are now exempt by virtue of the universal law which declares: Regulars, both men and women, including novices, except those nuns who are not subject to Regular superiors, are exempt from the jurisdiction of the local Ordinary, save in the cases explicitly mentioned in law (can. 615).

Regulars, as stated in canon 488, 7°, are religious who have made profession of vows in an order. Today, orders are generally classified as follows: Canons Regular, v.g., Premonstratensions, Canons Regular of the Lateran, Canons Regular of the Holy Cross (Crozier Fathers); monks, v.g., Benedictines, Cistercians, Carthusians, Trappists; mendicant friars, v.g., Dominicans, Franciscans, Augustinians, Carmelites; clerics Regular, v.g., Theatines, Jesuits, Barnabites.[11]

For the first time the exemption of Regulars has been incorporated in a universal law of the Church. This fact constitutes, theoretically at least, a change in the juridical status of members pertaining to religious Orders. Formerly, according to the common opinion of Canonists, only those who possessed a patent privilege were presumed exempt (N.B. For a considerable period prior to the Code, all Regulars had this patent privilege).[12] Now, however, the law proclaims that all Regulars, and all nuns subject to them are exempt except in the express cases stipulated in law. Exemption of Regulars, therefore, is the rule, and exceptions to it have to be proved.[13]

The enumeration of exempt Regulars in the Code (can. 615) leaves but little doubt as to the extension of the present law. Now, as previously, both professed religious and novices are withdrawn from the jurisdiction of local Ordinaries. The word "professed" signifies all Regulars who have pronounced public vows, whether the vows be simple or solemn, temporary or perpetual. Religious men and women subject to Regulars are expressly given this exemptive status.

Canon 615 makes no mention of postulants, hence, in view of the norm contained in canon 67, it would seem at first sight that they are not exempt. In the strict meaning of law they are neither novices nor professed, and are said by some[14] to be excluded from exemption. In reality, canon 615 declares Regular religious and their novices exempt, and it is to be remarked that the Code itself speaks of postulants only in the section entitled "Of religious." Hence, the law considers them religious in the broad but proper acceptation of the word, and, therefore, to include them under the terms of canon 615 is not an extension of terms. Hence they may be considered exempt.[15]

---

[11] Cf. Maire, op. cit.
[12] Cf. Leo XIII, Const., Romanos Pontifices; also Piat, II, p. 2, q. 5.
[13] Cf. Creusen, 310; W.-V., III, 400; Schäfer, 419; Epit., I, 774.
[14] Cf. W.-V., III, 400; Berutti, III, 128.
[15] Cf. Creusen, 2 edit., n. 254; in his 3 edit., n. 310, the author holds the contrary.

Students attending schools, like the Seraphic Schools of the Friars Minor, for the purpose of entering an exempt institute, have the same juridical relationship to local Ordinaries as have boarding students in general (can. 514). They are not, therefore, exempt, unless expressly declared so in a special Apostolic grant. The schools also, engaged in preparing such aspirants, are subject to episcopal visitation regarding the matters defined in canon 1382, unless they have a privilege to the contrary.[16]

Guests, boarding students, servants, etc., are not exempt from the jurisdiction of local Ordinaries; however, as members of the religious family, they enjoy many of the principal effects derived from exemption (cc. 514, 875, etc.)

As has been stated before, exempt religious are always under the jurisdiction of some ecclesiastical superior, for exemption does not withdraw them from the authority of the hierarchy, but only from that of local Ordinaries. According to the prescription of canon 118, only clerics may be endowed with jurisdictional power; hence, it follows, that lay orders, that is, institutes of nuns and brothers, are ordinarily subject to the authority of some person with clerical rank in the Church. Nuns who are under the jurisdiction of Regular superiors, are exempt from the authority of local Ordinaries; all other nuns are subject to that power. By express provisions of law, to be considered later, even exempt nuns do not enjoy so extensive an exemption as Regulars of clerical institutes.

It will be useful to consider the exemption of members of lay Orders of men and that of nuns separately.

EXEMPTION OF LAY ORDERS OF MEN

Since canon 615 declares all religious of male Orders exempt, it follows that members of lay male Orders enjoy this privilege. At first sight this is not easily seen. Because, on the one hand, of the intimate interrelation of exemption and jurisdiction, and on the other, of the jurisdictional incompetency of laymen, the Code seems at the same time to affirm (can. 615) and deny (cc. 501 and 118) their exemption. Yet this opposition does not really exist.

In reality, exemption of lay male Orders, though noticeably less extensive than that of clerical institutes, confers, nevertheless, definite immunity from the authority of local Ordinaries. The following instances exemplify this fact:

1. Government in the internal matters of these societies is entirely in the hands of their proper lay superiors. Further, these superiors have authority in all cases which do not require ecclesiastical jurisdiction.[17]

---

[16] Cf. Leo XIII, Const., *Romanos Pontifices*, par. 19; see *Per.*, XV, p. 57; *Goyeneche*, C.p.R., IV, pp. 224, 225.
[17] Cf. W.-V., III, 400, nota 28.

2. In matters requiring the intervention of jurisdictional power, the Code does not directly deny the competency of these lay institutes or their superiors. Canon 501 states that superiors and chapters, conformably to the constitutions and the universal law, have governing power (potestas dominativa) over their subjects, and in every exempt clerical institute they have ecclesiastical jurisdiction both in the internal and external forum. The provision herein contained and that of canon 118, appear to exclude any exercise of jurisdictional power on the part of superiors of lay Orders, and to imply, therefore, the necessary intervention of local Ordinaries.

Yet this implication is not correct in all cases.

If the Superior-General of such institutes is a priest, endowed with jurisdictional privileges, he has jurisdiction over his subjects and his religious are thereby exempt from the jurisdiction of local Ordinaries, save in the cases expressly defined by law (can. 615).[18]

If the superior has no jurisdiction, then, in accordance with their constitution and the universal law (can. 501), these religious must have recourse to the Holy See or to local Ordinaries for matters involving ecclesiastical jurisdiction.[19] The amplitude of their exemptive rights will be commensurate with their independence of local Ordinaries in jurisdictional matters. Yet it should be remarked that even those Orders which are most dependent possess rights not had by nonexempt lay religious, v.g., superiors appoint chaplains and preachers for their subjects (can. 529).[20]

It may be concluded, therefore, that exemption is conferred on members of lay male Orders just as on other Regulars, but in so far as the grant is not in opposition to the provisions of canons 118 and 501, for canon 615 when applied to religious of lay Orders must be understood and interpreted in the light of these two canons.

The Sovereign Pontiff, as is manifest, can delegate jurisdiction to whomsoever he pleases, and hence to lay religious.[21] Thus, at the present time, the Order of Hospitalers of St. John of God, an exempt institute of laymen, has the power of jurisdiction from a special grant of the Holy See. This power is exercised both by Chapters and by the lay superiors of the Order. Proof of this is found in the Bulls and other pontifical documents addressed to them, in constitutions of the Order, and in the constant and present mode of government of this institute.[22]

---

[18] Cf. W.-V., III, 400, nota 28.
[19] W.-V., loc. cit.
[20] Cf. Larraona, C.p.R., V, p. 291, nota (94).
[21] Cf. Reiff, I, tit. 29, n. 92; Suarez, Tom. 24, L. 4, c. 2, n. 12 ff.; Maroto, 576, C.
[22] Cf. R. Saucido, C.p.R., XIII, pp. 51–61, 106–114, 224–231, 291–302.

EXEMPTION OF NUNS

Since the promulgation of the Code, the general norm states that nuns subject to Regular superiors are exempt (cc. 501, 615). Others remain under the ordinary jurisdiction of diocesan Bishops,[23] and therefore are not exempt.[24]

According to the Code (can. 511, § 2) their constitutions determine whether or not the nuns are subject to Regulars. If the constitutions establish this subjection, nuns are withdrawn from the jurisdiction of local Ordinaries save in the cases expressly provided for in law; if the constitutions do not subject them to Regular superiors, then, generally speaking, they are not exempt.[25] The quality of vows, i.e., their simplicity or solemnity, in no way affects the exemptive status of these religious.[26]

At the present time the norm just cited (can. 500, § 2) is not applicable universally. In some countries, in spite of their constitutional subjection to Regulars, nuns are "de facto" subject to local Ordinaries, and hence possess no exemption. Thus, by a special papal indult, monasteries of nuns in Spain have been subjected to the Ordinaries of the places where they are located. This prescription is temporary in character and binding for periods of three years successively, but only under the express condition that the Holy See makes no other provision.[27] So, too, nuns in France, Belgium, and the United States have been placed under the jurisdiction of local Ordinaries.[28] This was their juridical status prior to the Code,[29] and after the promulgation of the Code the Sacred Congregation of Religious has declared that nothing is to be changed regarding the dependence of nuns in France and Belgium on the Ordinaries of places.[30] Later, the same Congregation stated that the monasteries of the aforesaid nuns, in the absence of a peculiar privilege, are not subject to Regular superiors, and hence have not the privilege of exemption under canon 615, but are subject to the jurisdiction of the Ordinaries of places in those matters in which the Code gives Bishops jurisdiction over monastic nuns.[31]

To avoid confusion, one should keep in mind the distinction between nuns who are immediately subject to Regular superiors of the male branch

---

[23] Cf. Maroto, C.p.R., I, p. 258.

[24] W.-V., III, 400, nota (28); *Epit.*, I, 400; Schäfer, 420.

[25] Cf. Maroto, C.p.R., *loc. cit.*

[26] Cf. Leo XIII, Decr., *Perpensis,* May 3, 1902, ap. Vermeersch, *De Rel.*, II, 64.

[27] Cf. AAS, III, p. 239.

[28] Cf. Vermeersch, *De Rel.*, I, 336; Piat, II, q. 6; Creusen, 53; Augustine III, p. 101; Melo, p. 48; Larraona, C.p.R., VI, p. 185, nota (86).

[29] Cf. Greg. XVI, Rescript to Bishop of Liege, Sept. 29, 1837; see also, Piat, II, q. 6; Vermeersch, *De Rel.*, I, 366.

[30] Cf. AAS, XI, 240.

[31] Cf. S. C. Rel., Decree, June 23, 1923, AAS, XV, 357; see also, Bouscaren, I, can. 500; *Per.*, XII, p. 77 and XIII, pp. 63 ff., XV, p. 230; Berutti, III, 128.

of their Order, v.g., Dominican nuns under provincials and the Master General of the Dominican Order; and nuns who merely profess the rule of an Order without being subject to its male superiors. The former, not the latter class, is exempt from the jurisdiction of local Ordinaries.[32]

ARTICLE II. LIMITATIONS OF PERSONAL EXEMPTION

The Code contains express cases in which local Ordinaries are given authority over religious endowed with exemption. Theoretically, only exceptions to *passive exemption* are, strictly speaking, exceptions to the exemption possessed by Regulars and other religious of exempt Congregations,[33] yet for practical purposes we list all cases in which local Ordinaries have authority over religious of exempt institutes.[34]

A. *Limitations of the Exemption of Clerical Exempt Religious*

1. Attendance at Diocesan Conferences

All exempt religious who have the care of souls, even though they have conferences in their houses, must attend the diocesan conference unless they have been expressly excused beforehand by the local Ordinary; the same is true of confessors approved by the local Ordinary, if they have not conferences in their religious house (can. 131, § 3). Religious who contumaciously disobey this prescription should be suspended from hearing confessions (can. 2377). If these conferences cannot be held, written solutions of the proposed cases should be submitted by the priests obliged to attend, according to the directions of the local Ordinary (can. 131, §§2 and 3).

2. The Care of Souls in Mission Territories

When there is a deficiency of secular priests in a vicariate or prefecture, the Vicar or Prefect can, after consulting the religious superior, compel exempt religious attached to the mission to undertake the care of souls, without prejudice to any special statutes that may have been approved by the Holy See (can. 297). The Holy See has declared that religious in the mission fields are obliged not only in charity but in justice to exercise the ministry in question.[35] Vicars or Prefects should settle as quickly as possible controversies that may arise between religious concerning the care of souls.

---

[32] Fanfani, 42, 352.

[33] Cf. Chaps. I and XIX.

[34] Exemptions of persons, places and things are so intimately connected that frequently we cannot logically treat of one type without including the other. Since the adopted division is quite arbitrary, in imitation of the divisions of the Code itself, we shall be forced to follow a rather arbitrary classification of the exceptions to exemption, especially to the exemptions of *persons* and *things*.

[35] Cf. S.C.P.F., Sept. 30, 1848, Col. P.F., 1033; see Coronata, I, 373, nota 4; cf. below, Chap. XIV, Art. I, "Missions."

Their decision must be followed by the religious, saving, however, the right of devolutive recourse to the Holy See (can. 298).[36]

3. Prescribed Prayers, Sacred Solemnities, etc.

Besides the prescription of canon 1345, if the local Ordinary prescribes from a motive of public utility, the ringing of the bells, certain prayers or sacred solemnities, all religious, even the exempt, must obey, without prejudice to the constitutions and privileges of each institute (can. 612). Authors commonly maintain that local Ordinaries cannot prescribe special functions whose celebration would be obligatory only in churches of religious.[37]

4. Explanation of the Gospel or Christian Doctrine

If the local Ordinary so orders it, exempt religious must give an explanation of the Gospel or of some part of Christian Doctrine to the faithful who assist at Mass in their churches, on Sundays or Holydays of Obligation (can. 1345).

5. The Celebret

Special norms issued by the local Ordinary concerning the *celebret,* which are in conformity with the prescriptions of canon 804, must be followed by exempt religious (can. 804, § 3; cf. Section III, Chapter XII, Article III).[38]

6. Mass Stipends

Exempt religious are subject to diocesan statutes and custom regulating Mass stipends (can. 831, § 3; cf. below, Chap. XII, Art. III).

7. Faculties for Hearing Confessions

Faculties for hearing the confessions of seculars and all female religious, even of nuns subject to Regulars (can. 874), must be obtained from the local Ordinary (cf. below, Chapter XII, Article IV).

8. Promulgation of Indulgences

Indulgences not yet promulgated in Rome may not be published, even in churches of Regulars, without consulting the local Ordinary (can. 919, § 1).

9. Ordinations

Ordinations are subject to the local or ordaining Bishop with regard to

---

[36] Cf. Bened. XIV, Const., *Ex quo,* July 11, 1742; *Fontes,* I, 239.
[37] Cf. *Epit.,* I, 614; Bondini, pp. 56, 57; Coronata, I, 617.
[38] Cf. Cappello, *De Sacr.,* I, 737.

the examination for and the reception of Holy Orders (cc. 965, 967, 996; cf. below, Chap. XII, Art. VI).

10. Governing Abbots

Legitimately elected Regular abbots who actually govern a community must be blessed by the Bishop in whose diocese the monastery is situated, within three months from the date of election; after being blessed, they enjoy both the power to confer orders, in conformity with the norm set forth in canon 964, 1°, and the privileges specified in canon 325, excepting the use of purple skullcap (can. 625).

The blessing is conferred by the Ordinary of the place where the exempt monastery is located, and after the blessing the abbot is entitled to confer first tonsure and minor orders and to pontificate.[39] The jurisdiction of an abbot over his monastery is in no way dependent upon the blessing; rather, full exercise of authority is enjoyed by the abbot previous to the reception of the benediction.[40]

Three conditions must be fulfilled for the abbot to *ordain validly*: he must be a priest; he must be blessed; and the candidate for orders must be his subject (can. 964, 1°).

The abbatial privilege of *pontificating* empowers the abbot to exercise pontifical functions and to use a throne and baldachino. Such functions, nevertheless, are restricted to his own churches (cf. cc. 625; 325), unless other prelates invite him to pontificate in their churches (cf. c. 337, § 3). He may not use this privilege outside the diocese, without the consent of the Ordinary of the place where he wishes to pontificate. He has not the privilege to consecrate churches or altars, for the canon 325 referred to does not specifically include such acts (cf. can. 1147, § 1).[41] Transference of an abbot from one monastery to another, even of a different diocese, does not require a new blessing.[42]

11. Rectors

Rectors, in the canonical sense of the term, are priests in charge of churches which are not parochial, nor capitular, nor ones attached to a religious community, such as a Regular church (can. 479, § 1).

N.B. These churches are sometimes called *chapels of ease*.[43]

When such churches belong to an exempt institute, the rector is named by the religious superior but must be approved by the local Ordinary (can.

---

[39] Augustine III, can. 625. For the meaning of the expression "to pontificate" or "to exercise pontificals" see below, Chap. X, Art. III, III, A.
[40] Cf. Bondini, p. 72.
[41] Augustine, III, can. 625.
[42] Cf. Bondini, p. 72.
[43] Cf. Augustine, II, can. 479.

480, § 2). "This approbation means nothing else than the ratification of the rectors presented."[44] The Bishop cannot subject them to the examination given to pastors, for the care of souls properly so called is not a function of their office. They are, however, subject to examinations which may be required for priests who request faculties to hear confessions.

In the removal of rectors of churches, local Ordinaries are governed by the same laws that regulate the removal of pastors or vicars (can. 486).[45]

12. Processions

Exempt religious must take part in Corpus Christi processions, and in any others ordered to be held for a public cause (cc. 1291, 1292), and, except in the case of the Corpus Christi procession mentioned in canon 1291, § 2, they may not hold processions outside of their churches or cloister, without the permission of the local Ordinary (can. 1293; cf. below, Chap. XIII, Art. V).[46]

13. Preaching and Catechetical Instruction

Exempt religious exercising these ministries for the benefit of secular persons are dependent upon the local Ordinary for faculties, and must exercise them in accordance with the prescriptions issued by him (cc. 1334, 1336, 1338; cf. below, Chap. XVI, Art. I).

14. Taxes

The exempt religious who are specified by law are obliged to pay the *seminary* tax and the *cathedraticum* (cc. 1355, f., 1504; cf. below, Chap. XVI, Art. III).

15. Parish and Mission Investments

For investments of money, the previous consent of the local Ordinary must be obtained by every religious, even a member of a Regular Order, if the money has been given to the parish or the mission, or to the religious for the benefit of the parish or mission. This holds, also, for every change of investments (can. 533, §1, 4°, and § 2; cf. below, Chap. XVII, Art. II).

16. Punitive Measures

Local Ordinaries can apply penal remedies in all cases in which religious are subject to them (can. 619). Though this prescription applies to all religious, exempt included, it does not embrace the cases in which mendi-

---

[44] Cf. Augustine, II, can. 480.
[45] Cf. Melo, p. 97.
[46] Cf. *Epit.*, II, 618–620; Ayrinhac, *Administrative Legislation*, 138.

cants are by special privilege exempted from the coercive power of local Ordinaries.[47]

17. Visitation

All houses of clerical *congregations* approved by the Holy See, even exempt ones, are subject to the quinquennial visitation of the local Ordinary or his delegate, concerning those matters which pertain to the church, the sacristy, the public oratory, and the confessionals (can. 512), unless endowed with a contrary privilege.

B. *Limitations of the Exemption of Nuns*

Local Ordinaries have more extensive jurisdiction over nuns than over exempt clerics. The following are the express exceptions to the exemption of nuns:

1. Right of Visitation

The local Ordinary must visit every five years, either in person or by delegate, the monasteries of nuns who are subject to Regulars, concerning those matters which pertain to the law of enclosure; nay more, even in all other matters, if the Regular superior has not visited them within the past five years. The local Ordinary has the same power of visitation over monasteries of nuns immediately subject to himself or to the Apostolic See (can. 512, §§ 1 and 2).

2. Confessors of Nuns

The local Ordinary *approves* the ordinary and extraordinary confessors for nuns subject to Regulars; he *selects* these confessors for all houses of religious women immediately subject to the Apostolic See or to himself (can. 525).

3. Removal of Confessors

According to the terms of canon 880, the local Ordinary can, for a serious cause, remove both the ordinary and extraordinary confessor of religious women, even when the monastery is subject to Regulars and the confessor himself is a Regular; nor is the Ordinary bound to make known the reason for the removal to anyone except to the Holy See, if it require the reason from him; he must, however, if the nuns are subject to Regulars, inform the Regular superior of the removal (can. 527).

4. Investments

In the investment of money, the previous consent of the local Ordinary

---

[47] Cf. Piat, II, pp. 8–12; Vermeersch, *De Rel.,* I, 380; *Epit.,* I, 624; Schäfer, 282; Coronata, I, 626; see above, Chap. VI.

must be obtained by the superioress of nuns; moreover, if the monastery of nuns be subject to a Regular superior, his consent also is necessary. The same regulation is to be observed for every change of investment (can. 533, § 1, 1°, and § 2).

5. Alienations

To effect the alienations determined in canon 534, nuns must have the written consent of the local Ordinary, as well as the consent of the Regular superior, if the monastery of nuns be subject to Regulars (can. 534).

6. Account of Administration

For every monastery of nuns, even exempt, the superioress must furnish, gratuitously, an account of her administration once a year, or even oftener, if the constitutions so prescribe it, to the local Ordinary, as well as to the Regular superior, if the monastery be subject to Regulars. If the Ordinary does not approve of the account furnished him, he can apply the necessary remedies, including even the removal from office, if the circumstances demand it, of the bursar and the other administrators; but if the monastery be subject to a Regular superior, the Ordinary shall request him to see to it; and if the Regular superior fail to do so, then the Ordinary himself must deal with the case (can. 535, § 1).

7. Dowry

After the first profession of the religious, the superioress, with her Council, and with the consent of the local Ordinary and of the Regular superior, if the house be dependent on Regulars, must place the dowry in a safe, lawful, and productive investment (can. 549). Local Ordinaries must diligently see that the dowries of the religious are conserved; and they must exact an account on the subject, especially on the pastoral visitation (can. 550; cf. above, Chap. VI, Art. II and III).

8. Examination of Aspirants

The superioress even of exempt religious must inform the local Ordinary, at least two months in advance, of the approaching admission to the novitiate and to the profession both of temporary and perpetual, or of solemn or simple vows.

The local Ordinary, or if he be absent or otherwise impeded, a priest delegated by him must, at least thirty days before the admission to the novitiate and to profession, carefully examine the dispositions of the aspirant, and this gratuitously, without, however, entering the cloister; he must inform himself as to whether she has been constrained or beguiled, and whether she understands the import of the step she is about to take; and if he is fully satisfied regarding her pious intentions and freedom of action, then the aspirant may be admitted to the novitiate, or, if already a novice, to profession (can. 552; cf. above, Chap. VI, n. VII).

9. Disposition of Property

In the case of nuns, any modification of the disposition of property treated of in canon 569, § 2, shall be made with the permission of the local Ordinary, as well as that of the Regular superior, if the monastery be subject to Regulars (can. 580, § 3).

10. Cloister

The local Ordinary canonically visiting the monastery of nuns, or other visitators delegated by him, may enter the enclosure, but only for the purpose of inspection, and on condition that he be accompanied by at least one cleric or male religious of mature age. Concerning further dependence upon the local Ordinary in this matter, consult below, Chapter IX, Article VII.

11. Prescribed Prayers, Sacred Solemnities, etc.

All religious, even exempt, must obey the local Ordinary, if from a motive of public utility he prescribes the ringing of bells, certain prayers or certain solemnities, without prejudice to the constitutions and privileges of each institute (can. 612).

12. Punishment

Local Ordinaries can coerce by penalties, even exempt religious, in all cases in which the religious are subject to them (can. 619).

The superioress even of exempt religious women shall be punished by the local Ordinary, according to the gravity of the fault, including, if necessary, even deposition from office: if, contrary to the prescription of canon 549, she has presumed to spend, in whatever manner, the dowries of the young girls received into the institute, always safeguarding the obligation mentioned in canon 551; if, contrary to the prescription of canon 552, she has omitted to inform the local Ordinary concerning the approaching admission of a subject to the novitiate or to profession (can. 2412).

If a superioress acts against the prescriptions of canons 521, § 3, 522, or 523 (concerning confessions), she shall be admonished by the local Ordinary; if again found delinquent, she shall be punished by removal from office, and the Sacred Congregation of Religious is to be immediately informed of the matter (can. 2415).

ARTICLE III. LOSS OF EXEMPTIVE RIGHTS

Under certain conditions, Regulars may suffer a total or a partial loss of their exemptive rights: total, if they are unlawfully absent from their house; partial, if after the commission of a crime outside their house they remain unpunished; cf. above, Chapter VI, Article II, n. I.

CHAPTER VIII

THE EXEMPTION OF MORAL PERSONS

Exemption liberates not only individual religious but also their Orders, provinces, and houses from the jurisdiction of local Ordinaries. These units are moral or juridical persons pertaining to exempt religious. An examination of their exemptive status will show that such corporations enjoy, in the main, that extensive freedom possessed by individual Regulars.[1]

ARTICLE I. THE EXEMPTION OF MORAL PERSONS PERTAINING TO EXEMPT INSTITUTES

Among the rights of religious societies in general is this fundamental one, that every institute legitimately organized is vested with, and enjoys moral personality (can. 99) according to law.[2] This is true also, as will be seen, of provinces and houses belonging to these institutes. When a religious juridical person is exempt, it possesses freedom from the jurisdiction of local Ordinaries by virtue of both its exemption and its legal personality. By reason of the official approbation from the Holy See religious institutes together with their provinces and houses, become moral persons of Pontifical law (cc. 448, 3°; 536).[3]

Hence, they receive all the rights of a papal organization, chief of which is a partial exemption from episcopal jurisdiction. Thereafter, Ordinaries cannot make alterations in the internal government of such bodies nor in the rules which have been approved by the Holy See, nor can they suppress any convent of the institute.[4] When the institutes approved by the Holy See are exempt, they and their various units are vested with the passive exemption enjoyed by the individual Regular religious, for, by the defini-

[1] Cf. Ojetti, Syn., v. *Exemptio.*

[2] Cf. S. C. Rel., Decree, Nov. 10, 1922, AAS, XIV, 644; see Bouscaren, I, can. 488; *Per.,* XI, 173.

[3] According to the Code the juridical personality in question is acquired in one of two ways (can. 100): either by law, as is the case with institutes and their ordinary units; or by the special concession of a person in authority, as is the case with pious foundations belonging to religious corporations (can. 1550). Concerning the first method of acquisition it should be noticed that the moral person need not be expressly established by the law itself; it is sufficient that this be done equivalently by means of legal recognition of the existence of this status, as is had in canon 536 in behalf of a religious institute, province, and house; see Gillet, p. 240; Maroto, I, 460.

[4] Cf. Piat, I, p. 22; Orth, *The Approbation of Religious Institutes,* p. 151.

tions given in the Code, they are withdrawn from the jurisdiction of local Ordinaries (can. 488, 2°) and subjected to that of their own superiors and Chapters (can. 501, § 1).[5]

Besides the moral persons just considered, all religious, according to the norms specified in their constitutions, have the right to establish within their organization offices which are legally recognized as moral persons; exempt religious can accept and erect pious foundations both in their own churches and in the parish churches entrusted to their care (can. 1550).[6] The moral persons of exempt religious enjoy the exemption with which the religious themselves are endowed.[7] Exemption of other moral persons, such as Third Orders, confraternities, and pious unions pertaining to Regulars will be explained in Article III of the present chapter.

RIGHTS AND OBLIGATIONS OF MORAL BODIES PERTAINING TO EXEMPT INSTITUTES

Save for the limitations expressly defined in law or those naturally arising from the nonphysical character of their personality, exempt moral persons have all the rights and obligations possessed by individual religious, and consequently, within the restrictions just stated, their exemption is co-extensive with that of the professed religious. They are withdrawn from the jurisdiction of local Ordinaries unless the law expressly states otherwise (can. 615).

Therefore, they have the right, independently of local Ordinaries: to acquire, own, and administer temporal goods under the provisions of their rules and constitutions (cc. 1495 and 531); to undertake contractual obligations (cc. 534–537; 1228, § 1; 1529, ff.; 1536; 1544); to use judicial means in order to protect their rights (cc. 1552, § 2; 1648 ff.); to elect their own superiors (cc. 506, 507); and in general to enact legislative measures for all matters which common or particular law has not withdrawn from their competency (can. 101, § 1, 1°).[8]

ACTION OF MORAL PERSONS PERTAINING TO EXEMPT INSTITUTES

It follows, as a corollary, that in the exercise of their rights moral persons of the institutes, in question, are exempt from the authority of local Ordinaries. This, too, is manifest from the general principle: unless expressly prescribed in general or particular law, that which has been decided by the

---

[5] Cf. Bened. XIV, Bull, *Apostolicum ministerium*, May 30, 1753; Bouix, II, p. 120; Chokier, Pars. I, q. 17.

[6] Cf. Maroto, I, 461, B; Coronata, II, 1028.

[7] Cf. Gasparri, *De Sanct. Euch.*, I, 559 ff.; Wernz, III, 200 ff.

[8] Cf. Chaps. III and IV; see also Maroto, I, 462.

absolute majority of those who vote, shall have the force of law (can. 101, § 1, 1°).

Though exempt institutes and their units are *collegiate* moral persons, yet some of their actions are performed in a collegiate and others in a noncollegiate manner. This fact is readily deduced from canon 501, § 1, which states that in exempt clerical institutes jurisdiction is exercised by superiors (noncollegiate action) and by Chapters or congregations (collegiate action).[9] Legislative enactments are generally restricted to collegiate action,[10] while ordinary daily government falls to the lot of the individual superiors.

JURISDICTION OF SUPERIORS OVER MORAL PERSONS

The Superior-General has jurisdiction over the entire religious institute and over its provinces, houses, and members in the manner prescribed by common law and the constitution (can. 502). Therefore, the legal capacity (cc. 534–537; 1298, § 1; 1508–1512, 1550, etc.), and the privileges resulting from juridical personality[11] remain under the government and control of the supreme moderator, and withdrawn from the authority of the local Ordinaries.

Other superiors of the institute have jurisdiction within the limits of their charge (can. 502), provincials over provinces, and local superiors over houses, churches, and the like. The management of the juridical person is not the concern of external superiors. For this reason, the religious superiors, and not local Ordinaries or others, are obliged at specified periods to send to the Holy See a written account of the state of the institute signed by themselves and by members of their council (can. 510).[12]

Administration of temporal goods pertaining to the moral persons here discussed, is of such importance in the matter of exemption that we shall give a detailed exposition of it, in Part III, Section III, when dealing with the exemption of things. The exemption of houses and churches of Regulars is studied under the exemption of places, in the next section.

Article II. Jurisdiction of Local Ordinaries Over Moral Persons Pertaining to Exempt Institutes

As has been seen, these moral persons are exempt generally, from the jurisdiction of local Ordinaries. Nevertheless, both before and since the promulgation of the Code there have existed exceptions to this exemption; especially in the case of nuns the law links together both local Ordinaries and Regular superiors in the supervision required for the principal acts of government which must be exercised by nuns subject to Regulars (cf.,

---

[9] Cf. Maroto, I, 465.
[10] Cf. Wernz, III, 690; Piat, I, p. 4; Bied.-Führ., 37; W.-V., III, 127.
[11] Cf. W.-V., II, 30; Gillet, pp. 253, 254.
[12] Cf. Coronata, I, 540.

v.g., cc. 506, § 2; 512, § 2, 1°; 525; 527; 533, § 1, 1°; 534, § 1; 535; 548; 552; 597, § 3; 601, § 2; 603, § 1; 652, § 2).[13]

We shall now consider the cases which form exceptions to the exemption of moral persons.

I. THE ELECTION OF SUPERIORS

In institutes of men, elections are exempt from any intervention on the part of local Ordinaries. The same, however, is not true of nuns, even of those who are subject to Regulars. The Code declares that in monasteries of nuns not subject to local Ordinaries, the assemblies for the election of a superioress shall be presided over by the Regular superior, but even in this case the local Ordinary should be duly informed of the day and hour of the election, at which he may assist, either in person or by a delegate, with the Regular superior, and, if he assists, he presides (can. 506, § 2).

The Regular superior's jurisdictional direction and presidency over the elections in question, entitles him to convoke the electoral assembly, determine the day and the hour for the election, designate the scrutators, receive and record the votes, issue instructions, advice, and warnings deemed necessary or useful for the correct management of the election. It seems, too, that he is the person competent to cast the deciding vote in case of a tie after the third ballot (cf. can. 101, § 1, 1°).[14]

Since, however, the local Ordinary has the right to be present, either in person or by his delegate, he should be informed in advance of the coming election.

If the Bishop attends in person or by his delegate, he or his delegate presides. The Code Commission was asked:

Whether in canon 506, § 2, the words: "secus, Superior regularis; sed etiam hoc in casu Ordinarius tempestive moneri debet de die et hora electionis, cui potest una cum Superiore regulari per se ipse vel per alium assistere, et, si assistat, praeesse," are to be understood to mean that the Ordinary of the place may, but need not, be present in person or by another at the election of the Superioress in monasteries of nuns who are subject to regular superiors (even exempt), and may preside, that is, govern the election, either in person or by another; or only in person?

The Commission replied: in the affirmative to the first part; in the negative to the second. That is, the Ordinary may preside whether he be present in person or by another.[15]

Even after this reply there still remained some obscurity concerning the

---

[13] Cf. Larraona, C.p.R., VIII, p. 26.

[14] Cf. Larraona, C.p.R., VIII, p. 29; Coronata, I, 538.

[15] Cf. AAS, XII, 575; Bouscaren, I, can. 506; Per., X, p. 252.

nature of the presidency to be exercised by the Ordinary.[16] In 1934 the Code Commission was asked:

Whether the words "to preside," which occur in canon 506, § 2, and in the interpretation of 24 Nov., 1920, are to be understood as designating a presidency of honor, or one of jurisdiction?

The Commission replied in the negative to the first part; in the affirmative to the second.[17]

II. CONTROVERSIES REGARDING PRECEDENCE

Controversies on matters of precedence have been sufficiently considered above, in Chapter V, II, B.

The relationship of exempt religious to the local Ordinary in matters pertaining to sacred processions is treated below, in Chapter XIII, Article V, V.

III. CONTROVERSIES IN MISSION TERRITORIES

The Vicar or Prefect Apostolic shall settle all controversies regarding the care of souls that might arise between different religious institutes. His decision must be followed, though the institutes involved have the right of devolutive recourse to the Holy See (can. 298).

ARTICLE III. ASSOCIATIONS OF THE FAITHFUL

The Church has always fostered pious associations of the faithful. Evidence of this is the fact that types of such organizations have flourished among Catholics since primitive times.[18] So today the Holy See encourages membership in societies which have been erected, or at least approved, by the Church, for the Code declares those persons praiseworthy who enroll in the same (can. 684).[19] Once, therefore, that an association has been erected or approved by the proper ecclesiastical authority, membership in it is considered beneficial to the faithful. It follows that either direct or indirect opposition to such societies is not compatible with Christian piety, and must be construed as a violation of the canonical provision just mentioned.

An association of the faithful is a voluntary union or society of persons, distinct from the religious institutes provided for in canons 487–681, which is established or approved by ecclesiastical authority for the promotion of

---

[16] Cf. Bied.-Führ., 33, nota 1; Ferreres, *Inst. Can.*, I, 812; Larraona, C.p.R., VIII, p. 28, nota 346.

[17] Cf. Cod. Com., July 30, 1934, AAS, XXVI, 494; Bouscaren, II, can. 506; *Per.*, XXIII, p. 147, E.R., XCI, 496; *Irish Ecclesiastical Record*, 1934, 638; *Clergy Review*, 1934, 491.

[18] Cf. Augustine, III, tit. XVIII; W.-V., Tom. III, 466.

[19] Cf. Ferreres, *Institutiones Canonicae*, I, 954; W.-V., Tom. III, 463; Vromant, *De Fidelium Associationibus* (Louvain, 1932), 3; Borkowski (Dissert. C.U., 1918), Prooemium and Caput I.

Christian perfection, or the performance of works of piety and charity, or the advancement of public cult[20] (can. 685).

At present we are concerned with the associations pertaining to exempt religious, and particularly with those which are properly constituted moral persons in the Church, namely, which have been granted a formal decree of erection by a legitimate ecclesiastical superior (can. 687).[21]

In considering this matter it will be of advantage to follow the order of the Code, Book II, Part III. Hence, we shall treat of the provisions affecting: (I) associations in general; and (II) particular associations.

I. ASSOCIATIONS IN GENERAL

Canons 684–699 contain the general norms regulating the relationship that exists between local Ordinaries and exempt religious with regard to the erection, government, temporal goods, visitation, etc., of these associations.

A. *Erection of Associations*

In the Church recognition is given to those associations only which have been erected or at least approved by legitimate ecclesiastical authority (can. 686, § 1). Generally this implies two things: the power to erect the society, and the consent of the local Ordinary.

1. Authority to Erect Associations

Erection or approval of associations must come from the Roman Pontiff, or the local Ordinary, or some person, v.g., the superior-general or provincial of a religious institute, endowed with the requisite privilege (can. 686, § 2).[22]

Canon 686, § 2, clearly indicates that the erection of associations may be reserved to certain specified persons. Actually the erection of some associations is reserved to the religious Orders which originally founded them.[23]

---

[20] Some societies, though strictly Catholic in character, have not received the approval of the Church. They are not ecclesiastical in the sense of can. 1489, § 1, though they enjoy the marked favor of the Church, cf. Greg. XVI, Jan. 10, and Aug. 12, 1845. A good example is the Society of St. Vincent de Paul founded for the relief of the poor, by Ozanam in 1833. No ecclesiastical approval is required for the erection of its units or "conferences." Such societies are not subject to local Ordinaries as to their existence, constitution, organization, rules, activities, and internal government. "They are not moral persons in the sense of canons 100 and 687. Hence canons 686–699, which apply to societies juridically erected or approved by ecclesiastical authority, have no application to them. However, by virtue of can. 336, even these societies are subject to the Bishop in the sense that he has the right and duty to exercise vigilance over them in all that concerns faith and morals"; S.C.C., Resolutio, Nov. 14, 1920, AAS, XIII, 135: cf. Bouscaren, I, can. 1489; *Per.*, X, p. 293. See Cappello, *Summa Iuris Canonici,* Vol. II, 645.

[21] Cf. Coronata, I, 669; W.-V., Tom. III, 465, especially nota 8; Vromant, *De Fidelium Associationibus,* 7.

[22] The expression "local Ordinary" employed here, does not signify the vicar-general or vicar-capitular; hence, they cannot *erect* associations, nor can they grant the permission required for their erection or aggregation. However, by virtue of a general mandate the vicar-general may possess the said authority; can. 686, § 4. It seems that the said vicars need no mandate to *approve* associations; cf. Cappello, *Summa Iuris Canonici,* II, 646. Local Ordinaries cannot erect Third Orders, Cappello, *loc. cit.;* Beringer-Steinen, II, 60.

[23] Cf. S. C. Indulg., July 16, 1887.

Such reservations may be divided into two classes: (*a*) erections reserved *exclusively* to religious institutes, and (*b*) erections reserved, but *not exclusively,* to these institutes.

a) Erections reserved exclusively to religious institutes

Without the intervention of the Superior-General the erection of associations of this type is null and void. However, there are degrees of exclusiveness even in these reservations.

i) The most exclusive power in this respect is that exercised by the Master General of the Dominicans over the Confraternity of the Most Holy Rosary. He alone is empowered to erect this society.[24]

ii) Less exclusive is the power had by the Generals of the Trinitarians, Carmelites, and Servites regarding the confraternities of the Most Holy Trinity, of the Blessed Virgin Mary of Mount Carmel, and of the Seven Dolors. For regions under its jurisdiction the S. C. of the Propaganda may grant faculties to erect the afore-mentioned confraternities, and when erected they participate in the same indulgences as those erected at the intervention of the respective generals.[25] The said Congregation has not this power with regard to the Confraternity of the Most Holy Rosary.[26]

b) Erections reserved, but not exclusively, to religious institutes

The erection of some associations, though reserved to religious institutes, may also be effected through the intervention of the local Ordinary. Nevertheless, when established by the latter's authority, they do not participate in the indulgences granted by the Roman Pontiff to the original association, unless they are aggregated by the general of the religious institute to the Primary confraternity.[27] Examples of this type of association are: the congregations of Our Lady of Perpetual Help and of St. Alphonsus, reserved to the Redemptorists; the Sodality of the Blessed Virgin Mary and the Society of Bona Mors, reserved to the General of the Society of Jesus; the congregation of St. Camillus de Lellis, reserved to the Clerics Regulars ministering to the infirm.[28]

2. The Consent of the Local Ordinary

To erect their associations exempt religious require the permission of the local Ordinary, for even when the existence of a privilege in this matter is

---

[24] Cf. S. Off., May 8, 1901; see Borkowski, *De Confraternitatibus Ecclesiasticis* (Dissert. C.U.), p. 44.

[25] Cf. Beringer-Steinen, II, 53; Borkowski, *op. cit.,* Wash., 1918, pp. 44 ff.

[26] Cf. S. C. Indulg., Aug. 10, 1899; S. Off., May 4, 1901; see Ferreres, *op. cit.,* I, 959; Beringer-Steinen, II, 53.

[27] Cf. Ferreres, *op. cit.,* I, 960; Vermeersch, *De Rel.,* I, 546; Beringer-Steinen, II, 55, 106 ff.; Coronata, I, 671, nota 2.

[28] Cf. Beringer-Steinen, II, 55; Ferreres, I, 960; W.-V., Tom. III, 468, and nota 16.

proven, the written consent of the local Ordinary is necessary for the validity of the erection, unless it be stated otherwise in the privilege itself. Consent of the local Ordinary granted for the erection of the religious house contains the permission to erect, in the house or church attached to it, an association which is not constituted after the manner of an organic body and which at the same time is an organization proper to the religious institute (can. 686, § 3).

Several matters connected with this norm are worthy of comment.

a) The Ordinary's consent should be obtained prior to the erection or aggregation of an association.[29]

b) The said consent may not be refused without a just cause.[30] Also, according to the more probable opinion, the Ordinary in giving permission to erect a religious house cannot impose conditions which deprive the religious of their right to establish associations, so long as these are not constituted after the manner of an organic body.[31]

c) The expression "constituted after the manner of an organic body," though occurring frequently in apostolic decrees, is not defined in law. Generally authors take it to mean a society established after the pattern of a religious institute,[32] one, namely, with an internal hierarchy made up of president and counselors who direct the internal government of the body. Also characteristic of such societies are: the trial period or novitiate for candidates, the reception according to a definite public rite and the investing with habit, scapular, or other distinctive insignia.[33] The following are associations which frequently are not constituted after the manner of an organic body, and which, therefore, can be erected in the houses of the religious institutes to which they properly pertain, without the consent of the local Ordinary: the confraternities of the Holy Rosary and of the Holy Name in churches of the Dominicans; the confraternities of the scapular of Our Lady of Mount Carmel and of the Seven Dolors in the churches of the Carmelites and the Servites; the sodality of the Blessed Virgin Mary and the Bona Mors society in the houses or churches of the Society of Jesus.[34]

B. *Statutes of Associations*

It pertains to the local Ordinary to examine and approve the statutes of an

---

[29] S. C. Indulg., Dec. 3, 1892, May 20, 1896; see Beringer-Steinen, II, 58; Ferreres, I, 961; W.-V., Tom. III, 469.

[30] Ferreres, *loc. cit.;* W.-V., *loc. cit.*

[31] This is held by: Vromant, 12; Schäfer, 617; Coronata, I, 671; Claeys Bouuaert-Simenon, 709; Goyeneche, *De Rel.,* 143, nota 10; and C.p.R., XII, pp. 360 ff.

[32] Woywod, I, 584.

[33] S. C. Indulg., Nov. 26, 1880: cf. Vromant, 12, nota 1; Woywod, I, 584; Cocchi, L. II, pars III, 172.

[34] S. C. Indulg., Aug. 25, 1897 and Nov. 15, 1905, ap. ASS, XXX, 276; Beringer-Steinen, II, 58; Goyeneche, *De Rel.,* 143, nota 10.

association, unless the Holy See has already done so;[35] and for a grave reason he may at any time amend the same (can. 687).[36] Approval of the local Ordinary is not required for the statutes of associations which religious are permitted to establish in their own churches without the consent of the local Ordinary.[37]

Statutes which need the approval of the local Ordinary may not be changed without his permission.[38]

C. Government of Associations

All associations, even those erected by the Apostolic See, unless they have a special privilege, are subject to the jurisdiction and vigilance of the local Ordinary, who has the right and duty to visit them in accordance with the sacred canons (can. 690, § 1).

Nevertheless, in the case of associations which by virtue of an apostolic privilege have been established by exempt religious in their own churches, this power is limited, for in such instances it cannot cover matters relating to the internal discipline or the spiritual direction of these bodies (can. 690, § 2). His visitation must comprise only the temporal affairs of the association.[39] This partial exemption applies to all, even to the parish churches of exempt religious,[40] and is subject to broad interpretation.[41]

By virtue of papal decrees, the government and administration of sodalities of either sex and in any institution belonging to or under the care of the Society of Jesus is entirely subject to the General or Vicar-General of the Society.[42]

The visitatorial power of the local Ordinary extends also to the chapels of associations erected in churches of exempt religious, unless the chapel and its upkeep is provided for by the religious themselves.[43] According to Vromant[44] privileges exempting associations from the jurisdiction and vigilance of local Ordinaries are extremely rare.

D. Temporal Goods

Unless the contrary has been expressly determined, a legitimately erected

---

[35] No Ordinary may change a statute approved by the Holy See, S.C.EE.RR., Feb. 17, 1605, ap. ASS, XV, 191.

[36] Beringer-Steinen, II, 81; Ferreres, I, 963; Bondini, p. 74.

[37] S. C. Indulg., May 20, 1882; cf. Ferreres, I, 963; Vromant, 18; also, S. C. Indulg., Nov. 15, 1905.

[38] S.C.C., May 20, 1882; S.C.EE.RR., July 31, 1637; Ferreres, I, 963.

[39] S.C.EE.RR., Sept. 20, 1844; Ferreres, I, 964.

[40] Cod. Com., July 25, 1926, AAS, XVIII, 393.

[41] Vromant, 20.

[42] Bened. XIV, Brief, *Laudabile Romanorum*, Feb. 15, 1758; Leo XII, Const., *Cum Multa*, May 17, 1821.

[43] Conc. Trid., sess. XXII, cc. 8, 9; S.C.EE.RR., July 31, 1637; ap. Biz. 250 ff.; Ferraris, v. *Confraternitates*, art. 3, nn. 38 ff.; Piat, II, pp. 59, 60; Beringer-Steinen, II, 38 ff.; Fanfani, *De Iure Religiosorum*, 535.

[44] Vromant, 19.

association may possess and administer temporal goods under the authority of the local Ordinary.[45] Associations must render the latter an account at least once a year, as stated in canon 1525 (can. 691, § 1). Local Ordinaries cannot assume the administration of goods belonging to these moral persons nor divert their funds to purposes other than those specified in the statutes,[46] for such goods are ecclesiastical in character (can. 1497, § 1), and are, therefore, subject to the norms set down in canons 1518–1551.[47]

If allowed by their statutes, associations may accept offerings, and dispose of them in accordance with the pious practices of their organization, always saving the will of the donor (can. 691, § 2).

Associations may not seek alms,[48] unless permitted by their statutes or constrained by necessity, in which cases they must have the consent of the local Ordinary and follow the norms he issues governing the matter (can. 691, § 3).

To collect alms outside the place of their establishment they need the written permission of the Ordinary in whose territory they seek this assistance (can. 691, § 4).

Associations are bound to give the Ordinary an exact account of the distribution they have made of offerings and alms received by them (can. 691, § 5).

E. *Dismissal of Members*

No one who has been legitimately inscribed in an association may be expelled from the same, except for a just cause as stipulated in the statutes (can. 696, § 1).

Even though no mention is made in the statutes, the local Ordinary has the right to dismiss members from any association; the religious superior has the same right with regard to associations which have been erected in virtue of an apostolic indult by the religious (can. 696, § 3). Power of dismissal may be delegated, v.g., to the moderator.[49]

F. *The Internal Government*

As has been seen (can. 690, § 1), all associations not endowed with special exemptive privileges are subject to the jurisdiction and vigilance of local Ordinaries. This authority extends to the convocation and acts of their meetings, and to the appointment of moderators and chaplains.

---

[45] Sodalities of our Lady erected in houses of the Society of Jesus cannot possess temporal goods. Property of these associations is property of the Jesuit house to which they are attached: cf. Constitutiones S. I., P. 6, c. 2, nn. 2, 5; Bened. XIV, Brief, *Laudabile Romanorum*, Feb. 15, 1758; see Elder Mullan, *Sodality of Our Lady*, nn. 442–469.

[46] Coronata, I, 676.

[47] Cf. W.-V., III, 473; Vromant, 21.

[48] Cf. below, Chap. XVI, Art. II, II, F.

[49] Vromant, 36.

1. Convocation of Meetings

Legitimately erected associations have the right, in conformity with their statutes and the sacred canons, to hold meetings, to issue norms which affect the organization itself, to elect administrators of their temporal goods, officers, and assistants, subject to the prescription of canon 715 (can. 697, § 1).

By reason of canon 715 the local Ordinary has the right to preside over ordinary and extraordinary meetings, even of those confraternities pertaining to the churches of exempt religious which, as stated in canon 690, § 2, enjoy exemption with regard to their discipline and internal direction. He has authority to confirm the election of worthy officers and assistants, and to disapprove of unfit ones. In the case of *pious unions,* however, the election of officers is not subject to his authority.[50]

The local Ordinary is empowered to correct or approve regulations made in these meetings. Yet this is not universally true, for regulations concerning the discipline and spiritual direction of associations which by apostolic privilege are erected in churches of exempt religious (can. 690, § 2) are not subject to the jurisdiction of the local Ordinary.

The local Ordinary or his delegate must be advised at an opportune time of any extraordinary meetings that are to be convened, so that he may preside, if he so wishes. If he is not given proper notice, he may prevent the meeting or nullify its acts.

Provisions contained in canons 161–182, and particular statutes not opposed to common law, should be observed with regard both to the convoking of meetings and to elections (can. 697, § 2).

2. Moderators and Chaplains

Unless an apostolic privilege provides otherwise in an express manner, the nomination of moderator and chaplain pertains to the local Ordinary in associations approved or erected by himself or the Apostolic See and in associations erected by religious, in virtue of a papal privilege, outside their own churches; in associations, however, erected in their own churches only the consent of the local Ordinary is required, if the moderator or chaplain is chosen from among the secular clergy (can. 698, § 1).[1]

For a just reason the moderator and chaplain may be removed from office by these who have authority to nominate them, or by their successors or delegates (can. 698, § 3).

From paragraph 1 of canon 698, it is clear that exempt religious may possess an apostolic privilege reserving the nomination of moderators or

---

[50] Cf. Vromant, 78.
[1] Generally the offices of moderator and chaplain are held by one individual (cf. can. 698, § 4); cf. Vromant, 38, 40.

chaplains to themselves, even in cases in which the law normally consigns this right to the local Ordinary. The Dominican Order enjoys such a privilege with regard to the confraternity of the Holy Rosary. In fact the local Ordinary's consent is only required for nominations in churches entrusted to the secular clergy.[2] The Franciscans also seem to have the right of nominating directors for sodalities of their Third Order, even when these are established outside their own churches. This appears to be confirmed not only by immemorial custom but by expressed concessions of the Holy See.[3]

It pertains to religious superiors to nominate the moderator or chaplain of associations which, by virtue of an apostolic indult, are established in their own churches. The consent of the local Ordinary is required only when they choose the moderator or chaplain from among the secular clergy.

G. *Cessation of Associations*

An association may cease to exist either because it has no members, or because it has been suppressed.

1. Defect of Membership

It is a general rule of the Code that a moral person, such as an association, does not cease to exist unless it entirely lacks members during the space of one hundred years (can. 102, § 1).[4]

2. Suppression

For grave reasons, and always saving the right of recourse to the Holy See, the local Ordinary may suppress not only the associations erected by himself or his predecessors, but also those erected with his consent by religious in virtue of an apostolic privilege (can. 699, § 1).

There are several types of associations over which the local Ordinary has no repressive power.

He has not authority to suppress associations established: (*a*) by the Apostolic See (can. 699, § 2); (*b*) by religious who, by virtue of a particular indult did not require the consent of the local Ordinary; (*c*) by religious with the implicit consent of the local Ordinary, as stated in canon 686, § 3, which are proper organizations of the religious institute in question and which at the same time are not constituted after the manner of organic bodies.[5]

---

[2] Leo XIII, Const., *Ubi primum,* Oct. 10, 1898: cf. Vromant, 39, nota 3.

[3] Cf. S.C.EE.RR., June 18, 1717, ap. Biz. 339; Leo XIII, Brief, *In tertium,* Sept. 21, 1900; Pius X, *Tertium Franciscalium,* Sept. 8, 1912: cf. Coronata, I, 683; Vromant, 39.

[4] Cf. Vromant, 42.

[5] Cf. Vromant, 42; Prümmer, p. 268; Maroto, I, 467; Claeys Bouuaert-Simenon, I, 714; Coronata, I, 684.

It is a disputed point whether or not religious superiors have the right to suppress those associations which required the consent of the local Ordinary for their establishment.[6] In such cases the more prudent procedure is to obtain the consent of both the religious superior and the local Ordinary.[7]

II. PARTICULAR ASSOCIATIONS

In view of their different purposes, associations are divided into three classes: Third Orders, Confraternities, and Pious Unions (can. 700).

A. *Third Orders*

The purpose of a Third Order is to procure the Christian perfection of persons in the world who enroll therein, under the guidance and according to the spirit of the religious Order to which it pertains and conformably with the rules approved by the Apostolic See (can. 702, § 1). Examples of such Orders are the Third Orders of the Franciscans, Dominicans, Carmelites, Trinitarians, Oblates of St. Benedict, Hermites of St. Augustine, etc.[8]

Even though endowed with an apostolic privilege, religious superiors cannot validly erect a sodality of a Third Order without the consent of the local Ordinary, as stated in canon 686, § 3. This consent is not necessary for the erection of sodalities in the churches of the religious, so long as such associations are not constituted after the manner of an organic body.[9] The prescription of canon 703, § 2, does not restrict the right of religious to receive candidates into Third Orders which have already been established. It should be remarked that local Ordinaries are not competent to erect Third Orders (cf. cc. 702, 703).[10]

In their government Third Orders are independent of local Ordinaries, and subject to religious superiors. This holds true of all sodalities of Tertiaries, whether they are erected in exempt or in secular churches.[11] Now, as previously,[12] the local Ordinary has the right to visit sodalities, but not concerning matters relating to the internal government or the spiritual direction of the organization (can. 690).[13] His visitatorial power is limited to the temporal affairs, as stated above.[14] Acquisition and administration of goods, nomination of moderators and chaplains are regulated by the general norms already explained.[15]

---

[6] Coronata, I, 684, affirms that they have such power; Maroto, I, 467, denies it.
[7] Coronata, I, 684.
[8] Cf. Beringer-Steinen, II, 350–409; Ferreres, I, 977.
[9] Coronata, I, 689.
[10] Coronata, I, 670, nota 6.
[11] Cf. Leo XIII, May 30, 1883; see Vermeersch, *De Rel.*, I, 536; Beringer-Steinen, II, 377; Coronata, I, 687.
[12] Cf. S. C. Indulg., Jan. 31, 1893, ap. N.R.T., XXV, 274.
[13] Cf. Piat, II, p. 59. By apostolic privilege Third Orders of the Franciscans are exempted from this visitation; Bened. XIII, Const., *Paterna Sedis*, Dec. 10, 1725; Vromant, 67.
[14] Present Article, I, C.   [15] Present Article, I, D, and F, 2.

Third Orders are permitted, but not obliged, to take part collegiately in public processions; if they do so, they must march under their own cross and standard, and wear the insignia of their order (can. 706).[16]

Superiors cannot permit sodalities established by them to wear a particular garb in sacred functions of a public nature, without the special permission of the local Ordinary (can. 703, § 3). This rule does not seem applicable to sacred functions which are conducted in their own churches or oratories.[17]

B. *Confraternities and Pious Unions*

A Pious Union is an association of the faithful erected for the practice of some work of piety or charity. When it is canonically established by a legitimate superior, it becomes an ecclesiastical moral person. Pious Unions erected after the manner of an organic body are called *sodalities.* Sodalities which have been established for the purpose of advancing public worship are given the special title, *confraternities* (can. 707). It is essential to a confraternity that it be vested with juridic personality.[18]

Norms governing the erection of associations in general, explained above,[19] are applicable to the erection of pious unions and confraternities. However, unlike pious unions, confraternities can only be instituted by a formal decree of erection (can. 708).

Several confraternities of the same title and institute should not be erected in the same place, unless this be allowed by special concession or by a provision of law; if, however, there be question of large cities, this is permitted so long as the local Ordinary judges that the confraternities are sufficiently distant from one another (can. 711, § 1). Third Orders being neither pious unions nor confraternities are not affected by the law of *distance.*[20]

Exempt from this same law are: sodalities of the Blessed Virgin Mary[21] and of the Children of Mary;[22] confraternities of Christian Doctrine and of the Blessed Sacrament;[23] associations of Bona Mors, of the Sacred Heart of Jesus, of Christian Mothers, etc.[24]

In churches or oratories of religious women, the local Ordinary can permit the erection of associations of women only, or of a pious union which is merely obliged to recite certain prayers and enjoys the communication of spiritual favors alone (can. 712, § 3).[25]

---

[16] S.R.C., Resp., June 30, 1905; cf. Vermeersch, *De Rel.,* I, 536.
[17] Coronata, I, 694.
[18] Coronata, I, 692.
[19] Cf. Present Article, I, A.
[20] Cf. S. C. Indulg., Jan. 12, 1893; Coronata, I, 694.
[21] Cf. S. C. Indulg., Aug. 29, 1864, Decr. auth. 413.
[22] Cf. S. C. Indulg., Aug. 30, 1866.
[23] Cf. S. C. Indulg., Aug. 22, 1842, and July 12, 1848.
[24] Cf. Beringer-Steinen, II, 74.
[25] Cf. Coronata, I, 695.

Care is to be taken that the exercises and functions of pious unions and confraternities do not cause harm to parochial ministries. If there be doubt as to the existence of such interference, the local Ordinary has the right to decide the matter and to issue the regulations to be observed (can. 716).

Confraternities and pious unions which are properly constituted moral persons have the right to acquire and administer temporal goods, according to the norms explained above.[26]

Confraternities and pious unions which are reserved to a religious institute may not be transferred from one place to another without the permission of the religious superior (can. 719, § 2). By an analogy of law, this same norm is applicable to Third Orders.[27]

Members of confraternities cannot officially assist at sacred functions unless they wear the habit or insignia of their association (can. 709, § 1). Confraternities are obliged to take part collegiately bearing their insignia and under their banner in the customary processions and in any others prescribed by the local Ordinary, unless the said Ordinary has ruled otherwise (can. 718).

Only the Ordinary of the place can authorize the faithful to wear the habit or insignia of their association, which according to canon 718, is to be used in public processions. Canon 713, § 2, expressly decrees this for confraternities that have been erected by religious institutes.

Confraternities cannot abandon or modify their proper habit or insignia without the permission of the local Ordinary (can. 714).

The local Ordinary has the right to preside either personally or by delegate at assemblies of confraternities, even when these are held in churches or oratories of Regulars, without, however, the right to vote. He has the right to confirm the election of worthy and capable officers, and to reject that of the unworthy and incapable; and he is empowered to correct and approve statutes or other norms, unless they have already had the approval of the Apostolic See (can. 715, § 1).

Notice should be given the local Ordinary of any extraordinary assemblies that are to be convened. If this rule is not observed the Ordinary can prevent the holding of the assembly or he can nullify its decrees (can. 715, § 2).

C. Archconfraternities and Primary Unions

Sodalities[28] which have the right to aggregate to themselves other associations of the same kind, are called archsodalities, or archconfraternities, or primary pious unions or congregations or societies (can. 720).

Without an apostolic indult no association can validly aggregate others to itself (can. 721, § 1).

---

[26] Present Article, I, D.

[27] Cf. Coronata, I, 699.

[28] The term "sodality" is not employed in the strict meaning defined in can. 707, but in a more general sense embracing all pious unions; cf. Vromant, 84.

In order that a valid aggregation be effected, written consent and testimonial letters must be obtained from the Ordinary of the place where the association to be aggregated is situated (can. 723, 2°). However, the consent of the local Ordinary does not seem to be necessary for the aggregation of confraternities or pious unions which are not constituted after the manner of an organic body and which at the same time are erected in the churches or oratories of the religious institutes to which they pertain.[29]

Indulgences, privileges, and other spiritual favors communicated by aggregation, must be enumerated in a list inspected by the Ordinary of the place in which the archconfraternity is located, which list must be transmitted to the aggregated association (can. 723, 3°).

---

[29] Cf. Coronata, I, 704; Ferreres, I, 994.

The Exemption of Places

Local exemption, as the term indicates, signifies the withdrawal of places, such as territories, houses, churches, etc., from the jurisdiction of local Ordinaries. Different types of withdrawal are met with, the diversity arising from the various kinds of exemption vested in religious. *Passive* exemption causes the direct withdrawal of persons, and as a consequence, of *places also,* from the jurisdiction of local Ordinaries. By a fiction of law,[1] places are considered outside of diocesan territory, and are therefore exempt from diocesan authority.[2]

Active exemption bestows on religious prelates full jurisdiction over places and over the people and clergy in these places, and as a consequence, effects the entire withdrawal of these persons and places from the jurisdictional power of local Ordinaries.[3] Territories of this sort which are withdrawn from dioceses, are not enumerated as dioceses but rather as prelacies or abbacies "nullius" (that is, of no diocese).[4]

In places enjoying passive exemption, the people and clergy, not the exempt religious, are subject to local Ordinaries; in those enjoying active exemption, all the persons and places are subject to the exempted prelates.

Both before and after the promulgation of the Code, authors have disputed about the nature of the local exemption which is normally possessed by the houses, churches, etc., of exempt religious (not pertaining to an abbacy "nullius"). Exemption of this kind some claim is *active,* directly freeing both persons and places from the jurisdiction of local Ordinaries, so that even *nonexempt people* in such places are withdrawn from this juris-

---

[1] Cf. Leo XIII, Const., *Romanos Pontifices.*

[2] Cf. Bened. XIV, *De Syn. Dioec.,* L. II, c. XI, 2; Suarez, *De Censuris,* V, IV, 6; Schmalz., L. V, XXXIII, 248; Piat, II, c. III, q. 2.

[3] Cf. Bened. XIV, Const., *Apostolicae servitutis,* pars. 6, 10, Feb. 25, 1741; and Const., *Inter multa,* Apr. 4, 1747 (*Fontes* II, pp. 102 ff.); see also Piat, II, p. 1, q. 2.

[4] Examples of such withdrawals are: the abbacy "nullius" of St. Peter, Muenster, Saskatchewan, erected by Benedict XV, May 6, 1921; and the abbacy "nullius," Mary Help of Christians, North Carolina, erected by Pius X, June 8, 1910. Both these territories have been placed under the jurisdiction of Benedictine prelates.

diction.[5] Others hold that only the religious to whom exemption is granted are directly freed from the authority of local Ordinaries and that their places benefit indirectly because of the personal exemption. The religious, therefore, enjoy only *passive* exemption, and other persons who are accidentally in their houses, churches, etc., remain under the jurisdiction of the local Ordinary.[6]

The more probable opinion seems to be this: places, such as houses and churches of exempt religious, are not endowed with that immunity which flows from active local exemption; they are exempt to that degree only which is demanded to insure the exempt status of the religious dwelling therein. They are not, therefore, so severed from diocesan territory as to become territories "nullius." Local Ordinaries still retain jurisdiction over subjects accidentally found in these places.[7]

In penal matters, one should interpret the law strictly (can. 19), thus favoring, as far as permitted by equity and justice, those subject to the legislation. Since both the opinions just discussed are supported by many noted authors, they have true extrinsic probability. Hence, in practice, it should be maintained that Bishops cannot inflict penalties on subjects in exempt places.[8]

The principal places of exempt religious with which we are concerned are their houses and sacred places. Hence, in the Chapters of this Section we shall consider exemption in so far as it affects the houses, churches, oratories, altars, and cemeteries of exempt religious. The general norms of the Code applying to religious houses are contained in canons 497 and 498; those referring to sacred places are found in Book III, Part III, canons 1154–1242.

---

[5] Cf. St. Alph., *Theol. Mor.* (ed. Gaude, p. 244), L. I, tr. II, cap. IV, *De Priv.*, n. 74; Laymann, *Theol. Mor.*, L. I, tr. IV, cap. XI, 5; Bonacina, *De Censuris*, Disp. I, q. 1; Bordonius, Resolut., VII, 4; Avila, *De Censuris*, part. II, cap. III, Disp. 2, dub. 3; Peyrinus, Tom. I, *Priv. Sixt.* IV, Const. 2, dub. 6; Schmalz., L. V, tit. XLVII, 56; Salmanticenses, *Theol. Mor.*, tr. XVIII, *De Priv.*, cap. III, p. 1, par. 1, n. 3; Ballerini-Palmieri, *Opus Theol. Mor.*, I, 346, VII, 68; Cappello, *De Censuris*, 20; Genicot-Salsmans, *Inst. Theol. Mor.*, I, 114; Noldin, *De Princ.*, 151; Chaupin-Gautrelet, *Nature et Obligations de l' Etat Religieux*, p. 495; Coronata, I, 621, nota 4 and 623, etc.

[6] Cf. Suarez, *De Censuris*, Disp. V, sect. IV, 6; Bened. XIV, *De Syn. Dioec.*, L. II, c. 11, 2; Salas, *De Legibus*, Disp. 14, 84; Azor, *Inst. Mor.*, L. I, XXVI, 94; Pignatelli, *Consult. Can.* VII, 8; Bouix, II, 87; Molitor, 241; *Epit.*, I, 774; De Meester, II, 1024; Chelodi, *De Personis*, p. 438; Cocchi, IV, 114; Fanfani, *De Jure Rel.*, 356; Prümmer, p. 304; Bondini, p. 6; Ojetti, *Comm. in Cod.*, I, pp. 19 ff.; d'Angelo, p. 25; Ramos, C.p.R., pp. 28–33, 82–25.

[7] Cf. Bened. XIV, *De Syn. Dioec.*, II, 11, 2, and Const., *Apostolicae servitutis*, Feb. 25, 1741; see also Creusen, 310; Augustine, III, can. 615; Ramos, C.p.R., VI, p. 83; Goyeneche, C.p.R., IV, pp. 219–221; Melo, p. 121.

[8] Cf. Cappello, *De Censuris*, 20; Coronata, I, 621, nota 4 and 623.

CHAPTER IX

THE EXEMPTION OF RELIGIOUS HOUSES

The Code states: "Regulars . . . are exempt together with their houses . . . from the jurisdiction of local Ordinaries except in the cases expressly provided for by law" (can. 615).

ARTICLE I. THE MEANING OF THE TERM "HOUSE"

Before the Code, the words "house" and "religious house" were used generically to designate all places, as monasteries, convents, churches, oratories, hospices, orphanages, hospitals, schools, and the like, which had been erected by the authority of the Bishop or of some other prelate. Likewise included under the term were congregations, confraternities, and other organizations established by a competent ecclesiastical superior and destined for merciful, charitable, or other pious uses.[1] Other pious houses or places were those privately established, that is, *without ecclesiastical erection or approbation,* which were destined for charitable or pious uses.[2]

According to the Code, a "religious house" is one belonging to any religious institute in general; a "Regular house," one belonging to a religious Order (can. 488, 5°). Since now, as formerly, the term "house" has a very extensive meaning, it will be well to consider briefly its general signification as found in the new Code.

The term "house" is used in a material and in a formal sense.

1. It is often used in its *material* and *common* meaning to signify a dwelling place or edifice, as a monastery, church, school, etc.[3] The extension of this meaning varies, sometimes denoting the particular dwelling of religious; sometimes embracing all edifices within the monastery walls. This latter is the sense employed, for example, in canon 514.[4] Hence, the term may signify the community house, or that dwelling together with all the other edifices attached to it, e.g., servants' quarters, schools, libraries, hospitals, oratories, churches, guest houses, etc. A religious house, in this

---

[1] Cf. *Decretales:* Greg. IX, L. III, t. 36; Bonif. VIII, L. III, t. 17; Clem. VIII, L. III, t. 20; *Etrav. Joan.,* XXII, t. 7; *Etrav. Comm.,* t. 9; see also Schmalz., IV, t. 36; nn. 1–3; W.-V., III, 43; Larraona, C.p.R., p. 46; *Per.,* X, pp. 34–35; Schäfer, 42.
[2] Cf. W.-V., III, 43.
[3] Cf. cc. 508; 540; 555, § 1, 3°; 556, § 1; 564, § 1; 597, §§ 1 and 2; 599, § 1; 604; 1477; 1483; 2156, etc.
[4] Cf. Larraona, C.p.R., IX, pp. 104 ff.

material sense, can be a noncollegiate moral person distinct juridically from the religious community.[5]

To be a properly constituted religious house, it is not necessary that the material structure be owned by the moral person or religious community; it may be leased or rented. However, it should be their permanent dwelling.[6] Because of the norms governing the founding of religious houses, there exists a strict relationship between the religious house and the religious community; so that, as Larraona points out, a transfer of the community's dwelling very often implies, practically speaking, a change in the moral person, for frequently such a transfer is equivalent to a new foundation.[7]

2. In the *formal* and more technical sense, the term "house" signifies a *collegiate moral person*. Thus, when the Code employs the word to mean the religious community, it uses it in this sense. This is apparent from canons 502, § 1, and 521, §§ 1 and 2, where "house" (domus) and "community" (communitas) refer to the same identical object.[8] In canon 536, § 1, the religious house is expressly called a *moral person*. Yet, it should be remarked that the expression "religious house," when used in the technical meaning, does not signify "community" in the abstract; it has, rather, a definite and concrete signification, namely, *a community inasmuch as it has a fixed abode* or dwelling.[9]

It is clear, from what has just been stated, that both the material and formal meanings are *proper* legal significations of the expression "religious house," or "Regular house." Presently, we shall see that the statement "Regulars, together with their houses, are exempt" means that the communities of these religious, together with their edifices are immune from the jurisdictional authority of local Ordinaries.

ARTICLE II. HOUSES POSSESSING EXEMPTION

Before the Code, the houses of Regulars, with the exception of small convents, were exempt from the jurisdiction of local Ordinaries. The different legislative measures which regulated small convents can be reduced to the following points:

1. Convents established after the decree *"Cum Saepe,"* of Urban VIII (June 21, 1625), were not exempt unless they contained at least twelve religious.

2. Likewise, convents in Italy and the adjacent islands established before that date, which were suppressed by Innocent X, and later re-established, did not enjoy exemption unless they had at least twelve religious.

---

[5] Cf. Schäfer, 42.
[6] Cf. W.-V., III, 402; Schäfer, 42; Larraona, C.p.R., VI, p. 47, nota 174.
[7] Cf. Larraona, C.p.R., III, p. 47, nota 174.
[8] Cf. cc. 531; 532, § 1; 582, 1°; 594, § 2.
[9] Cf. Larraona, C.p.R., III, p. 47.

3. Other convents in Italy which had not been suppressed, enjoyed exemption if they had at least six religious, four of whom were priests.

4. There were no legal provisions for convents established outside of Italy before the year 1625.[10]

On account of these different norms, great diversity was found in the decisions issuing from the Holy See.[11] In course of time, a new and more general discipline developed which recognized as exempt, convents containing at least six religious.[12] This was confirmed by Leo XIII, who declared: "It has been established by common law that houses which have not at least six religious should certainly be subject to the authority of Bishops" (Const., *Romanos Pontifices*, par. 8).[13]

Since the promulgation of the Code, all Regular houses, *irrespective of the number of religious occupants*, are exempt from the jurisdiction of local Ordinaries (can. 615). Nonformal houses, according to canon 617, § 2, are under the vigilance, but not the jurisdiction, of local Ordinaries.[14] Now, the sole fact required for exemption is that the house be lawfully erected (can. 497).[15]

From the different canonical meanings of the term "house," it is clear that the house of the religious community and all edifices within the confines of the convent, or not situated at a great distance from the same, are embraced by the law of exemption. The same is true of all property and of all edifices even though widely separated from the community dwelling, so long as they are within the walls or precincts of the monastery.[16]

The last article deals with the dependence of the cloister of nuns upon the authority of local Ordinaries.

The remaining articles of this chapter treating of the erection, alterations, suppression, extinction, etc., of a religious house, delineate in sufficient detail the extent of the jurisdiction granted to local Ordinaries.

ARTICLE III. THE ERECTION OF RELIGIOUS HOUSES

The Holy See has always favored the spread of religious institutes and has strongly protested against those who have endeavored to impede their progress or restrict their sacred ministries.[17]

Their work for souls has ever been most fruitful. The very nature of their

---

[10] Cf. W.-V., III, 401, nota 30.
[11] Cf. Ferraris, V, *Conventus*, Art. 2, nn. 23 ff., nn. 32 ff.
[12] Cf. Biz., pp. 396, 284.
[13] Cf. W.-V., III, 401, nota 30; Aichner, *Juris Can. Comp.*, p. 471, nota 14; Lucidi, II, 67, 68; Vermeersch, *De Rel.*, I, 365; ASS, Tom. 38, p. 144; Fagn., Cap. "*Auctoritate*," de censibus, III, 29.
[14] Cf. W.-V., III, 401; Schäfer, 42.
[15] W.-V., *loc. cit.*
[16] Cf. Schäfer, 42; Larraona, C.p.R., IX, p. 105.
[17] Cf. Pius VI, Br., *Quod aliquantum*, Mar. 10, 1791; and Const., *Auctorem fidei*, Aug. 28, 1794, contra prop., LXXX, Synodi Pistor. (cf. *Fontes*, II, p. 709).

life admirably equips religious for this, for they form a choice portion of the flock of Jesus Christ consecrated by vow to a life of evangelical perfection, and live and labor under the supreme direction of the Apostolic See.[18]

There can be no question as to the esteem which hierarchy and faithful have manifested at all times for religious and their apostolic activities.[19] The Church, too, declares that all must continue to hold in honor this state of life (can. 487).[20]

In the establishment of religious houses, particularly those pertaining to exempt institutes, the Holy See desires a systematic mode of procedure in which she obliges religious to abide by definite canonical formalities. Once a house is erected, certain juridical effects follow as a consequence. The present Article deals with both the formalities and the juridical effects of erecting a religious house.

1. Requisite Legal Formalities

In order to erect a religious house in general, or an institution dependent upon but separated from a religious house, definite prescriptions must be followed.

(A) *Religious Houses in General*

Before the Code. It has long been the practice of the Church to require the fulfillment of certain legal formalities in the erection of houses, convents, or monasteries pertaining to religious institutes. As early as the fifth century (451), the Council of Chalcedon (can. 4) forbade the establishment of monasteries without the permission of the Bishop. This law was repeated by particular councils and formed the common discipline which was in vogue till the thirteenth century, as evidenced in the Decree of Gratian (10, 12, 13, C. 18, q. 2). Toward the middle of the thirteenth century, noticeable modifications were effected through privileges granted to mendicant Orders.[21] The Council of Trent restored the ancient practice ("Nec de cetero similia loca erigantur sine Episcopi in cujus diocesi erigenda sunt licentia prius obtenta," Conc. Trid., sess. XXV, *de Regul.*, c. 3), without revoking the privileges of mendicants;[22] and later, Urban VIII, in his Constitution, *Romanus Pontifex,* August 28, 1624, revoked all privileges which permitted religious to erect houses without the consent of local Ordinaries.[23] Innocent X, in his Constitution, *Instaurandae,* October 15, 1652, further decreed that it was necessary to obtain the *special* and *express* permission of the Holy See

---

[18] Cf. Leo XIII, Ep., *Au Milieu,* Dec. 23, 1900 (cf. *Fontes,* III, p. 567, n. 2).

[19] Cf. Leo XIII, Ep., *Au Milieu* (cf. *Fontes,* p. 567, n. 2).

[20] Cf. Leo XIII, Ep., *Testem,* ad Card. Gibbons, Jan. 22, 1899 (cf. *Fontes,* III, p. 540, n. 11).

[21] Cf. Vermeersch, *De Rel.,* I, 104.

[22] Cf. Wernz, III, 616.

[23] Cf. De Franchis, 507, p. 158; Bouix, I, p. 261; Wernz, III, 616.

for the erection of any Regular house in Italy, or the adjacent islands. Through the practice of the Roman Curia,[24] the necessity of this Apostolic indult (the indult was issued in favor of Regulars and in view of their exemption, so as to prevent unnecessary controversies concerning the status of their establishments)[25] was extended to houses outside of Italy and gradually became the general discipline of the Church.[26] The need both of the consent of the Holy See and of the Bishop was proclaimed anew and confirmed by Leo XIII,[27] and by the Sacred Congregation of the Propaganda, December 7, 1901.[28] The same legislation held for houses of nuns in which solemn vows were pronounced.[29] To avoid disputes, the express, i.e., viva voce or written permission of the local Ordinary was required. Ordinarily the Holy See reserved to itself the faculty to erect novitiate houses.[30]

2. Legislation of the Code

The Code decrees: for the erection of an exempt religious house, whether formal or not, or a monastery of nuns, or in places subject to the Sacred Congregation of the Propaganda, any religious house whatever, the approval of the Apostolic See and the written consent of the local Ordinary are necessary; in other cases the permission of the Ordinary suffices (can. 497, § 1).

This introduces a notable change by requiring permission of the Holy See for the erection of the house of any exempt institute, whether religious Order or congregation.

N.B. "To found a monastery of nuns of simple vows in France and Belgium it is probable that the authorization of the Holy See is not required. This opinion, which is shared by good canonists,[31] rests on repeated declarations of the Holy See that nothing is changed in the dependence of these nuns in regard to Bishops."[32]

In all institutes approved by the Holy See, the permission of the Apostolic See is necessary for the erection of novitiate houses (can. 554).

The necessary *consent* of *local Ordinaries* for the erection of exempt houses is of particular importance since it constitutes an express limitation of exemptive rights.

---

[24]Cf. *Monitore Eccl.*, VI, p. 40.
[25] Cf. Wernz, III, 616.
[26] Cf. Bened. XIV, *De Syn. Dioec.*, L. 9, c. I; Wernz, III, 616.
[27] Cf. Const., *Romanos Pontifices*, May 8, 1881.
[28] Cf. Pius IX, epist. ad Archiep. Paris, Oct. 26, 1865; Bouix, I, pp. 260 ff.; Piat, II, pp. 270, 276 ff.; Wernz, III, 617.
[29] Cf. S.C.EE.RR., Dec. 6, 1839, Sept. 20, 1840, June 20, 1851, etc., ap. Biz., pp. 85, n. 1, 549, 650; see also Ferraris, v. *Moniales*, art. 2, n. 6; Piat, II, p. 281; Bouix, I, pp. 249 ff., 305 ff.; ASS, I, pp. 725 ff., and XXVII, p. 636; Wernz, III, 616.
[30] Cf. Wernz, III, 619.
[31] Cf. Jombart, "*Les moniales a voeux simples*," N.R.T. (1924), p. 197.
[32] Cf. Creusen, 34.

No religious house can be *validly* erected without the permission of the local Ordinary. His consent is a prerequisite, not a constituent element in the act of erection. The formal decree of erection is issued by the institute or province in accordance with the norms of their constitutions; for an abbey the Holy See alone is competent to give the decree.[33]

To avoid future disputes, *written* permission should be obtained. The manner of concession, however, whether written or oral, does not affect the validity of the action, since neither canon 497, par. 1, nor former regulations[34] either expressly or equivalently made such provision (can. 11).[35]

For the settlement of controversies concerning the juridical status of religious houses erected before the promulgation of the Code, two facts should be borne in mind:

a) Written permission of the local Ordinary was *not necessary*.[36] Express permission sufficed. At one time certain religious, as the Discalced Carmelites, Dominicans, Jesuits, could establish houses without permission of the Holy See, and sometimes without that of local Ordinaries.[37] Such privileges were later revoked.[38]

b) Even though no proof could be adduced, monasteries of Regulars were *presumed* to have been validly erected, and could, therefore, be lawfully retained by them. Authors based this conclusion on the privilege of Sixtus V, granted to the Friars Minor,[39] and on the prescriptive rights acquired by the houses.[40]

Does the expression "local Ordinary," in canon 497, § 1, include all those listed under this title in canon 198, § 2, or does it apply merely to the Bishop?

It would seem, as Goyeneche points out,[41] that the granting of permission to erect a religious house is not always restricted to the Bishop of the place. Other local Ordinaries have this faculty in accordance with the following conditions. Vicars General who have a special mandate are competent in this respect (cf. cc. 368; 435, § 3).[42] Vicars Capitular can give the permission so

---

[33] Cf. W.-V., III, 76, nota 23; Schäfer, 80; Coronata, I, 522; Larraona, C.p.R., V, p. 418, nota 338.

[34] Cf. Wernz, III, 617.

[35] Cf. *Epit.*, I, 607; Coronata, I, 523; however, Chelodi, *De Personis*, p. 384, nota 4, holds the contrary.

[36] Cf. Wernz, III, 617; Piat, II, p. 277; Bondini, p. 42.

[37] Cf. Pius V, Const., *Ad hoc nos Deus*, Sept. 23, 1571; Paul III, Const., *Licet debitum*, Oct. 18, 1549; Pius IV, Const., *Etsi ex debito*, Apr. 13, 1561; Greg. XIII, Const., *Salvatoris Domini*. Oct. 30, 1576.

[38] Cf. Urban VIII, Const., *Romanus Pontifex*, par. 4, Aug. 28, 1624; Leo XIII, Const., *Romanos Pontifices;* see also Piat II, p. 271.

[39] Cf. Sixtus V, Const., *Cum sicut nobis*, par. 1, Dec. 20, 1589.

[40] Cf. Piat, II, p. 271.

[41] Cf. C.p.R., I, pp. 114–117.

[42] Cf. Vermeersch, *De Rel.*, I, 104; Bondini, p. 43; De Meester, 941; Larraona, C.p.R., V, p. 424.

long as the new religious establishment is not of such importance that its existence will constitute a change in the status of the diocese ("Sede vacante nihil innovetur," can. 425).[43]

Failure to obtain either of the permissions required by canon 497 render the erection of a house null and void. To rectify this condition and thus establish the house canonically, the superior must obtain the permission heretofore omitted, v.g., that of the Bishop, if his was lacking.[44] The consent of the Bishop should, as a general rule, be obtained before seeking that of the Holy See.[45]

As will be seen more at length in Article IV, permission of the Holy See and the local Ordinary is also necessary, if a religious house is to be converted to uses which require an alteration in the external regime (can. 497, § 4), or imply a change contrary to stipulations contained in the original permissions.[46]

Before granting religious permission to erect a house, the local Ordinary and the religious superior should examine its prospective means of support, for no religious house may be established unless it can be prudently estimated that it will be able to provide suitably for the habitation and maintenance of its members from its own resources, or from habitual alms, or otherwise (can. 496). This does not mean that the necessary funds must be on hand before permission is given. The superior and Ordinary should give their consent if they judge that there are solidly reasonable grounds to expect that adequate support is forthcoming.[47]

Other requisite formalities which were in force prior to the Code are no longer necessary;[48] those, however, which are not opposed to present legislation may serve as useful norms and in some cases will be the means of guaranteeing equity toward other organizations affected by the new establishment.[49] Evidently it is important to restrict the establishing of houses which would endanger the existence of those already erected in a locality. If there be reasonable doubt concerning such impending harm, superiors of the other houses should be interrogated. Injured parties have the right of devolutive recourse to the Holy See.[50]

---

[43] Cf. Schäfer, p. 44, nota 7; Goyeneche, C.p.R., I, pp. 110, 111; Larraona, C.p.R., V, 436; others, however, deny this power: cf., v.g., Coronata, I, 523; Melo, p. 122; Bondini, p. 43.
[44] Cf. Pius IX, epist. ad Archiep. Darboy, ASS, XI, 217; see also Vermeersch, De Rel., I, 104; Coronata, I, 523, nota 8; Melo, p. 123; Bondini, p. 43.
[45] Cf. Leo III, Const., Romanos Pontifices; see also Piat, I, pp. 270, 273, nota I, 276 ff.; Wernz, III, 617; Battandier, 509; Larraona, C.p.R., V, 425.
[46] Cf. W.-V., III, 72.
[47] Cf. W.-V., III, 74; Larraona, C.p.R., V, pp. 332, 333.
[48] Cf. Vermeersch, De Rel., I, 104.
[49] Cf. W.-V., III, 75; Creusen, 38; Larraona, C.p.R., V, p. 332, n. IV.
[50] Cf. Schäfer, 83, h; Chelodi, De Personis, 249; Larraona, C.p.R., V, pp. 330–334.

(B) *Schools, Hospices, etc., Separated From the Religious House*

To build and open a school, hospice, or any other such edifice separated from the house, even exempt, the special written permission of the local Ordinary is necessary and sufficient (can. 497, § 3).

1. The expression "to build and open" should be understood in the disjunctive sense. Therefore, written permission of the local Ordinary is required if either a building of this type is to be constructed, or one already constructed is to be used, or a school, hospice, etc., conducted by others is to be placed under the authority of religious and made dependent upon their house.[1]

2. As is clear from the context, this canon is expressly concerned with the formalities required for erecting a religious house. Paragraph 3 treats of a type of edifice which, though not of itself a religious house in the strict canonical sense used in paragraph 1, yet partakes of its general character. Though it lacks juridical personality, it is destined, under the authority of a religious house, to be used for pious or charitable works in behalf of the faithful; and consequently, is quite different in status from a purely secular edifice, such as a farm, or villa.[2]

Houses of this kind are frequently called *filial houses,* in the *strict* sense of the term. In some congregations, filial houses are those which have been founded by the community of another house called the mother house, or which are of lower rank than the mother house. These are filial houses in the *broad sense.*

Certain characteristics distinguish filial from the autonomous houses spoken of in paragraph 1 of canon 497.[3]

a) The occupants do not constitute a proper and distinct religious community endowed with moral personality, but are, as it were, members or parts of some canonically erected religious house.

b) They do not possess their own temporal goods independently of others.

c) Their superior is merely a *delegate* of the superior of some autonomous house. The latter rules both communities.

N.B. Many other features are pointed out by Maroto, which may serve as aids in recognizing this type of house.[4]

It seems clear that schools, hospices, and the like, established by religious in behalf of their own subjects and dependent on a canonically erected house should not be classified as the type of pious institution envisaged by paragraph 3 of canon 497.[5]

---

[1] Cf. Larraona, C.p.R., V, p. 431.
[2] Cf. *Epit.,* I, 607; Schäfer, 86; Larraona, C.p.R., V, p. 431, and IX, p. 105, nota 554.
[3] Cf. Molitor, p. 377; Maroto, C.p.R., V, pp. 127 ff.; *Epit.,* I, 591.
[4] Cf. C.p.R., V, pp. 128 ff.
[5] Cf. Melo, pp. 128, 129; Bondini, p. 48.

3. The rule of canon 497, paragraph 3, applies to institutions *at the service of secular persons,* and which are at a distance from the religious house on which they depend. If such establishments constitute works proper to a religious house, they may be built and opened without the permission of the Holy See, or of the local Ordinary, so long as they are not separated from the house itself (can. 497, § 2).[6]

4. For the building and opening of schools, etc., separted from the religious house, the consent of the local Ordinary is *necessary* and *sufficient.* Even though these institutions belong to exempt religious, they are not exempt houses but rather parts of such establishments and hence do not require an Apostolic indult. The consent of the local Ordinary must be *special* and given *in writing;* special, because it is different from that obtained for the erection of the principal house upon which the separated one depends; written, because it should constitute documentary evidence sufficient to prove the lawful status of a house in the event of future controversies.

Though these separated houses may not be erected without the special consent of local Ordinaries, once lawfully established, they are not diocesan in character because of this dependence. Their juridical status is not determined by the manner of their erection. They pertain to the mother house, and in the proper meaning of the word "house" employed in the Code, are actually part of the mother house, though separated from it. If the mother house is exempt from the jurisdiction of local Ordinaries, so are its separated parts. Canon 615 makes no distinction between separated and nonseparated, dependent or independent, mother or filial houses; rather, it declares in general, that *Regulars, together with their houses,* are exempt from the jurisdiction of local Ordinaries.[7]

It should be remarked, however, that the local Ordinary can personally, or by delegate, make the juridical visitation of any schools, oratories, asylums, orphanages, etc., for the purpose of inspecting whatever pertains to religious and moral instruction. None, except internal schools for members of exempt institutes, is immune from this visitation (cf. cc. 1382, 1491). Nevertheless, contrary privileges enjoyed by nonparochial schools pertaining to Regulars[8] are not revoked by this provision of the Code.[9]

II. Juridical Effects

1. By virtue of the law itself, a religious house is endowed with at least noncollegiate moral personality, and if occupied by three or more religious,

[6] Cf. Schäfer, 86; Coronata, I, 524.
[7] Cf. Coronata, I, 524, and nota II; Fanfani, *De Jure Religiosorum,* 27; Schäfer, 86 and 420; Larraona, C.p.R., IX, p. 105.
[8] Cf. Leo XIII, Const., *Romanos Pontifices,* par. 19.
[9] Cf. below: Chap. XIV: The Teaching Office; see *Per.,* XV, pp. 59–61; Schäfer, 86; Melo, p. 157; Coronata, II, 950, 1031; Fanfani, *De Jure Religiosorum,* 444.

with collegiate personality.[10] As a consequence, it is of its nature perpetual (can. 102, § 1), and is accorded the legal protection enjoyed by minors (can. 101, § 3). By reason, too, of its juridical personality, it is entitled to acquire and possess temporal goods (can. 531), and participates in the local privileges of its institute.[11]

2. Permission to erect a religious house implies, for clerical institutes, authorization for a church or public oratory annexed to the house, without prejudice to the terms of canon 1162, paragraph 4, and for the celebration of sacred functions in conformity with the requirements of law (can. 497, § 2).[12]

3. For all institutes, permission to erect a religious house implies authorization to exercise their proper work of piety, without prejudice to conditions made at the time of the concession (can. 497, § 2).

Hence, such houses have the right to engage in all ministries peculiar to their institute. Only a reasonable and grave cause can justify a local Ordinary imposing restrictions on these activities, for by reason of their pontifical approbation, religious of the institutes in question have, within regulations of law, acquired the right to establish houses and conduct their works according to the plans approved by the Holy See in their constitutions.[13]

Conditions which limit the ministries of religious houses must not be of such a nature as to hamper any of the principal works of their apostolate; otherwise they would be in direct opposition to the prescriptions of this canon.[14] Placing restrictions on ministries in order to avoid the ordinary disputes, which are practically inevitable, is not reasonable in view of the spiritual good thus obstructed.[15] This is evident from the fact that the Church herself, though fully cognizant of past and possible future difficulties, has ruled that religious should normally be unimpeded in the exercise of works proper to their institute. If local Ordinaries should impose injurious limitations, religious have the right of devolutive recourse to the Holy See.[16]

ARTICLE IV. CHANGES IN A RELIGIOUS HOUSE

To convert to other uses a house already established, the same solemnities as in paragraph 1 are required, except the alteration be of such a nature that, without prejudice to the laws of the foundation, it affects only the internal regime and religious discipline (can. 497, § 4).

Local Ordinaries have authority with respect to certain changes that may be made in religious houses. For convenience, we shall discuss these cases

---

[10] Cf. Schäfer, 42–44, 80; Pejska, p. 54; W.-V., III, 76; Coronata, I, 524.
[11] Cf. Pejska, p. 55.
[12] Cf. below, Chap. X.
[13] Cf. W.-V., III, 76.
[14] Cf. Larraona, C.p.R., V, p. 430.
[15] Cf. Larraona, C.p.R., V, p. 430, nota 379.
[16] Cf. Bondini, p. 48.

under the classifications employed by canonists; considering first, *material changes,* and second, *formal changes.*[17]

1. Material Changes

Permission to repair, amplify, or rebuild a house must be obtained from religious superiors. The intervention of external superiors is necessary only when the cost of alterations is equivalent to the sums specified in the canons regulating the alienation of property (cf. cc. 534, § 1; 535, § 3, 1°; 1530 ff.; 2347).[18]

2. Formal Changes

These are changes which affect the end or destination of the religious house itself. They may be *external* or *internal.* Canon 497, paragraph 4, expresses the legislation regulating both types.

(A) *External Changes*

This manner of change produces alterations in the external ministries and public uses of a house, thus affecting generally the faithful or externs.[19] Since such changes are equivalent to the erection of a new religious house,[20] they demand the fulfillment of the formalities defined in canon 497, paragraph 1 (can. 497, § 4). Hence, to change an exempt house already established, into one devoted to a *different purpose,* as just explained, superiors need an Apostolic indult and episcopal permission. Examples of formal external changes are: the conversion of a school into a church; a convent into a college or boarding school or hospital, etc.; the addition of a boarding school to a day school; the transformation of an apostolic school or preparatory seminary into a college open to all students.[21]

Obviously, the undertaking of ministries, v.g., retreat work, not previously exercised in a house, does not constitute an external change when such ministries are proper to the house (proper ministries of a house can be learned from the constitutions of a religious institute), and have not been excluded by stipulations made at the time of its erection (can. 497, § 2). Only when the purpose of the house was clearly limited can the exercise of its proper ministries be subjected to restrictions.[22]

(B) *Internal Changes*

Changes are considered internal *only* when they touch merely the internal

---

[17] Cf. Schäfer, 87; Coronata, I, 525; Larraona, C.p.R., V, pp. 433–436; Bondini, p. 51; Pejska, p. 56; d'Angelo, *La Esenzione Dei Religiosi,* p. 34.

[18] Cf. Schäfer, 87; W.-V., III, 79; Coronata, I, 525; Melo, p. 129; Bondini, p. 51; Balmes, *Les Religieux à Voeux Simples,* p. 40.

[19] Cf. Larraona, C.p.R., V, p. 434; Coronata, I, 525.

[20] Cf. Schäfer, 87; Coronata, *loc. cit.*

[21] Cf. Augustine, III, can. 497; Creusen, 37; Schäfer, 87.

[22] Cf. Larraona, C.p.R., V, pp. 434, 435 and nota 396.

order of an institute, and alter the use or juridical status of the house with respect to the religious subjects.[23] The following, for example, would be classified as internal changes: conversion of a house of philosophy to one of theology; addition to the novitiate of a house of retirement for sick and infirm religious of the same institute; transference of the provincial's residence from one house to another.[24]

These changes do not require the formalities provided for in canon 497, paragraph 1, and are in nowise dependent upon the intervention of local Ordinaries. If, however, a change of this kind should imply the erection of a novitiate, permission of the Holy See must be previously obtained (can. 554).[25]

Internal changes may not be effected if the laws of foundation prohibit them; for alterations of this kind would constitute a violation of legitimately accepted obligations. In such cases the will of a founder must be evident; otherwise it is presumed that no provision was made to prevent internal changes.[26]

The translation of a religious house from one place to another

Generally speaking, the translation of a religious house from one place to another *in the same city* requires neither the permission of the Holy See, nor of the local Ordinary.[27] This doctrine has been held by many before, and even after, the promulgation of the constitution, *Romanos Pontifices,* by Leo XIII, regulating these matters (cf. par. 22).[28] Piat says that this interpretation is reasonable, for the Constitution of Leo XIII speaks of translations from *place* to *place,* and in the classical meaning, *place* signifies a city, town, or municipality. Larraona claims that this interpretation is amply confirmed by the Code and its various redactions, and by actual practice in Rome itself.[29]

Though this seems true generally, there are, however, some exceptional cases. Permission of the local Ordinary would be necessary if he had excluded such translations when he first allowed the erection of the house. The same permission would be required if the religious planned to erect a *church* or *public oratory* in the new locality (can. 1162, § 4). In such translations, privileges of other interested religious must be respected.[30]

---

[23] Cf. Larraona, C.p.R., V, p. 434; Coronata, I, 525.
[24] Cf. Creusen, 37; Augustine, III, can. 497; Pejska, p. 57; Larraona, C.p.R., V, p. 434.
[25] Cf. Coronata, I, 525; Pejska, p. 57.
[26] Cf. Augustine, III, can. 497.
[27] Cf. W.-V., III, 72; Balmes, *op. cit.,* p. 41; Coronata, I, 525; Schäfer, 87; Larraona, C.p.R., V, p. 419.
[28] Cf. Schmalz., L. III, t. 41, n. 41; Ferraris, v. *Conventus,* art. 1, nn. 11, 12, 46; Cespedes, VII, 2 ff.; Tamb., Disp. V, q. 1, n. 14; since the Const., *Romanos Pontifices:* Piat, II, p. 279; Wernz, III, 618; Vermeersch, *De Rel.,* I, 115.
[29] Cf. C.p.R., V, p. 419, and nota 340.
[30] Cf. Schäfer, 87; W.-V., III, 72.

The permission of both the Holy See and the local Ordinary is required for the translation of an exempt house to another city, for this is equivalent to erecting a religious house.[31]

ARTICLE V. THE SUPPRESSION AND EXTINCTION OF EXEMPT RELIGIOUS HOUSES

1. The Suppression of Houses

Concerning the suppression of exempt religious houses local Ordinaries have no authority whatever. Canon 498 decrees that no religious house, whether formal or not, belonging to an exempt institute, can be suppressed without Apostolic authority. "This is the logical consequence of canon 497, paragraph 1, which requires a papal indult for the foundation" (Augustine, III, can. 498, p. 76).[32]

Separated institutions, spoken of in canon 497, paragraph 3, are not autonomous or distinct religious houses in the sense of the expression employed in canon 498; hence, suppression of them is not regulated by this latter prescription. After the Ordinary of the place has consented to their establishment (can. 497, § 3), he cannot bring about their suppression. This action can only be taken by the competent religious superior. In the event that such houses are to be suppressed, natural equity will practically always demand that the local Ordinary be opportunely notified, in order that he may make plans to provide in some other way for the needs of the faithful.[33]

It is well to note Creusen's statement in this respect: "In certain cases the authorization to open these establishments supposes an agreement, at least tacit, not to suppress them without the authorization of the Ordinary. If the Bishop should have refrained from the establishment of a school himself so as to allow the religious to add such a school to their other works, it is hard to see how they could later on suppress the school without the Bishop's authorization; otherwise very serious conflicts may arise afterward from the divergent interests of the diocese or of the parish, and of the institute."[34]

Furthermore, if the Bishop, besides having given the permission to erect a school, was also its founder or quasi-founder, he may have acquired or reserved to himself certain contractual rights which preclude the possibility of suppression.[35]

It is not the practice of the Holy See to issue an indult permitting the

---

[31] Cf. Leo XIII, Const., *Romanos Pontifices;* Piat, II, 279; Wernz, III, 618; Vermeersch, *De Rel.,* I, 115; Balmes, *op. cit.,* p. 41; Coronata, I, 525; Augustine, III, p. 93; Chelodi, *De Personis,* 249.
[32] Cf. S.C.C., Feb. 23 and Mar. 16, 1715, ad I (*Fontes,* V, n. 3142); Berutti, III, 20.
[33] Cf. Larraona, C.p.R., VI, p. 15 and nota 410; Berutti, III, 20, n. IV.
[34] Cf. Creusen, 40.
[35] Cf. Larraona, C.p.R., VI, p. 15, nota 410.

suppression of any religious house without first obtaining the local Ordinary's opinion on the matter.[36]

Worthy of remark is the fact that no papal indult is necessary for the suppression of a monastery of nuns nor of religious houses located in territories subject to the Propaganda. Regular prelates and local Ordinaries can suppress any houses of these types that fall under their respective jurisdictions.[37]

2. The Extinction of Houses

If a religious house has ceased to exist for a period of one hundred years, it automatically becomes extinct (can. 102, § 1).

Do convents from which the religious have been expelled during a persecution, become extinct after a hundred years of vacancy?

Controversies have arisen between religious and local Ordinaries on this point,[38] and diverse settlements have been suggested by different canonists.[39]

The sufficiently common opinion, which seems to be founded on justice and equity, denies the extinction of such convents.[40] Those supporting this conclusion maintain that the dispersed religious may recover their houses and re-establish communities therein, without the permission of either the Holy See or the local Ordinaries. As Bouix states,[41] the right of erecting these houses and establishing the communities was granted to the religious orders which founded them, not to the individual religious; and the provincials and Generals retain the right of sending subjects back to the houses whence their religious were forcibly expelled. The title to dwell in these houses was not acquired merely by certain religious for a limited period, but in perpetuity by all the religious whom superiors should assign to the houses. Religious are not deprived of such rights obtained from and protected by pontifical authority, because persecutors of the Church have unjustly despoiled them of their possessions.

In practice, however, the following norms should be borne in mind:[42]

a) The Holy See has consigned some houses formerly pertaining to religious Orders to the unrestricted uses of local Ordinaries, and has ceded the latter the right to alienate these properties when circumstances justify such action. In these instances, the dispersed religious may not reclaim their goods.

b) When the absence of the dispersed religious has extended over a very

---

[36] Cf. Larraona, C.p.R., VI, p. 16.

[37] Cf. Coronata, I, 526; Schäfer, 88; Larraona, C.p.R., VI, p. 16.

[38] Cf. Goyeneche, C.p.R., VII, pp. 393–396.

[39] Cf. Piat, II, p. 280.

[40] Cf. Rotarius, I, III, V, II, 3; Bouix, I, pp. 309, 360 ff.; Coronata, I, 526; Goyeneche, *loc. cit.*

[41] Cf. Bouix, I, p. 301.

[42] Cf. Goyeneche, C.p.R., VII, p. 395.

long period of time, the practice of the Holy See has been to favor the local Ordinary, rather than the Regulars.

c) In particular cases, existing circumstances may not allow recognition of the right still possessed by Regulars of recovering their properties.

Even though the juridical personality of the houses in question is not extinguished, nevertheless churches attached to such houses lose the indulgences which had accrued to them by reason of their connection with the religious community formerly in charge.[43]

Properties of suppressed or extinct houses revert to the province or religious institute, or, if these no longer exist, to whatsoever cause the Roman Pontiff assigns then (cf. cc. 493; 494, § 2).[44]

ARTICLE VI. OTHER ESTABLISHMENTS PERTAINING TO EXEMPT RELIGIOUS

Besides the autonomous and the strictly filial houses already discussed, other places, such as farms, villas, mission stations, quasi-parishes, etc., pertaining to exempt religious, bear a definite relation to the exemptive rights under consideration.

1. Farms, Villas, Hospices for Religious, etc.

Farms and villas are places used for agricultural or recreational purposes, where groups of religious dwell for limited periods, or where a few may live continually (we exclude from this classification farms, villas, or the like, which are strictly filial houses, in the sense explained above, Article III, B).[45] Other places of this kind are temporary dwellings used in time of persecution, and hospices for the religious of an institute who are not engaged in ministerial works for the faithful.[46]

THE JURIDICAL STATUS OF THESE INSTITUTIONS

To acquire and possess places of this kind, no permission is needed either from the Holy See or from the Ordinary of the place.[47] These places are purely secular in character, and in no canonical sense can be termed religious houses.[48] The right of religious to acquire and hold such properties without the approval of local Ordinaries is clear from canon 531, which states that every institute, every province, and every house is capable of acquiring and

---

[43] Cf. S. C. Indulg., Feb. 10, 1818, Decr. auth. 243; see also Goyeneche, C.p.R., VI, pp. 434-435; Coronata, I, 526.

[44] Cf. Coronata, I, 526; Balmes, pp. 41-42.

[45] Cf. Piat, II, p. 230.

[46] Cf. Piat, II, p. 230; W.-V., III, 401; Schäfer, 42; Larraona, C.p.R., III, p. 48, nota 177.

[47] Cf. Vermeersch, *De Rel.,* I, 101; *Epit.,* I, 607, n. 2; W.-V., III, 72; Coronata, I, 523, nota 9; Balmes, p. 39; Chelodi, *De Personis,* 249, nota 3; Larraona, C.p.R., V, p. 431.

[48] Cf. Vermeersch, *De Rel.,* I, 101; Schäfer, 42.

possessing property with fixed or founded revenues, unless their capacity to do so be restricted by rules or constitutions.

Properties of this kind are ecclesiastical goods (can. 1497, § 1), and when they belong to an exempt moral person, neither their acquisition nor their ownership nor their administration is subject to the jurisdiction of local Ordinaries.[49] Hence, in these matters, exempt religious enjoy the same exemptive rights and privileges which they have with respect to their other possessions.

Since the places under discussion can in nowise be considered religious houses, they are not affected by the regulations of the Code governing these latter. Therefore, no legal formalities are required for their establishment or suppression. They are not subject to canonical visitation, for no law expressly states that local Ordinaries have that right (cf. can. 344, § 2). If, however, Regulars have committed a crime in such places and, after being warned of the fact, are not punished by their superior, they can be punished by the local Ordinary (can. 616, § 2).

2. Mission Stations and Quasi-Parishes

Stations and quasi-parishes in mission territories which pertain to a Vicariate or Prefecture Apostolic are not religious houses though they be entrusted to exempt religious. The fact that an institute owns the edifices or property does not change the status of these places.[50]

Hence, no Apostolic indult is necessary for the establishing of mission stations or quasi-parishes. If, however, exempt religious wish to erect a college or any religious house whatever, which is proper to their institute, they must obtain the consent both of the Holy See and of the Vicar or Prefect Apostolic. It should be remarked that the Holy See encourages the founding of such religious establishments.[1]

It seems that since these stations and quasi-parishes confided to exempt religious are not religious houses, they are not under papal cloister.[2] They are under the jurisdiction, visitation, and vigilance of the local Ordinaries, and enjoy no exemption. The same is true of the elementary schools attached to them.

ARTICLE VII. PAPAL CLOISTER

In all houses of Regulars, whether of men or of women, canonically established, even though not formal, papal enclosure must be observed (can. 597, § 1).

This law does not refer to houses of nuns where, by order of the Holy

---

[49] Cf. W.-V., III, 72.
[50] Cf. Coronata, I, 523, p. 615, nota 1; *Per.*, XII, p. 2.
[1] Cf. S.C.P.F., Instr., Dec. 8, 1929, AAS, XXII, 111.
[2] Cf. *Per.*, XII, p. 3.

See, only simple vows are taken;[3] nor to a temporary dwelling place, e.g., a villa, or a refuge in time of persecution.[4] (Actually houses of nuns not professing solemn vows observe the laws of papal cloister; they are not, however, protected by the sanctions of common law.)[5]

The law of papal cloister affects the whole house inhabited by the Regular community, including the orchards and gardens, the access to which shall be reserved to the religious, but excluding the public church with its sacristy, the guest house, if there be one, and the parlor, which last should, where possible, be situated near the entrance to the house (can. 597, § 2).

The cloister of houses pertaining to orders of men is under the jurisdiction, supervision, and vigilance of Regular superiors, and is not subject to local Ordinaries. The brief exposition, which follows, will show that the same is not true of the cloister of nuns.

1. The Boundaries of the Cloister

According to canon 594, paragraph 3, it pertains to the Bishop to determine exactly the limits of the enclosure in the monasteries of nuns, or to modify them for lawful reasons without prejudice to the provisions of paragraph 2 of the same canon.[6]

2. Egress From the Monastery

No nun, after profession, may, under whatever pretext, leave the monastery even for a short time, without a special indult of the Holy See, except in case of imminent danger of death or other very serious evil. This danger must, if time permits, be acknowledged in writing by the Ordinary of the place (can. 601).

Such dangers are: fire, flood, collapse of the building, the terrors of war, invasion by soldiers, etc. The danger in question might arise from one of the nuns themselves, for example, if one of them were afflicted with a dangerous insanity, or an infectious disease, in which case she ought to leave the cloister for the safety of the rest of the community. If there is time, however, the Ordinary of the place should, at the request of the nuns, acknowledge in writing the danger and the existence of a sufficient cause for leaving the monastery.[7]

"The Holy See sometimes grants to the Ordinary the special faculties necessary to permit an individual to leave the convent, e.g., for the purpose of having an important surgical operation, even when the case is not so urgent as to be a matter of life and death."[8]

---

[3] Cf. Cod. Com., Mar. 1, 1921, AAS, XIII, 177; see *Per.*, X, p. 325.
[4] Cf. *Epit.*, I, 754; Creusen, 282; Coronata, I, 611.
[5] Cf. *Epit.*, I, 761; Coronata, I, 613, p. 779, nota 3.
[6] Cf. Ojetti, v. *Clausura*, 1178; Melo, p. 141.
[7] Cf. S. C. Rel., Instr., Feb. 6, 1924, AAS, XVI, 96; Bouscaren, I, can. 600; *Per.*, XIII, 58.
[8] Cf. Creusen, 289, nota 10.

Postulants can freely leave the monastery without permission of the Holy See, when they either decide of their own accord to return to the world, or are dismissed by their superiors. The same is true of novices, and of the professed of temporary vows, when their vows have expired, or when they have been lawfully dismissed.[9]

3. Ingress Into a Monastery

Within the enclosure of nuns, no one, of whatever class, condition, sex, or age may be admitted, without the permission of the Holy See. The following exceptions, however, are provided for in the Code:

a) The local Ordinary, or the Regular superior, when they make a canonical visitation of the monastery, or other visitors delegated by them, may enter the cloister for the purpose of inspection only, and with the precaution that a least one cleric or male religious of mature age accompany them (can. 600, 1°).

The Visitor, therefore, may enter the cloister for the *local* visitation only. The *personal* visitation must be made outside the cloister at the screen. And the Ordinary or Regular superior or Visitor, may not enter the cloister except in the act of official visitation.[10]

b) If the Bishop or another priest is to preside at the reception of the habit or at the profession of the nuns, he may not enter the cloister, nor may the postulant or the one who is to pronounce her vows leave it.[11]

c) The confessor or his substitute can, with the due precautions, enter the enclosure to administer sacraments to the sick or to assist the dying. Rulers of states, with their wives and retinue, and Cardinals, may also enter the cloister of nuns (can. 600, 2°, 3°).[12]

d) The superioress, after taking due precautions, can permit the doctor, the surgeon, and others whose work is necessary, to enter the enclosure, having previously obtained at least the habitual approval of the local Ordinary; but if urgent necessity does not allow time to seek this approval, she may presume the permission (can. 600, 4°).

e) Aspirants to the religious habit enter the cloister with the permission of the Ordinary.[13]

The cloister of nuns, even of those who are under Regular superiors, is subject, as regards its exact observance, to the vigilance of the Ordinary of the place, who has power, after a violation of it has been committed, to punish the offenders even by penalties and censures, without any exception in favor of men of the Regular Orders, and by the same measures to bring

---

[9] Cf. S. C. Rel., Instr., just cited, III, e.
[10] Cf. S. C. Rel., Instr. cited, III, 2, a.
[11] Cf. S. C. Rel., Instr. cited, III, 2, d.
[12] Cf. S. C. Rel., Decree, Sept. 1, 1912.
[13] Cf. S. C. Rel., Instr., n. IV, Feb. 6, 1924.

pressure to bear upon them to prevent its violation. The Regular superior also has the custody of the cloister of nuns who are subject to him, and he also may punish with penalties either the nuns or others among his subjects who offend in this matter (can. 603).[14]

"By reason of an offense on this point, any lay person and any religious become subject to the Ordinary of the place where the sin is committed (cc. 201, § 1; 1556); the same thing is not true in regard to the superior of Regulars" (Creusen, 290).

These penalties may be added to the "ipso facto" excommunication, reserved simply to the Holy See, against persons violating the cloister of nuns (can. 2342, 1°°-3°).

---

[14] Cf. S. C. Rel., Instr., n. VI, Feb. 6, 1924.

CHAPTER X

CHURCHES AND PUBLIC ORATORIES
PRELIMINARY NOTIONS

The present and following chapters treat of the exemption of *sacred places*. A place is considered sacred when by liturgical consecration or blessing it is set apart for divine worship or for the burial of the faithful (can. 1154).

Consecration of places, even of those belonging to Regulars, pertains exclusively to the Ordinary of the territory where the place is situated, provided he has the episcopal character; not, however, to the Vicar-General unless he be endowed with a special mandate (can. 1155, § 1). Even when the episcopal see is vacant the consecration of Regular and other sacred places pertains to the Vicar Capitular, and may not be performed by another Bishop without the latter's consent.[1] This rule binds even Regular Bishops who wish to consecrate exempt places of their own institute.[2] The local Ordinary may grant the aforesaid permission to any Bishop of the same rite to which he belongs (can. 1155, § 2). The expression "local Ordinary" comprises Vicars and Prefects Apostolic and Vicars Capitular or Administrators of dioceses,[3] although these officials cannot personally discharge this office validly, unless they be Bishops. Any priest who by virtue of a special privilege or law enjoys the right to consecrate, e.g., a Vicar or Prefect Apostolic (can. 294, § 2) and, it would seem, an Abbot or Prelate "nullius" (can. 323, § 2),[4] can exercise it within the limits of the concession made to him (can. 1147, § 1). Though Regular places depend upon the local Ordinary in the matter under consideration, they are not to be consecrated by him without the consent of the religious Ordinary. Hence the latter retains some authority with regard to this solemn dedication of the places under his jurisdiction (can. 1157).[5] N.B. Bishops in the United States have faculties whereby they may delegate to simple priests the power to consecrate altars and chalices, but not churches, oratories, or cemeteries.[6]

The *right to bless* a place pertaining to clerical exempt religious is reserved to the major superior, and one belonging to exempt lay religious to the Ordinary of the territory. Both have the power to delegate some priest to perform this function (can. 1156).

---

[1] Cf. Coronata, II, 724.
[2] Cf. Ayrinhac, *Adminis. Legis.*, 2.
[3] Cf. Coronata, II, 724; Ayrinhac, *loc. cit.*

[4] Cf. Coronata, II, 724; *Epit.*, II, 471.
[5] Cf. *Epit.*, II, 471.
[6] Cf. Woywod, II, 1193.

No one may consecrate or bless a place without the consent of the proper Ordinary, all privileges to the contrary notwithstanding (can. 1157).

Documents are to be drawn up testifying to the consecration of an exempt place. It would seem that one copy is to be kept in the archives of the particular place, and one at the curia of the religious superior (can. 1159).[7]

ARTICLE I. THE EXEMPTION OF CHURCHES AND PUBLIC ORATORIES

Churches and public oratories are here discussed under the one head, because they are both governed by the same laws (cf. can. 1191, § 1). What difference distinguishes them from one another is apparent from the definitions given in the Code.

By the term "church" is meant a sacred edifice dedicated to divine worship, whose chief purpose is to afford all the faithful a place for public divine worship (can. 1161).

A *public oratory,* as the name implies, is a sacred edifice erected primarily for the convenience of a moral body or even private individuals, but open at least during religious services to all the faithful. During these times all have an established right to use it (can. 1188, § 2, 1°).[8]

The principal difference between a church and a public oratory consists in this: the church is erected primarily for the benefit of all the faithful; the public oratory for that of a distinct group of persons, v.g., a religious community.[9]

There are various kinds of churches pertaining to exempt religious. For convenience we may treat of them under the following classifications: the Regular or conventual church; the church incorporated with a religious house; the secular church, entrusted to religious.

Canon 615 declares that Regulars, *together with their churches,* are exempt from the jurisdiction of local Ordinaries, except in the cases expressly defined in law. We shall endeavor to determine to what extent this law applies to the different churches just enumerated.

A. *Regular or Conventual Churches*

This type of church is the one which according to common law (can. 497, § 2) and the constitutions of particular institutes normally forms part of a convent or religious house.

Such churches are exempt from the jurisdiction and visitation of local Ordinaries. Proof of this statement is contained in papal documents and in the Code itself. Formerly this privilege was bestowed principally on men-

---

[7] Cf. Coronata, II, 726; *Epit.,* II, 472.
[8] Cf. W.-V., IV, Vol. I, 377; Ayrinhac, *Adminis. Legis.,* 34; *Epit.,* II, 498.
[9] Cf. W.-V., *loc. cit.*

dicant Orders,[10] and gradually, by communication of privileges, was extended to all Regulars.[11] Some canonists maintained that the constitution, *Inscrutabili,* of Gregory XV (Feb. 5, 1622), derogated the exemption of Regular churches; this, however, was denied by the Sacred Congregation of the Council.[12] These various decrees demonstrate that until the promulgation of the Code, churches of Regulars were immune from the jurisdiction and visitation of local Ordinaries.

The Code (can. 615) declares that Regular churches are exempt from episcopal jurisdiction excepting in the cases expressly defined in law. Express cases of exception will be dealt with in the subsequent articles of the present chapter.

Concerning *canonical visitation,* the Code contains several canons which define the rights of the local Ordinary:

1. Persons, things, and pious places, even though exempt, which are in a territory are subject to episcopal visitation unless it can be proven that the Apostolic See has granted them a special exemption in this matter. A Bishop, however, can visit exempt religious in those cases only which are expressly mentioned in law (can. 344).

2. Every five years the local Ordinary must make a visitation, either personally or by delegate, of all houses belonging to clerical congregations of pontifical right, even though they be exempt. This visitation should cover those matters which pertain to the church, the sacristy, the public oratory, the confessionals (can. 512, § 2, 2°).

3. Local Ordinaries are obliged to see that the regulations laid down in the sacred canons on divine worship are faithfully observed, especially that no superstitious practices are introduced into public or private divine worship, nor into the daily lives of the faithful; and that nothing be admitted which is contrary to faith, out of harmony with ecclesiastical tradition, or has the appearance of sordid money-making. If a local Ordinary enacts laws for his territory concerning these matters, even religious, though they be exempt, are bound to observe them; and the Ordinary can visit their churches and public oratories to see that they are observed (can. 1261).

To interpret correctly and apply these norms, and thus to avoid misunderstandings which have arisen in this matter even since the Code, one must keep in mind the general principles of interpretation enunciated in canon 6.[13]

---

[10] Cf. Sixtus IV, Const., *Regimini,* Aug. 31, 1474; Julius II, Const., *Dudum,* July 28, 1506.

[11] Cf. Fine, pp. 725, 726.

[12] Cf. ap. Vermeersch, *De Rel.,* II, 261, pp. 554, 556; and Ferraris, v. *Regulares,* art. 2, n. 6; see also the reply of the S.C.EE.RR., which denies Bishops the right to visit such churches (ap. ASS, II, p. 151); Fine, pp. 726, 727; and the similar reply of the S. C. De Rel., Aug. 3, 1915, ap. *Per.,* VIII, p. 233.

[13] Cf. *Disquisitio circa jus Ordinarii dioecesani visitandi ecclesias Regularium,* published Ad Claras Aquas, 1936.

If canons restate the old law in its entirety, they are to be accepted according to their signification in that law, and therefore according to the interpretations already given by approved authors (can. 6, 2°). Canons which only partially agree with the old law must be interpreted according to the old law in those matters in which they agree with it, and according to the meaning of the words employed in those matters in which they differ from it (can. 6, 3°). When there is doubt whether the provisions of canons differ from the old law, the old law must be followed.

Canon 344, § 1, which obliges the local Ordinary to visit persons, things, and pious places, even though they be exempt, agrees at least partially with the former law promulgated by the Council of Trent[14] which stated: "Locorum Ordinarii ecclesias quascumque, quomodolibet exemptas, auctoritate Apostolica singulis annis visitare tenentur." It has just been seen, in the beginning of the present article, that the authentic interpretation of this law, given by the Sacred Congregation of the Council and often repeated by other congregations, declares that in virtue of the law, local Ordinaries *have not* the right to visit churches or public oratories pertaining to *Regulars*.

Paragraph 2 of canon 344 states that a Bishop can visit exempt religious in those cases only which are specified expressly by law. One case of exception in which local Ordinaries can visit churches and public oratories of exempt religious is that provided for in canon 1261.

The first paragraph of this canon deals with vigilance that local Ordinaries are to exercise with respect to the correct observance of the sacred canons on divine worship; the second paragraph obliges exempt religious to obey the particular enactment of Ordinaries with respect to the matters legislated on in the first paragraph, and grants local Ordinaries the right to visit churches and public oratories of these religious to see that his laws are observed. The right of vigilance is not a jurisdictional power, as is that of visitation.[15]

By the provision of paragraph 2 (can. 1261), therefore, exempt religious and their churches are subject to particular episcopal laws and decrees in matters of divine worship. If an Ordinary's prescriptions do not differ from those of the common law, he has the right of vigilance only (§ 1); if they differ, he has the right of visitation.[16]

Since paragraph 2 imposes a limitation on the exemption of religious, it is subject to strict interpretation.[17] Hence, one should conclude that a local Ordinary has the right of visiting churches of exempt religious when he has enacted particular laws *in the matter* contained in paragraph 1. The words

---

[14] Cf. Conc. Trid., sess. VII, *Decretum de Reform.*, c. 8.
[15] Cf. W.-V., III, 401, 402; Marcellus a P. Jesu, and Kraemer, C.p.R., IX, pp. 235–248.
[16] Cf. Bondini, p. 114.
[17] Cf. Marcellus a P. Jesu, C.p.R., IX, 242.

"in the matter" (hac in re) refer to the *elimination of abuses* in matters of divine worship. Therefore, unless the local Ordinary has positive knowledge that the aforesaid abuses existed, and still exist, in churches or public oratories of these religious, he has no right to make a visitation.[18]

Final confirmation of this doctrine is found in the authentic reply of Cardinal Gasparri, President of the Commission for interpreting the Code. The following is the case presented, together with the official reply:

In urbe N. tempore quo ecclesiae urbis quinquennali visitationi subdabantur, misit Ordinarius loci suum delegatum ad visitandum templum Ordinis N. in illa urbe existens. Superiore praedicti Ordinis non reluctante, delegatus Ordinarii visitavit templum et sacrarium eodem modo, quo ecclesiae non exemptae visitari solent.

Re audita, Provincialis praedicti Ordinis protestationem Ordinario porrexit, in qua cum debita reverentia ei inculcare conabatur, templum Ordinis vi exemptionis visitationi loci Ordinarii subjectum non esse. Quodsi vero de visitatione juxta can. 1261, par. 2 agatur, illam supponere leges particulares in materia in praedicto canone expresse latas, hancque visitationem totam quantam differre ab illa quinquennali. Ordinarius affirmat, se allatas rationes non agnoscere seque jus habere etiam exemptorum regularium templa visitandi. Ad rem dirimendam quaeritur:

I. Utrum Ordinarius loci templa Ordinis N. in sua dioecesi existentia modo praedicto quinto quoque anno visitare possit. Et quatenus negative:

II. Utrum in casu, quo leges dioecesanas (e. gr. synodales) non quidam novam materiam juxta can. 1261 afferunt, sed solum leges ecclesiasticas urgent, Ordinarius ad visitationem manum apponere possit. Et quatenus negative:

III. Utrum visitatio, de qua in canone 1261, par. 2, eodem modo instituenda sit, ac solita quinquennalis visitatio ecclesiarum non exemptarum. Et quatenus negative:

IV. Utrum ad visitationem juxta can. 1261, par. 2, extendi possint responsa S.C. EE. et RR. ante novum Codicem data, ut nempe Ordinarius visitationis jure in tantum solum generatim utatur, in quantum positivam habeat notitiam, leges particulares a se latas in ecclesiis regularium exemptorum non observari.

Ad dubia I, II, III, negative; ad IV affirmative.

Romae, die 8 aprilis, 1924

✠ P. card. Gasparri,

Praeses Commissionis

pro interpretatione Codicis.

---

[18] Cf. Marcellus a P. Jesu, C.p.R., IX, 242.

This reply[19] was a private reply, not published in the *Acta Apostolicae Sedis*. Yet this in no way diminishes its force or authority, for, as the Commission itself has officially stated, questions which are of lesser importance, or which offer no great difficulty, can be answered by the Eminent President of the Commission.[20]

The third canon defining visitatorial rights of local Ordinaries, viz., canon 512, accords the latter no power to visit churches or oratories of Regulars, for, as is manifest from the terms of the law, it refers merely to houses and churches of clerical *congregations* (can. 488, 2°).[21]

Thus far we have considered the status of normal, Regular, or conventual churches and public oratories. Their status or relationship with local Ordinaries is different from that just explained if these churches are burdened with the *care* of souls. In this latter case, Regular and conventual churches are subject to the jurisdiction and visitation of local Ordinaries in all matters relating to the aforesaid office (can. 631).[22] Hence, the jurisdictional and visitatorial rights of local Ordinaries over such churches extend *only to the matters connected with the care of souls*. These matters are clearly defined in the Constitution, *Firmandis,* of Benedict XIV, paragraph 7.[23] Religious superiors have this same authority cumulatively with the local Ordinary. In case of conflict in the exercise of such right, the decision of the local Ordinary prevails over that of the religious superior (can. 631, § 2).

B. *Churches Incorporated With Religious Houses*

There exist three types of incorporation or union: "plenissimo jure," "pleno jure," and "non pleno jure."

1. "Plenissimo Jure" Incorporations

If a church is united "plenissimo jure" to a religious house, the religious superior possesses full jurisdiction over its spiritual and temporal affairs. Such a church, therefore, enjoys the most complete exemption, for it is withdrawn entirely from the jurisdiction of local Ordinaries, and is a legally constituted prelacy or abbacy "nullius."[24]

2. "Pleno Jure" Incorporations

If a church is united "pleno jure" to a religious house, it is withdrawn

---

[19] Cf. W.-V., III, 402, nota 32.

[20] Cf. Cod. Com., Dec. 9, 1917, AAS, XI, 480; see Bouscaren, I, can. 1251, note.

[21] Cf. *Disquisitio circa Ordinarii*, etc., Ad Claras Aquas, 1936; Larraona, C.p.R., VIII, 446; *Epit.*, I, 631; Prümmer, q. 187, n. 5; Cocchi, IV, p. 52.

[22] Cf. Leo X, Const., *Dum intra*, par. 3, Dec. 19, 1516; Conc. Trid., sess. XXV, *de Regul.*, c. 11; Greg. XV, Const., *Inscrutabile*, Feb. 5, 1622; Bened. XIV, Const., *Firmandis*, pars. 7, 8, 9, Nov. 6, 1744 (ap. *Fontes*, I, 349, p. 858); S.C.EE.RR., Apr. 8, 1839 (ap. *Fontes*, IV, 1921, p. 884).

[23] Cf. below, II, 2, b.

[24] Cf. W.-V., III, 175.

both in spiritual and temporal matters from the jurisdiction of the local Ordinary and placed under that of the religious superiors.

The incorporated church may be either parochial or nonparochial, v.g., a devotional shrine.

(A) *Nonparochial Church*

By the incorporation of this kind of church with a religious house, the church becomes a religious church, and is endowed with exemptive rights similar to those possessed by a Regular or conventual church. It should be remarked that the distinction formerly made between *small* houses[25] and others, does not affect the exemptive rights of the religious house, for the law now declares that all houses, without distinction, pertaining to Regulars are exempt (can. 615).

(B) *Parochial Church*

A "pleno jure" union of a parochial church withdraws it from the jurisdiction of the local Ordinary with respect to all matters, spiritual and temporal, save the *care of souls*.

Apparently its exemption is less extensive than that of the nonparochial church. The house with which it is united has the right to the *revenue* of the parish (this will be treated under temporal goods) and the *care of souls*, the latter under the authority of the local Ordinary.[26] By its incorporation it becomes a religious parish church (can. 1425, § 2).[27] The pastor is the *moral person* with which the church is incorporated, that is, the religious house (can. 452);[28] the religious superior of the house must appoint one of his subjects as vicar (can. 471) to exercise the care of souls (can. 1425, § 2).

With the sole exception of religious discipline, religious pastors or vicars, although exercising their ministry in a house or place where the major superiors of the institute have their habitual residence, are, like secular pastors, subject to the full jurisdiction, visitation, and correction of the local Ordinary (cc. 631, 1425).

The local Ordinary's right of visitation extends both to the persons engaged in the parochial ministries and *to the church* itself. With regard to the church, however, he can visit those objects only which pertain to the service of the parish. Benedict XIV in his constitution, *Firmandis*, paragraph 7,

---

[25] In former legislation, a small house was one containing less than 12 religious, cf. Urban VIII, Decretum, *Cum saepe*, June 21, 1625; more recent legislation designates "small houses," those having less than 6 religious, cf., v.g., S. C. Super Statu Rel., Nov. 29, 1657 (ap. Biz. p. 255); S.C.EE.RR., May 12, 1741 (ap. Biz. p. 357); Leo XIII, Const., *Romanos Pontifices*, par. 8.

[26] Cf. Leurenius, *Forum Beneficiale*, P. I, q. 167, and P. II, qq. 878, 889; Bouix, II, pp. 15 ff.; W.-V., II, 175; Fanfani, *De Jure Parochorum*, 421.

[27] Cf. W.-V., II, 175, and III, 414.

[28] Cf. W.-V., *loc. cit.*; Fanfani, *De Jure Religiosorum*, 421.

gives the following list of the objects in question: the tabernacle and the altar where the Blessed Sacrament is reserved — not the other altars; the baptismal font; the confessional which the pastor is accustomed to use; the pulpit; the sacristy where the objects for the administration of the sacraments are kept; the sepulchers and cemeteries for the use of the parishioners; the bell tower, if the bell pertains to the parish; and, finally, besides the above mentioned, all sacred vessels which are used for the Blessed Sacrament, the holy oils, the baptismal water, and holy-water fonts.[29] This discipline is in force at the present time since the Code has made no changes with regard to these visitations.[30] (The Bishop has not the right to visit the religious houses with which these parish churches are incorporated.)[31]

3. "Non Pleno Jure" Incorporations

In the case of incorporation of this kind, the religious house has the right to the revenues only, derived from the benefice. The superior of the house must present a priest of the secular clergy to the local Ordinary to be instituted as pastor, assigning to the latter his proper portion of the revenue (can. 1425, § 1).

Such parishes and churches do not become religious or Regular benefices; they retain their secular character, and save for the two instances just mentioned, remain under the jurisdiction of local Ordinaries.[32]

It is to be noted that a Bishop must appoint the secular priest presented by the superior, provided this priest is endowed with the necessary qualifications. To act otherwise would be a violation of the rights of the religious house.[33]

(C) Secular Parishes Entrusted to Religious

Parishes entrusted to religious which are not incorporated with a religious house, are generally secular in character. The fact that they are put under such care does not alter their juridical status, so that they remain in all things subject to the jurisdiction and visitation of the diocesan Ordinary.

(D) Churches in Mission Territories

The Vicar or Prefect Apostolic or simple superior appointed by the Holy See has full jurisdiction over the mission territory. It is his business to establish mission stations and to build chapels and churches. Without him, no one, whatever be his authority, can establish, change, or discontinue any

---

[29] Cf. *Fontes,* I, 349, p. 858.
[30] Cf. *Disquisitio circa jus Ordinarii,* etc., Ad Claras Aquas, 1936; Fanfani, *De Jure Parochorum,* 424.
[31] Cf. Fagn., I, in cap., *Grave,* 19, *De officio judicis ordinarii,* L. I, t. 31; Fine, p. 730.
[32] Cf. Fanfani, *De Jure Parochorum,* 421.
[33] Cf. S.C.C., July 18, 1761; see Augustine, VI, can. 1425.

work in the mission.[34] Churches, therefore, in mission stations are under the authority of the mission superior, not the religious superior, and are governed the same way as secular parishes.[35]

It is not forbidden to erect religious houses, even exempt ones, and religious provinces in mission territories,[36] so long as the requirements of law are complied with. From this it follows that religious may, with the requisite authorization, establish any type of church enumerated above and enjoy the exemption proper to such edifices. The Sacred Congregation of the Propaganda welcomes such foundations not only because they are entirely in accord with the wishes expressed by our Holy Father, Pius XI, in his Encyclical, *Rerum Ecclesiae,*[37] but also because they are of the highest usefulness.[38]

ARTICLE II. ERECTION, DEDICATION, AND RECONCILIATION OF CHURCHES

Definite limitations to the exemptive rights of Regular churches arise, as seen in Article I, from the very nature of the church itself. Besides these, the law expressly defines other limitations. The latter are the subject of the present article.

1. The Erection of Religious Churches (or Public Oratories)

No church, whether exempt or not, may be erected without the *express written permission* of the local Ordinary. Unless endowed with a special mandate, the Vicar-General cannot give this permission (can. 1162, § 1; and can. 497, § 2).

Express and written consent of the local Ordinary is required for the liceity, express consent alone for the validity of the act.[39]

The consent of the local Ordinary is also required in the event that Regulars wish to add a church to a Regular house which is already established in a place not withdrawn from the diocesan territory.[40] For all clerical institutes the permission to erect a religious house contains the juridical permission or authorization to have a church or public oratory annexed to the house, without prejudice to the terms of canon 1162, § 4 (can. 497, § 2). This right to erect a church or public oratory, which is now defined in law, manifests in clear and definite terms that the Holy See now,

---

[34] Cf. S.C.P.F., Instr., Dec. 8, 1929, AAS, XXII, 111; Bouscaren, I, can. 1350; *Per.,* XIX, 260.
[35] Cf. Vromant, VI, *De Bonis Eccl. Temp.,* 197 bis.
[36] Cf. S.C.P.F., Instr., Dec. 8, 1929.
[37] Pius XI, Encyl., *Rerum Ecclesiae,* Feb. 28, 1926, AAS, XVIII, 18–65.
[38] Cf. S.C.P.F., Instr., Dec. 8, 1929.
[39] Cf. *Epit.,* II, 477; Coronata, II, 732; Goyeneche, *De Rel.,* 15.
[40] Cf. W.-V., IV, Vol. I, 354.

as formerly,[41] wishes religious houses of clerical institutes to have their own proper churches. Since the institutes in question are *essentially clerical,* practically speaking, they must of necessity possess their own churches in order to exercise the ministries and fulfill the purpose of their apostolate according to the norms set down in their constitutions. The church or public oratory has always been looked upon as an integral and principal part of the houses pertaining to clerics, and for this reason the right of such religious to possess their own churches has been considered inherent in the very nature of their institutions.[42]

In view of these considerations, it is clear that the right of the religious in question to have their own proper churches, as decreed in canon 497, § 2, cannot be limited or restricted by local Ordinaries. This is now held by practically all canonists.[43] Vidal states that *in the rigor of the law* a local Ordinary may refuse permission for a church or public oratory in the case of nonclerical institutes even though exempt, but that he can scarcely have a reasonable cause for this refusal.[44]

Canon 497, § 2, declares that the prescription of canon 1162, § 4, must be safeguarded, namely, that even though religious of a clerical institute have obtained the local Ordinary's consent to establish a new house in a city or diocese, they should have his permission before building the church *in a certain definite place.*

Therefore, from a comparative study of canons 497, § 2, and 1162, § 4, it is clear that a new permission, different from the one for the erection of the house, must be obtained from the local Ordinary, authorizing the religious to build their church or public oratory in a certain locality. From this, it follows that local Ordinaries have the right of preventing Regulars from building churches or public oratories in places where the Ordinaries do not wish to have such establishments, and thus they can determine, in a more or less negative manner, the location of the churches. As De Meester says

---

[41] Such a privilege was granted in ancient times to monasteries in general, and later to mendicant orders, cf. Fine, cap. XV, nn. 17 ff.; nor was this revoked by the Council of Trent. After the Council, similar concessions were made by Gregory XIII, in his Constitution, *Salvatoris Domini,* Oct. 30, 1576. The Constitution, *Romanos Pontifices,* of Leo XIII, did not change this discipline.

[42] Cf. Vermeersch, *De Rel.,* I, 111; De Buck-Tinnerbroeck, c. 21, n. 12–16; Piat, II, p. 277; Oswald, *Comm. In Decem Partes Const. S.J.* (3 Ed.), pp. 156 ff.; Toso, *Comm.,* L. 2, *De Personis,* Pars II, can. 497.

[43] Cf. W.-V., III, 77; Coronata, I, 524; Chelodi, *De Personis,* 249, p. 414, n. 1; Schäfer, 84; Larraona, C.p.R., V. pp. 426, 427; Goyeneche, *De Rel.,* 15; De Meester, II, 942; Claeys Bouuaert-Simenon, I, 604; Vromant, II, 341; Toso, *Comm.,* L. II, *De Personis,* Pars II, can. 497; Fanfani, *De Jure Religiosorum,* 21, and 369; Vermeersch, *Per.,* XVIII, p. 93. Jombart (*Per.,* XII, pp. 60 f.) maintains that Bishops may refuse permission for a church or oratory, but, as Coronata remarks, the writer supposes a condition to be contained in canon 497, § 2, which in reality does not exist, and which, if it did, would render the juridic right under discussion useless. Such a condition, too, would confer on Bishops authority far in excess of that granted by canon 1162, § 4 (cf. Coronata, I, 524).

[44] Cf. W.-V., III, 77.

(II, 943), "Consensus Ordinarii *tantum* respicit determinationem loci ubi ecclesia est aedificanda."

Evidently this permission requisite for building in a certain locality provides a legal safeguard against unwarranted injury to already existing churches which might be caused by new ones, and enables local Ordinaries to aid the religious in making their choice of a suitable locality. As a matter of fact, the manner of procuring the first-mentioned result is explicitly decreed in canon 1162, § 3, which states: in order that the new church may not, without proportionate spiritual benefit, cause injury to churches already established, the local Ordinary shall, before giving his consent, hear the interested rectors of the neighboring churches, due regard being had for the rule contained in canon 1676.[45] By virtue of canon 1676, the pastor of a neighboring church who believes that the spiritual good to be effected by the new enterprise will be disproportionate to the injury done his church, may sue for an injunction before the Bishop, and ask for an interruption of the new work until such time as the rights of both parties have been defined. If such a suit is filed, the religious must stop further work on their church. Pending the trial, the builder may be permitted to continue his work, provided he gives security to restore everything to the former condition, in the event of an adverse sentence. The plaintiff is granted two months within which he must prove his contention. The judge may prolong or shorten this period for a just and necessary reason, after hearing the other party.

2. Dedication and Reconciliation of Churches

Cases in which the intervention of local Ordinaries is necessary for the dedication and reconciliation of exempt churches are expressly defined in law.

(A) *The Dedication of Churches*

A church may be dedicated to divine services by either solemn consecration or benediction (can. 1165, § 1).[46]

Concerning the persons competent to perform these functions consult what has been stated previously in the present chapter.

(B) *Reconciliation of Churches*

Reconciliation of desecrated churches (can. 1172) which pertain to exempt *clerical* institutes, can be effected by major superiors (can. 1176, § 2).[47] The minister competent to reconcile a church of exempt *lay* institutes is: the

---

[45] Cf. Schäfer, 464.
[46] Cf. above, Art. I.
[47] Cf. Paul III, Const., *Licet debitum*, Oct. 18, 1549; Leo XII, Br., *Plura inter*, July 11, 1826.

local Ordinary, if the church in question had been consecrated (can. 1176, § 2); the rector, or any other priest with at least the presumed permission of the rector, if the church had been dedicated with the simple blessing (can. 1176, § 1). In urgent cases when the local Ordinary cannot be reached, the rector has the right to reconcile a *consecrated* church, but he must afterward notify the Ordinary of his action (can. 1176, § 3).

Article III. The Use of Churches and Public Oratories

1. THE RIGHT TO CELEBRATE SACRED FUNCTIONS

a) Religious of clerical institutes not only have the right to build a church or public oratory in connection with their houses, but they are also entitled *to perform the sacred ministries* in these places, in conformity, of course, with the requirements of law (can. 497, § 2). Wherefore, when such places have been legitimately dedicated, all sacred rites may be carried on in them, safeguarding, however, parochial rights, privileges, lawful customs, and contrary rubrical prescriptions (can. 1171; can. 1191, § 1).

Within the limitations just mentioned, the law declares that religious have the right to exercise all ministries, as those proper to the priestly state, v.g., to celebrate the Holy Sacrifice of the Mass, to hear confessions, to preach, to conduct funeral services, to assist at marriages, to baptize, etc.[48] The prescription stipulates that the requirements of law must be observed (servatis de jure servandis). Thus, for example, diocesan faculties must be obtained to preach or to hear the confessions of the faithful (can. 877); the faculty to assist at a marriage in such churches (which are nonparochial) must be obtained from the Ordinary or pastor of the place by a specified priest for a specified marriage (can. 1095, § 2; 1096, § 1); permission of the pastor or Ordinary of the place must be had in order to hold solemn baptisms in these churches (can. 738, § 1); consent of the local Ordinary must be obtained for Exposition of the Blessed Sacrament outside the times permitted by law (can. 1274); special permission of the local Ordinary is required for the celebration of marriage in churches or oratories of religious women (can. 1109, § 2); generally speaking, funeral services for secular persons are not to be held in churches of nuns (can. 1225), etc.

Since the free exercise of sacred ministries in churches and public oratories is a concession of common law, it cannot be interfered with or restricted by local Ordinaries.[49] Stipulations, therefore, which prevent the full discharge of these functions are null and void, even though they had been agreed upon by Bishop and religious at the founding of the church or oratory.

b) All religious churches, like houses, have the right to perform the *pious works proper to their institute*. This is manifest from the fact that units of

---

[48] Cf. Larraona, C.p.R., V, pp. 428, 429.
[49] Cf. Larraona, C.p.R., V, p. 429.

any clerical religious institute are established to afford opportunities for priestly administrations and for works of zeal and charity which are characteristically peculiar to the religious society operating them. As has been remarked before, when treating of religious houses, all pontifical institutes have, by reason of their papal approbation, an *acquired right* to establish such units, as houses and churches, everywhere, and to designate subjects to live and labor in them conformably to the manner approved by the Holy See in their rules and constitutions.[1]

Only for a grave and reasonable cause can local Ordinaries impose restrictions on these activities. When, as is rarely verified, such measures are justifiable, an agreement should be signed by the Ordinary and the institute before the church or oratory has been erected (can. 497, § 2).[2]

II. PARTICULAR NORMS REGULATING SERVICES HELD IN EXEMPT CHURCHES

Some writers have erroneously maintained that Regulars should be employed in administering to the faithful *only* when the scarcity of secular priests forces local Ordinaries to call on them. This error, which seems to have originated with William of St. Amour, was ably refuted by St. Thomas.[3] Later, it was espoused by the Jansenistic synod of Pistoia (prop. 80) and met with condemnation by the Holy See.[4] In recent times, a similar doctrine was proposed by M. Verhoeven.[5]

The truth is that *all clerics* are *auxiliaries* of the divinely constituted hierarchy, that is to say, of the *Roman Pontiff* and of *Bishops*. By their exemption, Regulars and some religious congregations have been withdrawn from the jurisdiction of local Ordinaries. They remain, necessarily, under the immediate jurisdiction of the Sovereign Pontiff. It is under such government that they normally operate, and in their ministries to the faithful they are subjected in such a way to the local Ordinaries that their exemption does not detract from the authority of the latter.[6]

All clerical institutes have a twofold end: they are founded to procure the spiritual perfection of their members; and to aid, by their clerical administrations, in the salvation of others.[7] In order that they might accomplish this latter purpose, in accordance with their rules and constitutions, the Holy See has decreed that their houses shall have churches or public oratories attached to them for the service of the faithful (can. 497, § 2). From this provision of law, and from the very nature of such edifices, it is manifest

---

[1] Cf. W.-V., III, 76; Vermeersch, *De Rel.*, I, 494.
[2] Cf. W.-V., III, 76.
[3] Cf. St. Thomas, Edit. Vivés, *Opusculum* I, *Contra impugnantes Dei cultum et religionem, pars*, II, *cap.* 12–26.
[4] Pius VI, Const., *Auctorem fidei*, Aug. 28, 1794.
[5] Cf. De Buck-Tinnebroek, *Examen Hist. et Can. Libri* R.D. M. Verhoeven.
[6] Cf. Vermeersch, *De Rel.*, I, 494.
[7] Cf. Leo XIII, *Epist. ad Archiep. Paris.*, Dec. 23, 1900.

that the faithful in general have a right to gather in them, at least during the hours of sacred services.

A. *Masses in Exempt Churches and Public Oratories*

Some centuries ago, the faithful were obliged to be present at Mass in their parochial church on Sundays and Holydays.[8] This rule, however, has long since been abolished. At present, Catholics should be reminded to visit frequently their parish church, when they can conveniently do so, and to assist at divine offices and hear the word of God (can. 467, § 2). It is wrong to assert that they have an obligation to attend the Sunday parochial Mass.

The evolution of this doctrine is clearly outlined by Benedict XIV.[9] In the sixteenth century, St. Antoninus[10] taught that where the custom prevailed of hearing Mass in any church, it was not a sin for people to assist at Mass on feast days outside their own parish. He implies that this custom existed in many places. Contemporaneous papal documents confirm his theory and show a transitional stage between the ancient and modern discipline. For example, Clement VIII, in his Brief, *Significatum*, 1592, stated: "Praesenti nostro decreto sancimus, saecularibus universis libere Missas diebus Dominicis, et aliis majoribus festis audire in ecclesia tam Fratrum Praedicatorum quam aliorum Mendicantium, necnon etiam Societatis Jesu, licere posse, dummodo in contemptum parochialium ecclesiarum non faciant."[11]

Though some few authors[12] wrongly interpreted these decrees, Benedict XIV declares that the freedom of the faithful to attend Mass in Regular churches any day of the year is beyond dispute. Further, he states: "Today, everyone has the right to attend the sacred mysteries *in any church whatever,* so long as it is not a chapel, that is, a private oratory; for by contrary custom, now accepted by the whole of Christendom, the precept of attending the parochial Mass is abrogated. This is the teaching also of Sylvester, Novarrus, and Treulench. Barbosa and others add that today a Bishop cannot order his subjects to assist at the parochial Mass, for it is not within his power to abolish a custom which is followed throughout the world and already has the nature of a common law"[13] (De Syn. Dioec., Lib. XI, c. xiv, 10).

---

[8] Cf. Sixtus IV, Const., *Vices illius*, June 17, 1478.

[9] Cf. Bened., XIV, *De Syn. Dioec.*, L. XI, c. XIV, par. VIII.

[10] Cf. *Summ. Theol.*, P. II, t. 9, c. 10.

[11] Cf. also Leo X, Lit. ap., *Intelleximus*, Nov. 13, 1517 (ap. *Fontes*, I, p. 127); S. Pius V, Lit. ap., Aug. 16, 1567.

[12] Cf. Jeunin, *De Sacramentis Dissent.* V, q. 7, c. 2, art. 2; Van Espen, *Jus. Eccl.* P. II, t. 5, c. 2.

[13] Cf. Sylvester, v. *Missa*, 2, q. 5; Novarrus, *Manual*, cap. 21, n. 5; Treulench, *In Praecepta Decl.*, Tom. I, L. 3, cap. 1, dub. 6, n. 5; Barbosa, *In collect. ad Trid.*, sess. 22, de observ. et evitan. in celebr. Miss., n. 21, and *De offic. et potest. Parochi*, c. 11, nn. 14 ff.

What is maintained by Benedict XIV is "a fortiori" true today. Nor is there opposition between this right of the faithful and canon 467, § 2, which declares that they should be reminded to attend frequently their parish church.

Can local Ordinaries *fix the time* and *limit the number* of Masses in exempt churches?

They cannot, for no such authority has been expressly accorded them by law (cc. 500, 615). In fact, when this power concerning Masses is explicitly dealt with in the Code, exempt churches are expressly declared not to be effected by it. Canon 1171 decrees that local Ordinaries can, for a just reason, fix especially the hours for sacred functions *in churches not belonging to exempt religious.* The canon cited states that the provision of canon 609, § 3, is to be safeguarded.

By this latter, superiors are reminded to take care that the divine offices performed in their churches do not cause harm to the catechetical instruction or to the explanation of the Gospel given in parish churches. The canon adds that it pertains to the local Ordinary to judge whether or not harm is done.

Neither canon 1171 nor 609, § 3, expressly gives local Ordinaries any authority over exempt religious or their churches. In referring to these prescriptions, Berutti remarks that local Ordinaries have the right to warn superiors in order that they themselves might opportunely adjust such matters.[14]

The commentary of Vermeersch on canon 609, § 3, helps much to clarify the subject. He says: "The parish priest, whose office it is, after the Bishop, to teach catechism and explain the Gospel to his people, should not be hindered by Regulars from faithfully carrying out his charge. However, Regulars, too, have the right to admit the faithful to their Masses and sermons, even though the increase of numbers in their church cause a corresponding decrease in the other. Such harm is in reality offset by much good. For in the last analysis, the important point is that the people increase in devotion, and that they hear an explanation of the catechism and Gospel. It is of but secondary importance that this useful work be accomplished in one place, rather than in the other.

"In his Epistle *Etsi minime* (Feb. 7, 1742), whence this canon is derived, Benedict XIV states that in some cities, because of special celebrations conducted by Regulars on certain days, no one attends his parish church. The Pontiff, therefore, referred to celebrations which caused extraordinary harm to the ministry of the parish church.

"It is the Bishop's right to judge whether or not such harm is done. Because of this, however, *he does not acquire any repressive jurisdiction over*

---

[14] Cf. Berutti, III, 122.

Regulars. Yet the superior, when warned by the Bishop, should see to it that the divine services in his church are not of such a character as to cause direct harm to parochial functions. Should the superior neglect to remedy matters, the local Ordinary may have recourse to the Holy See, which will take the measures deemed proper."[15]

B. *Preaching*[16]

Exempt religious need the approval of the local Ordinary in order to preach to the faithful or to nuns subject to them (can. 1338, § 2).[17]

For religious of clerical institutes, the ministry of preaching constitutes one of the principal functions of their apostolate, and, generally speaking, its exercise may not be impeded by the local Ordinary.[18]

There is one instance in which a Bishop has the authority to forbid Regulars and others to preach in their own churches. The provision is contained in canon 1343, § 2, which runs as follows: unless there be question of large cities, a Bishop may forbid sermons to the faithful in other churches of the same place at the time when he himself is preaching or when he has a sermon delivered in his presence, to which, for some public and extraordinary reason, he has convoked the faithful. Hence, in small cities (that is, those with less than 100,000 inhabitants),[19] when, in the specified circumstances there is a sermon *by* or *before* the Bishop, even Regular churches may be obliged to omit their sermons. A prohibition of this kind may be issued only when there is a verification of the conditions which have been specified by the Sacred Congregation of the Council,[20] and which are now contained in canon 1343, § 2.[21]

A Bishop may not force Regulars to omit sermons in their churches at times when pastors are preaching in parish churches.[22] As stated before, the law allows the faithful freedom to hear sermons anywhere and does not *oblige* them to attend those in the parish church, nor may the Bishop enact a particular law restricting the liberty sanctioned by common law.[23]

It is to be desired that a brief explanation of the Gospel or of some portion of Christian doctrine be given in all churches and public oratories where the faithful assist at Mass on Sundays and Holydays of Obligation.

[15] *Epit.*, I, 767.
[16] Cf. below, Chap. XIV.
[17] To preach in public places outside their churches or oratories, no special permission distinct from the general approval seems to be required. Regulars, however, should obey, if the Bishop forbids this practice; cf. Piat, II, 260; Vermeersch, *De Rel.*, I, 515, p. 345, nota 1.
[18] Cf. Fine, p. 828.
[19] Cf. Coronata, II, 927; *Epit.*, II, 678; De Meester, III, 1298, p. 202, nota 1.
[20] Cf. Bened. XIV, *De Syn. Dioec.*, L. IX, cap. 17, nn. 6, 7, 8; Ferraris, v. *Praedicare*, nn. 25, 26.
[21] Cf. W.-V., IV, Vol. II, 644; *Epit.*, II, 678; Coronata, II, 927; Bondini, p. 129.
[22] Cf. S.C.C., July 2, 1620, and May 19, June 9, 1708; S.C.EE.RR., Mar. 14, 1879.
[23] Cf. Bened. XIV, *De Syn. Dioec.*, L. IX, cap. 14, nn. 12, 13; Pignatelli, *Cons. Can.*, Tom. IV, cons. 206, n. 61; Piat, II, pp. 255, 256; W.-V., IV, Vol. II, 644.

Should the local Ordinary opportunely issue regulations on this matter, they must be observed by both the secular and religious clergy, including the exempt, even when there be question of their own churches (can. 1345).

Though this is an express exception to the exemptive privileges of exempt religious churches, its manifest reasonableness and great utility is beyond dispute. Bishops are the pastors in their respective territories, and should have the authority to see to it that their flock receives adequate spiritual nourishment from those engaged in the sacred ministries. Though this provision of the Code is new,[24] yet elements of it are contained in documents published before the promulgation of the Code. Thus, the Sacred Congregation of the Council (Mar. 2, 1861) approved the mandate of a Bishop couched in the following terms: "In diebus dominicis aliisque festis de praecepto in prima Missa in omnibus ecclesiis et publicis oratoriis post Evangelium clara et intelligibili voce, sacerdote verbo ad verbum praeveniente, et populo comitante, recitari debet brevis instructio, quae scienda necessitate medii vel praecepti continet," and the Congregation declared that in the proposed case, because of special existing circumstances, even Regulars were bound to follow out the Bishop's instructions.[25]

Preaching in parochial churches pertaining to exempt religious is subject to the local Ordinary and must be carried on according to his wishes and the prescription of law; the same is true for missions which must be arranged for parishioners at least once every ten years (can. 1349).[26]

C. Catechetical Instruction[27]

If in the judgment of the local Ordinary the aid of religious is necessary for the catechetical instruction of the people, superiors, even of exempt religious, upon request of the same local Ordinary, are obliged to accord that assistance either personally or through their subjects, especially in their own churches, when harm will not thereby be done to religious discipline (can. 1334). Regulations which local Ordinaries have issued concerning the teaching of Christian doctrine must be followed by exempt religious in their instruction to nonexempt persons (can. 1336).

It is not the exclusive right of parish churches to instruct people in the rudiments of the faith and to conduct classes in catechism; religious may exercise such ministries in their exempt churches and elsewhere, without the approbation of the local Ordinary.[28]

---

[24] Cf. Coronata, II, 927; Bondini, p. 130.
[25] Cf. ASS, II, 184 f.; see Piat, II, p. 259; Bondini, p. 130.
[26] Cf. S.C.EE.RR., July 23, 1694, ap. Biz., p. 281; Wernz, III, 59; Bondini, p. 131; Coronata, II, 931.
[27] Cf. below, Chap. XIV.
[28] Cf. S.C.C., Mar. 30, 1726; see Wernz, III, 45; Piat, II, p. 259; Bondini, pp. 123, 124.

D. *Prescribed Public Prayers, Sacred Solemnities, etc.*

Besides the prescription of canon 1345, if, for a public reason, the local Ordinary prescribes the ringing of bells, certain prayers or sacred solemnities, all religious, even exempt, must obey, without prejudice to the constitutions and privileges of each institute (can. 612).

A *public* cause would be one which affects a whole diocese. The Bishop, consequently, has not the right to prescribe the ringing of bells, prayers, or sacred solemnities for exempt churches exclusively; he can only use authority over such churches when he issues the orders in question for all churches indiscriminately.[29] In general, outside of the prescription here considered, exempt religious enjoy freedom with regard to the ringing of their church bells and the celebrating of solemn and extraordinary functions in their churches.[30] Nevertheless, exempt churches cannot hold *public* exposition or benediction of the Blessed Sacrament without the permission of the local Ordinary, except on the feast and during the octave of Corpus Christi (can. 1274, § 1).[31]

III. PREROGATIVES OF BISHOPS WITH RESPECT TO EXEMPT CHURCHES

The law expressly mentions certain functions which local Ordinaries may perform in exempt churches.

A. *The Exercise of Pontifical Functions*

The Metropolitan is entitled to perform pontifical functions, or as the Code says, "to exercise pontificals." In law "to exercise pontificals" means to perform those functions which by liturgical law require the use of the crozier and miter (can. 337, § 2). The functions included in this definition are: solemn Pontifical Mass; Pontifical Vespers; Pontifical assistance at Mass and choir; the conferring of orders; the consecration of Bishops; the blessing of Abbots; the veiling of virgins consecrated to God; the coronation of kings; the consecration of bells, churches, sacred vessels; the blessing of cornerstones and of cemeteries; the reconciliation of churches or cemeteries; the solemn conferring of confirmation.[32]

Within the limits designated by law both Metropolitan and Diocesan Bishops may exercise pontifical functions in exempt churches.

---

[29] Cf. S.R.C., Reply, April 8, 1821; see Claeys Bouuaert-Simenon, I, 668; Bondini, pp. 56, 57; Fanfani, *De Jure Rel.,* p. 151.

[30] Cf. S.R.C., Sept. 24, 1633, and Nov. 21, 1671; S.C.EE.RR., Reply, Mar. 14, 1879, and Feb. 18, 1723, ap. Biz., p. 313.

[31] Cf. S.C.C., Decr., Aug. 17, 1630; S.R.C., Reply, Apr. 3, 1821 (Decr. auth. 2613); see Bened. XIV, *De Syn. Dioec.,* L. IX, cap. 15, n. 4.

[32] Cf. S.C.C., Resolutio, Monopolitana, Feb. 9, 1924, AAS, XVII, 245; *Per.,* 14, 90; Bouscaren, I, can. 337.

1. The Metropolitan

Canon 274, 6°, states: in all churches, even exempt ones, and in cathedral churches after notifying the Bishop, the Metropolitan may exercise pontifical functions as a Bishop in his diocese, and may bless the people and have the cross carried before him, but he may not perform other acts which imply jurisdiction.[33]

The same prelate has the right to use his pallium at solemn Masses in exempt churches of his province on the days determined by the Roman Pontifical (cf. *Pontificale Romanum*, L. I, c. 16, nn. 4, 6) or on any other days for which he has received special concessions (can. 277) .

2. The Diocesan Bishop

A Diocesan Bishop may exercise pontifical functions anywhere in his diocese, even in exempt places; to do so in an exempt church outside his diocese he needs the consent both of the local Ordinary and of the religious superior (can. 337, § 1).

This law of the Code is the same as that contained in the Constitution of Clement V, and in the decree of the Sacred Congregation of Bishops and Regulars, June 10, 1603. Therefore, as stated in canon 6, 2°, it should be understood as formerly, that is, according to the interpretations of approved authors. Authors before the Code generally maintained that in the case of exempt churches Bishops were permitted to perform only those pontifical functions which did not import the exercise of jurisdiction.[34] After the Code Melo[35] and Bondini[36] seem to hold this same opinion.

B. *Conferring of Confirmation*

Bishops have the right to administer the sacrament of confirmation in churches, oratories, or, for a just and reasonable cause, in other places belonging to exempt religious, when such places are within the confines of their dioceses (can. 792).[37]

C. *Celebration of Mass*

Bishops have the right to celebrate the Holy Sacrifice of the Mass in places belonging to exempt religious; it is probable, however, that they cannot grant this faculty to other persons.[38]

---

[33] Cf. Clem. V, *Conc. Viennensi* (ap. c. 1, *de priv. et excess.*, V, 7, in Clem.).

[34] Cf. Tamb. I, XV, XV, 10 ff.; Peyr., *Priv. Const. XXVI Leonis X*, 45; Donatus, I, II, LXXIV, 9; Pign., X, CVI, 21; Rot., III, II, II, I, 155; Piat, II, p. 63; Fine, p. 761; Vermeersch, *De Rel.*, I, 375; Appeltern, *Compendium Praelectionum Juris Regularium*, q. 573, n. 2; Prümmer, *Manuale Juris Ecclesiastici*, II, q. 194, n. 1.

[35] Cf. Melo, p. 150.

[36] Cf. Bondini, p. 26.

[37] Cf. Bened. XIV, Const., *Firmandis*, par. 6, Nov. 6, 1744; see Piat, II, p. 63; *Epit.*, II, 69.

[38] Cf. Clem. V, *Conc. Viennensi* (ap. c. 1, *de priv. et excess.*, V, 7, in Clem.): see Tamb., I, Disp. XV, q. XV, nn. 9, 15.

D. *Preaching*

Local Ordinaries have the right to preach in all churches including exempt ones, within their territories (can. 1343, § 1). The expression "local Ordinaries," employed in this canon includes residential Bishops, Abbots, and Prelates "nullius," Vicars and Prefects Apostolic; Vicars General or Capitular.[39] The right to preach in exempt churches does not enable local Ordinaries to assign others to do so; the law grants them this latter authority only in definite cases which apply exclusively to *parish* churches of exempt religious.[40]

E. *Ordinations and Other Functions*

From the interpretation given by authors prior to the promulgation of the Code, as seen above under A, it seems that a Bishop may not ordain a person in an exempt church, oratory, or other place, without permission of the religious superior;[41] nor may he grant indulgences or the remission of sins in such places without the same permission.[42]

---

[39] Cf. cc. 198; 294; 435, par. 1.
[40] Cf. Bened. XIV, Const., *Firmandis,* par. 5, Nov. 6, 1744; S.C.C., Sept. 13, 1749; S.C.EE.RR., July 23, 1694 (ap. Biz., p. 281); see Piat, II, p. 256; Vermeersch, *De Rel.,* I, 515.
[41] Cf. Pignatelli, Cons. Can. X, Cons. 106, n. 21; Tamb., I. Disp. XV, q. XV, 10; Ferraris, v., *Episcopus,* Art. 4, n. 22; Piat, II, 63; Gasparri, *De Sacra Ordinatione,* I, 100.
[42] Cf. Tamb., I, XV, XV, 13; Piat, II, 63.

CHAPTER XI

OTHER EXEMPT PLACES

Local exemption, as has been seen,[1] is enjoyed by religious houses, churches, and public oratories. The exemptive status of semipublic oratories, altars, and cemeteries will be discussed in the present chapter.

ARTICLE I. SEMIPUBLIC ORATORIES

To determine the amplitude or extent of exemption had by these oratories, it is necessary to understand the juridical norms and principles which specify and control their nature, erection or establishment, dedication and use. The present article purposes to explain these norms and principles.

I. NATURE OF A SEMIPUBLIC ORATORY OR CHAPEL

The threefold division of oratories into public, semipublic, and private[2] or domestic (can. 1182, § 2), is of recent origin. Decrees prior to the past century generally classified oratories as public or private; public, being those now described in canon 1188, § 2, 1°, and private, those in numbers 2° and 3° of the same paragraph.[3] Authors recognized three distinct classes under the twofold division, and many canonists, following Petra, enumerated three species: public, semipublic, and private.[4]

Within the past century, the three species have been mentioned in decrees of the Holy See.[5] In the Decree of January 23, 1899, the Sacred Congregation of Rites gave definite and official recognition to this manner of classifying oratories, when it declared the precise canonical meaning of semipublic Oratory. The Congregation decreed as follows:

"Ut autem quaelibet ambiguitas circa haec oratoria amoveatur Sanctissimus Dominus Noster Leo Papa XIII, ex Sacrorum Rituum Congregationis consulto, statuit et declaravit: Oratoria semipublica ea esse quae, etsi in loco quodammodo privato, vel non absolute publico, auctoritate Ordinarii erecta sunt, commodo tamen non Fidelium omnium nec privatae tantum personae

---

[1] Cf. above, Chaps. IX and X.
[2] Cf. Feldhaus, *Oratories* (Dissert. Cath. U., 1927).
[3] Cf. Gatticus, c. III.
[4] Cf. De Meester, 1146; *N.R.T.*, VII, pp. 391 ff., and XXIX, p. 615.
[5] Cf. S.R.C., Mar. 8, 1879, Decr. auth. 3484, Aug. 10, 1884, ap. Gardelin, 5920; July 18, 1885, Decr. auth. 3638; July 9, 1895, Decr. auth. 3832; May 22, 1896, Decr. auth. 3910: see also, Many, *De Locis Sacris*, 106 ff.; Fine, pp. 830 ff.; De Meester, 1146.

aut familiae, sed alicujus communitatis vel personarum coetus inserviunt. In his, sicut auctoritate Ordinarii sacrosanctum Missae sacrificium offerri potest, ita omnes qui eidem, intersint, praecepto audiendi Sacrum satisfacere valent. Hujus genera oratoria sunt quae pertinent ad Seminaria et Collegia ecclesiastica; ad pia Instituta et Societates votorum simplicium, aliasque Communitates sub regula sive statutis ab Ordinario approbatis; ad Domus spiritualibus exercitiis addictas; ad Convictus et Hospitia juventuti litteris, scientiis aut artibus instruendae destinata; ad Nosocomia, Orphanotrophia, nec non ad Arces et Carceres; atque similia oratoria, in quibus ex instituto aliquis Christifidelium coetus convenire solet ad audiendam Missam. Quibus adjungi debent Capellae in Coemeterio rite erectae, dummodo in Missae celebratione non iis tantum ad quos pertinet, sed aliis etiam Fidelibus aditus pateat.

"Voluit autem Sanctitas Sua sarta et tecta jura ac privilegia Oratoriorum quibus fruentur Emi. S. R. E. Cardinales, Rmi. Sacrorum Antistites atque Ordines Congregationesque Regulares, ac praeterea confirmare dignata est Decretum in una Nivernen. diei 8 Martii, 1879.

"Contrariis non obstantibus quibuscumque."

To interpret correctly the more ancient decrees applying to these sacred places, one must always bear in mind that the expression "private oratory of religious" means precisely the same as the expression "semipublic oratory" defined in canon 1188, § 2, 2°, of the Code.

Semipublic oratories, according to the Code, are those which are erected for the benefit of a community or group of the faithful who assemble in them, and to which others have not free access (can. 1188, § 2, 2°). They differ, therefore, from public oratories, because in the case of the latter, the faithful have the right of free access at least during times of divine services (can. 1188, § 2, 1°). In other words, the community or group of persons have exclusive right to use their own semipublic oratories; others may be permitted to use them, although they cannot claim a right to do so.[6]

Religious communities and the various institutions governed by them generally have their own semipublic oratories. As Creusen states: "All chapels of religious communities are certainly semipublic oratories; so also are the chapels of third orders, sodalities, and confraternities, provided divine services are held in them. The chapels erected in a country house or villa of a religious community likewise come under the definition of a semipublic oratory, even though the community live there for only a few weeks during the year. Finally, the secondary chapels erected in a religious house or in a seminary to provide facilities for saying Mass on the part of a large number of priests, or in which distinct groups of religious assist at the Holy Sacrifice, are to be classed as semipublic oratories.

---

[6] Cf. Coronata, II, 762.

"A chapel in the infirmary of a religious house is, therefore, a semipublic oratory, contrary to what was the case under the former law."[7]

Semipublic oratories are of their very nature an integral part of a religious house, and consequently participate fully in the local exemption enjoyed by exempt institutes, as will be manifest from what follows.[8]

II. THE ERECTION OF SEMIPUBLIC ORATORIES

The canonical erection of these oratories will be discussed under two heads: (A) the erection of those attached to religious houses; (B) the erection of those in farms, villas, hospices, and the like, which are not attached to a religious house.

(A) *Oratories Attached to Religious Houses*
FORMER DISCIPLINE

Prior to the council of Trent, Generals and Provincials of Regulars had authority, independently of local Ordinaries, to erect semipublic oratories (at that period called private oratories) in their religious houses and in the institutions connected with them, so long as these places were set apart exclusively for divine worship.[9] Thus, Clement IV granted the Friars Minor the right to establish semipublic oratories wherever these religious dwelt,[10] and Sixtus IV reaffirmed this in favor of both the Franciscans and Dominicans.[11] Paul III made a similar concession to the Society of Jesus.[12]

Did the Council of Trent revoke these privileges?

Some authors maintained that the Decree *"De observandis et vitandis in celebratione Missae"* (sess. XXII) contained such a revocation, and that thereafter authorization of the Bishop had to be obtained for the erection of semipublic oratories;[13] others denied that this Decree affected the privileges of Regulars.[14]

Whatever be the correct solution, most Regular institutes were soon after granted a new privilege. On May 3, 1575, Gregory XIII made the following concession to the Society of Jesus: "Volumus ut in oratoriis et capellis, quae ipsius Societatis Provinciales per se in domibus, collegiis, et aliis locis, ubi

---

[7] Cf. Creusen, 135.

[8] Cf. Pejska, p. 262.

[9] Cf. Ferraris, v. *Oratorium*, 72.

[10] Cf. Clem. IV, Const., *Virtute conspicuos*, par. 8, July 21, 1265.

[11] Cf. Sixtus IV, Const., *Regimini*, Aug. 31, 1476.

[12] "Liceatque Praepositis et eorum facultate universis Fratribus et Sociis Societatis hujusmodi in presbyteratus ordine constitutis, in locis in quibus degunt et eos pro tempore morari contigerit, habere oratoria; et in eis ac quocumque alio honesto et congruenti loco in altari portatili reverentia et honore . . . missas et alia divina officia celebrare, ac ecclesiastica sacramenta recipere et aliis ministrare," Paul III, Const., *Licet debitum*, Oct. 18, 1549.

[13] Cf. Fagn., C. *In his*, 30, *de priv.*, 22 ff.; Gatticus, c. XVIII, 2; Schmalz., III, XLI, 47; Van Gameren, *De oratoriis publicis et privatis*, p. 273; Piat, II, p. 229, q. 5; Many, *De Locis Sacris*, 106.

[14] Cf. Reiff., L. III, t. 41, nn. 19–21; Ferraris, v. *Oratorium*, 72; Bouix, II, p. 191.

aliqui Societatis residebunt, approbaverint et ad divinum dumtaxat cultum deputaverint, missae et alia divina officia, alterius licentia minime requisita, celebrare possint."[15]

The rights contained in this privilege are most extensive. No limitations are made concerning the *number* of chapels to be erected in any place, nor the nature of the place where they are to be established. They may be erected any place where a member of the Order resides, even though the residence be temporary in character.[16] The privilege contains no terms forbidding its communication, consequently it is enjoyed by all religious to whom the privileges of the Society of Jesus are communicated.[17] This privilege is still in force.[18]

To use it lawfully, the following conditions must be fulfilled:

1. The oratory must be established in a place where a religious of the privileged institute resides, at least temporarily;

2. The place must be reserved exclusively for divine worship;

3. It must have the approval of the Provincial, after he or his delegate has made sure of its fitness for the celebration of Mass.[19]

It should be remarked that the existence of the rights in question have been recognized in recent replies of the Sacred Congregation of Rites.[20] In particular, the Decree of 1906 declared: "If there be question of Regulars (or, for the same reason, of clerical exempt religious), permission of the Bishop is not to be sought by the religious Ordinary for the erection of these oratories; the permission of the Superior-General, or of the Provincial, suffices, according to the Decree of January 23, 1899 (Decr. auth. 4007)."

THE LAW OF THE CODE

Canon 1192, § 1, states that semipublic oratories cannot be erected without permission of the Ordinary.

Since the Code employs the general term "Ordinary," and not "local Ordinary," all the persons enumerated in canon 198, § 1, may grant this permission. Hence, permission of major superiors must be obtained for the erection of semipublic oratories in houses pertaining to exempt clerical

---

[15] Greg. XIII, Const., *Decet Romanum*, May 3, 1575.

[16] Cf. Gatticus, XVIII, 3.

[17] Cf. Thomas Tamburini, *De Sacr. Missae*, c. VI, par. 3, n. 2; Petra, Tom. II, ad const. VIII, Honor. II, 47; Tamb., *De Jure Abb.*, II, Disp., 5, q. 6, n. 4; Gatticus, XVIII, 3; Ferraris, v. *Oratorium*, 74; Piat, II, p. 280, q. 5; Many, *De Locis Sacris*, 106; Vermeersch, *De Rel.*, I, 511; d'Angelo, p. 40.

[18] Melo, p. 132.

[19] Cf. Ferraris, v. *Oratorium*, 79; De Lugo, *Resp. Mor.*, L. I, dub. 14; Diana, part. 9, tr. 1, resolut. 32, 34; Vermeersch, *De Rel.*, I, 511; Ojetti, *Syn.* v., *Oratorium*; Melo, p. 131.

[20] Cf. Jan. 23, 1899, Decr. auth. 4007, ap. ASS, XXXI, pp. 412, 413; Nov. 10, 1906, Decr. auth. 4190.

religious.[21] It seems that major superiors are also empowered to grant this permission in favor of convents of nuns subject to them.[22]

As a general rule, in the case of colleges, boarding schools, etc., permission should be given for the erection of only *one* chapel. However, for reasons of necessity or great utility, the religious Ordinary may allow a plurality of semipublic oratories (can. 1192, § 4). Since the major superior has such authority with regard to the institutions in question, it is manifest that he may more readily authorize the erection of additional chapels in the religious house proper.

Thus far we have considered the formalities required for the erection of semipublic oratories in religious houses and in other institutions either materially or formally connected with them.[23] We shall now explain the norms governing the establishing of such chapels in other places pertaining to exempt institutes.

(B) *Semipublic Oratories in Farms, Villas, Hospices, and Other Places not Attached to the Exempt House*

The places under consideration are secular in character; that is, they are neither religious houses nor small dependent or filial houses united with a canonically erected house.

1. By common law, expressed in the Council of Trent[24] and reaffirmed in replies of the Roman Congregations, v.g., S.C.C., March 1, 1687,[25] permission of the local Ordinary must be obtained in order that religious may erect semipublic oratories in the aforesaid places.[26] This same law is now in force.[27]

2. In virtue of special privileges granted by Gregory XIII to the Society of Jesus,[28] by Clement XII to the Carthusians,[29] and by Benedict XIV to the Dominicans,[30] these religious institutes and those to whom their privileges have been communicated, may with the permission of their major superiors erect semipublic oratories in farms, villas, hospices, and in any other place where their religious reside even temporarily. No authorization of local Ordinaries is needed.[31]

---

[21] Cf. Melo, p. 131.

[22] Cf. Schäfer, 464; Coronata, II, 524, p. 616, nota 5.

[23] Cf. De Meester, 1149.

[24] Sess. XXII, Decr., *de observand. et evitand., in celebrat. Miss.*

[25] Cf. Gatticus, XVIII, 24: for other replies, consult Fagn., *Disputatio de granciis* (after the chapter *Auctoritate*), q. 27, *De censibus;* Petra, In Const. VIII, Honorii III, n. 51 ff., Tom. II.

[26] Cf. S.R.C., Decr., Nov. 10, 1906; see Many, 106.

[27] Cf. De Meester, 1149; Coronata, *De Locis et Temporibus Sacris,* 85; Feldhaus, *Oratories* (Dissert., Cath. U.), p. 112.

[28] Cf. Greg. XIII, Const., *Decet Romanum,* May 3, 1575.

[29] Cf. Clem. XII, Const., *Exponi Nobis,* Aug. 19, 1737.

[30] Cf. Bened. XIV, Br., *Exponi Nobis,* Jan. 22, 1755.

[31] Cf. Gatticus, XVIII, 24; Piat, II, p. 231, q. 6; Vermeersch, *De Rel.,* I, 511; Many, *De Locis Sacris,* 107; Gasparri, *De Eucharistia,* I, 221.

Since these privileges have not been revoked by the Code, they retain their full juridical force.[32]

Ordinaries should not grant permission for the erection of such a chapel before they have visited the place personally or through a delegate, and have been assured of its suitableness. Since the chapel is destined for the Holy Sacrifice of the Mass and for other sacred functions, its inspection and approval is to be made especially with a view to the fitness of the place for these specific purposes.

III. DEDICATION OF SEMIPUBLIC ORATORIES

It is not necessary to bless a semipublic oratory. The blessing conferred on the house or place where it is situated suffices, although even this does not seem to be a strict requirement.[33]

The type of oratory in question may, nevertheless, be blessed or consecrated, if the structure, stability, and importance of the edifice warrants it. Consecration is reserved to the Bishop of the place; benediction, to major superiors.[34]

IV. SACRED FUNCTIONS IN SEMIPUBLIC ORATORIES

In their use, as in their erection, these oratories are exempt from the jurisdiction of the local Ordinary; that is to say, the services conducted in them are under the control of the religious and cannot be interfered with by others.[35]

A. *The General Rule*

The celebration of all sacred functions is permitted in semipublic oratories, with the exception of those forbidden either by the liturgy or by a precept of the Ordinary (can. 1193). Regulations, therefore, restricting the exercise of sacred functions in these places may issue either from law or from the ordinances of a competent Ordinary.

Legal limitations may arise from liturgical law, as the canon states, v.g., if the other functions of Holy Week are not celebrated, it is not permitted to hold the adoration and reposition of the Blessed Sacrament on Maundy Thursday.[36] Besides these, there are limitations expressed in the Code itself. Obviously, restrictions limiting functions performed for the faithful in exempt churches and public oratories[37] are especially applicable to semi-

---

[32] Cf. *Epit.*, I, 785; Schäfer, 442; d'Angelo, p. 40; De Meester, 1149; Coronata, *De Locis et Temporibus Sacris*, 85.

[33] Cf. Coronata, II, 767; *Epit.*, II, 501.

[34] Cf. above, Chap. X, Art. I; see Pejska, p. 259.

[35] Cf. S.R.C., Resp., Secovien, Nov. 10, 1906; Mostaza, *Per.*, XXII, 145*; Feldhaus, p. 116.

[36] Cf. S.R.C., Nov. 30, 1889, Decr. auth. 3716; see Coronata, *De Locis et Temporibus Sacris*, 73, p. 73, nota 2, and 79.

[37] Cf. can. 497, par. 2; see explanation given above, Chap. X, Art. III.

public oratories. Thus, for example, functions reserved to parochial churches (cf. can. 462), as, performing the solemn rite of baptism, are not permitted in these chapels.[38]

Limitations imposed by the Ordinary may prevent the exercise of certain functions. Only major superiors have this power over the semipublic oratories of their institutes; local Ordinaries, in other cases.[39] In no case has an Ordinary authority to impose restrictions which are contrary to the provisions of the Code.

Regulars and other religious enjoying the privilege of Gregory XIII,[40] cited above, may, with the permission of their own superiors, conduct sacred functions in their semipublic oratories wherever situated, whether in a religious house or in villas, farms, etc., or in any place where the religious even temporarily reside. Local Ordinaries may not interfere with the exercise of this right.[41]

B. *Particular Norms Governing Various Functions*

As the celebration of certain functions sometimes occasions disputes and difficulties, it will be useful to consider somewhat in detail the principal ones which are performed in oratories.

THE HOLY SACRIFICE OF THE MASS

The rights of semipublic oratories comprise both the celebration of Mass and the assistance of the faithful at this sacred function.

1. The Celebration of Mass

The Church permits the celebrations of a plurality of Masses daily, even on the more solemn feast days, in these chapels. Superiors of exempt institutes may allow extraneous priests to offer Holy Mass in these places. This discipline has been in force both before and since the promulgation of the Code.[42] A detailed explanation is given below in Chapter XII, article III.

2. Assistance of the Faithful at Mass

Before the Code it was commonly taught[43] that the faithful could hear Mass on any day and could satisfy their obligation of hearing Mass on Sundays and Holydays by assisting at the Holy Sacrifice in semipublic oratories.

---

[38] Cf. cc. 481, 482, 483, 716, 1171.
[39] Cf. S.R.C., Secovien, Nov. 10, 1906; Mostaza, *Per.*, XXII, p. 145*; *Epit.*, 501.
[40] Cf. Greg. XIII, Const., *Decet Romanum*, May 3, 1575.
[41] Cf. S.R.C., Secovien, Nov. 10, 1906; Rosignoli, *De Euch.*, q. 8, art. 14, nn. 4 ff.; Gatticus, XVIII, 7, 8; Ferraris, v. *Oratorium*, 74, 78; Piat, II, p. 230; Fine, pp. 831, 832; Many, *De Locis Sacris*, 106, 107; Ojetti, *Syn.*, 2936.
[42] Cf. S.R.C., Decr., Mar. 8, 1879 ad 1, Decr. auth. 3484; Jan. 23, 1899; Nov. 10, 1906, Decr. auth. 4192; Mar. 31, 1909, Decr. auth. 4335: see also Gatticus, XVIII, 6; Vermeersch, *De Rel.*, I, 513; *Per.*, VI (14); De Meester, 1149, III, p. 55, n. 1.
[43] Cf. Ferraris, v. *Oratorium*, 76.

It was argued that oratories of this kind enjoyed the privileges of public oratories,[44] since they had been habitually set aside for divine worship exclusively. And since the aforesaid privileges were local, not personal, they could be shared by anybody assisting at Mass in such places.[45]

From the very nature of the semipublic oratory, explained above in Article I, n. I, it is clear that the superior of an exempt institute, who has authority over the chapel, may allow the faithful to assist at Mass there, and from canon 1249 it is also clear that people may satisfy their obligations of hearing Mass on Sundays and Holydays by assisting at the Holy Sacrifice in this type of chapel.

Local Ordinaries cannot issue precepts which militate against these rights. We follow Mostaza's explanation of the Code on this point.[46]

Religious superiors of clerical exempt institutes have jurisdiction over the chapel in question and may allow the faithful free access to the same at any time. Local Ordinaries have no restrictive authority in this matter. Therefore, even indirect measures taken by them in order to prevent religious superiors from granting access to the chapels would be usurpations of authority and consequently ineffective juridically.

The Code manifestly implies this since even in the matter of quinquennial visitations it grants local Ordinaries no right to visit these places or investigate anything pertaining to them. Hence, this precludes the possibility of the Ordinaries imposing any conditions on either the celebration of Mass or the attendance of the faithful in the chapels.

In view of the ancient practice on this point Mostaza seems correct in maintaining that, without special and grave reason the imposition by the local Ordinary of any even indirect measures for the purpose of hindering the faithful from attending services in *whatever semipublic oratory they choose,* is an abuse of authority which is directly opposed to the Regula Juris: "Quum quid una via prohibetur alicui, ad id alia non debet admitti" (cf. Reg. jur. 84, in VI). It is useful to note in this connection that the Council of Trent, which was more insistent than the Code on attendance at parochial functions, did not decree that the faithful should be *ordered,* but only that they should be *exhorted* to attend their parish churches frequently on Sundays and Holydays of Obligation.[47] A good example of the correct manner of interpreting this decree is found in the measures adopted by St. Charles Borromeo, in the Sixth Council of Milan, cited by Benedict

---

[44] Cf. Many, *De Locis Sacris,* 106.

[45] Cf. Thomas Tamburini, *De Sacr. Missae,* L. L, c. 4, par. 3, n. 6; (who cites Azorius, Suarez, Diana, Quarti): Rosignoli, *De Euch.,* q. 8, art. 14, n. 7, says, "Omnes indifferenter et libere audiunt sacrum, nec ullus est qui dubitet, quin praecepto satisfaciant," ap. Ferraris, v. *Oratorium,* 76.

[46] Cf. Mostaza, *Per.,* XXII, pp. 141*–146*.

[47] Cf. Conc. Trid., sess. XXII, Decr. *de observand. et evitand. in celebrat. Miss.*

XIV.[48] Incorrect interpretations, in which Bishops attempted to prescribe assistance at the parish church, have often been declared excessive and have been expunged by the Sacred Congregation of the Council from synodal statutes. See, for example, the prescription of the Bishop of Meath, cited by Benedict XIV (*loc. cit.*, n. 11); and others cited by Azorius,[49] Pasqualigo,[50] and Barbosa.[1]

N.B. Other matters relating to the Holy Sacrifice of the Mass, as the time for Mass, the right to offer Midnight Mass on Christmas, etc., are discussed below: Chapter XII, Article III.

RESERVATION OF THE BLESSED SACRAMENT

Permission to reserve the Blessed Sacrament in a semipublic oratory must be obtained from the local Ordinary (cf. can. 1265). This law applies to the oratories of exempt religious.[2] However, privileges and immemorial customs entitling some institutes to reserve the Blessed Sacrament in their semipublic chapels[3] have not been revoked by the Code.[4]

EXPOSITION AND BENEDICTION OF THE BLESSED SACRAMENT

The consent of the local Ordinary is needed for *public* Exposition or Benediction[5] of the Blessed Sacrament.[6] It is probable that if the doors of the chapel are kept closed, thus excluding the assistance of the faithful, public Exposition and Benediction may be held with the consent of the religious prelate.[7]

PREACHING TO THE FAITHFUL

Religious having diocesan faculties may preach to the faithful assembled in their semipublic oratories.[8]

Are the faithful free to attend such sermons?

If the religious superior permits it, they may do so. Nor may the local Ordinary force them to attend sermons in their parish church and thereby restrict this freedom. When treating this question, the Council of Trent declared: "Let the Bishop diligently remind the people that all should hear

---

[48] *De Syn. Dioec.*, L. XI, c. XIV, 10.

[49] *Inst.*, p. I, L. 7, c. 6.

[50] *De Sacr. Novae Legis*, q. 1258.

[1] Collect. in Trid., sess. XXII, *de observand. et evitand. in celebrat. Miss.*, n. 11.

[2] Cf. below, Chap. XIII; see also, Gattico, XVIII, 10; Piat, II, p. 241; *Epit.*, II, 589.

[3] Cf. Bened. XIV, Br., *Quemadmodum Presbyteri,* July 15, 1749; see also Pignatelli, X, 84; Gatticus, XVIII, 10 ff.; Piat, II, p. 241.

[4] Cf. *Epit.*, I, 505, and II, 589; Bondini, p. 118; Cappello, *De Euch.*, 358, n. 4; De Meester, 1149, n. III, p. 55, nota 4.

[5] Cf. Cod. Com., Mar. 6, 1927, ad III, AAS, XIX, 161; *Per.*, XVI, 55; *N.R.T.*, LIV, 476.

[6] See below, Chap. XIII; *Epit.*, II, 599.

[7] Cf. Wernz, III, 353, nota 235; *Epit.*, II, 599; *Per.*, XVI, p. 60.

[8] Cf. De Meester, 834.

the word of God in their parish church, when this can be conveniently done."[9]

On account of the attenuating force of the clause, "when this can be conveniently done," Suarez and others held that the Council did not impose an absolute precept upon the faithful, but issued, rather, an admonition and exhortation.[10] Zerola, Trullench, and others[11] asserted that the obligation of hearing the parish sermon, if it ever existed, is now abrogated by virtue of the contrary custom, since pious and learned people freely go where they please to attend sermons. Zerola further states that, according to frequent declarations of the Sacred Congregation of the Council, the local Ordinary may not impose fines or other penalties in order to constrain subjects to attend parish sermons. The same is affirmed by Barbosa.[12]

"From this it is readily seen," says Mostaza, "that the recommendation of canon 467, paragraph 2, together with other concordant canons, concerning attendance at the parochial church for divine services (Mass) and sermons, neither deprives the faithful of their freedom to hear Mass and the word of God elsewhere, nor does it permit an Ordinary, wishing to foster attendance at the parish church, to order this or to limit people's right of frequenting other churches or oratories, even semipublic, on Sundays and Holydays of Obligation.

"For if before the Code, according to Benedict the XIV and the Sacred Congregation of the Council, Bishops were not permitted to impose such limitations, they are certainly not to be attributed this authority from the Code, since the present legislation is much more favorable to liberty of the faithful in these matters than was the former."[13]

OTHER SACRED FUNCTIONS

Not only the sacred offices thus far enumerated, but all other functions which are characteristically sacerdotal, may be discharged in these oratories.[14] The expression "sacerdotal functions" is employed here in contradistinction to "parochial functions," to signify those ministries and sacred rites which priests may perform outside of parish churches without the permission of pastors. Examples of such functions, drawn from the common law, are, besides those mentioned above in nn. 1–5: public recitation of the Breviary; Forty Hours' Devotion; churching of women; blessing of ashes, candles, palms, etc.; enthroning of the Sacred Heart; all the functions of

---

[9] Cf. Conc. Trid., XXIV, c. 4, *de reform.*

[10] Cf. Suarez, *De Rel.*, L. II, c. 16, n. 10; see also, Roderico, *Quaest. Regul.*, Tom. I, q. 43, art. 7; Bonacina, Disp. V, *De Tertio Decalogi Praecepto*, Q. unic., punct. 2, nn. 27 ff.

[11] Ap. Bened. XIV, *De Syn. Dioec.*, L., XI, c. XIV, 13.

[12] Cf. Collect. ad Trid., sess. XXIV, c. 4, n. 17; see Bened. XIV, *De Syn. Dioec.*, L. XI, c. XIV, 13.

[14] Cf. De Meester, 1148, 1149.

[13] Cf. Mostaza, *Per.*, XXII, p. 143*; De Meester, 834.

Holy Week, to be performed only in chapels where the Blessed Sacrament is reserved (can. 1265); etc.[15]

PRIVATE OR PROFANE USES FORBIDDEN

Semipublic oratories, like churches and other oratories, are essentially places of worship. Although such oratories are not necessarily consecrated or blessed in such a way as to constitute them sacred places in the strict sense (cf. can. 1154), they are reserved exclusively for divine service and, consequently, may not be used for domestic purposes (can. 1196, § 2).[16]

Ordinarily, therefore, the chapels in question should retain their sacred character. Either a temporary or a permanent change is, nevertheless, possible, yet neither may be effected without the permission of the major superior (cf. cc. 1192, § 3 and 1196, § 2).

ARTICLE II. ALTARS

Altars pertaining to exempt religious are under the supervision and authority of the religious superiors and, consequently, are not subject to the jurisdiction of local Ordinaries. The altars here spoken of are those which are not used for obligatory care of the souls of the faithful, as is the case, v.g., with the altar used by a pastor. These latter connected with this spiritual care are subject to the jurisdiction and canonical visitation of the local Ordinary.

Some doubt and confusion concerning the exemption of altars arose after Gregory XV promulgated his Constitution, *Inscrutabile*.[17] The Sacred Congregation of the Council, having been consulted on the matter, replied that Bishops could not, by virtue of the cited constitution, lawfully make a visitation of those altars in Regular churches which were not burdened with the spiritual care of the faithful.[18] From this it is seen that the altars pertaining to Regulars, with the specified exception, enjoy full exemption.[19] The establishing, construction, dedication, and use of the altars are subject to the supervision, authority, and visitation of the major superiors of exempt institutes.

The definite extent and limitation of these exemptive rights are more clearly determined by norms governing the dedication of altars and the privilege of portable altars belonging to exempt institutes.

---

[15] Cf. S.R.C., Mar. 3, 1866; S.R.C., decr., Dec. 10, 1703; Bened. XIV, Const., *Etsi minime*, pars. 14, 15, Feb. 7, 1742: see also De Meester, 834, 1149.
[16] Cf. S. C. Consist., Dec. 10, 1912, AAS, IV, 724; S.R.C., May 11, 1641, Decr. auth. 756; Sept. 12, 1840, Decr. auth. 2812; July 27, 1878, Decr. auth. 3460; Nov. 23, 1880, Decr. auth. 3525: see also, Many, *De Locis Sacris*, 157; Augustine, VI, can. 1192, § 3.
[17] Cf. Greg. XV, Const., *Inscrutabile*, Feb. 5, 1622.
[18] Cf. *Bullarium Romanum*, t. 5, p. 5, p. 3, ap. Vermeersch, *De Rel.*, II, n. 261, p. 553.
[19] Cf. Del Bene, Pars II, cap. XII, dub. I, sect. II, n. 20.

1. Dedication of Altars

The Code distinguishes two kinds of altars, the immovable or fixed, and the movable or portable altar. For the fixed altar, the table, and for the portable altar, the sacred stone must be a single piece of natural, solid stone, without fractures or crevices. In the case of the fixed altar, the stone must extend the full length and breadth of the table and rest on its support or base so as to form one whole (cf. cc. 1197, 1198).[20]

Altars on which the Holy Sacrifice of the Mass is to be celebrated must be consecrated, in accordance with the liturgical laws, the whole altar in the case of fixed altars, and the altar stone, in the case of portable ones (can. 1199).

All Bishops as well as persons especially privileged can consecrate *portable* altars. Hence, exempt religious may request any Bishop to perform this function. Titular Bishops are competent in the matter. Only the persons specified in canon 1155[21] can consecrate a *fixed* altar (can. 1199, § 2). In the latter case, therefore, exempt religious are dependent upon the local Bishop for the consecration of fixed altars, whether these be constructed in their churches or oratories. Canon 1199 expressly states that privileges concerning the consecration of altars are not affected by its provision; hence, Franciscans and Jesuits retain the right to consecrate altars erected in mission territories.[22]

Altars may *lose* their consecration in several ways. The *fixed* altar suffers this loss if the table is separated even momentarily from its supports. Both *fixed* and *portable* altars lose consecration if they suffer enormous fracture, or, if the relics are removed; or if the cover of the sepulcher is broken or removed. Exceptions to the last mentioned are defined in canon 1200, § 2.

In the case of separation of the table from its supports, Ordinaries may grant any priest delegation to reconsecrate the altar (can. 1200, § 1). The Code uses the term "Ordinaries" not "local Ordinaries"; consequently, major superiors of exempt clerical institutes may grant this delegation.[23] For this the short formula published by the Sacred Congregation of Rites, September 9, 1920, may be employed.[24]

When consecration is lost in the other ways specified in canon 1200, § 2, only the *local Bishop* can reconsecrate immovable altars; all Bishops can

---

[20] Cf. Ayrinhac, *Administrative Legislation*, 41.
[21] Cf. above, Chap. X, Art. III.
[22] Cf. Honorius IV, Const., *In parte vestro*, ap. Roderico, *Bullarium*, 2; Leo XII, Br., *Plura Inter*, July 11, 1826; see Ferraris, v. *Altare*, 10; Coronata, *De Locis et Temporibus Sacris*, 107.
[23] Cf. Melo, p. 133; Coronata, *De Locis* etc., 112; *Epit.*, II, 507; De Meester, 1156, p. 67, nota 7.
[24] Cf. AAS, XII, 450; *Rit Rom.*, *Appendix De consecr. altarium*, excr. I.: see Woywod, II, 1232.

reconsecrate movable ones, for by loss of consecration, altars are the same as though never consecrated and are, therefore, subject to the provisions of canon 1199, § 2.

Religious Ordinaries may grant permission to change the title of an altar. This does not permit changing the title of the main altar, which must remain the same as that of the church (can. 1201).[25]

2. Privilege of the Portable Altar

The privilege of the portable altar means the right to celebrate Mass on an altar stone in any proper and respectable place (can. 822, § 3).[26] By means of this privilege, the holder is permitted to offer up the Holy Sacrifice in places which have not been dedicated or designated for divine worship.

Mass may be celebrated on all days not excluded by liturgical law nor by the terms of the indult.[27]

The privilege of the portable altar has been accorded certain exempt clerical institutes. Though the Council of Trent abrogated all grants of this kind,[28] after the Council Roman Pontiffs have conceded new privileges. Thus, Pius IV granted *infirm members* of the Canons Regular of the Lateran the right to have any priest say Mass in their room, if the sick person was unable to leave the same.[29] According to many authors, Innocent XIII (May 23, 1723) revoked this privilege. Gregory XIII gave this privilege to priests of the Society of Jesus engaged in giving missions.[30] The same privilege was communicated to other institutes.[31] Priests of the Society of Jesus who are on a voyage also enjoy the privilege.[32] Clement XIV granted the Redemptorists who are *conducting missions* permission to say Mass in places where they reside while engaged in this work.[33] Their privilege seems

---

[25] Cf. Coronata, *De Locis* etc., 119, p. 121, nota 3.

[26] Cf. Ojetti, *Syn.* v., *Altare portabile;* Gasparri, *De Euch.*, I, 272; De Meester, 1165; Coronata, *De Locis*, 123.

[27] Cf. Gasparri, *De Euch.*, I, 272; Coronata, *De Locis*, 123.

[28] Cf. Conc. Trid., sess. XXII, *Decr. de observand. et evitand. in celebrat. Miss.;* see also Gatticus, *De usu altaris portalis*, XIII, nn. 1–13; Fine, p. 856; Gasparri, *De Euch.*, I, 262; Van Gameren, *De Oratoriis*, pp. 266 ff.; Piat II, p. 226; Vermeersch, *De Rel.*, I, 468; Coronata, *De Locis* etc., 124, p. 127, nota 5.

[29] Cf. Pius IV, Mar. 8, 1565; see Gatticus, *De usu altaris portatilis*, XIII, n. 13.

[30] The grant declares: "Usum altaris viatici, Societati vestrae a fel. rec. Paulo Papa III concessum, deinde a Concilio Tridentino universe sublatum, vobis eatenus restituimus, ut inter missiones, quae a superioribus fiunt, Presbyteri vestri, servata alias forma dictae concessionis, Missae sacrificium licite valeant celebrare super hujusmodi altari ubique gentium, etiam in castris militum; modo loca etsi communia et profana, tuta et honesta sint, et Generalis aut per eum Provinciales Praepositi eo tum utendum fore judicaverint; itidemque possint ibi Presbyteri ipsi Sanctissimum Eucharistiae Sacramentum ministrare fidelibus ad illud sumendum debite praeparatis. Non obstantibus praemissis ac constitutionibus et ordinationibus apostolicis, caeterisque contrariis quibuscumque," Greg. XIII, Br., *Usum altaris*, Oct. 1, 1579, ap. *Institutum S.J.,* Vol. I, *Bullarium*, p. 78: see Vermeersch, *De Rel.*, I, 468; Gasparri, *De Euch.*, I, 262.

[31] Cf. Lezana, Tom. I, c. XXI, 14; Gatticus, *De usu altaris portatilis*, XIII, 18; Gasparri, *De Euch.*, I, 262.

[32] Cf. S.C. Neg. Eccl. Ext., June 28, 1898.

[33] Cf. Clem. XIV, Rescript. June 19, 1773.

to have been communicated to other religious, as, the Dominicans, in Poland; the Discalced Carmelites, in Italy; and the Trinitarians in Africa. Other institutes, within certain specifications, were given direct concessions of this kind.[34]

The privileges of the portable altar just enumerated were in use up till the promulgation of the Code,[35] and since they have not been revoked by the new law, they retain their juridic force at present.[36]

Further, the Code itself permits a grant of this kind under certain conditions. Canon 822, § 4, entitles local and religious Ordinaries, for a just and reasonable cause, to permit the celebration of Mass on a consecrated stone in a decent place outside a church or oratory. This concession may be made only in an extraordinary case and by way of act, not habitually, as the canon stipulates.[37]

Since the traditional discipline of the Church enunciated in canon 822, § 1, declares: "Mass is to be celebrated on a consecrated stone and in a church or oratory," etc., it is readily inferred that the faculties of Ordinaries contained in paragraph 4, are limited and may not be exercised except in an extraordinary case, nor without just and reasonable cause, which must be inspired by the highest motives connected with divine worship and the spiritual welfare of the faithful.[38]

Communion may be given at such Masses.[39] Those who hear Mass celebrated at a portable altar, even outside a church or oratory, seem to satisfy the obligation, since the Code mentions only the strictly private oratory as the one place where the obligation of hearing Mass cannot be fulfilled[40] (cf. can. 1249).

ARTICLE III. ECCLESIASTICAL BURIAL

Definite juridical norms establish the relationship of exempt religious and local Ordinaries in matters relating to Christian burial. The exemptive rights of religious are clearly defined. To understand them and their amplitude it will be necessary to evaluate correctly the regulations which govern: (I) Cemeteries of exempt institutes; (II) Funeral services and interment of religious; (III) Funeral services and interment of the faithful in exempt places; (IV) Funeral taxes.

---

[34] Cf. Novarius, *Lucerna Regularium*, v. *Altare*; Vermeersch, *De Rel.*, I, 468; Gasparri, *De Euch.*, I, 262.

[35] Cf. Vermeersch, *De Rel.*, I, 468; Gasparri, *De Euch.*, I, 262.

[36] Cf. Coronata, *De Locis* etc., 124, p. 127, nota 5; De Meester, 1166.

[37] Cf. De Meester, 1166.

[38] Cf. S. C. Sacr., Letter, July 26, 1924, AAS, XVI, 370; Bouscaren, I, can. 822; *Per.*, XIII, 161.

[39] Cf. S. C. Sacr., Reply, July 29, 1927; AAS, XX, 79; Bouscaren, I, can. 822.

[40] Cf. Coronata, *De Locis* etc., 123.

I. CEMETERIES OF EXEMPT RELIGIOUS

Exempt religious institutes have the right, independently of local Ordinaries, to establish, use, and govern their own cemeteries.

A. *Establishment of Cemeteries*

Prior to the promulgation of the Code, express declarations of Roman Pontiffs are proof of the fact that Regulars had the right to establish and own cemeteries.[41] Clement V made a statement in behalf of the Franciscans and Dominicans which is typical of those made by other Pontiffs. His words themselves adequately explain the rights of the orders in question: "Hujusmodi quoque statuto et ordinationibus nostris adjicimus, ut fratres dictorum ordinum (Praedicatores et Minores) in ecclesiis vel locis suis ubilibet constitutis liberam (ut sequitur) habeant sepulturam, videlicet, quod omnes ad eam recipere valeant, qui sepeliri elegerint in locis et ecclesiis memoratis."[42] As has been said, the same privilege was directly granted to other institutes, and by communication of privileges has been shared by all Regulars.[43]

The Code has not restricted the exemption of cemeteries but, on the contrary, has granted it to others for, according to canon 1208, § 2, the right to own them is extended to *all* exempt religious. Hence *all exempt institutes,* whether clerical or lay, now enjoy this right. Manifestly, nuns, as was the case before the Code,[44] share the same privilege.[45]

If, as is the case in some countries, the State usurps authority in this matter and forces religious to use the common or municipal burial ground, exempt institutes may, if it be possible, reserve a plot of ground there, which, in the circumstance, will be considered to be canonically their proper cemetery, and therefore will be exempt from the jurisdiction of the local Ordinary. For only "per accidens," on account of unjust legislation, is it outside the monastery.[46] The Holy See maintains that rights and privileges of religious in these matters are not abrogated because of adverse civil laws.[47]

It is not necessary to erect a cemetery within the precincts of the monastery nor to obtain the permission of the local Ordinary before establishing

---

[41] Cf. Reiff, L. III, t. 28, n. 18.

[42] Cf. c. 2, *De sepulturis*, III, 7, in Clem.: these are the identical terms employed by Boniface VIII, in his decree, *Super cathedram* (ap. c. 2, *De sepulturis*, III, 7, *in Extravag. com.*). Though the provisions of Boniface were revoked by his successor, Benedict XI (ap. c. 1, *De sepulturis*, III, 7, *in Extravag. com.*), they were restored by Clement V in the decree just quoted: see Many, *De Locis Sacris*, 157.

[43] Cf. Leo XIII, Const., *Romanos Pontifices*, par. 17; c. 16, X, *de excess. prelat. et. subd.*, V, 31; see Many, *De Locis Sacris*, 157; Fine, p. 760; Vermeersch, *De Rel.*, I, 485.

[44] Cf. Many, *De Locis Sacris*, 158; Vermeersch, *De Rel.*, I, 485.

[45] Cf. Creusen, 152.

[46] Cf. S.R.C., Decr., Jan. 23, 1849.

[47] Cf. S.C.C., Jan. 23, 1886, ASS, XVIII, 457; S.C.C., Sept. 16, 1871; ASS, VII, 36; see Wernz, III, 777; Coronata, *De Locis* etc., nn. 85, 139.

it.[48] Canon 1208, § 2, grants exempt institutes unrestricted right to own their proper cemeteries.

B. *Use of Cemeteries*

Exempt religious, as will be seen below, should be buried in their own cemeteries (cf. can. 1224, 2°, together with can. 1208, § 2), if they have such.

Furthermore, superiors of exempt institutes may allow the faithful who so desire to be interred in their cemeteries (can. 1228, § 2).[49] Once their convent and cemetery is established, religious cannot renounce their right to grant this permission, although they may refuse to exercise it in favor of the faithful.[50]

C. *Government of Cemeteries*

Since the cemeteries being discussed are exempt, they are under the jurisdiction of the religious superiors. The erection and blessing of these places pertain to these superiors (cf. can. 1156); the consecration, to the Ordinary of the place where they are situated (cf. can. 1155).

Superiors are, therefore, responsible for the proper administration and government of their cemeteries. Hence they are obliged to see that the cemetery is properly closed on all sides and carefully guarded (can. 1210). It is their duty to take care that epitaphs, inscriptions, and adornments contain nothing which is discordant with Catholic faith or piety (can. 1211). Exhumation is not allowed without their consent, which may be given only when the body in question can certainly be distinguished from other bodies (can. 1214).[1] They should not permit burials, especially in cases of sudden death, until sufficient time has elapsed to remove every vestige of doubt as to the reality of the death (can. 1213).[2]

With the consent of the major or local superior, the faithful may arrange for their own special burial places, which, with the same authorization, they may likewise alienate (can. 1209, § 1). "Alienation is, of course, here to be understood of a conveyance for burial purposes," as Augustine points out (Augustine, VI, can. 1209, § 1).[3] Finally, superiors are obliged to see that the prescriptions of law concerning the registration of death, and the denial of burial, are faithfully observed (cf. cc. 1238–1242).[4]

---

[48] Cf. Pejska, p. 328.

[49] Cf. Clem. V, decree quoted above, n. I; Clem. X, Br., Jan. 18, 1672, and Br., Aug. 3, 1672; Clem. XI, June 3, 1716; see Reiff., tit. *De Sepulturis,* n. 31; Many, *De Locis Sacris,* 157; Coronata, *De Locis* etc., 139.

[50] Cf. Ferraris, v. *Sepultura,* 142; Many, *De Locis Sacris,* 157.

[1] Cf. c. 12, X, *de sepulturis,* III, 28; see Coronata, *De Locis* etc., 151.

[2] Cf. S. Off., Sutchuen, Apr. 10, 1777, ad 2; S.C.P.F., Mar. 21, 1774; *Rit. Rom.,* tit. VI, c. 1, *de exsequiis,* n. 3; see Coronata, *De Locis* etc., 150.

[3] Cf. Woywod, II, 1240.

[4] For provisions of civil law in the United States affecting cemeteries owned by ecclesiastical corporations, consult Zollman, *American Church Law,* pars. 433–443.

II. FUNERAL SERVICES OF EXEMPT RELIGIOUS

Funeral services in general consist of three elements: transfer of the body to the church; service over the body in the church; and interment in a cemetery legitimately established for the burial of the faithful departed (can. 1204).

Funerals of religious men are regulated by canons 1221 and 1222, and those of religious women by canon 1230, § 5.

A. *Funerals of Religious Men*
1. TRANSFER OF A BODY TO THE CHURCH OR ORATORY

At death a professed religious or novice, must be translated for the funeral service to the church or oratory of his own religious house, or at least to a church or oratory of the institute, except the novice will have selected another church for his funeral service; but the right of removing the body and having it borne to the church for the funeral service always belongs to the religious superior (can. 1221, § 1).

The classes of persons governed by this law are clearly determined by the Code.

PROFESSED RELIGIOUS AND NOVICES

Only religious superiors, not pastors or local Ordinaries, have the right to remove and transfer the bodies of professed religious and novices. This rule applies to exempt and nonexempt novices. This term "professed" embraces all religious who have pronounced vows, whether temporary or perpetual. Other persons are not permitted to interfere or to claim compensation for unauthorized participation in such services.[5]

If the deceased belongs to a *lay order of men,* the superior must ordinarily designate some priest, v.g., the chaplain, to exercise his right, since generally speaking such a superior is not himself a priest. If he were, he could exercise the function, and, it seems certain, he may always designate a priest of his order to do so.

Funerals of *exclaustrated religious* and of *fugitives* and *apostates* from religion, are regulated by the cited canon, since the religious mentioned are still professed of vows (cf. cc. 638, f., 645 § 1).[6] On the contrary, *secularized* and *dismissed* religious, being released from their vows, are governed by the prescriptions of canons 1216–1218, regulating the funerals of secular persons.[7]

Are funerals of *postulants* and of *students in apostolic schools* regulated by the same norms as those of novices?

---

[5] Cf. c. 16, X, V, 31; c. 5, III, 12 in VI; S.C.EE.RR., July 21, 1848, ap. Biz. pp. 563–566: see Many, *De Locis Sacris,* 181, 182; Augustine, VI, can. 1221.

[6] Cf. Piat, II, p. 314; Coronata, *De Locis* etc., 176.

[7] Cf. Ferraris, v. *Sepultura,* 47; Many, *De Locis Sacris,* 180; Piat, II, 314; Coronata, *De Locis* etc., 176.

Both before and since the promulgation of the Code, some authors have answered this question affirmatively.[8] However, when the Code Commission was asked whether the prescription of canon 1221 extended also to postulants and to students of apostolic schools in religious institutes, *it replied in the negative*.[9] After this authentic reply, there can be no further dispute on the matter.

According to M. a Coronata,[10] funerals of *secular tertiaries* enjoy the same privileges as those of Regulars, and are, therefore, to be conducted in accordance with the prescriptions of canon 1221. He bases his contention on two decisions of the Holy See issued prior to the Code.[11] Coronata is certainly correct, if custom and usage make membership tantamount to a choice by the deceased of the church of the tertiaries as that from which he wishes to be buried, for this would satisfy the requirements of canon 1226, § 1.[12] In other cases, the opinion of this author seems at least probable. However, Piat contends that declarations of the Holy See prove the opposite.[13]

Mere membership in a *confraternity* does not necessarily imply the right on the part of the confraternity to conduct the funeral, for not all confraternities have this right by law.[14]

SERVANTS LIVING IN A RELIGIOUS HOUSE

What has been said of novices applies also to the persons actually employed in the service and permanently dwelling within the precincts of the religious house; but if they die outside the religious house, the funeral must be celebrated according to the prescriptions of canons 1216–1218 (can. 1221, § 3).

To be a servant in the sense employed by the Code, two conditions must be verified: the person must live within the confines of the monastery, in the material or common meaning of the term,[15] and must be actually employed by the religious. No definite period of residence is required; it is sufficient that one has taken up residence and has the intention of remaining indefinitely with the religious.[16]

The difference between the provision for novices and the one for servants consists in this: the body of a novice who died outside the house is to be

---

[8] Cf. Piat, II, 247, nota 5; Many, *De Locis Sacris*, 182; Vermeersch, *De Rel.*, I, 163; Fanfani, *De Jure Religiosorum*, 421; Pejska, p. 330.

[9] Cf. Cod. Com., July 20, 1929, IV, AAS, XXI, 573: see *Per.*, XVIII, 254.

[10] Cf. Coronata, *De Locis* etc., 182.

[11] Cf. S.C.EE.RR., in causa Tricaricen, Mar. 18, 1887; ASS, XXVI, 238 ff.; see also *Monit.*, VIII, part. I, p. 124, and V, part. I, p. 119.

[12] Cf. S.C.C., Resol., May 25, and Nov. 15, 1930, AAS, XXV, 155; Bouscaren, I, can. 1226.

[13] Cf. Piat, II, p. 310, q. 5.

[14] Cf. S.C.C., Resol, May 25, and Nov. 15, 1930, AAS, XXV, 155.

[15] Cf. above, Chap. IX, Art. I, 1.

[16] Cf. Coronata, *De Locis* etc., 179.

removed to a church of the institute, unless the superior decides that this cannot be conveniently done, or the novice has chosen some other church (can. 1221, § 2); the body of a servant who died outside the house is to be cared for in accordance with the prescriptions of canons 1216–1218 (can. 1221, § 3).

It is to be remarked that even if a religious novice die far away from his religious house, his superior always has the right of translating the body to the church of his house or at least of his institute. He must, of course, defray the expenses of the transportation (cf. cc. 1218, 1221). If the superior be unwilling to have the body transported to one of his churches or oratories, the funeral services must take place in the church of the parish where the person died, unless the novice has selected some other church (can. 1221. § 2).

Funerals of guests, boarding students, and the like, are to be conducted according to the provisions regulating the burial of the faithful in general. This is clear from the Code which decrees that the funerals of those who were dwelling in a religious house, even of Regulars, or in a college, by reason of hospitality, education, or infirmity, and of those who die in a hospital, are to be celebrated according to the prescriptions of canons 1216–1218, except a particular law or privilege provides otherwise (can. 1222).[17] The clause safeguarding provisions of particular laws or privileges refers to all the classes of persons specified in the canon. A particular law can be established either by prescription or by custom; a privilege, by concession from the Holy See, or from the local Ordinary for the case under consideration.[18]

2. FUNERAL SERVICES IN THE CHURCH

Professed religious of whatever rank or dignity, except they be Bishops, are not permitted to designate the church from which they are to be buried (can. 1224, 3°); but must be buried from the church of their house or institute (can. 1221). Their superior is the one canonically qualified to perform the funeral services (cf. can. 1230, § 3). The same rule holds for novices and servants who have died in the house, unless they have selected some other church for their burial (cf. can. 1221).[19]

3. INTERMENT

After conducting the services in the church, the superior, or priest designated by him, has the right and duty to accompany the body to the burial place (can. 1231, § 2). This is the rule even when the interment takes place in the common parochial cemetery.[20]

---

[17] Cf. S.C.EE.RR., July 21, 1848; see Ferrari, 78.
[18] Cf. Wernz, I, 160; Coronata, De Locis etc., 181.
[19] Cf. Coronata, op. cit., 191.
[20] Cf. Pejska, p. 330.

B. *Religious Women*

The norms just explained, governing the burial of religious men, are applicable practically in their entirety to the burial of religious women. Before the Code, this was the common teaching of canonists and was based on declarations of the Holy See.[21] The dispositions of the Code concerning religious, even when expressed in the masculine gender, apply equally to religious women, except it appears otherwise from the context and from the nature of the case (can. 490).

Therefore, funerals of nuns, novices, and servants, etc., dwelling within the confines of the monastery, are celebrated according to the following rules.[22]

1. Exempt nuns and their novices, whether they die within or outside their house, are to be removed to the church or oratory of the house, or at least of the institute, for funeral services (cf. cc. 1221, § 2; 490, 1218, 1230, § 5). Canon 1230, § 5, declares that for the funerals of religious women who die outside their house "the general dispositions of the canons are to be observed." This refers to the general dispositions for religious contained in canon 1221, § 2.[23]

2. If the nun or novice dies far away from the religious house and the superior decides that the body of the deceased is not to be translated to one of their churches, funeral services must take place in the church of the parish where she dies, unless, if a novice, she may have selected another church for this purpose.

3. Women who live permanently, not accidentally, within the cloister, either as servants or guests, or for reasons of education or sickness, may choose the church of nuns as their funeral church (can. 1225).

4. For funerals of nuns, the chaplain of the convents conducts the body to the proper church or oratory and celebrates the services (can. 1230, § 5).

III. FUNERALS OF THE FAITHFUL IN EXEMPT CHURCHES AND CEMETERIES

Any Catholic, unless expressly forbidden by law, is free to select the church and cemetery of his funeral (can. 1223). By virtue of canon 1225, the church of Regulars or any other which is entitled to celebrate funeral services may be chosen. The church of nuns may be chosen by those only who live permanently within the enclosure, as servants, guests, the infirm, and persons there for educational purposes (can. 1225).

---

[21] Cf. S.R.C., Mar. 16, 1805, ap. Gard., 4496, III, 50; S.C.EE.RR., May 30, 1856, ap. Biz., 648; Sept. 17, 1858, ap. Biz., 657; S.C.C., Feb. 24, 1872, ap. ASS, VII, 167; Aug. 12, 1872, ap. N.R.T., V, 235: see Tamb., IV, XXXIV, 1; Piat, II, p. 310, q. 6; Vermeersch, *De Rel.*, I, 485; Cappello, *De Visitatione SS. Liminum*, etc., II, p. 227.

[22] Cf. Coronata, *De Locis*, etc., 177, p. 172, nota 4; Creusen, 154; Pejska, p. 331; Melo, p. 65.

[23] Cf. Coronata, *De Locis etc.*, 177, p. 172, nota 4.

This choice may be made by a person either directly or by another authorized by him to act in his stead; the proof of the choice and of the authority given to the agent to make it may be established in any legitimate manner (can. 1226). Heirs and relatives, for example, are legitimate witnesses concerning the fact of the choice made by the deceased, and concerning the fact that he authorized others to make the choice for him. Manifestly, a signed statement left by the deceased is sufficient evidence of his choice. But it does not follow that if the deceased made no choice and authorized no one else to make it for him, the heirs, relatives, or anyone else may, as it were, supply the omission, or exercise the choice without showing any authority to do so. If that were true, such choice could be exercised by relatives in every case, thus imperiling the very rights of the pastor, which the Code wishes to protect (cf. can. 1216).[24]

The one instance in which the law allows persons any independence to choose for another is defined in canon 1224, 1°, whereby parents are accorded the right to select the church and cemetery for the funerals of their children who die before the age of puberty.

Even when choice of a Regular or other church exempt from the jurisdiction of the pastor has been made, the proper pastor of the deceased has the right to conduct the body from the house to the church where services are to be held, according to the norm set down in canon 1230, § 3.

It should be noted that a person may select the church in which the funeral is to take place, or the cemetery of burial, or both. These selections are quite separable.

Canon 1231, § 2, declares it to be the right and duty of the priest who conducts the funeral to accompany the remains to the burial ground, except in case of grave necessity, and canon 1232 permits him, in doing so, to pass in procession through the parishes without special permission.[25]

Worthy of remark is the fact that the church which the faithful may choose is one pertaining to a Regular institute, not a religious congregation, even though exempt, unless the latter enjoys a special privilege to bury secular persons (can. 1225).[26]

Although the faithful may choose the cemetery of Regulars for burial, they require the permission of the religious superior to execute this right. The constitutions will determine which superior is competent in this respect. No other authorization is needed (cf. cc. 1209, § 1; 1228, § 2).

In order that abuses might be avoided, the secular and religious clergy are strictly forbidden to induce anyone to vow, swear, or otherwise promise, with or without an oath, to select their church or cemetery for the funeral

---

[24] Cf. S.C.C., Resol., July 9, 1921, AAS, XIII, 534; *Per.*, X, 354; Bouscaren, I, can. 1223.
[25] Cf. S.C.C., Resol., Apuana, Nov. 12, 1927, AAS, XX, 142; *Per.*, XVII, 136; Bouscaren, I, can. 1230.
[26] Cf. Pejska, p. 332.

or to have them change a selection already made. Violation of this precept will render any choice null and void (can. 1227). This provision is derived from the former decree of Boniface VIII.[27]

Except for a grave and just reason approved by the local Ordinary, the pastor has no right to prevent religious, or pious societies such as confraternities, when the family or heirs wish to invite them, from accompanying the body of the deceased to the church and to the cemetery, and assisting at the funeral (can. 1233, § 1).[28]

IV. FUNERAL FEES

Two distinct fees are spoken of in law, the funeral tax levied on the faithful, and the parochial portion of that tax which is due to the pastor of the deceased.

A. *Funeral Tax*

Local Ordinaries are obliged to draw up for their territories a list of funeral taxes or alms, if such does not already exist, having due regard for lawful custom and the particular circumstances of all persons and places subject to them (can. 1234, § 1).

All are strictly forbidden to exact taxes in excess of those specified in the diocesan list (can. 1235, § 1). The Code Commission has declared that even exempt religious are bound by the schedule of funeral taxes mentioned in canon 1234.[29]

Prior to this authentic interpretation, which seems extensive in character, the opposite opinion appeared preferable, namely that Regulars were not bound by the diocesan schedule, because they are *not expressly* mentioned in canon 1224 (cf. can. 615), as they are, for example, in the prescriptions regulating manual Mass (cf. can. 831, § 3), and seminary taxes (can. 1536, § 1). Hence, the decision of the Commission seems based on the end of the law, that is, the avoidance of scandal and disputes, rather than on the words of the canon itself.[30]

B. *The Parochial Portion*

The parochial portion must be given the pastor of the deceased, if the funeral is not held in the parish church. In two instances, the portion is not to be paid, namely, when the body cannot be conveniently brought to the proper parish, or when a particular law exempts from such payment (can. 1236, § 1). Money for payment of the parochial portion is to be taken

---

[27] Cf. c. 1, *de sepulturis*, III, 12, in VI: see also, c. 3, *de poenis*, V, 8, in Clem.; S.C.EE.RR., May 15, 1590; S.C.C., July 13, and Aug. 3, 1743, ad. 6, 7.
[28] Cf. Melo, p. 164; Augustine, VI, can. 1233.
[29] Cf. Cod. Com., Reply, Mar. 6, 1927, ad II, AAS, XIX, 161.
[30] Cf. Vermeersch, *Per.*, XVI, p. 59; Schäfer, 476.

solely from the entire offerings fixed by diocesan tariff for funeral services and burial (can. 1237, § 1).

The portion must be paid by Regulars for the funerals of the faithful celebrated in their churches. Nevertheless, many religious Orders are exempt from this obligation of paying the parochial portion. Carmelites,[31] Friars Minor,[32] Friars Preachers,[33] and by communication of privileges, all mendicants[34] enjoy exemptive privileges in this matter.[35] Furthermore, in some places, as in many parts of France, custom and legitimate prescription exempt churches from these payments.[36]

---

[31] Cf. Paul V, Const., *Decet Romanum,* Aug. 20, 1605.

[32] Cf. S.C.EE.RR., Sept. 9, 1709, ap. *An. J.P.,* XIV, col. 204, n. 1137.

[33] Cf. S.C.EE.RR., April, 1709, ap. *An. J.P.,* XIV, col. 202, n. 1134.

[34] Cf. Woywod, II, 1266.

[35] Cf. Piat, II, p. 326, nota 3; Many, *De Locis Sacris,* 203; Coronata, *De Locis* etc., 249; Melo, pp. 163, 164.

[36] Cf. Many, *De Locis Sacris,* 203; Melo, p. 163.

The Exemption of Things

PRELIMINARY NOTIONS

The Church has in general granted exempt institutes the right to employ the means which are necessary and useful to fulfill the ends for which they were established. In the present section we shall endeavor to determine the extension of exemption which religious enjoy in the use of these various means. Comformably with the terminology of the Third Book of the Code, we classify these means as "things," and discuss them in the order followed in the Code.

Before entering upon a detailed investigation of the subject, it is useful to recall that exempt religious generally enjoy a *passive* exemption, whereby they are withdrawn from the jurisdiction of local Ordinaries and given independent and inviolable jurisdictional rights over all matters pertaining to their institute.[1] Superiors are vested with ecclesiastical jurisdiction. By means of this power they govern the spiritual and temporal affairs of their institutes, provinces, houses, and religious subjects, in accordance with the norms set down in common law, the constitutions and the special privileges accorded them. Local Ordinaries have jurisdictional authority over exempt religious in those matters only which are expressly mentioned in law (can. 615). Hence exemption does not directly provide the religious with any freedom or immunity in their administrations to the faithful. Their status in this respect is like that of the diocesan clergy. As will be seen, however, in the chapters that follow, even in their spiritual works among the people they do enjoy definite immunities from diocesan authority, but this is due chiefly to positive canonical provisions (cf., v.g., can. 497, § 2) and special privileges rather than to exemptive rights.

General exemption in the spiritual and temporal affairs of their institute is clearly testified to in many declarations of the Holy See and in the works of canonists.

Different Roman Pontiffs have asserted that full and inviolable power of ruling and governing the temporal and spiritual affairs of their mon-

---

[1] Cf. above, Chap. II.

asteries ("plena et libera potestas regendi et gubernandi monasterium in temporalibus et spiritualibus") has been committed to Regulars.[2] Sixtus IV stated[3] that jurisdiction in the Dominican Order is: "magisterii officium plane et libere in omnibus"; and that all clerical exempt Orders have: "omnimodam jurisdictionem ordinariam in spiritualibus et temporalibus."[4] In explaining the exemption of the Society of Jesus, Paul III says, "Ipsamque Societatem et universos illius socios et personas illorumque bona quaecumque, ab omni superioritate, jurisdictione, correctione quorumcumque Ordinariorum eximimus, et liberamus, ac sub nostra et praefatae Sedis protectione suscipimus."[5] Paul V, speaking of the authority of Regular superiors declared: "in spiritualibus et temporalibus . . . supremam jurisdictionem."[6] This same extensive scope of jurisdiction and hence of independence of Regulars from other authorities is likewise clear from documents which assert that religious superiors have that power in their order which Bishops have in their dioceses. Thus, Paul V[7] says: "Ipsi per seipsos possunt in *fratres et moniales* . . . sibi subditos, quod possunt episcopi in laicos sibi subditos, tam quoad absolvendi et dispensandi hujusmodi, quam alias quascumque facultates, eadem facultate et tenore etiam perpetuo concedimus, et indulgemus ac etiam declaramus."[8]

It will be seen in the chapters which follow that the Code has made no essential change in the discipline just described.[9]

In this section there is a natural division of the matter into spiritual and material or temporal things. This classification is time honored and has been adopted by the Code.[10] Much has already been said about the exclusive jurisdiction of superiors over spiritual matters pertaining to their own institutes and religious subjects. We, therefore, confine the remaining preliminary remarks to those spiritual affairs which bear a direct relationship to the faithful; and we offer, at the end, a few general notions about temporal matters.

---

[2] The force of the formula quoted is found in c. 42, I, 6, in VI: see also Molitor, 184.

[3] Cf. Sixtus IV, Const., *Regimini universalis*, par. 1, Aug. 31, 1474.

[4] Cf. Sixtus IV, const., *Sedes Apostolica*, par. 5, May 27, 1474.

[5] Cf. Paul III, *Licet debitum*, Oct. 18, 1549; concerning the same Order consult also: Pope Pius VII, Br., *Catholicae Fidei*, Mar. 7, 1801; Br., *Per alias*, July 30, 1804; Const., *Solicitudo*, Aug. 7, 1814; Leo XIII, Br., *Dolemus inter*, July 13, 1886; Pius XI, *Paterna caritas*, Mar. 12, 1933, confirming all privileges except those expressly revoked by the Code, AAS, XXV, pp. 245, 246.

[6] Cf. Paul V, Const., *Ad Immarcessibilem*, par. 3, Feb. 13, 1567: see also, Molitor, nn. 159, 184; Cappello, *De Visitatione SS. Liminum*, etc., II, pp. 405 ff.

[7] Cf. Paul V, Const., *Romani Pontificis*, par. 3, July 21, 1571.

[8] Cf. also: c. 3, V, 7, in VI; Suarez, *De Rel.*, tr. VIII, L. 2, cap. 9, nn. 3, 4; Reiff. L. V, t. 7, par. 9, nn. 417 ff.; Wernz, III, 683; Piat, I, 563; Pell., IX, III, 6; Donatus, II, I, X, III; Vermeersch, *De Rel.*, I, 415; Molitor, 181-183.

[9] See also above, Chaps. II–VI.

[10] In Book III, the first three parts deal with spiritual affairs, the fourth part, with benefices which are mixed in character containing both spiritual and temporal elements and with temporal ecclesiastical goods.

SPIRITUAL THINGS

Most religious, like secular priests, are destined by their state of life to undertake an active apostolate for the salvation of souls. By vocation members of noncontemplative institutes are occupied in administering the sacraments, preaching, teaching, and practically all other spiritual and charitable functions connected with the supernatural end of the Church.

False theories have often opposed and done harm to the ministry of religious. Some have maintained that religious should not engage in those ministries which are exercised by secular priests. (For a refutation, consult Letters of Leo XIII, Dec. 23, 1900, July 10, 1901.) Others, through excessive zeal for diocesan and parochial organizations and activities, have cast suspicion on the works and even the status of religious. It has been stated that religious occupied in the sacred ministries and the care of souls are but auxiliaries of the secular clergy and should be thus employed only so long as there remains a deficiency of the latter.[11] Statements occasionally made would lead one to believe that persons who participate in activities or devotions conducted by Regulars are doing something abnormal, less Catholic, individualistic, or, at least not in harmony with the strict plan and organization of the Church. Authors of such assertions have declared that there exist but three grades of jurisdictional or administrative authority: the Church universal, the diocese, and the parish. Accordingly, the proponents of such theories maintain that the works of Regulars are at best tolerated, for, as they claim they lie on the border or even outside the hierarchial order and plan adopted by the Church.[12]

What is the true status of religious with respect to these sacred ministries?

1. Aptitude of religious for these functions: The Church has always held that the religious state itself in nowise prevents its followers from exercising such clerical ministries as the care of souls, the administration of the sacraments, etc., or from assuming prelacies in the ecclesiastical hierarchy. She condemned the contrary doctrine as false, pernicious, and injurious to the teaching of the Fathers, and contrary to her pious, ancient and approved tradition and to declarations of the Sovereign Pontiffs.[13] Leo XIII wrote in the same sense to Cardinal Richard, Archbishop of Paris.[14]

---

[11] Cf. Verhoeven, ap. De Buck-Tinnebroech, *op. cit.,* 400.

[12] For refutation of these theories consult Creusen, *N.R.T.,* 55, pp. 492 ff.

[13] Cf. Pius VI, Const., *Auctorem fidei,* 1794, Condemnation of Proposition 80 of the Council of Pistoia.

[14] "Scopus votorum religiosorum duplex est: primo eos qui hujusmodi vota emittunt, ad altius perfectionis gradum erigere; deinde ipsos praeparare, eorum mentes purificando et roborando, ad externum ministerium in salutem aeternam proximi et levamentum tantarum generis humani miseriarum. Sic laborando sub suprema Sedis Apostolicae auctoritate. . . . Instituta religiosa plurimum ad divinam Ecclesiae missionem cooperantur, quae in sanctificandis animis et bono hominum consistit." N. 2, Dec. 28, 1900, ap. Vermeersch, *De Rel.,* II, pp. 46–56; Fine, p. 787; cf. also, *Epist.,* June 29, 1901, ap. Vermeersch, *op. cit.,* II, pp. 57–65.

Reason itself, and the statements of the Holy See just cited, show that religious, above all, are especially well equipped for the sacred ministries. "For," as St. Thomas asserts, "it is foolish to say that a man is rendered less fit for spiritual duties through advancing himself in holiness; and consequently it is a foolish opinion of those who declare that the religious state is an obstacle to the fulfillment of suchlike duties" (2. 2ᵃᵉ, q. 187, a. 1).

2. It is the manifest intention of the Holy See that the religious, as well as the secular clergy, should be employed in procuring the salvation of souls through their priestly administrations.[15]

In further proof of this, we have the testimony of all the Roman Pontiffs who from early days till the present have approved, confirmed, and praised religious institutes destined for the sacred ministry, and of all those who have encouraged and furthered their work by extending to these religious special means for helping the faithful, such as privileges, indulgences, and extraordinary faculties.

The very essence, too, of clerical institutes requires their members to undertake works for souls.[16]

In the case of Orders of Canons or Clerics Regular, the *clerical state* constitutes the specific nature of their organization; the rule or religious constitution is but an element added to the former, and not vice versa.[17]

TEMPORAL THINGS

As has been seen, exemptive rights extend to temporal goods. Temporal goods include all external objects that have an economic value, that is to say, a value in use or exchange which can be computed in money, e.g., land, buildings, furniture, personal annuities, stocks, shares, patents, copyrights, and the like.[18] The word "goods" employed by the Code is a very broad term embracing every class of lawful acquisition which a person can own or have an interest in.

The exemption of temporal goods touches questions both of ownership and of administration of property. It involves, too, the goods of individual religious and of moral corporations.

As will be explained in Chapter XVI, the rights of exempt religious, independently of local Ordinaries, to acquire, own, and administer temporal goods are far reaching. There exist but few cases of exception to this type of exemption.

Division of the subject matter of Section III is as follows: Chapters XII-

---

[15] For direct references consult Melot, *De Habilitate Regularium Ad Munera Ecclesiastica*, ap. Vermeersch, *De Rel.*, II, Suppl. VIII.

[16] Cf. Greg. XIII, Const., *Ascendente Domino*, May 25, 1584; also Vermeersch, *De Rel.*, I, 54, 55, 77, 78, 493; De Buck-Tinnebroech, *op. cit.*, cap. VIII, especially pp. 417 ff.

[17] Cf. *Epit.*, I, 586.

[18] Cf. Laymann, *Theol. Mor.*, L. IV, tr. V, c. VII, 3; Creusen, 155.

XIV treat of spiritual things; Chapter XV of mixed[19] things, that is, matters containing spiritual and temporal elements; Chapter XVI of ecclesiastical temporal goods.

[19] In law "mixed things" are objects that can be or are both spiritual and temporal in character, as, e.g., benefices, or sacred utensils which have been blessed or consecrated. *Per se* things of this kind have an economic value independently of both their spiritual purpose and their blessing or consecration. Because, therefore, they are composed of spiritual and temporal elements they are called "mixed things" (cf. can. 726).

CHAPTER XII

THE SACRAMENTS

In the Church, power over sacramentary functions resides in the ecclesiastical hierarchy. No one, therefore, may administer the sacraments unless he has received legitimate deputation to do so. As a result priests of exempt institutes cannot lawfully perform these sacred ministries without first obtaining the requisite faculty or permission.[1] The source of this faculty or permission, and the consequent subjection of exempt religious to higher authority, varies, depending on whether the sacraments are to be administered to members of their institute, or to other persons.

1. With Regard to Members of Exempt Institutes

In exempt clerical institutes, the celebration and administration of sacraments for the benefit of the religious or members of the household (can. 514) are under the authority of the religious Ordinaries and other superiors.[2] Regulars enjoy full exemption in this respect.[3]

Likewise in the administration of the sacraments in their oratories and churches, not burdened with the care of souls, Regulars are exempt from the jurisdiction of local Ordinaries (can. 615). From this it follows that these sacred functions in such places are not subject to the canonical visitation of local Ordinaries. Hence, too, altars, shrines, or confessionals, even though they be for the use of the faithful in general, enjoy the same immunity[4] (cf. cc. 344, § 2; 511; 512; 615). Furthermore, local Ordinaries cannot issue prescriptions affecting the time, place, or persons involved in the

---

[1] Cf. Suarez, *Opera Omnia,* 20, p. 297; Cappello, *De Sacramentis,* I, 63.

[2] Cf. Barbosa, Trid. XXV, Regul. XI, 21; Cesp. CXXV, 2 sq.; Tamb., Tom. III, Disp. V, q. XI, 46; Piat, II, p. 24.

[3] S.C.C., 1623, with the approbation of Urban VIII, "Censuit, nequaquam subjicere Regulares exemptos, quibus animarum saecularium cura non incumbit, jurisdictioni Episcoporum in his quae Sacramentorum administrationem concernunt, nisi cum in Sacramentis administrandis personis saecularibus iidem Regulares delinquent. Similiter constituit, non licere in vim supradictae constitutionis Episcopo visitare altare Ecclesiarum Regularium, quibus non incumbit animarum cura personarum saecularium, nec loca ubi in iisdem ecclesiis asservatur Sanctissimum Eucharistiae Sacramentum, vel ubi confessiones personarum saecularium audiuntur" (Tamb., *loc. cit.*).

[4] Cf. S. C. Rel., Resp., Aug. 3, 1915; Cod. Com., Aug. 8, 1924 (a private reply by the president of the Commission, Card. Gasparri); see also, Tamb., *loc. cit.;* Ferraris, v, *Regulares,* a. 3, n. 4; W.-V., III, 402; Schäfer, 97b; Prümmer, Q. 187; C.p.R., VIII, p. 446.

confessions heard by Regulars, in their nonparochial churches.[5] Nor can they restrict or alter any privileges enjoyed by these religious in the celebration or administration of the sacraments.[6]

2. With Regard to Others

Regulars exercising these ministries in parishes and places other than the above mentioned, are subject to the jurisdiction, visitation, and correction of the local Ordinary. Pastors and their assistants are governed by this Ordinary in all matters, with the sole exception of religious discipline (can. 631).[7] The same is true of Regulars in charge of mission stations.[8]

Exemptive rights of Regulars vary in the administration of the different sacraments. It will be useful, therefore, to consider each sacrament separately.

ARTICLE I. BAPTISM

The priest is the ordinary minister of baptism. However, exempt religious, unless they be entrusted with the care of souls may not administer this without the authorization of the pastor or local Ordinary (can. 738, § 1).

No reason need be had by the one who petitions or the one who grants this faculty.[9] Pastors, therefore, should not embarrass or estrange their parishioners by uncalled-for refusals. For cases of necessity, it is always lawful to presume authorization (can. 738, § 1).[10]

Churches of Regulars which by statute, privilege, or custom have acquired a right to a baptismal font, retain the same cumulatively with the parish church. Blat defines this cumulative right as one whereby the faithful might lawfully be baptized at such a font as well as in their own parish churches.[11] Churches can no longer have exclusive right to a font in preference to other parish churches.[12]

ARTICLE II. CONFIRMATION

The only ordinary minister of Confirmation is a Bishop (can. 782).[13]

By law, abbots and prelates "nullius" may administer this sacrament, but only within the boundaries of their territories and during their term of office (can. 782, § 3). Regulars and other priests laboring on the missions

---

[5] Cf. Tamb., *loc. cit.*
[6] Barbosa, *loc. cit.,* Tamb., *loc. cit.;* Piat, II, p. 25.
[7] Cf. Conc. Trid., sess. XXV, cap. 11, *de Regul.;* Greg. XV, Const., *Inscrutabile,* par. 4, Feb. 5, 1622; Bened. XIV, Const., *Firmandis,* par. 3, 9, 10; Nov. 6, 1744, S.C.P.F., May 13, 1839, ap. Coll. P.F., 886 and 348.
[8] Cf. Leo XIII, Const., *Romanos Pontifices;* Vromant II, 280.
[9] Cf. W.-V., IV, Vol. I, 32.
[10] Cf. Can. 462; *Rit. Rom.,* II, c. 1, n. 12.
[11] Cf. Blat, *De Rebus,* I, 64.
[12] Cf. Cod. Com., Nov. 12, 1922; AAS, XIV, 662; Bouscaren, I, can. 774.
[13] Conc. Trid., sess. VII, *de Confirm.,* can. 3.

are sometimes granted this faculty, but in the exercise thereof they must always use chrism blessed by a Catholic Bishop (can. 781, § 1).[14]

A Bishop may administer the sacrament of confirmation in any, even an exempt, place within the confines of his territory (can. 792).[15] According to this law, Augustine well says that the exempt places are monasteries, convents, academies, churches, chapels, and the like, of exempt religious or other persons, but not exempt territories of abbots or prelates nullius.[16]

ARTICLE III. THE HOLY EUCHARIST

In discussing the extension and restriction of the exemptive rights of Regulars, with respect to matters pertaining to the Holy Eucharist, we shall follow the order employed by the Code.[17]

THE HOLY SACRIFICE OF THE MASS

The celebrant

Regulars are free from the jurisdiction of local Ordinaries with regard to the celebration of Mass in their churches and oratories (cc. 615, 1171, 1191).[18]

The Holy See desires that special precaution be taken when there is question of the celebration of Mass by strangers, even in churches of Regulars. The Council of Trent recommended that Bishops forbid strange or unknown priests to say Mass within the confines of their territories,[19] unless they showed letters of recommendation from their own Bishops.[20] Some authors maintained that such prohibitions would be binding on churches pertaining to religious Orders even though these churches were not in character parochial.[21] However, no authorization was needed by Regulars who wished to say Mass in churches of their own order, or in those of nuns subject to the same.[22]

A Regular having commendatory letters from his superior could be permitted to offer the Holy Sacrifice in any secular or religious church, provided diocesan statutes did not decree otherwise.[23] A secular priest could not be

---

[14] Cf. S.C.P.F., May 4, 1774, ap. Coll., P.F., 502; Bened. XIX, *De Syn. Dioec.*, L. VII, c. 8, nn. 1–2; Noldin, III, n. 86; see Augustine, IV, can. 782, Woywod, *A Practical Com.*, I, 681.
[15] Cf. Bened. XIV, Const., *"Firmandis,"* June 10, 1603.
[16] Augustine, IV, *loc. cit.*
[17] Book III, Part I, tit. III.
[18] Cf. Clement IV, Const., *Virtute Conspicuos,* par. 8, July 21, 1265; Sixtus IV, Const., *Regimini,* Aug. 31, 1474; Paul III, Const., *Licet Debitum,* Oct. 18, 1549; Greg. XIII, Const., *Decet Romanum,* May 3, 1575; see also Ferraris, v, *Oratorium,* 72; Piat, II, p. 230.
[19] Cf. Sess. XXII, *de observandis,* etc.
[20] Cf. Sess. XXIII, *de Reform.* cap. 16.
[21] Cf. Fine, p. 838.
[22] Cf. Bened. XIV, Const., *Quam grave,* par. 12, Aug. 2, 1757.
[23] Cf. Piat, II, p. 239.

granted this permission unless he were known or had commendatory letters from his local Ordinary.[24]

In the case of certain orders, like the Carthusian, the Society of Jesus, and the Dominican, special privileges were granted by the Holy See enabling them to permit any worthy priest to say Mass without the authorization required by law.[25] Since the legislation of the Code on this matter contains no revocatory clause, these grants are still in force.

Present legislation

The law of the Code is practically the same as that just described. If a stranger wishes to celebrate Mass, he must have the *celebret* (commendatory letters) from his Ordinary or his religious superior. One without a *celebret* may be given permission if he is known to be a priest in good standing. Even though unknown to the rector of a church, he may be allowed the privilege once or twice, provided he wears the ecclesiastical garb, accepts nothing from the church for saying Mass, and enters his name, office, and diocese in the book kept for that purpose (can. 804, §§ 1, 2).

Any special diocesan regulations on this point which are not contrary to the prescriptions of the canon last cited, must be observed by all, including exempt religious, unless they say Mass in a church of their own Order (can. 804, § 3). Norms issued by a local Ordinary which are opposed to the provisions of this general law are null and void. Thus, no Ordinary could prevent priests not possessing a *celebret* from saying Mass, nor demand that the *celebret* be first submitted to the chancery office before its holder be allowed to offer up the Holy Sacrifice.[26]

Should a Regular wish to say Mass in a church not belonging to his institute, he is bound, as formerly, by both general and particular laws governing such cases.[27]

Time and place for celebrating Mass

1. Time

The Sacrifice of the Mass may be offered up on all days except those excluded by the proper rite of the celebrant (can. 820).

Mass must not be said outside of the hours specified in law, namely, it is not to be started earlier than an hour before dawn, nor later than an hour after noon (can. 821).

---

[24] Cf. Bened. XIV, *Quam grave*, par. 10.
[25] Cf. Bened. XIV, Const., *Exponi nobis*, 1755.
[26] Cf. Cappello, *De Sacr.*, I, 737.
[27] Cf. Augustine, IV, can. 804; Ayrinhac, *Legislation on the Sacraments*, 69.

For a just reason, the local Ordinary may determine the hours of services in all nonexempt churches (can. 1171). He may, therefore, take such measures in order to settle controversies, to arouse and augment the piety of the faithful, or to procure a better attendance at Mass.[28] It is plain from this law and from several decisions of the Holy See that the local Ordinary cannot fix the hours of Masses in churches or public oratories of exempt religious.[29] On the other hand, religious superiors must prevent the services in their churches from doing harm to the catechetical instruction or the explanation of the Gospel given in the parish church. When there is question of such harm, it is the right of the local Ordinary to pass judgment and the obligation of the religious superior to apply the proper remedy (can. 609, § 3); i.e., the latter must either change the hours of Mass, or give the same instructions offered in the parish church.[30]

Local Ordinaries cannot interfere with the concessions made by general law or privilege to Regulars.

By virtue of apostolic privileges, Regulars, and many other religious, may commence Mass two hours before dawn and two hours after midday.[31] Under certain conditions, some also have the privilege of starting Mass two hours after midnight.[32] Redemptorists and others to whom this privilege has been communicated, can commence Mass three hours after noon.[33] Since the promulgation of the Code, the Congregation of the Blessed Sacrament has been given most extensive faculties for this matter.[34]

In harmony with the ancient and widespread practice of celebrating midnight Mass on Christmas,[35] the Code grants leave to start the conventual or parochial Mass at midnight on this day. In the conventual or parochial churches, these designated Masses are the only ones permitted at that hour, unless fuller rights have been ceded by Apostolic indult (can. 821, § 2). Only in particular cases, and because of grave reasons, such as local abuses,[36] may the Ordinary of the place forbid the parochial or conventual midnight Mass, for the right to celebrate them being a concession of common law is not committed entirely to his discretionary measures.[37]

---

[28] Cf. Cappello, *De Sacr.*, I, 796.

[29] Cf. S.C.C., Oct. 6, 1625; S.C.P.F., Jan. 26, 1688; ap. *Coll.*, P.F., 166; see also Augustine, VI, can. 1171; Coronata, II, 742; Ayrinhac, *Administrative Legislation*, 20.

[30] Cf. Ayrinhac, *Administrative Legislation*, 20; Coronata, II, 742; *Epit.*, I, 611.

[31] Given by Pius VI, 1783, and later declared authentic by Cardinal Prefect of S.C.EE.RR., 1834; see Fine, p. 860; Gasparri, *De Sanct. Euch.*, 113; Piat, II, pp. 233–234; Ferrari, 94; *Epit.*, I, 785, and II, 96; Coronata, I, 619, bis.; Claeys Bouuaert-Simenon, I, 680.

[32] Cf. Clement VIII, Const., *Romanus Pontifex*, Sept. 30, 1592; Gregory XVI, Indult, 1838; see Fine, *loc. cit.*, Piat, II, p. 234; *Epit*, I, 785.

[33] Cf. Fine, p. 860.

[34] Cf. S. C. Sacr., Rescript, Mar. 5, 1928; ap. *Per.*, XVII, p. 139.

[35] Cf. Woywod, I, 720.

[36] Cf. Can. 1261.

[37] Cf. Ayrinhac, *Legislation on the Sacraments*, 106; *Monit.*, 1923, p. 24 (Gennaio).

Religious and pious institutions having a chapel where the Blessed Sacrament is habitually reserved, are permitted to have midnight Mass. Their right in this matter is more extensive than that of the parochial and conventual churches, for by it one priest may say one or three Masses, according to the liturgy of the day. Those who assist at the Holy Sacrifice may, if they wish, receive Holy Communion, and they fulfill their obligation of hearing Mass (can. 821, § 3).

The source of this provision is the "Motu proprio" of Pius X, Aug. 1, 1907. Concessions contained therein, though made to religious and pious institutions, purpose to benefit the *faithful* in general, and public worship. For the Pontiff expressly declares that through this grant he desires to arouse the piety of the faithful and to excite in their souls gratitude for the ineffable mystery of the Incarnation.[38] Keeping in mind this his intention and his explicit mention of the fact that those attending such Masses fulfill their obligation and may receive Holy Communion, it is clear that religious may allow and even invite secular persons to the midnight Mass said in their oratories.[39]

The Code Commission has been asked if canon 867, § 4, when compared with canon 821, § 2, is to be understood in the sense that Holy Communion may be distributed at a Mass which is celebrated at midnight on Christmas, whether according to law or in virtue of an apostolic privilege. The Commission replied that Holy Communion may be distributed in either instance, unless the Ordinary of the place has, for a just cause in particular cases, forbidden it as provided for in canon 869.[40]

When Mass and the other functions are celebrated on Holy Thursday the solemn manner prescribed in liturgical law must be observed. This norm applies to all churches and oratories, even to those pertaining to exempt religious. However, Regulars enjoy certain privileges which form exceptions to this rule. Thus, although the solemnities of Holy Week be omitted, Regular prelates may permit the celebration of a Low Mass in order that Holy Communion may be distributed to the members of their communities. Likewise, even when the solemnities of Holy Week are observed, Regular prelates may permit that a Low Mass be said for the convenience of their infirm subjects. In both the cases mentioned Mass may be celebrated in either the churches or the oratories of these religious, provided that the doors of the churches or of the oratories are closed to the faithful.[41]

---

[38] Cf. *Motu proprio*, cited.
[39] Cf. *Per.*, III, pp. 169, 171.
[40] Col. Com., Mar. 16, 1936, ap. AAS, 28, 179; see Bouscaren, II, can. 867.
[41] Cf. S.R.C., Rescripts: Aug. 31, 1839; Dec. 9, 1899; ap. Vermeersch, *De Rel.*, I, 467, and II, 220; see also Cappello, *De Sacr.*, I, 784; Creusen, 141.

2. Place for Mass

Ancient custom requiring that Mass be said in a church or oratory has been retained by the Code.[42]

Mass, therefore, may be said on a consecrated altar in a church or oratory consecrated or blessed according to the law, and with regard for the prescriptions contained in canon 1196. The major superior of an exempt religious house can grant permission to celebrate Mass outside a church or oratory on a consecrated altar stone in a decent place, but never in a bedroom. The permission here stated can only be given in an extraordinary case, for a just and reasonable cause and by way of act, i.e., not habitually (can. 822).

It is readily inferred that this faculty is rather limited and may only be exercised under the specified conditions, for the Holy See does not look with favor on the celebration of Mass outside the church.[43] The superior's reason for granting it must be inspired by the highest motives connected with divine worship, and the spiritual welfare of the faithful.[44] The jurisdiction of religious superiors in this matter is ordinary and consequently may be delegated to local superiors (can. 199, § 2).[45]

Religious superiors may exercise this faculty independently of local Ordinaries but only for Masses to be said in places pertaining to their exempt religious institute. For other places, the competent superior is the Ordinary of the territory where the Mass is to be celebrated.

Many religious, like Redemptorists, Dominicans, and Jesuits, enjoy more extensive faculties than those granted by canon 822.[46]

Mass stipends

Exempt religious are subject to prescriptions of local Ordinaries regulating manual Mass stipends. They may not demand more than the amount fixed by diocesan decrees or custom (can. 831).[47] If a priest exacts more than the determined tax, he violates not only the law but commutative justice as well, and is bound to make restitution.[48]

A Bishop, however, cannot forbid the offering or the accepting of a sum which exceeds the fixed amount (can. 832).[49]

---

[42] Cf. S. C. Sacr., Reply, May 3, 1926, AAS, XVIII, 388.

[43] Cf. S. C. Sacr., Reply, May 3, 1926, AAS, XVIII, 388.

[44] Cf. S. C. Sacr., Letter, July 26, 1924, AAS, XVI, 370; ap. Bouscaren I, can. 822.

[45] Cf. S. C. Sacr., Reply, Jan. 5, 1928, AAS, XX, 79.

[46] Cf. Greg. XIII, Const., *Usum altaris*, Oct. 1, 1579; Bened. XIV, Const., *Magno cum,* par. 31, 32, Jan. 2, 1751; Leo XII, Const., *Plura inter,* July 11, 1826: see also Piat, II, p. 226; Fine, pp. 855–859.

[47] Cf. Bened. XIV, *De Sacrif. Miss.,* Part II, 89; Many, *De Missa,* 44; Bondini, p. 82.

[48] Cf. Bened. XIV, *De Sacrif. Miss.,* Part II, 189; Many, *loc. cit.,* 46; Cappello, *De Sacr.,* I, 673.

[49] Cf. S.C.C., Jan. 16, 1648; Bened. XVI, *loc. cit.;* Many, *loc. cit.*

Acceptance of stipends smaller than the diocesan tax is allowed so long as this has not been forbidden by the local Ordinary (can. 832).[50] Furthermore, a priest may renounce entirely his right to a stipend and say Mass gratuitously.

Taxes for founded Masses, fixed by local Ordinaries, do not affect exempt religious, for these are regulated by the superiors of their institute (can. 1550).[1]

Superiors and not local Ordinaries have the right and duty to see to it that the Mass obligations of their subjects have been properly fulfilled (cc. 1550 ff.). This legislation is in conformity with previous decrees of the Holy See.[2] The Code states that superiors have this authority in the churches of religious. As no distinction is drawn between churches which are perpetually or temporarily intrusted to religious, both types fall under their jurisdiction.[3]

In his diocesan visitation, a Bishop has no right to inspect the records of either the founded or the manual Masses pertaining to exempt religious, for this office belongs to the religious superior (can. 843, § 2). This holds true for records of the parochial and other churches cared for by these religious (cc. 842, and 1550).[4]

THE HOLY EUCHARIST

The priest alone is the ordinary minister of the Holy Eucharist (can. 845).

Regulars may administer Holy Communion to the faithful in their churches during all the hours and days when the celebration of Mass is permitted.[5] The former restriction, excluding the distribution of Holy Communion in churches of Regulars on Easter Sunday, is no longer in force.[6] Neither pastors nor local Ordinaries can hinder the faithful or Regulars from exercising this freedom given them by law.[7]

Likewise Holy Communion may be distributed to the faithful wherever the celebration of Mass is permitted, even in private oratories, unless for just reasons the local Ordinary has issued a prohibition in particular cases (cc. 869, 846).

---

[50] Cf. S.C.C., July 16, 1689; Bened. XIV, *De Syn. Dioec.*, L. V., c. 9, n. 2.

[1] Cf. S.C.C., Jan. 15, 1698; Bened. XIV, *De Sacrif. Miss.*, Part III, 22, 9; Augustine, IV, can. 831.

[2] Cf. S.C.EE.RR., May 11, 1904; ASS, XXXVI, p. 718; S.C.C., Feb. 27, 1905; ASS, XXXVII, p. 526: see also Cappello, *De Sacr.*, I, 713; Woywod, I, 740.

[3] Cf. Augustine, IV, can. 842.

[4] Cf. S.C.EE.RR., May 11, 1904; see Cappello, *De Sacr.*, I, 714.

[5] Cf. Julius II, Const., *Dudum ad sacrum*, par. 39, July 28, 1506; Paul III, Const., *Dudum felicis*, par. 7, July 25, 1535, and Const., *Licet Debitum*, Oct. 18, 1549; Bened. XIV, Const., *Magno cum animi*, Jan. 2, 1751: S.R.C., Sept. 7, 1816; and Jan. 11, 1904, ASS, XXXVII, p. 109.

[6] Cf. can. 859, par. 3; S.C.C., Nov. 28, 1912, AAS, IV, p. 726; see Woywod, I, 766; Melo, p. 146.

[7] Cf. Pius V, Const., *Etsi mendicantium*, May 16, 1567; S.C.C., Jan. 31, 1682; see Bened. XIV, *De Syn Dioec.*, L. IX, c. 16, n. 3; Piat, II, p. 244; Fine, pp. 840, 841.

From the wording of canon 869, it is manifest that a local Ordinary may by way of act (not habitually) forbid the distribution of Holy Communion, when he has a proportionately just cause. He is not competent, therefore, to effect this through the enactment of a diocesan law, or statute, or general precept, but only through a particular precept, on account of extraordinary circumstances, and merely for the duration of such circumstances.[8]

By virtue of special privileges some Regulars may distribute communion wherever they are allowed to celebrate Mass. This permits them to do this even outside of churches and oratories, when the conditions specified in their privileges are verified.[9]

Communion to the sick

The rights of Regulars are different for public and private administration of the Eucharist to the sick. Only in cases of necessity, or with at least the presumed permission of the pastor or local Ordinary may Regulars carry Holy Communion *publicly* to the sick within a parish (cc. 462, 848). On the other hand, the Church permits any priest, religious or secular, to administer this sacrament privately. In this latter instance, if the priest wishes to take the Blessed Sacrament from a church in the locality, he may presume the permission of the person to whom the custody of the Blessed Sacrament is intrusted (can. 849, § 1). It is to be noted that in the United States, Holy Communion is administered to the sick privately.[10]

Holy Viaticum

The administration of Holy Viaticum, whether public or private, belongs to the pastor alone, without prejudice to the prescriptions of canons 397, 3°, and 514, §§ 1-3 (can. 850). Since this is an exclusive parochial right (can. 462, 3°), outside of cases of necessity an exempt religious cannot exercise it without the pastor's leave.[11]

In clerical religious institutes the right and duty of administering Holy Viaticum to subjects and other persons of the household pertains to the superiors; in a house of nuns to the ordinary confessor or the priest taking his place (can. 514).

First Communion

Before the promulgation of the Code, authors disputed whether the pastor had exclusive right to administer First Communion to his parishoners.[12] Keeping in mind canons 462 and 854, it now seems clear that pastors

---

[8] Cf. Cappello, *De Sacr.*, I, 442; Ayrinhac, *Legislation on the Sacraments*, 160; *Epit.*, II, 111, where Vermeersch limits the restricting power of the Ordinary to private chapels.

[9] Cf. Leo XII, *Plura inter*, July 11, 1826.

[10] Cf. II Conc. Balt., 264; see Woywod, I, 745.

[11] Cf. S.C.P.F., Jan. 13, 1633, Coll. P.F., 73; S.R.C., Jan. 20, 1609, *Decr. Auth.* 271: see Bondini, p. 85.

[12] Cf. Cappello, *De Sacr.*, I, 531.

have not exclusive right to either the simple or solemn administration of First Communion. Hence, a pastor cannot prevent others, such as Regulars, from exercising this function.[13] From this it follows that children who are educated in Catholic schools belonging to religious may receive their First Communion at these institutions.[14]

ARTICLE IV. THE SACRAMENT OF PENANCE

It is a general principle of law that jurisdiction can be directly exercised only over subjects (can. 210, § 1), for it is nothing else than the power of governing subjects. This holds true for jurisdiction of both the internal and external forums, and, as a result, a confessor can absolve penitents only in so far as they are his subjects.

A person is constituted the appropriate subject of an ecclesiastical superior either by the possession of a domicile or quasi-domicile in the latter's territory, or by aggregation in the family of a religious institute.[15]

With respect to the reception of the sacrament of penance, all penitents are now (i.e., by the law of the Code) given the status of inhabitants (incolae) of the place where they confess: hence, by virtue of their confession, they become in this matter the confessor's subjects.

Wherefore priests having ordinary or delegated faculties in a territory may validly and licitly absolve all who come there for confession, whether the penitents be seculars or religious, and whether they be "vagi" or "peregrini" (cc. 881, 874).

From this it is seen that an exempt religious can voluntarily render himself subject to the sacramental jurisdiction of local Ordinaries or their delegates. As a consequence the local Ordinary becomes a superior of the religious in the internal forum over the conscience matters that the latter has submitted to his spiritual government.

At one time confessors for Regulars received jurisdiction and approbation from prelates of their own institute only, not from Bishops.[16] Regulars properly so called were obliged to confess to priests designated by their superiors and, ordinarily, could not be absolved by those outside their Order.[17]

Similarly, members of exempt clerical congregations had to confess to the priests approved by their superiors. Confessions made to others, without the superior's permission, were considered invalid. Only in two cases were these religious able to confess to others: when it was difficult to go to a

---

[13] Cf. Cappello, *loc. cit.*; Woywod, I, 752.
[14] Cf. S.C.EE.RR., Mar. 4, 1908: see Cappello, *loc. cit.*
[15] Cf. Cappello, *De Sacr.*, II, pars I, 377.
[16] Cf. Piat, I, pp. 400 ff.
[17] Cf. Bouix, *De Jure Regul.*, II, pars 5, sect. III, cap. 3; Piat, I, p. 405.

priest approved in their institute; and when superiors granted them permission to do so.

On August 5, 1913, through a decree of the Congregation of Religious, Pius X established new legislation for the confessions of religious which, with few modifications, has been retained by the Code.[18] He laid down the general principle that all religious, without the consent of their superiors, could licitly and validly confess to any priest approved by the local Ordinary, and could be absolved from all sins and censures reserved in their institutes. At the same time he revoked all privileges contrary to this provision which had formerly been granted to Orders and congregations.[19]

I. CONFESSIONS OF RELIGIOUS

A. *Clerical Exempt Institutes*

1. Superiors of exempt clerical institutes have ordinary jurisdiction to hear the confessions of their religious, excluding the nuns subject to them, in accordance with the provisions of their constitution (can. 873, § 2). Unless constitutions state otherwise, this power is possessed by both major and local superiors.[20]

Nevertheless, they may hear the confessions of those subjects only who spontaneously and freely approach them for that purpose, and may not, without grave reason, hear them habitually (can. 518, § 1). Further, they must take care not to induce personally, or through others, by force, by fear or by importunate persuasion, or by other means, any of their subjects to confess his sins to them (can. 518, § 2).

Since their jurisdiction is ordinary, these superiors may delegate others to hear the confessions of the professed members, novices, and other persons specified in canon 514, unless otherwise expressly stated in law (can. 199, § 1). Both previous legislation and that of the Code make it clear that the existence of any express modification of this power will be learned from the constitutions of each religious institute.[21]

This right to delegate facilitates certain ministries. Thus, for example, priests from other dioceses who are engaged in giving seculars a closed retreat in the house of an exempt clerical institute need not seek faculties at the chancery, but may obtain them from the religious superior.[22]

---

[18] Cf. AAS, V, 431.
[19] Cf. Cappello, *De Sacr.*, II, pars I, 433–436.
[20] Cf. Cappello, *De Sacr.*, II, pars I, 386; Melo, p. 58; C.p.R., IV, p. 341.
[21] Cf. Vermeersch, *De Rel.*, I, 416; Schäfer, 166; *Per.*, XVI, pp. 175*, 176*; C.p.R., IV, p. 341.
[22] Cf. Schäfer, *loc. cit.*; *Per.*, XVI, p. 175*; cf. *De Sacr.*, II, pars I, 432. The opinion of Cappello concerning the jurisdiction of these religious over the boarding students attending their schools, seems well founded. He maintains that this jurisdiction remains in force so long as the students are subject to the discipline of the school. Hence, during vacation periods confessors of the school may absolve those who have not graduated, nor been dismissed or withdrawn from the school.

Major and local superiors may likewise grant secular and religious priests of other institutes faculties to absolve their subjects and those of their household (can. 875). To receive or exercise this faculty such priests do not require the approval of the local Ordinary.[23]

This delegated jurisdiction generally includes faculties to absolve from sins and censures reserved in the institute, but not from diocesan reservations.[24]

2. Local Ordinaries have ordinary jurisdiction to hear the confessions of all in their territories, even of exempt religious (can. 873, § 1).

They may delegate this to any priest, secular or religious.[25] One who has received such delegation may absolve religious from sins and censures reserved in their institute, so long as the censures are not "ab homine" (for absolution from "ab homine" censures, consult Cappello, *De Censuris*, 113). Manifestly these absolutions are valid only in the internal forum, so that a superior, if he deems it necessary, may refuse to recognize them in the external forum.[26]

Local Ordinaries may confer faculties on exempt religious even against the wish of religious superiors. Religious, however, may not use faculties received from a local Ordinary without at least the presumed permission of their superiors, due allowance, however, being made for the case provided for in canon 519 (can. 874, § 1).

Canon 519 grants religious most extensive freedom in the choice of confessors. The words of the law place this fact beyond dispute.

"Without prejudice to the constitutions which prescribe confession to be made at stated times or counsel that it be made to designated confessors, if any religious, even the exempt, have recourse, for the peace of his conscience, to any confessor approved by the local Ordinary, even though not one of the number of the designated confessors, that confession, every contrary privilege being revoked, is valid and lawful, and the confessor may absolve the religious even from sins and censures reserved in the institutes" (can. 519).

B. *Exempt Lay Institutes*

In exempt lay institutes superiors propose the confessors, who, however, must receive jurisdiction from the Ordinary of the place in which the religious house is situated (can. 875).

Nevertheless, privileges contrary to this prescription are not revoked by the Code. Therefore, former papal concessions to lay Orders which empowered their priests and the chaplains designated by superiors to absolve

---

[23] Cf. Melo, p. 58; Cappello, *De Sacr.*, II, pars I, 418, 430.
[24] Cf. Cappello, *loc. cit.*, 418.
[25] Cf. Cappello, *De Sacr.*, II, pars I, 416.
[26] Cf. Cappello, *De Sacr.*, II, pars I, 417.

subjects and others of the household, remain in force.[27] This jurisdiction, it should be remarked, is in no way dependent upon the local Ordinary. The Order of St. John of God is an example of institutes possessing such faculties. Any priest designated by the Prior can hear the confessions of his subjects.[28]

C. Institutes of Nuns

It may be said in general that nuns and other religious women have not the same liberty enjoyed by the ordinary faithful in the choice of confessors. Though at present they have more freedom than formerly, and though recent provisions show a marked inclination to grant larger concessions, nevertheless the Church, while safeguarding their liberty of conscience, strives in her legislation to protect the cloister and to guarantee these religious the experienced and enlightened confessors required by their state of life.[29]

1. Before the Code

Formerly the Holy See prescribed that ordinary and extraordinary confessors of religious women could not validly absolve them, unless they had first received special approval from the local Ordinary.[30]

In the case of nuns subject to Regulars, religious superiors had only the right to present confessors; local Ordinaries gave the aforesaid approval required for the validity of confessions.[31]

2. Present Legislation

For all houses of religious women immediately subject to the Apostolic See or to the local Ordinary, the latter selects both ordinary and extraordinary confessors; for those subject to a Regular superior, this superior presents the confessors to the Ordinary, who will grant them the approval to hear the confession of nuns; the Ordinary shall also supply, if necessary, for the negligence of the Regular superior (can. 525).

Every contrary law or privilege being revoked, all priests, secular and religious, no matter what may be their dignity or offices, must have special jurisdiction to hear validly and licitly the confessions of religious women and novices, safeguarding, however, the prescriptions of canons 239, § 1, 1°; 522; 523 (can. 876, § 1).

---

[27] Cf. Bied.-Führ., 50; Melo, p. 59; C.p.R., XII, p. 21, nota 365.
[28] See constitutions of this Order, n. 19, recently reapproved and confirmed by Pius XI, in his Brief of July 20, 1926. Cf. also Pius V "Salvatoris," Aug. 8, 1571; Bened. XIV, Br., Creditae Nobis, Feb. 7, 1757; Saucedo, C.p.R., XIII, pp. 52, 299; Larraona, C.p.R., XII, p. 21; Bied-Führ., 50; Melo, p. 59.
[29] Cf. Creusen, 110.
[30] Greg. XV, Const., Inscrutabili, Feb. 5, 1622; Clem. X., Const., Superna, June 21, 1670; Bened. XIV, Const., Pastoralis curae, Aug. 5, 1748.
[31] Cf. Clem. X, Const., Superna; see Schäfer, 170.

This jurisdiction is conferred by the Ordinary of the place in which the religious house is located, according to the norm of canon 525 (can. 876, § 2).

The importance and contents of this canon are quite clear. As Creusen remarks: "This law is absolute and no reason for making exception is of value against it, such as: the fact that a regular is of the same Order as the penitent; the fact that one has jurisdiction *in foro externo* over the nuns; the episcopal dignity; the office of director of an entire institute or of the mother house; any immemorial custom; special privileges conceded directly by the Holy See, etc. The text of canon 876 sums up or completes in a definite way legislation already in use and it is designed to put an end to the claims of some regulars, especially in this matter" (Creusen, 110).

Canon 876 declares that its provisions are in no way opposed to the following laws:

a) "If notwithstanding the prescriptions of canons 520 and 521, any religious, for the peace of her conscience, has recourse to a confessor approved by the local Ordinary to hear the confessions of women, this confession, whether made in a church or oratory, even a semipublic oratory, is valid and lawful, every contrary privilege being revoked; nor may the superioress prohibit it or make any inquiry concerning it, even indirectly; and the religious are under no obligation to inform the superioress on the matter" (can. 522).

b) "All religious women when seriously ill, even if not in danger of death, may, as often as they wish during their serious illness, invite any priest whatever to hear their confession, provided that he be approved to hear the confessions of women, though not designated for religious women, nor can the superioress either directly or indirectly prevent them from doing so" (can. 523).

For the validity of the confessions specified in canon 522, two conditions must be fulfilled: first, the priest must be approved to hear the confessions of women; and second, he must exercise his faculties in the places mentioned in canon 522 and in the Reply of the Code Commission, November 4, 1920.[32] Therefore, he must hear confessions in a church, oratory, even a semipublic one, or in a place which is legitimately destined for the confessions of women.[33] "A place legitimately destined" for these confessions signifies not only a place habitually so designated but also a place designated by way of act, or chosen in accordance with canon 901, § 1.[34]

The Church desires that religious women enjoy the fullest freedom and the greatest spiritual aid and benefit possible, in the matter of confession.

---

[32] Cf. Cod. Com., Dec. 28, 1927, AAS, XX, 61; see also *Per.*, XVII, pp. 37–39.

[33] Cf. Cod. Com., Nov. 24, 1920, AAS, XII, 575.

[34] Cf. Cod. Com., Feb. 12, 1935, AAS, XXVII, 92; ap. Bouscaren II, can. 522; *Per.*, XXIV, p. 95; consult Cappello, *De Sacr.*, II, pars I, 450.

We can readily understand, therefore, as Creusen asserts, that "It is always lawful for superiors to make known to the Ordinary their wishes concerning the choice of confessors. This is especially the case if the community wishes to have as extraordinary confessor a religious of some special institute; the superior of the community of religious women, after she has made sure that the priest in question will give his lawful consent, may ask the Ordinary of the place to give him the necessary faculties. It is hardly necessary to add that the Bishop is still entirely free in the matter" (Creusen, 125).

In saying that Bishops are entirely free, the author does not imply that they may act in an arbitrary fashion. In granting or refusing faculties they must always respect the freedom and promote the spiritual good of the religious. Any other manner of acting would be unlawful and a violation of one's office.

II. CONFESSIONS OF THE FAITHFUL

At one time Regular superiors could delegate their priests to hear the confessions of the faithful in any diocese.[35] This power was abrogated by the Council of Trent, which decreed that to hear the confessions of secular persons validly, Regulars required approval from the Bishop of the place where this ministry was to be exercised.[36] Bishops, however, were not permitted to refuse faculties to those who were endowed with the appropriate qualifications for this work.[37]

According to present legislation to hear confessions of the faithful, all priests, Regulars included, must have faculties from the local Ordinary (can. 874).[38] Yet it should be remarked that the Code contains no clause revoking privileges or rights contrary to this provision; and consequently, those whereby some religious Orders had faculties for the confession of secular persons, are still in force. Jurisdiction of this nature, however, is not had for territories ruled by a Bishop or his vicar, but in places where there are no such Ordinaries. In these cases, Regulars once approved by their superiors or a local Ordinary, can hear the confessions of the faithful.[39]

Regulars approved by the local Ordinary can be given faculties by their superiors to absolve any penitents from papal censures which have been reserved by common law to local Ordinaries.[40]

With the same faculties they have the jurisdiction, either in or outside

---

[35] Cf. Boniface VIII, Bull, *Super cathedram,* ap. c. 2, *de sep.* III, 6, in Extravag. com.

[36] Cf. Conc. Trid., sess. XXIII, cap. 15, *de reform.; Epit.,* II, 143.

[37] Cf. Clem. X, Bull, *Superna,* Jan. 21, 1670; see also Vermeersch, *De Rel.,* I, 516.

[38] Cf. Cappello, *De Sacr.,* II, pars I, 393.

[39] Cf. Greg. XIII, Const., *Decet Romanum Pontificem,* May 3, 1575; Leo X, Const., *Plura inter,* July 11, 1826; consult Coronata, I, 619 bis.

[40] Cf. Piat, II, pp. 329 ff.; Vermeersch, *De Rel,* I, 517; *Epit.,* I, 785; Claeys Bouuaert-Simenon, I, 680; Coronata, I, 619 bis.

the confessional, to dispense from nonreserved vows and from oaths, so long as no injury is thereby done to a third party.[41]

Concession of Faculties

Local Ordinaries should grant habitual faculties to those religious only who have been presented to them by their superiors, nor should they without grave reason refuse these faculties, saving, however, the prescription of canon 877 (can. 874).

All priests presented for faculties should be endowed with the qualifications necessary for hearing confession. It is the duty of those in authority to see that this is so. Therefore, local Ordinaries and religious superiors shall grant jurisdiction or permission to hear confessions to those priests only who *by examination* have been found fit for this ministry, unless there be question of priests whose theological knowledge is otherwise manifest (can. 877, § 1). Regulars, as well as others, are obliged to submit to such examinations. Apparently local Ordinaries may abide by the attestation of religious superiors concerning the qualifications of their subjects, since there is no necessity to have a priest undergo a twofold examination.[42]

Should there arise just reason to doubt the fitness of a confessor, the local Ordinary or religious superior shall investigate the case and, when necessary, subject the priest to another examination (can. 877, § 2).

Confessors are not generally delegated to hear the confessions of all persons indiscriminately. Ordinarily they are not granted faculties for religious women or their novices.[43] Besides this, their jurisdiction may be restricted to a definite time (v.g., for one year) or place (v.g., the parish church), etc. (can. 878). Nevertheless, both superiors and local Ordinaries are warned against placing unreasonable limits on the jurisdiction which they grant to confessors (can. 878, § 2). No one can restrict the faculties conferred by law. Thus, for instance, an Ordinary cannot alter or revoke the powers granted by canons 899 and 900.

It is clear that priests of exempt institutes cannot absolve from sins or censures which a local Ordinary has reserved to himself (can. 893), except in cases specified by law[44] (cf., v.g., cc. 899, 900, 2252, 2254).

When it is necessary to absolve women, outside the confessional, priests of exempt institutes, as well as others, are obliged to abide by any prescriptions which the local Ordinary has issued on the matter (can. 910, § 1).

Suspension and Revocation of Faculties

For grave reasons superiors and local Ordinaries may suspend a confessor

---

[41] Cf. Piat, II, pp. 330 ff.; *Epit.*, *loc. cit.*; Claeys Bouuaert-Simenon, *loc. cit.*; Coronata, *loc. cit.*
[42] Cf. Woywod, I, 779.
[43] Cf. cc. 524, 876.
[44] Cf. Clem. X, Const., *Superna*, June 21, 1670; consult also Bened. XIV, *De Syn.*, L. V, c. 5, nn. 6, 7; Chokier, pp. 337–340; Melo, p. 103.

or revoke his faculties (can. 880, § 1). Revocation of jurisdiction prevents a priest from validly administering the sacrament of penance; suspension renders his administration illicit.[45]

Revocation and suspension can be effected by those only who have conferred the faculties. A religious superior can, however, forbid his subject to exercise jurisdiction given by a local Ordinary, and such a prohibition would make the use of the faculties illicit but not invalid.[46]

The Code states that local Ordinaries and superiors should suspend or revoke faculties only when they have grave causes for doing so. The reason for this law is evident. Suspension and "a fortiori" revocation is odious, for it is injurious to the confessor and is likely to prove detrimental to souls. Hence not only a just but a *grave* cause is required in order that an Ordinary or superior may take such repressive actions.

According to the terms of canon 880, the local Ordinary can, for a serious cause, remove both the ordinary and extraordinary confessor of religious women, even when the monastery is subject to Regulars, and the confessor is himself a Regular, nor is the Ordinary bound to make known the reason for the removal to anyone except to the Holy See, if it should require the reason from him; he must, however, if the nuns are subject to Regulars, inform the Regular superior of the removal (can. 527).

After a removal of this type the confessor cannot *per se* validly hear the confessions of religious women, for by the removal his faculties for this particular ministry have been revoked.[47] This follows as a juridical corollary from the prescription (cc. 876, § 2; 525), which requires that a confessor have special jurisdiction from the local Ordinary in order that he might absolve religious women and their novices.[48]

It should be noted that the local Ordinaries or superiors have the right to decide whether a grave cause exists which warrants the withdrawal of faculties. In all cases the priest is allowed a devolutive recourse to the Holy See; in the meanwhile, however, pending a reply, he must abide by the decision of the superior or Ordinary.

The power of local Ordinaries to suspend or revoke the faculties of all confessors of a religious house is more limited than their repressive authority over individual confessors. Even a grave reason is not sufficient to justify this collective suspension or revocation, for a drastic measure of this character would do grave harm to the religious community, and very likely cause irreparable scandal to the faithful.[49] Hence, the Code forbids Bishops to effect any simultaneous withdrawal of faculties from all the

[45] Cf. Cappello, *De Sacr.*, II, pars I, 401.
[46] Cf. S.C.EE.RR., Mar. 2, 1866, Pejska, p. 295.
[47] Cf. W.-V., III, 173, note (17); Schäfer, 180.
[48] Cf. W.-V., *loc. cit.*
[49] Cf. Cappello, *De Sacr.*, II, pars I, 402.

confessors of a formal religious house without first consulting the Apostolic See (can. 880, § 3).

Formerly Bishops were forbidden to take such measures in the case of monasteries of exempt religious;[50] now this prohibition applies to houses of all religious institutes.

INDULGENCES

I. PUBLICATION OF NEW INDULGENCES

The Church always keeps strict watch over the divulgation of indulgences. *New* indulgences granted to churches, which have not been promulgated at Rome, may not be published or divulged without first consulting the local Ordinary. This rule is binding on all churches, those of Regulars included (can. 919, § 1).[1]

The prescription of canon 919 envisages the protection of the faithful. It does not, therefore, affect all new indulgences, but only those which are not personal (i.e., conceded to individuals); such, for instance, as have been granted to a church, or altar, or group of persons (cf. can. 713, § 1).[2] Authorization by the local Ordinary adds nothing to the efficacy of the indulgence itself; it merely safeguards the faithful from possible fraud.[3]

No authorization of the local Ordinary is needed for the divulgation of grants contained in any authentic catalogue approved by the S. C. of Indulgences. Some religious institutes possess such catalogues.[4] These, however, should be shown to the Bishop, if he asks to see them.

Promulgation at Rome is generally effected by publishing the concessions in the *Acta Apostolicae Sedis*. Once this is done, indulgences may be made known to the faithful without any further submission to local Ordinaries.[5]

Anyone publishing books, pamphlets, and the like which contain prayers and pious works with indulgences attached, must follow the norms set down in canon 1388 (can. 919, § 2). These demand: *(a)* that permission of the local Ordinary be obtained for the publication of works which contain concessions of indulgences;[6] *(b)* that express authorization of the Apostolic See be had for editing in any language, *authentic* collections of prayers and good works to which the Holy See has attached indulgences, lists of papal indulgences, summaries of indulgences previously collected but never approved, and new summaries made from various concessions.[7]

---

[50] Cf. Clem. X, Const., *Superna,* June 21, 1670.

[1] Cf. Conc. Trid., sess. XXI, c. 9, *de reform.;* see Pallotini, V, *Indulgentia,* nn. 44, 45.

[2] Cf. Beringer-Steinen, I, 195–197; Cappello, *De Sacr.,* I, pars II, 962; *Epit.,* II, 207; W.-V., IV, Vol. I, 157.

[3] Cf. S. C. Indulg., Aug. 31, 1844; W.-V., *loc. cit.;* Cappello, *loc. cit.;* *Epit., loc. cit.*

[4] Cf. Fine, p. 746.

[5] Cf. S. C. Indulg., July 1, 1839; see Woywod, I, 835; Ayrinhac, *Legislation on the Sacraments,* 239.

[6] Cf. Leo XIII, Jan. 25, 1897.

[7] Cf. Cappello, *De Sacr.,* I, pars II, 962; W.-V., IV, Vol. I, 157.

II. SPECIAL CONCESSIONS

(A) *Papal Blessing and Indulgences*

Regulars are often endowed with the privilege of imparting to the faithful the papal blessing with a plenary indulgence attached thereto.[8] They may use this right only in their own churches, and in the churches of nuns and tertiaries legitimately aggregated to their Order; but they must not do so at the same place (city) or time when the Bishop gives it (can. 915). In conferring the blessing they are obliged to use the formula prescribed by Benedict XIV.[9]

The following cases are not subject to this prescription: papal blessings which some religious can give at the close of retreats or missions;[10] the general Apostolic absolution and plenary indulgence granted several times a year to members of certain religious Orders, or to tertiaries of some institutes;[11] plenary indulgences some Regulars are entitled to grant to persons when they are first converted from heresy and to penitents at the moment of death.[12]

It should be remarked that, besides the papal blessing with its plenary indulgence, many other plenary and partial indulgences have been granted to churches belonging to Regulars and to those intrusted to their care.[13] In a number of cases these concessions of the Holy See have been further extended to the oratories and domestic chapels of these religious.[14]

(B) *Privileged Altars*

The Church grants a plenary indulgence for Masses celebrated at altars which have been declared by legitimate superiors to be *privileged* altars. The privilege may benefit both living and dead, but it is generally granted only in favor of the latter.

Major superiors of clerical exempt institutes have the right to declare one altar in each of their churches to be a privileged altar (can. 916).[15] Besides this provision of common law, some orders enjoy particular privileges which entitle their superiors to designate a privileged altar in one of their oratories and domestic chapels, provided these places have no other altar indulgenced in this way.[16]

---

[8] Cf. Ayrinhac, *Legislation on the Sacraments*, 243.
[9] Cf. Bened. XIV, *Exemplis praedecessorum*, Mar. 19, 1748; see, Rit. Rom., tit. VIII, c. 32; Beringer-Steinen, II, 52; W.-V., IV, Vol. II, 163.
[10] Cf. S.R.C., May 11, 1911.
[11] Cf. Leo XIII, *Quo universi*, July 7, 1882; see Beringer-Steinen II, 53; Ayrinhac, *Legislation on the Sacraments*, 235.
[12] Cf. Leo XII, Br., *Plura inter*, July 11, 1826.
[13] Cf. S. C. Indulg., Aug. 18, 1868.
[14] Cf. S. C. Indulg., Jan. 8, 1861, and Aug. 10, 1899.
[15] Cf. Bened. XIV, Bull, *Quemadmodum presbyteri*, July 15, 1749.
[16] Cf. Pius X, Apr. 15, 1907, grant to the Society of Jesus; see Fine, pp. 854, 855.

ARTICLE V. EXTREME UNCTION

Administration of the sacrament of extreme unction by exempt religious will be discussed under the following heads: (I) Administration to persons subject to religious; (II) Administration to the faithful in general.

I. ADMINISTRATION TO PERSONS SUBJECT TO RELIGIOUS

In ancient times, any priest could validly and licitly administer the sacrament of extreme unction. It was only toward the close of the thirteenth century that particular Councils began reserving this ministry to the pastor of the infirm party. Gradually such reservation of the right became the common law of the Church.[17]

Before the Code, Regular Prelates and superiors in exempt clerical congregations had the right to anoint their own subjects, but they could exercise this only in their religious houses.[18]

Legislation of the Code on this matter is contained in canon 514. The canon provides norms for houses of clerical religious, of nuns, and of other lay institutes.

A. *Houses of Men*

"In every clerical institute the superior has the right and duty to administer either personally or by a delegate Holy Viaticum and Extreme Unction, in case of sickness, to the professed members, to the novices, and to other persons dwelling day and night in the religious house by reason of service, education, hospitality, or health" (can. 514).[19]

The law of the Code increases the exemptive rights of religious in the administration of extreme unction. What before the promulgation of the Code was permitted only to Regular prelates and superiors of exempt clerical congregations is now the right and duty of superiors *in every clerical institute*. Formerly those endowed with this right were allowed to anoint only professed religious, novices, and persons truly considered part of their family or community;[20] now, this authority extends to all the persons enumerated in canon 514, § 1.

In the cited canon, two distinct groups are provided for:

1. The first group comprises *professed religious* and *novices*. Canon 514, § 1, states that the religious superior has the right and duty to anoint such persons, and it makes no distinction as to places where the sacrament may

---

[17] Cf. c. 1, *de priv. et excess.*, etc., V, 7, in Clem.; Leo X, Const., *Dum intra,* par. 7, Dec. 19, 1516, ap. *Fontes,* n. 72: see Cappello, *De Extrema Unctione,* 112; Kilker, p. 92.

[18] Cf. *Epit.,* I, 632.

[19] It is clear that the law for the administration of extreme unction applies equally to Holy Viaticum, so that the explanation here given covers both administrations.

[20] Cf. Conc. Trid., sess. XXV, c. 11, *de Regul.;* S.C.C., June, 1587, and Jan. 25, 1738: see Melo, p. 62.

be administered. Hence, the religious superior is authorized to perform this spiritual function in behalf of professed and novices, whether they be inside or outside the monastery. Unlimited exercise of this kind flows from the personal nature of the exemptive right involved.[21]

An authentic declaration has been issued confirming this interpretation. The Code Commission was asked: Whether canon 514, § 1, is to be understood in the sense that, in a clerical religious institute, superiors have the right and duty of administering to all the persons mentioned in that canon Eucharistic Viaticum and extreme unction when they are ill outside the religious house. The Commission replied in the affirmative as regards the professed religious and novices, but without prejudice to the prescription of canon 848; otherwise in the negative.[22]

2. The second group comprises persons who actually dwell in a religious house, although they are not members of the institute.

Persons expressly mentioned as included in the group are: servants, boarding students, guests, and the infirm. This list includes in reality anyone who dwells in the religious house. Postulants, it is true, are not specifically mentioned, yet they may certainly be considered guests, if not servants or students.[23]

In order that superiors may licitly anoint these persons, two conditions must be verified.

a) The persons must actually dwell *in the religious house*. The expression "religious house" is to be accepted in the *material sense* as signifying any place within the premises belonging and attached to the house.[24] Generally, servants, boarding students, and the like, are lodged in buildings on the property which are separated from the one occupied by the religious community.

b) These persons must dwell *day and night* in the religious house. The expression "day and night" (diu noctuque) means that the residence must be prolonged for *an entire day,* i.e., a canonical day of 24 hours, or it signifies at least a person's actual presence in the house with the intention of remaining that length of time.[25]

The religious superior has the duty to administer the last sacraments to the persons enumerated in both groups, and in doing so he is in nowise obliged to consult or inform the pastor or local Ordinary. He may, nevertheless, fulfill his duty, as the canon states, by delegating another priest to anoint the sick.

---

[21] Cf. Schäfer, 148.
[22] Cf. Cod. Com., June 16, 1931, AAS, XXIII, 353; ap. Bouscaren, I, can. 514; see *Per.,* XXI, 38.
[23] Cf. Fanfani, *De Jure Religiosorum,* 415; Pejska, p. 88; Kilker, p. 94.
[24] Cf. above, Chap. IX, Art. I; see also Kilker, p. 94.
[25] Cf. *Epit.,* I, 632; Augustine, III, can. 514; Fanfani, *De Jure Religiosorum,* 93; Kilker, p. 95.

B. *Houses of Nuns*

"In houses of nuns, the ordinary confessor or his substitute has the same right and duty" (can. 514, § 2). Houses of nuns both of solemn and of simple vows are included in this provision. Kilker limits this right to houses of nuns professed of solemn vows.[26] He bases his opinion on an incomplete and incorrect citation of canon 488, 7°, when he states: "Only nuns of solemn vows are 'moniales.'" The full and correct citation reads "(In the following canons) we mean by *nuns*: religious women with solemn vows or, unless it appears otherwise from the nature of the case or from the context, religious women whose vows are normally solemn, but which by a dispensation of the Holy See, are simple in certain regions."[27] Neither the nature of the matter in question nor the context of canon 514 excludes nuns of simple vows from enjoying the granted benefit.

For nuns, therefore, the ordinary confessor or a priest taking his place is the minister of extreme unction. By "ordinary" confessor is meant the one appointed in accordance with the rule given in canon 520, § 1. If there are several confessors of this type, they are all competent.[28]

The confessor substituting for the ordinary one, may be the chaplain, a delegated priest, or in the case of necessity any priest at all.[29]

Canon 514, paragraph 2, states that the confessor, or his substitute has the same right and duty as that attributed to the religious superior in paragraph 1. Hence, he should administer the sacrament to all the persons specified therein.[30]

C. *Houses of Other Lay Institutes*

"In other lay institutes, this right and duty belongs to the local parish priest or to the chaplain designated by the Ordinary to replace the parish priest according to the terms of canon 464, § 3."

According to most authors this includes all lay institutes, with the exception of nuns.[31] However, as Vermeersch observes,[32] the prescription does not abrogate privileges whereby lay institutes, v.g., the Brothers Hospitalers of St. John of God, may obtain their proper chaplains who have the right to administer this sacrament.[33]

---

[26] Cf. Kilker, p. 96, and note 84.
[27] Cf. above, Chap. I, 4.
[28] Cf. Blat, II, 537; Kilker, p. 96.
[29] Cf. Fanfani, *De Jure Religiosorum*, 416. Under the expression "one taking his place," Melo includes the extraordinary confessor (Melo, p. 62); Kilker excludes him (Kilker, p. 96).
[30] Cf. S.C.EE.RR., May, 1788, ap. Biz., 348; Melo, p. 62; Fanfani, *De Jure Religiosorum*, 416; Kilker, p. 96.
[31] Cf. *Epit.*, I, 632; Kilker, p. 97; Melo, p. 63; Pejska, p. 289.
[32] Cf. *Epit.*, I, 632.
[33] Cf. Melo, p. 63.

D. *Seminaries*

If exempt religious are in charge of a seminary, the rector or his delegate has the right and duty to anoint the students and the other persons mentioned in canon 514 (can. 1368).[34]

II. ADMINISTRATION TO THE FAITHFUL IN GENERAL

Unless they be pastors or their assistants, exempt religious are forbidden to anoint any of the faithful who do not belong to their religious houses, as stated in canon 514. Regulars who, without proper authorization and outside of cases of necessity, presumed to anoint such persons, formerly incurred excommunication reserved to the Sovereign Pontiff.[35] This penal law has been abrogated by the Code (cf. can. 6, 5°).[36]

It is the general rule that the pastor has exclusive right to administer the sacrament of extreme unction to his parishioners. Of course, in case of necessity, as just stated, or with at least the presumed permission of the pastor or local Ordinary, any priest may anoint the sick (can. 938).

Caution, however, should always be used by exempt religious in administering to the faithful. Regulars have often been reminded not to interfere with this parochial right.[37] Religious superiors, too, are forbidden to anoint tertiaries pertaining to their own order.[38]

ARTICLE VI. HOLY ORDERS
FORMER DISCIPLINE

For the reception of holy orders, which requires the intervention of the episcopal power of orders, exempt religious are generally dependent upon local Ordinaries. According to the general law which had long been in force, Regulars were forbidden to be ordained by any save their proper Bishop.[39] The term *proper Bishop* signifies the one governing the diocese where the religious house of the one to be ordained is located.[40]

After the rise of mendicant Orders in the thirteenth century, Popes granted privileges permitting members of these institutes to be presented

---

[34] Cf. Kilker, p. 96.

[35] Cf. Pius, IX, Const., *Apostolicae Sedis*, Oct. 12, 1869: see also Suarez, *De Censuris*, Disp. 22, sect. 4, n. 6; D'Annibale, Com. in Const., *Apostolicae Sedis*, n. 145; Cappello, *De Extrema Unctione*, 112.

[36] Cf. Cappello, *De Extrema Unctione*, 112; Schäfer, 443.

[37] Cf. c. 1, *de priv. et excess.*, V, 7, in Clem.; S.C.C., June 7, 1698; S.C.P.F., June 13, 1633, Coll., P.F., 73: see Bened. XIV, *De Syn. Dioec.*, VIII, c. 4, 7, and IX, c. 16, n. 2; Augustine, IV, can. 938; Kilker, pp. 96, 97.

[38] Cf. S.R.C., Mar. 17, 1663, Decr. auth. 1255; Dec. 18, 1756, Decr. auth. 2441: see Augustine, IV, can. 939; Kilker, p. 97.

[39] Cf. Conc. Trid., sess. 23, *de Reform.*, cap. 8.

[40] Cf. Bened. XIV, Const., *Impositi Nobis*, Feb. 27, 1747; S.C.C., Resp., Aug. 18, 1888, ap. ASS, XXI, p. 364; Vermeersch, *De Rel.*, I, 480; Piat, II, p. 290.

for ordinations to any Bishop in communion with the Holy See.[41] According to some authors, the legislation of the Council of Trent revoked these privileges.[42] Pope St. Pius V, however, declared authoritatively that the decrees of the Council did not apply to Regulars;[43] later, Gregory XIII[44] extended the Tridentine laws to all religious. Benedict XIV more definitely determined the status of Regulars in these matters by decreeing that only those privileges against the common law remained in force which had been expressly and directly (not by communication) granted to religious Orders after the Council of Trent.[45]

By common law Regular superiors had the right to grant their subjects dimissorial letters, but they were obliged to present the religious to the diocesan Bishop except in two specified cases; namely, when the Bishop was absent, and, when he was not to hold ordinations at the next period designated in law.[46] In the two cases of exception mentioned, Regular superiors could have their religious ordained by any Bishop they chose.[47]

After the Council of Trent, several Orders were given particular privileges whereby they could send their subjects to any Bishop in communion with the Holy See. Such a concession was granted to the Society of Jesus, by Gregory XIII;[48] to the Congregation of Clerics Regular ministering to the infirm, by Gregory XIV;[49] to the Friars Minor in the West Indies, by Urban VIII;[50] and to the Spanish members of the Discalced Friars of St. Augustine in the Philippines and West Indies, by Urban VIII.[1]

PRESENT LAW

I. A governing abbot of Regulars, even though he be not an abbot "nullius," may confer tonsure and minor orders on those who are subject to him by virtue of at least simple profession, provided the abbot himself be a priest and has lawfully received the abbatial blessing. Outside of these limits, ordination is invalid unless the abbot has episcopal powers. All privileges contrary to this provision are revoked (can. 964, 1°).

From this it is clear that the abbot must be one who is actually ruling;

---

[41] Cf. Clem. IV, *Virtute conspicuos*, par. 7, 1265; Sixtus IV, Const., *Regimini Universali*, par. 7, 1474.
[42] Cf. Many, *De Sacra Ord.*, 157.
[43] Cf. Const., *Etsi Mendicantium*, 1567.
[44] Cf. Const., *In tanta rerum*, Mar. 1, 1583.
[45] Cf. Const., *Impositi Nobis*, par. 3, Feb. 27, 1747; see also Wernz, II, 28; Piat, II, p. 292; Many, *De Sacra Ord.*, 147; Cappello, *De Sacra Ord.*, 340.
[46] Cf. Bened. XIV, Const., *Impositi Nobis*, par. 12.
[47] Cf. Many, *De Sacra Ord.*, 159; Vermeersch, *De Rel.*, I, 480.
[48] Cf. Const., *Pium et utile*, par. 3, Sept. 22, 1582.
[49] Cf. Const., *Illius qui*, par. 28, Sept. 21, 1591.
[50] Cf. Const., *Cum sicut*, par. 2, June 30, 1625.
[1] Cf. *Jus Pontificium de Prop. Fide.*, Par. 1, Vol. I, pp. 155 and 173; see also Piat, II, p. 294; Many, *De Sacra Ord.*, 160; Vermeersch, *De Rel.*, I, 480.

a titular or commendatory abbot, or one who has entirely renounced his office, can neither validly nor licitly confer tonsure or minor orders.[2]

Any major superior who is a consecrated Bishop can confer all orders on his exempt subjects (can. 959).[3]

2. Generally exempt religious are ordained by a Bishop who is not a superior of their institute. In this case, the candidate must be presented to the Bishop by his major religious superior. This is clear from the Code, which states that exempt religious cannot be licitly ordained by any Bishop without dimissorial letters from their own major superiors (can. 964, 2°).

The character of these letters is determined by law. They are documents certifying that a legitimate religious superior grants his subject the faculty to be ordained, and simultaneously testifying to the fulfillment of other requirements of law (can. 995, § 1). The contents, therefore, furnish information concerning the religious profession of the candidate, his character, reputation, domicile, the completion of his studies, spiritual exercises, etc.[4] These are the only testimonial letters needed by the ordaining Bishop (can. 995).

Superiors are bound in conscience to transmit the above-mentioned attestation to the ordaining Bishop; the latter, however, is free also to question the candidates further, as he sees fit.[5] If, after this, there exist no well-founded doubts as to the qualifications of the religious, the Bishop may not carry on other investigations. Should some positive doubt arise, the Bishop may *per se* make other inquiries, but he is not bound to do so.[6] Bishops may, before God and the Church, accept the favorable testimonials of the superiors and leave to them full responsibility regarding the due training and worthiness of the candidates (cc. 970; 995, § 2).[7]

A Bishop shall not confer sacred orders upon anyone unless from positive proof, v.g., from testimonial letters or personal investigation he is morally certain of the candidate's canonical fitness; otherwise he not only commits a most grievous sin, but exposes himself to the danger of being a partaker of other men's sins (can. 973, § 3).

For ordinations to the diaconate and the priesthood, it is not necessary to secure the full information mentioned above, nor to get new testimonials, yet superiors should take the precautions deemed prudent.[8]

It is a disputed point as to whether or not major superiors of *lay* exempt institutes, v.g., members of the Order of St. John of God, may grant dimis-

---

[2] Cf. S.C.C., Sept. 20, 1788; S.O., July 15, 1903, ap. ASS, XXXIII, p. 167; S.C.EE.RR., Sept. 20, 1697, ap. Biz., p. 281: see also Augustine, IV, can. 964; Cappello, *De Sacra Ord.*, 394.
[3] Cf. W.-V., IV, Vol. I, 197.
[4] Cf. S. C. Rel., Instr., Par. 12, Dec. 1, 1931, ap. AAS, XXIV, 74; *Per.*, XXI, p. 188; Cappello, *De Sacra Ord.*, 344.
[5] Cf. S. C. Rel., Instr., par. 19.
[6] Cf. Cappello, *loc. cit.*
[7] Cf. S. C. Rel., Instr., par. 12.
[8] Cf. S. C. Rel., Instr., par. 20.

sorial letters for the subjects whom they intend to advance to orders. The affirmative opinion seems certain, for canon 964, 2°, makes no distinction between lay and clerical institutes, but merely sets down the rule to be followed by major superiors of exempt institutes in general.[9]

The following provisions are to be observed by all superiors of religious and clerical societies. Novices before their profession of temporary vows may not be promoted to tonsure or minor orders (can. 567, § 2).[10] Religious with temporary vows may be advanced only to tonsure and minor orders (can. 964, 3°). As regards the reception of major orders, religious superiors must remember that they may by no means allow their subjects to be promoted to them before they have made their religious profession, either perpetual or solemn (can. 964, 3°, 4°).

EXAMINATION OF CANDIDATES

Prior to the reception of orders, Regulars, like seculars, must be carefully examined concerning the order they are about to receive, and those being advanced to sacred orders should also be examined on other sections of theology (can. 996). Major superiors of clerical exempt religious have the right and obligation to conduct these examinations. The truth of this statement is evident, for these superiors are obliged in their dimissorial letters to testify to the fact that the candidate has completed his studies (can. 995, § 1), and has been subjected to the proper examinations (can. 997, § 2).[11]

According to law (can. 997, § 2), ordaining Bishops may refuse to acquiesce to the testimonials of the superiors, and may themselves examine the religious candidates for orders, yet they are not bound to do so. As has been stated above, they may leave the full responsibility to the religious superiors.[12]

Certain Orders, such as the Society of Jesus,[13] possess a privilege which exempts their subjects from examinations by the ordaining Bishop.[14]

THE ORDAINING BISHOP

The dimissorial letters must be transmitted to the Bishop of the diocese where the candidate for orders is dwelling (can. 965). Religious superiors have a grave obligation to comply with this prescription of the Code.[15]

---

[9] Cf. Cappello, *De Sacra Orrd.,* 344, n. 2; Fanfani, *De Jure Rel.,* 285; *Epit.,* II, 241.

[10] Cf. S.C.EE.RR., decr., *Auctis admodum,* Nov. 4, 1892; S. C. Rel., Instr., par. 14, Dec. 1, 1931.

[11] Cf. Cappello, *De Sacra Ord.,* 542; Vermeersch, *Theologia Moralis,* III, 672; Piscetta-Gennaro, VI, 85.

[12] Cf. S. C. Rel., Instr., par. 12, Dec. 1, 1931; see also Cappello, *De Sacra Ord.,* 542.

[13] Cf. Greg. XIII, Const., *Pium et utile,* Sept. 22, 1582; this privilege was confirmed by Paul V in his Constitution, *Quantum,* Sept. 5, 1606; and since it has not been revoked by the Code, it is again confirmed by Pius XI in his Apostolic Letter, *Paterna Caritas,* Mar. 12, 1933, ap. AAS, XXV, pp. 245–246.

[14] Cf. Cappello, *De Sacra Ord.,* 545.

[15] Cf. Cappello, *De Sacra Ord.,* 344, n. 8.

There are, however, several instances in which a religious may be presented to another Bishop for ordination. This can be done: (1) when the diocesan Bishop permits it; (2) when the Bishop belongs to a rite different from that of the religious; (3) when the Bishop is absent from the diocese; (4) when he is not to hold ordinations at the next legitimate time designated in law; (5) when the diocesan see is vacant and the regent is not endowed with episcopal power (can. 966).

In any of these cases the ordaining Bishop must have an authentic attestation from the chancery of the proper Bishop vouching for the truth of the situation (can. 966, § 2).

The case of absence is verified even though the proper Bishop brings another to the diocese to hold ordinations in his place.[16] The *legitimate times designated by law* are the following: the four Ember Saturdays, the Saturday before Passion Sunday, and Holy Saturday (can. 1006, § 2). If ordinations are not to be had on the approaching day of those enumerated, even though they will be had on one of the other days permitted by canon 1006, § 3, the superior is free to send his subjects to any Bishop he chooses.[17]

It seems that even though the Bishop hold ordinations in a remote part of the diocese, superiors, in spite of inconveniences, are obliged to have their religious ordained by him.[18] Extraordinary circumstances, such as great distances or difficult journeys, constitute an excusing cause, as long as the ordination cannot be delayed without grave harm being done the religious and especially his institute.[19] Superiors are cautioned not to act deceitfully in this matter, either by sending their subjects to another house in order to avoid presenting them to the proper Bishop, or by purposely delaying the issuance of dimissorial letters until a time when the Bishop will be absent or will not be having ordinations (can. 967). Transference to another house for reasons of health, study, vacation, or the like, would not be a violation of this provision. Fraud in these matters is not to be presumed but must be proved.[20]

If a Bishop unjustly refuses to ordain a religious or to grant him leave to go to another Bishop, the superior may have recourse to the Holy See, but, pending the reply, he must abide by the decision of the Bishop.[21] Religious superiors who violate the norms set down in canons 965–967 are "ipso facto" suspended from celebrating Mass for a period of one month (can. 2410).[22] Since this vindicative penalty of canon 2410 is incurred only

[16] Cf. Many, *De Sacra Ord.*, 159 n. 3; Augustine, IV, can. 966.
[17] Cf. Augustine, IV, can. 966.
[18] Cf. Cappello, *De Sacra Ord.*, 344, n. 9.
[19] Cf. S.C.C., Feb. 11, 1703; Bondini, p. 102.
[20] Cf. Many, *De Sacra Ord.*, 159, n. 4; Augustine, IV, can. 967.
[21] Cf. S.C.C., Feb. 11, 1703, and Apr. 20, 1604; see Bondini, p. 102.
[22] Cf. Cappello, *De Censuris*, 561 ff.; Melo, p. 107.

by those who *presume* to violate these provisions, any ignorance, except it be affected, will excuse from the punishment (cf. can. 2229, § 2).

Privileges in force before the Code, whereby superiors of certain institutes had the right to send dimissorial letters to any Catholic Bishop, are still in force. This is clear from canon 4, and also from canon 2373, 4°, which latter expressly states this fact (by the words "salvo legitimo privilegio").[23]

ARTICLE VII. MATRIMONY

Exempt religious not engaged in parochial work have but few rights or faculties with regard to marriages of the faithful. Publication of marriage banns, assistance at marriage and bestowal of the nuptial blessings are functions reserved to parish priests (can. 462, 4°). Other priests are not permitted to exercise these functions without authorization by a competent authority (cf. cc. 1094, 1095) or by positive provisions of law (cf. cc. 1044, 1098).[24]

Interference in marriage matters reserved to pastors has generally been severely punished, for it has been considered an offense particularly harmful to public order. Formerly Regulars who dared assist at a marriage or bestow the nuptial blessing without permission of the pastor were "ipso facto" suspended. This penalty was primarily inflicted as a remedial measure to restore the public order disturbed by the offense. This is clear from the nature of the penalty: the suspension incurred was vindicative in character for the delinquent Regular remained under the reservation until such time as the Ordinary absolved him.[25] Though the penalty is abrogated by the new Code (cf. can. 6, 5°), interference with the exclusive rights of a pastor is now, as formerly, strictly forbidden.

In spite of these general principles, there are several instances defined by law in which priests not engaged in parochial work have rights over marriage matters.

I. THE RIGHT TO ASSIST AT MARRIAGES

Common law makes provision for three specific cases in which simple priests (that is, nonparochial priests) may lawfully assist at marriages.[26]

---

[23] Cf. Cappello, *De Sacra Ord.*, 344, n. 8; Ayrinhac, *Legis. on the Sacr.*, 286; Melo, p. 107; Augustine, IV, can. 967; W.-V., IV, Vol. II, 107. Thus, for example, the privileges of the Society of Jesus formerly in force and not expressly revoked by the Code, are retained, and have been further explicitly confirmed by Pius XI, in his Apostolic Letter, *"Paterna Caritas,"* March 12, 1933 (cf. AAS, XXV, pp. 245-246).

[24] The churching of women is not a strict parochial function (cf. can. 462): see also S.R.C., July 20, 1630, Decr. auth. 538, ad 1; Jan. 12, 1704, Decr. auth. 2123, ad 6; Nov. 21, 1893, Decr. auth. 3813; see Cappello, *De Matr.*, 730; Claeys Bouuaert-Simenon, II, 313 f.

[25] Cf. Conc. Trid., sess. XXIV, c. 1, *De reform. matr.;* Pius IX, Const., *Apostolicae Sedis*, par. *Denique:* see Piat, Com. in Const., *Apostolicae Sedis*, 321: see also Piat, II, p. 621.

[26] Cf. Pejska, p. 312.

A. *By Virtue of Delegated Faculties*

Canon 1094 declares: "Those marriages alone are valid which are contracted before the parish priest, or local Ordinary, or priest delegated by either, and at least two witnesses. . . ." Hence, priests pertaining to exempt institutes may be delegated to assist at marriages.

Assistance by delegated priests is regulated by the following norms:

1. In order that a priest, secular or religious, may validly assist at a marriage, he needs delegation from the pastor or Ordinary of the place where the marriage is to be contracted, even though neither of the contracting parties has a domicile or quasi-domicile there. In other words, only the pastor and Ordinary of this place can validly delegate, and not the proper pastor of the contracting parties.[27]

2. The delegated priest can validly assist at the marriage only within the limits of the territory of the person who granted him the delegation, that is, within the parish of the delegating pastor, or within the diocese of the delegating local Ordinary (cf. can. 1095, § 2).

3. Delegation must be given expressly to a specified priest for a specified marriage. General delegation to priests other than regularly appointed parish assistants is invalid (can. 1096, § 1).

4. Pastors and Ordinaries should not grant delegation before everything has been done which the law requires for the proof of the parties' freedom to marry (can. 1096, § 1).

5. The priest who has been delegated must assist at the marriage in the parish church unless he has permission of the pastor or Ordinary to perform this function in another church or oratory (public or semipublic) located within their respective territories. Prior to the Code there existed no common provision restricting the celebration of marriages to churches or oratories.[28]

According to the present law local Ordinaries and pastors may delegate religious priests to assist at marriages even in their exempt church.

Occasionally Ordinaries and pastors are found who are of the opinion that all marriages should be celebrated in the parish church and that any other procedure is not in conformity with the intention of the legislator. The Code clearly expresses the contrary. Churches and oratories of religious *women* are the only ones from which marriages should be normally excluded. Though canon 462, 4°, defines assistance at marriage as an exclusive parochial function it would be false to conclude that the Holy See wishes all marriages to be celebrated in the parish church. If this were the mind of the Church she would have expressed it in her legislation, and would

---

[27] Cf. Pejska, p. 312.
[28] Cf. Gasparri, *De Matr.*, 1264; Cappello, *De Matr.*, 729.

have omitted canon 1109, paragraph 1, of the Code. This canon makes explicit provision for assistance of priests other than the pastor, and in churches other than the parish.

Pastors and Ordinaries may grant this permission in any case whatever. No special reason is required on the part either of the petitioner or of the grantor. In practice it should be the desire of all priests concerned to contribute, as far as they may do so legitimately, to the happiness of the faithful on such solemn occasions.[29] Lack of priestly kindness and courtesy, in cases especially in which the faithful know that their desires may be readily acceded to, can be provocative of much bitterness and harm to souls.

6. The pastor, not the delegated priest, should procure all documents and attend to all the requirements prescribed as necessary preliminaries to the celebration of marriage (cf. cc. 1097, 1103).

7. The priest delegated to assist at a marriage is entitled to impart the solemn blessing during the nuptial Mass (can. 1101, § 1).

B. *In Danger of Death*

A person in danger of death who cannot without grave inconvenience summon or go to the pastor, local Ordinary, or delegated priest can validly and licitly contract marriage before two witnesses (can. 1098, 1°). If a priest, even without faculties is at hand he should be summoned to assist at the marriage together with two witnesses (can. 1098, 2°).

For the lawful use of the faculty granted in canon 1098, it is not necessary that the danger of death be imminent or of a most grave type, common danger suffices. In virtue of the faculty any priest who is present can rectify civil and other invalid marriages.

C. *In the Absence of Pastor or Ordinary*

Even when there is no danger of death, if the Ordinary, or pastor, or priest delegated to assist at marriage in accordance with the norm of canons 1095 and 1096, can neither be had nor approached without grave inconvenience, e.g., in mission territories or during persecutions, a marriage may be contracted before two witnesses, so long as it is foreseen that this state of affairs will continue for at least a month (can. 1098, 1°). In this case, also, if another priest is at hand who can be present, he should be asked to assist at the marriage.

A priest assisting at the marriage under the conditions just described may give the simple liturgical blessing, but not the solemn nuptial blessing imparted at nuptial Masses (can. 1102, § 2). This latter can be supplied

---

[29] Cf. Woywod, *Homiletic and Pastoral Review*, XXXVIII, p. 414.

any time afterward by the local Ordinary or pastor or priest delegated by either.

It is the duty of the priest or witnesses assisting at marriages, in accordance with canon 1098, to have them registered as soon as possible in the books designated for that purpose (can. 1103, § 3). The right to grant dispensations, which will be explained presently, may be exercised by priests assisting at the marriages just described under A and B.

II. THE RIGHT TO DISPENSE FROM IMPEDIMENTS

Exempt religious priests, like others, cannot dispense from matrimonial impediments, except for cases in which they have faculties from either common law or indult (can. 1040).

A. *In Two Cases the Law Grants All Priests Extensive Dispensatory Rights*

1. In Urgent Danger of Death

When there is urgent danger of death and recourse even to the local Ordinary is impossible, all priests enjoy the faculties accorded by canon 1044 to be used in the internal forum only and during sacramental confession.[30]

By means of this faculty priests are empowered to dispense: from the form prescribed for the celebration of marriage and from both occult and public impediments imposed by ecclesiastical law, whether they be impedient or diriment impediments. Dispensations given in these cases are not juridically effective in the external forum (cf. can. 1757, § 3). By the faculty here spoken of, priests have not power over impediments arising from the *sacred order* of the *priesthood* or from *affinity* in the direct line when the marriage producing the affinity has already been consummated. Manifestly the faculty is valueless for impediments arising from the natural or divine law, such as impotency, consanguinity in the direct line, etc.

In using the faculty the priest should see to it that scandal is avoided. Particular attention must be given to cases involving sacred orders, v.g., the diaconate or subdiaconate, or solemn vows. Since persons in these conditions may possibly recover from their illness, the Holy Office[31] has declared that they must betake themselves to some locality where they are unknown, or at least that they must adopt a manner of living which will provide an edifying example to the faithful.

Priests rectifying marriages should record the details as soon as possible, when they were matters of external forum (can. 1046). A confessor on the other hand may not do this since he is bound by the sacramental seal.

---

[30] Cf. can. 882: see, Cappello, *De Matr.*, 238.
[31] Cf. S. Off., Decr., Feb. 20, 1888.

2. When All Things Are in Readiness for the Marriage

In *occult* cases, the pastor, delegated priest, or confessor may grant dispensations for any impediment specified in canon 1043, so long as the impediment has only been detected after all things have been prepared for the wedding, and the marriage cannot be delayed, pending recourse to the Ordinary, without the probability of grave harm resulting, or without danger of violating the seal of confession (can. 1045, § 3).[32]

B. *Faculties From Indults*

Exempt religious may likewise dispense from impediments, if they have an indult granting them this power. Such an indult may be either general or particular. It is particular when given for one or two cases or in favor of several specified persons; otherwise it is general. The latter type may be valid in perpetuity, or for a period of three, five, or more years. It may be granted to a priest directly by the Holy See, v.g., the Sacred Penitentiary, or by Ordinaries having such authority.[33] Religious, or others vested with such powers, must be careful that they do not employ them beyond the limits specified in the indult.[34]

III. FACULTIES TO DISPENSE FROM INTERPELLATIONS

By virtue of the Constitution, *Populis,* of Gregory XIII, certain religious have been accorded faculties to dispense from the interpellations normally required in the dissolution of marriages between infidels. This concession, which is contained in canon 1125, now constitutes a general provision of the Code.

A. *The Concession of Faculties*

From the wording of the Constitution it is clear that local Ordinaries, pastors, and priests of the Society of Jesus who have been approved for confessions can grant a dispensation in favor of any convert who before being baptized had contracted marriage with another infidel. Provided it be certain from a summary and extrajudicial inquiry that the partner of the former marriage cannot be admonished according to law, or having been admonished has failed to reply within the time stipulated in the admonition, the dispensation enables the convert lawfully to contract a new marriage without interpellating the spouse who is still alive; to solemnize the marriage in the Church; to consummate it; and to live in the union for

---

[32] Cf. Cod. Com., Nov. 12, 1922, AAS, XIV, 662; Mar. 1, 1921, AAS, X, 177; Dec. 28, 1927, AAS, XX, 61: see Bouscaren, I, can. 1045; *Per.,* XVII, 42; Cappello, *De Matr.,* 238.

[33] Cf. Cappello, *De Matr.,* 235, 240, 245 ff.

[34] Cf. Cappello, *De Matr.,* 254.

life. A marriage entered into with this dispensation is never to be rescinded, even though afterward it becomes known that the former infidel partner was prevented by some just cause from manifesting his or her intention, and further, even though at the time of the second marriage the former spouse had been already converted to the faith.[35]

The dispensatory faculties contained in this Constitution are, by virtue of canon 1125, now extended to all cases in which the essential conditions required by the papal grant are verified.[36] Hence those possessing these faculties may use them in any part of the world.[37]

B. *Conditions Essential for the Use of the Faculties*

The faculties of dispensing can only be used validly: (1) when the absent spouse cannot be interpellated, or, (2) when the spouse, whether present or absent, has not communicated his or her intention within the time stipulated in the admonition.

1. The impossibility of making interpellations can arise in different ways: for example, because the hostility of a country prevents the transmission of interpellations, or, because the dwelling place of the spouse cannot be ascertained, or, because the length of the journey involved presents grave difficulty.[38] It seems to be the common opinion of authors that any moral impossibility suffices.[39]

2. Failure of the spouse, whether present or absent, to reply to the interpellations within the fixed time, constitutes a sufficient cause for granting the dispensation.[40] A reasonable amount of time for making the reply should be allowed the infidel spouse.[41] This period will vary depending upon the different circumstances of each case.

For each case in which a dispensation from the interpellations is to be applied a summary and extrajudicial process should be employed. This should contain a brief statement showing the necessity for granting the dispensation.[42]

---

[35] Cf. Document VIII of the Code of Canon Law.

[36] This Constitution was originally granted for Angola, Ethiopia, Brazil, and other countries of the Indies. Later, in 1777, it was extended to China, and afterward to the whole of Asia: cf. Woods, *Constitutions of Canon 1125*, p. 72; Feije, *De Impedimentis Et Dispensationibus Matrimonialibus*, 3 ed., 1885, n. 48.

[37] Cf. W.-V., V, 633; Cappello, *De Matrimonio*, 787; *Epit.*, II, 436; Vermeersch, *Per.*, XX, pp. 1*–5*; Bouscaren, *Miscellanea Vermeersch* (Roma, 1935), Vol. I, pp. 283–286; Vromant, *De Matrimonio*, 340; Woods, *op. cit.*, pp. 76–82; Petrovits, *The New Church Law on Matrimony*, 574; Joyce, *Christian Marriage*, p. 492; Payen, *De Matrimonio*, II, 2404 ff.; etc.

[38] S. Off., Resp., Nov. 29, 1882, *Fontes*, 1075; Payen, *op. cit.*, 2409; Vromant, *De Matrimonio*, 348; Burton, *A Commentary On Canon 1125* (Dissert. C. U., 1940), p. 168.

[39] Cf. Cappello, *op. cit.*, 4 ed., 787; De Lery, *Le Privilege de la Foi*, p. 89; Payen, *op. cit.*, II, 2409; Bouscaren, *op. cit.*, p. 294; Vromant, *Per.*, XX, p. 116*; Burton, *op. cit.*, p. 169.

[40] Cf. Payen, *op. cit.*, 2409; Burton, *op. cit.*, p. 171.

[41] Cf. Burton, *op. cit.*, p. 171.

[42] S. Off., Inst., June 11, 1760, *Fontes*, IV, 811; Payen, *op. cit.*, 2409; Burton, *op. cit.*, p. 171.

C. *Persons Endowed With These Faculties*

According to the Code Commission the tenor of the Constitution, *Populis,* is the norm which must be used for determining the persons who enjoy these faculties.[43] In the papal document jurisdiction is expressly granted to local Ordinaries, pastors, and priests of the Society of Jesus who have been approved for hearing confessions by superiors of their order.

1. Local Ordinaries

By the expression "local Ordinaries" is meant all persons mentioned in canon 198, § 1, excepting religious superiors (can. 198, § 2).

2. Priests of the Society of Jesus Approved for Confessions

Priests of the Society of Jesus who are approved for confessions by their superiors and who for the time being are either sent to the countries specified or are admitted to them, possess the powers in question. At present, according to the general norm of the Code (can. 874, § 1), priests of the Society are constituted confessors for the faithful only when they have received faculties from the Ordinary of the place where they hear confessions.[44] Hence outside of the countries mentioned in the Gregorian Constitution, they require faculties from the local Ordinary in order that they might validly exercise the jurisdiction granted by can. 1125.[45]

3. Religious of Other Institutes

Religious pertaining to other institutes which by communication have shared in the privileges of the Society of Jesus enjoy the same jurisdiction as Jesuit confessors,[46] so long as they acquired the privileges before the promulgation of the Code (can. 613).[47]

4. Pastors and Quasi-Pastors

All pastors and quasi-pastors have the faculties under consideration. The Constitution of Gregory XIII expressly mentions pastors, and the Code Commission has authentically declared that, in virtue of canon 1125, quasi-pastors receive by law the same faculty to dispense.[48] It follows that all pastors and quasi-pastors of exempt institutes possess this power.

---

[43] Cod. Com., Reply (Private), Jan. 26, 1919, Bouscaren, *The Canon Law Digest,* Supplement — 1941, can. 1125.

[44] Bouscaren, *Miscellanea Vermeersch,* I, p. 298; Woods, *op. cit.,* p. 69; Vromant, *Per.,* XX, p. 117*; Burton, *op. cit.,* p. 175.

[45] Cf. Cappello, *De Matrimonio,* 787.

[46] Cf. Clericatus, *Decisiones De Matrimonio* (Venetiis, 1716), Dec. XI, n. 28; Burton, *op. cit.,* p. 70, note 29, and p. 174.

[47] Cod. Com., Reply, Dec. 30, 1937, AAS. XXX, 73; Bouscaren, *The Canon Law Digest,* Supplement — 1941, can. 613.

[48] Cod. Com. Reply (Private), Aug. 3, 1919; Bouscaren, *op. cit.,* can. 1125.

5. Confessors in General

Some authors maintain that canon 1125 extends the faculties of the Gregorian Constitution to all confessors.[49] However, the more common opinion denying this extention seems to be the correct one. The Code Commission appears to have settled the issue when it declared that the persons having these powers are determined in the Constitution itself.[50] From the tenor of the papal document confessors in general are accorded no jurisdiction whatever.

D. *Nature of the Faculties*

By law the faculties in question are attached to the offices of local Ordinaries, pastors, and quasi-pastors, and hence are ordinary in character (can. 197, § 1). In the case of confessors of the Society of Jesus and of other institutes the jurisdiction granted by canon 1125 is delegated; for confessors, as such, do not hold an ecclesiastical office in the strict sense of the term (can. 145). Nevertheless these confessors may subdelegate such faculties, and even habitually, since the power of subdelegation is not forbidden (cf. can. 199, § 2).[1]

Jurisdiction granted by the Constitution, *Populis,* may be employed both in the internal and external forum.[2] Since, by canon 1125, the exempt religious mentioned above (C. nn. 2, 3) are directly empowered to grant the dispensations in question, neither their own superiors nor local Ordinaries can impede them in this matter.

The local Ordinary may exact a statement of cases which have been handled in the external forum. Nevertheless, such a statement would merely constitute an instrument to furnish evidence that the dispensation had been granted, and would in nowise affect the validity of the dispensation. It is clear from the Constitution itself that the validity of the dispensation and of the subsequent marriage depends only on whether or not the privileged person who performed the ministry had faculties to hear confessions.[3]

Article VIII. Sacramentals

Sacramentals are objects or actions which the Church makes use of, in imitation of the sacraments, for the purpose of obtaining favors, especially those of a spiritual nature, through her intercession (can. 1144). Examples

---

[49] Payen, *op. cit.,* II, 2409; Aertnys-Damen, *Theologia Moralis,* Vol. II, n. 922, footnote.
[50] Cf. Woods, *op. cit.,* p. 68; *Epit.,* II, 435; De Lery, *op. cit.,* p. 120; Burton, *op. cit.,* p. 175; Vromant, *De Matrimonio,* 351, nota 2.
[1] Cf. Bouscaren, *Miscellanea Vermeersch,* I, p. 298; Burton, *op. cit.,* p. 175.
[2] Cf. Cappello, *op. cit.,* 787; Vromant, *Per.,* XX, p. 117*; Bouscaren, *Miscellanea Vermeersch,* I, p. 298.
[3] Cf. Cappello, *op. cit.,* 787.

of such objects are: blessed candles, palms, holy water, rosaries; examples of actions are: consecrations, blessings, exorcisms.

All priests, hence those of exempt institutes, are by virtue of their ordination legitimate ministers of sacramentals (can. 1146). In all cases not reserved to particular persons, they may confer blessings (can. 1147, § 2).[4]

The power of conferring sacramentals is *reserved* to particular persons, in many cases. Some blessings are reserved to Bishops, and others to religious and parish priests, as may be seen in the Roman Ritual.[5]

1. Thus *only Bishops* can bless holy oils, relic cases, etc. So, too, only Bishops, and ecclesiastics authorized by common law or papal indult, can consecrate (can. 1147, § 1). An example of papal indults conferring such faculties is that possessed by the Franciscans and the Jesuits, whereby their priests laboring on the missions are entitled to consecrate chalices and patens, in the absence of the Bishop[6] (cf. Chap. X preliminary notions).

According to the latest Formula of Quinquennial Faculties for local Ordinaries of the United States these Ordinaries are entitled *"to depute priests —* if possible such as hold some ecclesiastical dignity: to consecrate fixed and portable altars, observing the rite and form of the Roman Pontifical, and as regards portable altars, also using merely the approved short ritual formula; . . . to consecrate fixed and portable altars which have lost their consecration, using the shorter formula, B, for cases coming under canon 1200, § 2, of the Code, while in cases coming under canon 1200, § 1, the canon itself gives the faculty, and formula A is to be used; . . . to consecrate chalices and patens, observing the rite and form of the Roman Pontifical" (cf. Bouscaren, *The Canon Law Digest,* Supplement — 1941, can. 66, Faculties from the Sacred Congregation of Rites, nn. 1, 2, 3).

2. To *parish* priests are reserved the rights to confer the nuptial blessing, and the solemn blessing of homes on Easter Saturday. It is also their exclusive right to bless the baptismal font in their churches (can. 462).

3. Certain blessings have been reserved to *religious,* e.g., the blessings of the Stations of the Cross to the Friars Minor, of the rosary to the Friars Preachers, of the scapulars of Mount Carmel to the Carmelites.[7]

For their own churches and oratories, and for those of nuns subject to them, religious superiors and priests of their own institute whom they have delegated have the faculty to bless those sacred furnishings which, according to liturgical law, should be blessed before being put to their

---

[4] Cf. *Pontificale Romanum, De ordin. presbyt.;* see Ferraris, v, *Benedictio,* art. I, 14, 15; Gasparri, *De Sacra Ordin.,* nn. 1137 f.; W.-V., IV, Vol. I, 309; d'Angelo, p. 76.
[5] Cf. Rit. Rom., tit. VIII, Appendix.
[6] Cf. Adrian, VI, Const., *Exponi Nobis;* Paul III, Const., *Licet debitum,* par. 35, Oct. 18, 1549: see, Piat, II, p. 360.
[7] Cf. Ayrinhac, *Legislation on the Sacraments,* 340; when authorized other priests, whether religious or secular, may confer these blessings, cf. Beringer-Steinen, I, 683, 903, 923, 924.

destined use (can. 1304, 5°).[8] Thus, they can bless the tabernacle, altar cloths, vestments, and other such objects.

As stated above, many blessings are not reserved to any particular ecclesiastic. Thus, for example, when asked to do so, religious may impart a simple (i.e., a nonsolemn) blessing to crops, ships, fields, bridges, roads, animals, houses, etc.[9]

The effect of the reservation renders unlawful, not invalid, blessings imparted without permission of the one to whom they are reserved, unless the Holy See has expressly provided otherwise in the reservation (can. 1147, § 3).

Exorcisms are reserved to the local Ordinary. Hence, to exorcise a possessed person, a priest, even though he be an exempt religious, must obtain special and express permission of the local Ordinary (can. 1151).[10]

---

[8] Cf. S.R.C., Aug. 18, 1629; Cameracen, March 13, 1632; decr., Sept. 27, 1659, nn. 18, 19, etc.; cf. *Fontes* for this canon.

[9] Cf. S.R.C., June 13, 1893, ad 6; S.C.C., Aug. 31, 1629; S.C.EE.RR., Nov. 28, 1664, Biz., 262; Sept. 15, 1788, ap. J. P., XVI, 635, n. 1412; cf. *Monit.*. VII, part I, p. 217: see Piat, II, p. 364; d'Angelo, p. 76; W.-V., IV, Vol. I, 309, nota 29.

[10] Cf. Bened. XIV, ep., *Sollicitudini,* par. 43, Oct. 1, 1745; ep. encycl., *Magno cum,* par. 34, June 2, 1751; S.C.P.F. instr. (ad Ep. Scodren.), n. 1, Sept. 11, 1779.

CHAPTER XIII

DIVINE WORSHIP

After issuing provisions for the administration and reception of the sacraments, the legislator sets down norms which regulate some of the principal acts of divine worship. In the discharge of their ministries exempt religious must of necessity participate in many of these functions. The purpose of the present chapter is to review briefly those in which the Code establishes a definite relationship between exempt religious and local Ordinaries.

Article I. The Approbation of Prayers and Pious Exercises

Prayers and pious exercises in general constitute an important element of Catholic worship. For this reason they must always be consonant with faith and piety.

It is not permitted, therefore, to use prayers and pious exercises in churches or oratories, unless they have been revised and authorized by the local Ordinary beforehand. The opportuneness, and the dogmatic and traditional correctness of all such matters should always be carefully studied. Utmost caution is demanded. In the more difficult cases the Ordinary should submit the entire affair to the Apostolic See (can. 1259, § 1).

To gain a reasonable understanding of this canon several points are worthy of attention.

The prayers and exercises referred to are those which have not yet been approved for common use in the Church.[1] Oratories are mentioned, without a distinction being made between the public and semipublic ones. Likewise no distinction is drawn between exempt and nonexempt churches and oratories, so that now, as formerly,[2] the regulation refers to both.[3]

The rule given in canon 1259, § 1, does not, however, apply to every manner of use. If prayers and exercises are used for the faithful, that is, publicly, they need the approbation of the local Ordinary; if used privately in chapels or semipublic oratories of exempt clerical institutes for these religious, they require the approval of the religious Ordinary alone.[4]

Even the approval of local Ordinaries is not sufficient for the use of all

---

[1] Cf. *Epit.*, II, 579; Claeys Bouuaert-Simenon, 824.
[2] Cf. Conc. Trid., sess. XXV, *de invocat.*
[3] Cf. Ayrinhac, *Administrative Legislation,* 107.
[4] Cf. *Epit.*, II, 579.

types of prayer. That is clear from canon 1259, § 2, which states that local Ordinaries are not competent to approve *new litanies* destined for public use. This rule having been in force prior to the Code, must be interpreted in the sense of the former legislation, as referring only to the liturgical use, or the public recitation.[5] The recitation of litanies by a number of people together in a church or public oratory, even though not conducted by a person acting as minister, is considered public recitation.[6] Nuns in choir are forbidden to recite litanies not approved by the Holy See even if the choir be separated from the church by grates.[7]

The Holy See forbids interpolations of invocations and all deviations from the form in which the litany has been approved. Some religious are permitted to insert the name of their founder or patriarch but of no other saint.[8]

ARTICLE II. SUPERVISION OF LOCAL ORDINARIES OVER MATTERS OF DIVINE WORSHIP

The Church has committed to local Ordinaries the duty of seeing that the sacred canons on divine worship are faithfully observed and that abuses are eliminated. They should eradicate from private or public worship and from the daily lives of the faithful all superstitious practices and whatever is contrary to faith, discordant with ecclesiastical tradition, or has the appearance of sordid money-making (can. 1261). The last-mentioned abuse must be particularly guarded against for it can readily manifest itself in popular exercise of devotion.

The local Ordinary must be vigilant in these matters even over exempt religious. If he publishes any regulations different from the common law, even exempt religious must observe them, and the Ordinary may visit their churches and public oratories to see that they are carried out (can. 1261, § 2). He has no authority to visit their semipublic oratories.

The power of visitation here given does not derogate particular privileges which free some Regulars from all episcopal visitation.[9] It is subject, too, to the limitations expressed in the canon and in the authentic interpretation given by the President of the Code Commission.[10]

---

[5] Cf. S.R.C., Aug. 29, 1882, Decr. auth. 3555: see *Epit.*, II, 580.

[6] Cf. S.R.C., Mar. 6, 1894, Decr. auth. 3820, and June 20, 1896, Decr. auth. 3916.

[7] Cf. S.R.C., June 1, 1896, Decr. auth. 3916: see Woywod, II, 1286. The following have Apostolic approval: the litany of the Saints contained in the Breviary and in the Clementine instruction on the Forty Hours' Devotion; the litany of the Holy Name of Jesus; the litany of the Sacred Heart; the litany of the Blessed Virgin (Laurentine); the litany of St. Joseph; the litany to be recited for persons in their last agony (cf. *Rit. Rom.*): see, *Epit.*, II, 580; Augustine, VI, can. 1259.

[8] Cf. S.R.C., June 16, 1674, Decr. auth. 1518; Feb. 11, 1702, Decr. auth. 2093; Mar. 20, 1706, Decr. auth. 2166.

[9] Cf. *Epit.*, II, 583.

[10] Cf. above, Chap. X, Art. I; see also, Coronata, II ,834; C.p.R., Goyeneche, VI, pp. 357–360, Marcellus a P. Jesu, IX, pp. 235–244, Kraemer, IX, 245–248.

ARTICLE III. RESERVATION AND WORSHIP OF THE BLESSED SACRAMENT

I. RESERVATION OF THE BLESSED SACRAMENT

Certain places of exempt institutes *must* reserve the Blessed Sacrament; others *may* do so with the authorization of competent superiors.

A. The Blessed Sacrament *must* be kept in churches attached to the canonically erected houses of exempt religious, whether they be men or women (can. 1265, § 1, 1°). It would seem that even nuns who no longer enjoy exemption, v.g., those in France, Belgium, the United States, and elsewhere, are bound by this law.[11] This canon applies also to public oratories (cf. can. 1191, § 1).[12]

B. With the permission of the local Ordinary, the Blessed Sacrament *may* be kept in collegiate churches, in the principal public and semipublic oratories of religious or pious houses and in ecclesiastical colleges in charge of the secular or religious clergy (can. 1265).

A *pious house* is one established for pious works. Such would be orphanages and hospitals whose spiritual care is in the hands of a priest or religious, and Catholic schools in general.[13] The expression "ecclesiastical college," used in this canon, means, an institution in which young men are prepared for the clerical or religious state.[14]

Permission of the local Ordinary is required even by Regulars if they wish to reserve the Blessed Sacrament in public or semipublic oratories of their community houses or of any pious houses or seminaries under their authority. Oral or written, explicit or implicit, and even presumed permission of the local Ordinary suffices in the cases spoken of in canon 1265, paragraph 1, 2°.[15] The rights to reserve the Blessed Sacrament which have been acquired through immemorial custom or special privileges retain their juridical force.[16] For examples of such privileges, consult the Constitution, *Licet debitum,* of Paul III,[17] and the Brief, *Quemadmodum Presbyteri,* of Benedict XIV.[18]

In religious and pious houses the Blessed Sacrament may be kept only in the church or principal oratory; in monasteries of nuns it may not be reserved within the choir or enclosure. All privileges contrary to this prescription are revoked (can. 1267).

This canon contains a twofold prohibition: on the one hand, it excludes

---

[11] Cf. *Epit.*, II, 588.
[12] Cf. Pejska, p. 284.
[13] Cf. *Epit.*, II, 589.
[14] Cf. *Epit.*, II, 589; Claeys Bouuaert-Simenon, 833; De Meester, 1259; *Per.,* V, 33, 39.
[15] Cf. Ayrinhac, *Administrative Legislation,* 113; Augustine, VI, can. 1265.
[16] Cf. Gatticus, XVIII, 10; Piat, II, p. 241; Vermeersch, *De Rel.,* I, 505; *Epit.,* II, 589; Bondini, p. 118; Ayrinhac, *Administrative Legislation,* 113.
[17] Cf. Paul III, Const., *Licet debitum,* Oct. 18, 1549.
[18] Cf. Bened. XIV, Br., *Quemadmodum Presbyteri,* July 15, 1749.

a plurality of places of reservation for one house; on the other, it forbids reservation within the choir or cloister of nuns.

The meaning of the first prohibition is this: "If a house of religion or piety is connected with a public church and makes use of it for its ordinary daily exercises of piety, the Blessed Sacrament may be kept there only; otherwise it may be kept in the principal oratory of the said house of religion or piety (without prejudice to the right of the church, if any), and nowhere else, unless in the same material building there are distinct and separate families, so that formally they constitute distinct houses of religion or piety (cf. Cod. Com., June 3, 1918, Bouscaren, I, 1267).[19]

The meaning of the second prohibition is clear in the light of paragraph 1, 1° (can. 1265); for since nuns are under the strict rules of papal cloister, reservation of the Blessed Sacrament within that choir or cloister would prevent a priest from celebrating the prescribed weekly Mass.[20]

Because of the revocatory clause of canon 1267, religious organizations may no longer claim the rights formerly granted them by special privilege.[21]

C. To reserve the Blessed Sacrament in churches or oratories other than those mentioned in paragraph 1 of canon 1265, requires an apostolic indult; for a just cause, the local Ordinary may grant this permission to a church or public oratory, but only by way of act, not habitually (can. 1265, § 2).

This prescription would hold, for example, in the case of *churches* of *confraternities,* which are neither parish churches nor churches of exempt institutes; in the case of *all private* oratories except those of cardinals or Bishops; and in the case of semipublic oratories which do not serve as the main chapel of the religious community.[22]

II. CUSTODY OF THE TABERNACLE

In her utmost care for the Blessed Sacrament, the Church has always supplied local Ordinaries with protective and precautionary measures by which the Holy Eucharist which is reserved in churches should always be carefully guarded and protected against profanation.

The Code decrees that the Blessed Sacrament must be kept in an immovable tabernacle in the middle of the altar. The tabernacle should be securely closed on all sides, and so carefully guarded that there is no danger of sacrilegious profanation. For grave reasons, and with the authorization of the local Ordinary, it is permitted to take the Blessed Sacrament out of the tabernacle overnight, and to keep it in a more secure but decent place, always on a corporal and with a light burning before it. The key of the

---

[19] Cf. AAS, X, 346: see *Epit.,* II, 592; *Per.,* IX, p. 151; J. P., 1922, p. 54.
[20] Cf. *Epit.,* II, 592.
[21] Cf. Bondini, p. 116.
[22] Cf. Augustine, VI, can. 1265.

tabernacle in which the Blessed Sacrament is kept must be carefully guarded; this is a grave obligation which rests on the conscience of the priest who is in charge of the church or oratory (can. 1269).

Detailed instruction as to the obligations and the manner of fulfilling them has been issued by the Sacred Congregation of the Sacraments on the Feast of the Ascension, 1938, and these norms must be strictly followed by all local Ordinaries and by others to whom they particularly apply, all things to the contrary notwithstanding.

1. Exempt religious must have permission of the local Ordinary if they wish to remove the Blessed Sacrament from the tabernacle and keep it during the night in a safer place (can. 1269, § 3).[23]

2. The Holy See instructs Bishops and local Ordinaries to use the greatest care and vigilance in order to obtain the fullest cooperation of all concerned in the custody of the Blessed Sacrament.

3. Should profanations occur, the local Ordinary, either himself or by delegate, must draw up a process against the pastor or against any other priest, either secular or religious, *even exempt,* who had the custody of the Blessed Sacrament. This process must be transmitted to the Sacred Congregation of the Sacraments together with the Bishop's own denunciation, in which he is to describe the particulars of the case, report whose was the fault or culpable negligence, propose the canonical penalties which should be inflicted on the culprit, and await the orders of the congregation.[24]

4. This office of Bishops and local Ordinaries with respect to Regulars is provided for in canon 617. Before the Code both local Ordinaries and religious superiors were competent to punish one who proved delinquent in his custody of the tabernacle key.[25] Local Ordinaries can no longer directly apply punitive measures in these cases.[26]

5. Olive oil or beeswax is to be used in the sanctuary lamp which is to burn continually before the tabernacle in which the Blessed Sacrament is reserved. When the aforesaid materials are not available, other vegetable oils may be used, with the permission of the local Ordinary (can. 1271). Regulars are obliged to obey this precept.[27]

6. Hosts consecrated for the Communion of the faithful or for the Exposition of the Blessed Sacrament must be fresh and frequently renewed;[28] old particles must be consumed as prescribed so that all danger of corruption may be avoided. Instructions and regulations of local Ordinaries

---

[23] Cf. Bondini, p. 144.

[24] Cf. S. C. Sacr., May 26, 1938, AAS, XXXVIII, pp. 198–207; E.R., XCIX, 2, p. 167.

[25] Cf. S.C.EE.RR., Feb. 9, 1751, ap. Lucidi, L. I, c. 1, n. 101; Bened. XIV, *De Syn. Dioec.,* L. IX, c. 15, n. 4; Vermeersch, *De Rel.,* I, 505.

[26] Cf. Bondini, p. 83; Melo, p. 144.

[27] Cf. S.R.C., July 14, 1864, Decr. auth. 3121; Melo, p. 144.

[28] Cf. S. C. Sacr., Aug. 2, 1922, AAS, XI, 8, and Mar. 26, 1929, AAS, XXI, 621: see *Per.,* XVIII, 305.

in these matters must be faithfully observed (can. 1272) even by exempt religious.[29]

III. EXPOSITION OF THE BLESSED SACRAMENT

In canon 1274, the distinction is drawn between *private* exposition, that is, with a pyx or ciborium, and *public,* with a monstrance. The expression "public exposition," employed in canon 1274, paragraph 1, includes also Eucharistic Benediction, which is usually given with the Blessed Sacrament openly exposed in the monstrance.[30] Private exposition is permitted for any just cause. No authorization of the local Ordinary is required.

Public exposition may be held in all churches where the Blessed Sacrament is reserved[31] on the Feast of Corpus Christi and during the octave at either Mass or Vespers. At other times, public exposition may be held only for a real and grave reason and with the permission of the local Ordinary. This provision holds for churches and oratories of exempt religious. Nothing is defined as to the manner in which the Bishop should accord this permission. Hence he may give it explicitly or implicitly, expressly or tacitly.[32]

The Sacred Congregation of Rites has decreed that the custom of holding public exposition without the consent of the local Ordinary cannot be sustained,[33] unless the custom be immemorial in character.[34]

It is probable that Regulars of male institutes may hold public exposition in their churches and oratories if the doors are kept closed, without asking permission of the local Ordinary. Under such circumstances, the authorization of their proper prelate seems sufficient.[35]

Regulations of the local Ordinary regarding the public exposition of the Blessed Sacrament and Vespers service must be observed even in churches of Regulars.[36]

Canon 1275 recommends that the Forty Hours' Devotion be held each year in all churches in which the Blessed Sacrament is habitually reserved. These sacred functions should be carried on with all possible solemnity, on fixed days, with the approval of the local Ordinary. Manifestly, this recommendation is extended to churches of Regulars.[37] The prescription of canon 1275 does not accord local Ordinaries direct power to determine

---

[29] Cf. *Epit.,* II, 597; Melo, p. 145.
[30] Cf. Cod Com., Reply, Mar. 6, 1927, III, AAS, XIX, 161; *Per.,* XVI, 60; J. P., 1927, 7; E.R. 76, 610.
[31] Cf. Cod. Com., July 14, 1922, AAS, XIV, 529.
[32] Cf. Bondini, pp. 118, 119.
[33] Cf. S.R.C., Resp., Mar. 16, 1861, Decr. auth. 3104: see *Epit.,* II, 599.
[34] Cf. S.C.C., Decr., June 12, 1658, ad Episc. Urbaniae, and April 3, 1821: see Bondini, p. 118.
[35] Cf. Wernz, III, 353, nota 235; *Epit.,* II, 599.
[36] Cf. *Epit.,* I, 505; Bondini, p. 119.
[37] Cf. Bondini, p. 118; Woywod, II, 1303.

definite days for the different churches of the diocese, but demands that their approval be sought for the days on which the pastors or superiors of churches wish to hold these services.[38]

The Second Plenary Council of Baltimore obtained for the churches of the United States the indulgences and privileges of the Forty Hours' Devotion granted by Clement VIII, with special permission to expose the Blessed Sacrament during the day only, and to omit the procession if the pastor cannot hold it with convenience.[39]

ARTICLE IV. THE CULT OF SACRED IMAGES AND RELICS

The dogmatic foundation, and the usefulness of the cult of images and relics is beyond dispute (can. 1276).[40] In her solicitude for such matters, the Church affirms that local Ordinaries have the right and duty to guard against errors and abuses even with respect to churches of exempt religious.

I. CULT OF SACRED IMAGES

Canon 1279 declares that without the approval of the local Ordinary, no one may place nor arrange for the placing of an image that is unusual in character, in churches even of exempt religious, or in other sacred places.

This is practically a repetition of the rule issued by the Council of Trent against the display of images which depart from traditional representations.[41] The term "images" comprises statues, painted or printed pictures, medallions, etc.[42]

Subjection of exempt churches to the local Ordinary is expressly stated in the law. Furthermore, it is clear from the purpose of the law that public oratories are affected by it. Approbations for images to be placed in semipublic oratories of exempt institutes pertains to the religious Ordinary.[43]

Neither the local nor the religious Ordinary should permit images to be exhibited for public veneration which are not in keeping with approved usage (can. 1279, § 2). They must never allow the exhibition, in churches or other sacred places, of images which convey false dogmatic notions, or offend against propriety and decency, or are likely to lead the ignorant into error (can. 1279, § 3). A number of specific prohibitions have been issued. Thus, for example, it is forbidden to represent saints in modern form or costume,[44] or the Blessed Virgin clothed in the habit of a religious

---

[38] Cf. *Epit.*, II, 600.

[39] Cf. Conc. Balt. II, Decr. IV, 377; S.C.P.F., Jan. 24, 1868; see Woywod, II, 1303; Ayrinhac, *Administrative Legislation*, 126.

[40] Cf. *c. un. de reliquiis et reveratione sanctorum*, III, 22 in VI; Conc. Trid., sess. XXV, *de invocat. venerat. et reliquis sanctorum et sac. imag.*

[41] Cf. Conc. Trid., sess. XXV, *de invocat.*, etc.

[42] Cf. Augustine, VI, can. 1279.

[43] Cf. Pejska, p. 321.

[44] Cf. Urban VIII, const., *Sacrosancta*, March 15, 1642.

order,[45] or in priestly vestments.[46] The Holy Ghost may not be represented in human form either together with the Father and the Son, or separately.[47] Benedict XIV established a positive norm, by declaring that God and the Divine Persons should be depicted in the forms in which they have appeared according to scriptural accounts, v.g., the Holy Ghost in the form of a dove, not as a youth.[48]

On the occasion of the dedication of the new Vatican Picture Gallery, Oct. 27, 1932, His Holiness Pius XI declared the so-called "New Sacred Art" unworthy to have part in the building or decoration of the house of God.[49]

It should be noted that sacred pictures are not to be printed without the previous censorship of the local Ordinary (cf. can. 1399, 12°).

Major superiors of exempt clerical institutes may personally, or by a delegate, solemnly bless images to be placed in their churches, oratories, etc. (can. 1279, § 4). To do this in the case of places not subject to them they require the permission of the local Ordinary. Any priest is allowed to bless, with the simple rite, images venerated in private houses.[50]

II. CULT OF RELICS

Relics may not be exposed for public veneration in any, even exempt, churches unless their genuineness is attested to by authentic documents from a Cardinal, or local Ordinary, or any ecclesiastic endowed with an apostolic indult to authenticate them (can. 1283, § 1). Generally the Postulator General has the faculty to authenticate relics of Servants of God pertaining to his institute.

Relics which are certainly unauthentic should be prudently removed from public veneration (can. 1284) and destroyed.[1] If, however, through civil disturbances or other causes, the authenticating documents have been lost, relics should not be exposed for public veneration until they have been previously approved by the local Ordinary. Unless he has a special mandate, the Vicar-General cannot grant this approval (can. 1285, § 1). Ancient relics which have been venerated by the faithful should be retained unless certain evidence shows that they are manifestly spurious (can. 1285, § 2).[2]

Local Ordinaries should not permit public discussion which calls in

---

[45] Cf. Urban VIII, *loc. cit.*
[46] Cf. S. Off., Reply, April 8, 1916, AAS, VIII, 146; *Per.,* VIII, 174: see also S.R.C., Nov. 29, 1879, Decr. auth. 3470; Feb. 23, 1894, Decr. auth. 3818.
[47] Cf. S. Off., Reply, Mar. 16, 1928, AAS, XX, 103.
[48] Cf. Bened. XIV, Epist., *Sollicitudini nostrae,* par. 8, Oct. 1, 1745.
[49] Cf. Pius XI, Address, Oct. 27, 1932, AAS, XXIV, 355, Bouscaren, I, can. 1164; *Per.,* XXII, 31: see also, S. Off., Mar. 30, 1921, AAS, XIII, 197.
[50] Cf. Pejska, p. 322.
[1] Cf. S.R.C., Aug. 3, 1687, Decr. auth. 1977.
[2] Cf. Pius X, *Sacrorum Antistitum,* Sept. 1, 1910, AAS, II, 664: see also, S. C. Indulg., Feb. 22, 1847, and Jan. 20, 1896; S.R.C., June 23, 1892, Decr. auth. 3779.

question the authenticity of sacred relics, if the arguments adduced are based on mere conjecture, or pure probability, or prejudice; especially if the methods employed are liable to arouse ridicule or contempt. Discussions concerning the genuiness of relics are to be excluded especially from sermons and from books, periodicals, or pamphlets dedicated to the furthering of piety and devotion.[3]

ARTICLE V. SACRED PROCESSIONS

Sacred processions are liturgical in character and consequently are regulated by the disciplinary measures governing such matters.

Unless altered by the Code, the rights and obligations of exempt religious with respect to liturgical processions remain the same as they were prior to the promulgation of the Code. This follows from the fact that the Code of Canon Law, for the most part, decrees nothing about the rites and ceremonies prescribed by the approved liturgical books. Hence liturgical laws, which are not penal (can. 6, 5°, 6°), retain their force unless they have been expressly corrected by the Code (can. 2). Therefore, pontifical constitutions and authentic decrees of the Sacred Congregation of Rites which are not contrary to the liturgical provisions contained in the Code constitute the juridical norms for such matters as sacred processions.[4]

I. THE MEANING AND KINDS OF PROCESSIONS

The expression "sacred procession" means the solemn supplications made by the faithful marching from one sacred place to another under the leadership of the clergy, for the purpose of promoting piety, commemorating God's benefits, thanking Him for His graces, and imploring His help (can. 1290, § 1). It is to be remarked that the leadership of the clergy constitutes an essential element in ecclesiastical processions.

Processions are of two types, ordinary and extraordinary. *Ordinary* processions are those held on fixed days during the year, according to the sacred liturgy or the custom of churches (can. 1290, § 2). Those determined in the Roman Ritual[5] are held on Candlemas Day, on Palm Sunday, on April 25 (the so-called greater litanies), on the three Rogation Days preceding the Feast of the Ascension, and on the Feast of Corpus Christi. As canon 1290 states, custom may establish other sacred processions for particular churches. *Extraordinary* processions are those held on other than the fixed days, for some public reason. Under this second type, according to the Roman Ritual, would be classified those held in special emergencies,

---

[3] Cf. Pius X, Litt. encycl., *Pascendi*, Sept. 8, 1907, and Const., *Sacrorum Antistitum*, n. VI, Sept. 1, 1910.
[4] Cf. Van Hove, Vol. I, Tom. II, 8.
[5] Cf. *Rit. Rom.*, tit. IX, c. 1, n. 8.

v.g., to obtain rain, or fair weather, or peace; to avert storm, famine, pestilence, war, or other calamities; to return thanks, etc.

II. THE RIGHTS AND OBLIGATIONS OF EXEMPT RELIGIOUS

According to the former law, Regulars, not other exempt religious,[6] were obliged to assist at sacred processions if the Bishop had invited them to do so.[7] Although formerly Bishops could impose penalties on those refusing to participate,[8] they have not now this coactive power (cf. can. 6, 5°, 6°).

The law of the Code declares that the local Ordinary, after taking advice of his chapter or consultors, may, for a public cause, prescribe extraordinary processions. All persons who according to canon 1291, § 1, are obliged to be present at the Corpus Christi procession must attend such extraordinary processions, and also the ordinary ones which have been established by custom or law (can. 1292).

There are express exceptions to this general law. Thus, the following are exempted from attendance at processions:

1. Those bound by strict cloister or living at a considerable distance from the place in which the procession is held (can. 1291, par. 1).[9]

2. Those favored by a legitimate contrary custom (can. 1291, par. 1).[10]

3. Those who, after the Council of Trent, have been granted a special privilege,[11] such as the Discalced Carmelites,[12] the Clerics Regular of St. Paul,[13] the Theatines,[14] the Jesuits,[15] the Clerics of the pious schools of the Mother of God.[16]

Privileges of this kind were noncommunicable.[17]

4. Those who are not summoned or invited to the procession[18] (can. 1291, par. 1).

---

[6] Cf. S.C.EE.RR., Reply in Pinerolien, July 30, 1667, Biz., pp. 428–434: Vermeersch, *De Rel.*, I, 454, n. 5.

[7] Cf. Conc. Trid., sess. XXV, c. 13, *de Regul.*

[8] Cf. Urban, VIII, Decr., July 27, 1628: S.C.C., July 27, 1627 and Aug. 3, 1658, ap. Pignatelli, III, cons, XLVI, 12 ff.

[9] Cf. Conc. Trid., sess. XXV, c. 13, *de Regul.;* Leo X, Const., *Dum intra,* par. 5, Dec. 19, 1516.

[10] Cf. Urban VIII, Const., *Nuper,* par. 2, Oct. 16, 1640; S.R.C., June 10, 1602: see Peyr., Priv. III, II, 29; Cesp., CCX, 1; Pell., V, XI, 13; Piat, II, p. 39.

[11] Cf. Urban VIII, Decr., July 27, 1628.

[12] Cf. Clem. VIII, Const., *Romanum Pontificem,* par. 4, Sept. 9, 1603.

[13] Cf. Sixtus V, Const., *Rationi congruit,* par. 1, May 1, 1585.

[14] Cf. St. Pius V, Const., *Ad immarcesibilem,* par. 10, Feb. 13, 1567.

[15] Cf. Greg. XIII, Const., *Quaecumque,* par. 3, July 16, 1576.

[16] Cf. Urban VIII, Const., *Debitum,* par. 2, June 1, 1629.

[17] Cf. S.C.EE.RR., in Pinarolien, July 30, 1667, Biz., 429; see Pell., V, XI, 5; Giraldi, *Jus. Pont.,* II, sect. 168; Piat, II, p. 40.

[18] Cf. S.C.EE.RR., May 1, 1649; Conc. Trid., *loc. cit.;* see Pell., V, XI, 4; Tamb., I, XXIV, VIII, 2; Ferraris, v, *Processiones,* 20; Piat, II, p. 40.

III. CORPUS CHRISTI PROCESSION

The procession of Corpus Christi which is devoted to the cult of the Blessed Sacrament ranks chief among the ordinary processions.

The Code makes special provisions for its celebration.

A. Unless, in the Bishop's judgment, local circumstances or immemorial custom favors other arrangements, the following rules are in force (can. 1291):

1. On the Feast of Corpus Christi only one solemn procession may be held in the public streets of a city.

2. This should be conducted by the principal church of the place.

3. The secular clergy, religious communities of men, even though exempt, and members of lay confraternities must take part in the procession.

4. Regulars who live in perpetual and strict enclosure, or who dwell at a considerable distance (about three miles) from the city, are not obliged to participate.

From this it is seen that unlike the former law, which obliged only Regulars to assist at this procession, canon 1291 requires the assistance of all religious. Since the cited canon contains no revocatory expressions, exemptive rights, such as those just explained above (n. II), are still in force.[19]

B. Other parochial and Regular churches may hold their processions outside in the public streets during the octave of Corpus Christi (can. 1291, § 2). This is a concession of common law and cannot be abrogated by local Ordinaries. However, if there are many churches in a city, the local Ordinary has authority to assign the day, hour, and route for each procession (can. 1291, § 2).

Unless endowed with a particular privilege, all are obliged to follow the local Ordinary's direction in this matter. By reason of a special grant of St. Pius V, confirmed by Clement VIII and Benedict XIII, the Dominicans may hold their Corpus Christi procession on the Sunday within the octave, or on the Sunday after, where, as in the United States, the solemnity of the feast and the procession are transferred to the Sunday within the octave.[20]

IV. OTHER PROCESSIONS

As stated above (n. II), other processions are regulated in the same way as before the Code.

A. *Extraordinary Processions*

The Code states that after learning the advice of his Cathedral Chapter

---

[19] Cf. *Epit.*, II, 618.
[20] Cf. S.R.C., Indult., Feb. 28, 1912, AAS, IV, 177: see *Per.*, VI, pp. 202, 203; Ayrinhac, *Administrative Legislation*, 138; Prümmer, Q. 395; *Epit.*, II, 620.

or Consultors, the local Ordinary may, for a public cause, order extra-ordinary processions, which, like the ordinary ones, must be attended by all the persons obliged to attend the Corpus Christi procession (can. 1292).

Hence, under the conditions enumerated, namely, after asking the opinion of his consultors, and in the event that there exists some public reason, the local Ordinary can oblige all religious of male institutes, even though exempt, to attend processions, if the religious have not been withdrawn from his authority in this matter, either by virtue of a special privilege or by virtue of a legitimate contrary custom.[21]

B. *Processions Not Prescribed by the Local Ordinary*

With the exception of the procession permitted during the octave of Corpus Christi, exempt religious may not hold others outside their churches or cloisters without leave of the local Ordinary (can. 1293).[22] Religious, however, who possess a special papal indult or can prove the existence of a legitimate contrary custom need not seek the consent of the local Ordinary.[23]

The prescription of canon 1293 does not prevent religious from holding processions inside their churches or cloisters. Local Ordinaries have no authority over exempt religious in such cases. Furthermore, if these re-ligious have no cloister grounds, they may conduct processions of this kind outside the church, so long as they confine them to the streets nearest the church.[24]

V. PRECEDENCE IN PROCESSIONS

The general norm of precedence is this: the higher the rank of persons, the nearer they should be to the celebrant.[25]

Rules of precedence such as canons 106 and 491[26] must be complied with. Within certain restrictions, local Ordinaries have jurisdiction to settle disputes in this matter, even though exempt religious be involved in them.[27] The religious have not the right of suspensive appeal against the decision of a local Ordinary (can. 106, 7°).

The order of precedence among Regulars is as follows: Canons Regular, Monks, and the other Regulars (cf. can. 491, § 1).

---

[21] Cf. S.R.C., June 23, 1670, Decr. auth. 2116; Dec. 22, 1770, ad 2, Decr. auth. 2490: see Augustine, VI, can. 1292.

[22] Cf. Greg. XIII, Const., *Dum intra*, Mar. 11, 1573; Innoc. XII, Const., *Sua nobis*, Feb. 25, 1696: see Ferraris, v, *Processiones*, 28; Vermeersch, *De Rel.*, I, 527.

[23] Cf. S.R.C., Nov. 14, 1676; Decr. auth. 1581; Nov. 24, 1691, Decr. auth. 1859; April 8, 1702, Decr. auth. 2099.

[24] Cf. S.R.C., July 27, 1628; Sept. 28, 1658, Decr. auth. 1096; June 21, 1690: see Augustine, VI, can. 1293; Ayrinhac, *Administrative Legislation*, 139; *Epit.*, II, 620.

[25] Cf. Augustine, *Liturgical Law*, p. 291.

[26] Cf. also cc. 239, 269, 280, 347, 370, 408, 478, 701.

[27] Cf. above, Chap. V, n. II, b.

For confraternities of laymen that of the Blessed Sacrament has precedence in theophoric processions;[28] otherwise, precedence is reckoned according to the antiquity of confraternities in the parish.[29]

---

[28] Cf. S.R.C., Jan. 17, 1887, Decr. auth. 3668.
[29] Cf. Augustine, *Liturgical Law*, p. 291, note 13.

CHAPTER XIV

THE TEACHING OFFICE OF THE CHURCH

General principles affecting the teaching office of the Church, and the relationship of local Ordinaries and exempt religious with respect to this office, have already been discussed.[1] The purpose of the present chapter is to explain the juridical status of exempt religious with relation to the particular teaching ministries treated in Book III of the Code.[2]

Among the preliminary canons referring to this office several norms are given which are pertinent to all persons, even exempt religious.

1. Catholics are not permitted to take part in disputes or conferences—especially if they be public—regarding matters of faith, with non-Catholics, unless they have the approval of the Holy See, or, in urgent cases, of the local Ordinary (can. 1325). This prohibition extends to laymen and clerics, including exempt religious. Any public participation of this nature requires a canonical mission, or commission, from the competent ecclesiastical authorities expressly mentioned in the cited canon.[3] The norm here given is similar to that formerly in force.[4]

Canon 1325 forbids public discussions with non-Catholics; not private ones, nor conferences on apologetics in which some questioning by non-Catholics is permitted, nor discussion which a Catholic might become engaged in accidentally in defense of the faith.[5] Religious congresses in which various religions or denominations are represented are, at least indirectly, included in this prohibition. Participation of Catholics in gatherings of this kind has frequently been expressly disapproved by the Holy See.[6]

2. Though Bishops neither singly nor united in particular councils enjoy

---

[1] Cf. above; Chap. III, Art. III.
[2] Cf. Code of Canon Law, Bk. III, part IV.
[3] Cf. W.-V., IV, Vol. II, 619.
[4] Cf. c. 2., V, 2 in VI; 36, C. XXVI, Q. III; S.C.P.F., Mar. 8, 1625; Feb. 7, 1645; Dec. 18, 1662; S. C. Neg. Eccl. Ext., Instr., Jan. 27, 1902, n. VIII.
[5] Cf. W.-V., IV, Vol. II, 619; Coronata, II, 912; Ayrinhac, *Administrative Legislation,* 165.
[6] Cf. Leo XIII, ep. to the Apostolic Delegate of the United States, Sept. 18, 1895; Pius XI, encycl., *Mortalium animos,* Jan. 6, 1928, AAS, XX, 5; see S. Off., Letter to Bishops of England, Sept. 16, 1864, and Letter, Nov. 8, 1865, texts in AAS, XI, 310, 311; Decree July 4, 1919, AAS, XI, 309; July 8, 1927, AAS, XIX, 278; consult *Per.,* XVII, 11; W.-V., IV, Vol. II, 619.

infallibility, nevertheless, under the jurisdiction of the Roman Pontiff, they are true teachers of the faithful confided to their care (can. 1326).[7]

The responsibility and authority of Bishops is a dogmatic truth. They are the divinely constituted pastors of their flock, and the successors of the Apostles, to whom Christ said, "Teach all nations."[8]

The canons considered at present, referring to the teaching office of the Church, are concerned with the twofold purpose of this function, namely, with the dissemination and the faithful custody of revealed truth. Titles XX–XXII of Book III, of the Code, directly apply to the dissemination of the Christian religion; titles XXIII and XXIV primarily to the custody of the faith. The present chapter treats of the status of exempt religious relative to the norms set down in the titles just cited.

ARTICLE I. PREACHING

Preaching, which has always been the most important function of the teaching office, is committed primarily to the Roman Pontiff for the whole Church and to the Bishops for their respective dioceses (can. 1327, § 1).

A Bishop must personally perform this office unless he be lawfully impeded. He is aided, of course, by pastors. He should use other priests and persons whom he judges capable of assisting him (can. 1327, § 2).

No one is allowed to preach until he has obtained the canonical mission from a legitimate superior, that is from the Sovereign Pontiff or the Bishop (can. 1328). Hence, exempt religious must not undertake this ministry unless they receive a positive deputation to do so.[9]

It should be remarked that the term "preaching" used in title XX of the Code, is employed in the broad sense to embrace catechetical instructions, sermons, and sacred missions.

CATECHETICAL INSTRUCTION

The expression "catechetical instruction" used by the Code (cc. 1329-1336) is taken to mean a simple presentation of the principal articles of faith, moral precepts, and the means of salvation.[10]

Ordinarily it signifies the methodical, progressive instruction imparted to children or others ignorant of Catholic truths, or even to the faithful in

---

[7] Cf. Pius VI, Const., *Auctorem fidei*, Aug. 28, 1794, prop. 6, Synodi Pistorien, damn.; Greg. XVI, encycl., *Mirari vos*, Aug. 15, 1832; Pius IX, ep., *Tuas libenter*, Dec. 21, 1863; Leo XIII, ep., *Est sane molestum*, Dec. 17, 1888; Pius X, encycl., *Acerbo nimis*, Apr. 15, 1905.

[8] Cf. *Epit.*, II, 662; Wernz, II, 756, scholion.

[9] Cf. Conc. Trid., sess. XXIII, C. 1, and sess. V, *de ref.;* see also W.-V., IV, Vol. II, 633; Coronata, II, 914; De Meester, III, 1288.

[10] Cf. W.-V., IV, Vol. II, 646; Jansen, *Canonical Provisions for Catechetical Instruction,* p. 5; Augustine, VI, can. 1329; Cocchi, *De Rebus, L,* III, Pars IV; 16.

general. It embraces the instructions given not only in churches but in schools, halls, private homes, and the like.[11]

I. JURISDICTION OF LOCAL ORDINARIES

Since the local Ordinaries have jurisdiction over the spiritual matters in the dioceses committed to their care (can. 335, § 1), it is their right and duty to set down norms regulating religious instruction in their dioceses (can. 1336).[12] As a consequence, they have the right to select teachers and textbooks, and to determine the course of instructions that is to be followed. Diocesan norms, however, cannot be in opposition to the general law; rather they must be further determinations of that law adapted to the exigencies of the locality (can. 6, § 1).[13]

II. DEPENDENCE OF EXEMPT RELIGIOUS

a) Exempt religious engaged in instructing nonexempt persons are obliged to observe the regulations of the local Ordinary (can. 1336). Hence, they must conform their teaching to any program respecting the matter, form, time, place, and other conditions set down by the said Ordinary.[14] (Concerning courses, textbooks, teachers, etc., consult what is indicated below, art. III, with reference to schools belonging to Regulars.)

Regulars who in accordance with the authorization of the Holy See and their particular privileges, are destined to teach Christian doctrine, may with permission of their superiors explain the fundamentals of the faith in their own churches. They need not ask leave of the local Ordinary in such cases.[15] It follows that the teaching of catechism is not the exclusive right of pastors.[16]

Regulars may teach catechism in other churches not pertaining to their institute without the previous permission of the local Ordinary. Consent of the rector of the church suffices.

It should be observed that the rules of the Council of Trent regulating the preaching are not applicable to the catechetical instructing done by Regulars.[17] Furthermore, often by reason of stipulations made in pious foundations, Regulars are obliged to engage in this ministry.[18] The Code

---

[11] Cf. W.-V., *loc. cit.;* Ayrinhac, *Administrative Legislation,* 169; Coronata, II, 915.

[12] Cf. Conc. Trid., sess. XXIV, *de ref.,* cap. 7; see also W.-V., IV, Vol. II, 648; Jansen, *op. cit.,* p. 42.

[13] Cf. Conc. Trid.: sess. XXIV, *de ref.,* cap. 4, 7, and sess. XXV, *de indice et catechismo,* Conc. Balt. III, 199, 217; *Coll. Lac.,* V, *Catechismus:* see W.-V., IV, Vol. II, 651; Coronata, II, 915; *Epit.,* I, 271; Jansen, *op. cit.,* p. 42.

[14] Cf. S.C.EE.RR., Mar. 16, 1866, ap. ASS, II, 151–157, 189; see also, W.-V., IV, Vol. II, 650; Coronata, II, 615; Jansen *op. cit.,* p. 60; Bondini, p. 123; De Meester, III, 1293.

[15] Cf. S.C.C., Mar. 2, 1861, ap. ASS, II, p. 189; S.C.EE.RR., Mar. 16, 1866, ASS, p. 157.

[16] Cf. Piat, II, p. V, c. II; W.-V., IV, Vol. II, 648; Bondini, p. 124; Jansen, *op. cit.,* p. 64; Coronata, II, 253.

[17] Cf. W.-V., *loc. cit.,* Coronata, *loc. cit.*

[18] W.-V., *loc. cit.*

itself contains no provisions restricting their activities in this respect.[19]

b) The prescription of canon 1333, permitting local Ordinaries to compel ecclesiastics to assist in the catechetical instruction *of children,* does not apply to exempt religious.[20]

For the instruction *of adults,* however, the local Ordinary may, if he thinks it necessary, ask the assistance even of exempt religious, whether they be clerical or lay. The superior is obliged either personally or through his subjects to fulfill this request (can. 1334),[21] if he can do so without harming the religious discipline of his subjects.[22]

It is clear from the words of the canon that in ordinary circumstances local Ordinaries cannot oblige exempt religious to give catechetical instructions outside their own churches.[23]

The authority of the local Ordinary as here set forth constitutes a derogation of the exemptive rights of religious; hence, it must be exercised only within the strict limits of the terms used in the law.[24]

It should be remembered that all religious institutes of either sex have been exhorted by the Holy See not only to help the Bishops in this work, but also to so conduct religious instruction in their schools that their students may be able not only to defend their faith against common objections, but also to teach it and cause it to be embraced by as many as possible.[25]

Superiors in houses of religious of both sexes should choose among their subjects some who are either to direct such schools or to teach religion to boys and girls.[26]

Superiors must see to it that the celebration of divine offices in their churches does not harm the catechetical instruction or explanation of the Gospel given in parochial churches. It pertains to the local Ordinary to judge whether or not these offices are harmful (can. 609, § 3). In case of a conflict in such functions, the local Ordinary should warn superiors in order that the latter may opportunely adjust matters[27] (cf. Chap. XIX ad finem).

SERMONS

The term sermon (concio) in this section of the Code (cc. 1337, 1348) is employed in a broad sense to signify any sacred discourse, whether it be

---

[19] Cf. S.C.C., June 29, 1923; ap. AAS, XV, p. 327; *Per.,* XII, p. 122; Bondini, p. 124.
[20] Cf. *Epit.,* II, 668; De Meester, III, 1291, nota 6; Ayrinhac, *Administrative Legislation,* 174.
[21] Cf. can. 608.
[22] Coronata, II, 918; Blat, III, 219.
[23] Cf. cc. 604, 1345; also Cocchi, *De Rebus,* III, pars. IV, 19; De Meester, III, 1291; Coronata, II, 918; *Epit.,* II, 668; Prümmer, 404, 2.
[24] Cf. Bondini, p. 52; Jansen, *op. cit.,* p. 63; *Epit.,* II, 668.
[25] Cf. Pius XI, *Motu Proprio,* n. 3, June 29, 1923, ap. Bouscaren I, can. 1329.
[26] Cf. Pius XI, *Motu Proprio,* just cited, n. 4.
[27] Cf. *Epit.,* I, 775; Berutti, III, 122.

a formal oration, homily, exhortation, or other form of preaching distinct from catechetical instruction treated in the preceding pages.[28]

Dependence of Regulars on local Ordinaries in this ministry has varied at different periods.

Before the Code

At one time (from the thirteenth century until the Council of Trent) Regulars, particularly mendicants, enjoyed most extensive privileges in the exercise of this function.[29] Later, these grants were restricted.[30] Under this modified discipline, which was in force till the promulgation of the Code, Regulars, with the permission of their superiors and independently of local Ordinaries, could preach to members of their institutes and to their domestic servants.[31]

In order to preach to the faithful, even in their own churches, these religious needed the permission of their own superiors; and further, had to be presented to the local Ordinary and to ask his benediction. To preach in other churches they required the permission of both the local Ordinary and their superiors.

Present Legislation

The work of preaching in a diocese belongs primarily to the Bishop.[32] It is his right and duty to choose or deputize those who shall assist him in fulfilling this most important function. He also has authority to impose conditions which he may deem necessary even upon those who by virtue of their office have received the mission to preach.[33]

The general rule regulating sermons is this: in order to preach to the people in public churches or oratories, even those belonging to exempt religious, all, including priests of exempt institutes, must obtain permission from the Ordinary of the diocese.[34]

Superiors of exempt clerical institutes who are designated by their constitutions, can permit preaching (by secular clerics or religious) to any audience composed exclusively of their subjects or of persons who share their privileges, such as boarding students, servants, and the like, specified in canon 514 (can. 1338, § 1).

Faculties for preaching to nuns who are subject to Regulars, and to

---

[28] Cf. Ayrinhac, *Administrative Legislation*, 177; W.-V., IV, Vol. II, 637; *Epit.*, II, 673.

[29] Given by Gregory IX, 1227–1237; Innocent IV, 1244; Alexander IV, 1254; Martin IV, 1282.

[30] Cf. Conc. Trid., sess V, *de ref.*, cap. 2; Greg. XV, Const., *Inscrutabile*, Feb. 5, 1622; Clement X, Const., *Superna*, June 21, 1670.

[31] Cf. Bouix, II, pp. 264 ff.; W.-V., IV, Vol. II, 640; Melo, pp. 110 ff.

[32] Cf. cc. 1327, 1328, 1337.

[33] Cf. S. C. Consist., "Norms for sacred preaching," nn. 2, 3, June 28, 1917, ap. AAS, IX, 328; see Bouscaren, *op. cit.*, I, can. 1327; *Per.*, IX, p. 37.

[34] Cf. S. C. Consist., cited instruction, n. 4; cf. cc. 1337, 1338, § 2.

religious of exempt lay institutes must be obtained from the local Ordinary. Even priests belonging to exempt institutes need this deputation (can. 1338, §§ 2 and 3). Furthermore, for sermons to exempt nuns permission of the Regular superior is required; for those to exempt lay institutes, the assent of the religious superior must be obtained (can. *cit.*).

There appears to be a disparity between the provisions of canon 529 and canon 1338, §§ 2 and 3. The first states that the Regular superior appoints chaplains and preachers for exempt lay institutes; the second, that the local Ordinary grants faculties for preaching to these religious and the superior gives the required permission. The seeming disagreement can be explained as follows: Permission (can. 1338, §§ 2 and 3) and designation (appointment) (can. 529) of the superior, are one and the same thing. Hence, the meaning of the cited canons is this: Regular superiors designate chaplains and preachers for exempt lay institutes. However, the priest to be designated should be chosen from those approved by the local Ordinary; i.e., those having the general faculties to preach in a diocese.[35]

Superiors of nuns subject to Regulars or of exempt lay religious cannot be forced to accept a preacher sent them by the Bishop; the contrary is true for nonexempt religious.[36] In general, it is not the intention of the legislator to have Ordinaries impose preachers upon the religious, but rather to grant them a choice among the properly approved priests, especially for more solemn sermons or spiritual exercises.[37]

Faculties for preaching to nonexempt lay congregations must be obtained from the local Ordinary (can. 1338, § 3). Superiors of such institutes may freely invite an exempt or a nonexempt priest to preach to their subjects, as long as this priest has received authorization to preach in the diocese where the religious are located (Creusen, 147).

Must Regulars conducting the Spiritual Exercises according to the traditional method, obtain the faculty to preach from the local Ordinary?

If these Exercises are given in the form of a mission, or the like, the priest is bound to obtain the aforesaid faculty, for in this case the Exercises are in reality a series of sermons.[38] However, this canonical statute cannot be applied to Spiritual Exercises conducted in a house of Regulars whose rules, approved by the Holy See, designate that this is a ministry proper to their work. In this case the priest need not obtain the faculty in question even though his retreatants be secular persons so long as these latter are living day and night, with the religious.[39]

[35] Cf. Coronata, I, 556; Prümmer, Q. 191.
[36] Cf. *Epit.*, II, 673; Coronata, II, 921; Cocchi, L. III, pars IV, 22.
[37] Cf. *Epit.*, II, 673.
[38] Cf. can. 1388, § 2.
[39] Cf. W.-V., IV, Vol. II, 662.

Examination of Candidates

Ordinaries are gravely obliged in conscience not to permit anyone to preach unless they are assured beforehand of his piety, learning, and fitness; or, if there is question of priests from outside the diocese or from some religious order, unless they shall have previously questioned the proper Ordinary and superior, and shall have obtained a favorable reply (can. 1340).[40]

The ordinary means to determine a person's fitness for preaching, especially as regards learning, piety, etc., are examinations in accordance with the norms just cited (can. 1340).

According to the result of these examinations the Ordinary may declare the candidate qualified either in general or for only a particular kind of preaching, for a limited time, or by way of trial and under certain conditions, or absolutely and perpetually, or he may simply deny him the permission to preach.[41]

In particular cases and by way of exception, Ordinaries may permit one to preach without the previous examination, provided the candidate's fitness is certain from other sources.[42]

Denial and Withdrawal of Faculties

Unfit candidates should be denied the faculty to preach. However, a gentle, discreet use of this restricting power is recommended. Therefore, only a grave reason should lead a local Ordinary to refuse authorizing a religious who has been presented to him by the proper superior (can. 1339, § 1).[43] Arbitrariness, caprice, dislike, etc., should in nowise affect the decision of Ordinaries.[44]

Generally, too, they should not hesitate to accept the attestation of religious superiors concerning the qualifications of their subjects. If the superiors have examined their candidate, local Ordinaries need not do so.[45]

The faculty or permission to preach should be revoked if the possessor shows he lacks the necessary qualifications. When doubt arises concerning a preacher's learning, new examinations may, if necessary, be imposed on him, in order to gain assurance of his fitness. A priest is bound to abide by a decision effecting the withdrawal of his faculty or permission to preach, though he is allowed a devolutive recourse against such a judgment (can. 1340).

Ordinaries should refrain from simultaneously revoking the faculty from

---

[40] Cf. S. C. Consist., Norms . . . n. 10, June, 28, 1917.
[41] S. C. Consist., Norms . . . n. 15.
[42] S. C. Consist., Norms . . . n. 16.
[43] Cf. Epit., II, 674.
[44] Cf. S.C.EE.RR., Jan. 13, 1610 (ap. Biz., p. 243); and Dec. 14, 1674 (ap. Biz., p. 273).
[45] Cf. Coronata, II, 923, nota 2; Epit., II, 675; Per., IX, p. 40.

all the religious of one house, saving, however, cases provided for in canon 1340 (can. 1339, §1).

Extradiocesan Preachers

Neither secular nor religious priests from outside a diocese should be invited to preach, before permission has been obtained from the Ordinary of the place where the sermon is to be delivered (can. 1341, § 1).

The request for a preacher must be made at an opportune time, thus enabling the Ordinary to obtain necessary assurance of the priest's qualifications (can. 1341, § 1). This will in general be not less than two months beforehand; without prejudice, however, to the right of an Ordinary to fix a shorter period, if he so desires.[46]

The Ordinary and the religious superior who shall be asked by another Ordinary for information regarding the piety, learning, and fitness to preach, of any one of their subjects, are bound by a grave obligation to give the information truthfully according to their knowledge and conscience, as prescribed in canon 1341, § 1. The Ordinary who receives the information is bound to act in accordance with it, keeping absolute secrecy as to the information received.[47]

No Ordinary is obliged to manifest his reasons for refusing the faculty.[48]

Rights of the Local Ordinary

1. A local Ordinary can preach anywhere in his diocese, even in the churches of exempt religious (can. 1343, § 1).

2. Furthermore, in all places except large cities, he can, within the limits defined in law, forbid others to preach. (A city is considered *large* if it contains over 100,000 inhabitants. This count does not refer solely to Catholics, but embraces all the people.)[49]

Two distinct cases are given in canon 1343, § 2:

a) A Bishop has the right to forbid others to preach to the people when he is *personally* doing so in the same city. The fact alone that he personally is giving the sermon is sufficient to justify this prohibition.

b) When he has appointed someone else to preach in his presence, he also has this restrictive power, but in a limited way. He can prevent others from preaching in the same city only when, for a public and extraordinary reason, he has summoned the faithful to attend the sermon to be given in his presence.[50]

---

[46] Cf. S. C. Consist., Norms . . . n. 7; W.-V., IV, Vol. II, 642.
[47] S. C. Consist., Norms . . . n. 11.
[48] S. C. Consist., Norms . . . n. 12.
[49] Cf. Epit., II, 678; Coronata, II, 927; De Meester, III, 1298, nota 1.
[50] Cf. Bened. XIV, De Syn. Dioec., L. IX, cap. 17, nn. 6, 7, 8; Ojetti, Synopsis, v, concio, 1396; Epit., II, 678; W.-V., IV, Vol. II, 644; Coronata, II, 927; Prümmer, 405, 5; Augustine, VI, can. 1343.

Unless a Bishop has issued this prohibition, other sermons may be given at the same time as that of the Bishop.[1]

3. It is within the jurisdiction of the local Ordinary to set down regulations on preaching that will be binding even in the churches of exempt religious.

According to canon 1345, it is desired that in churches and public oratories a brief explanation of the Gospel or some element of Christian doctrine be given at the Masses attended by the faithful on Holydays of Obligation. If the local Ordinary issues timely instructions to this effect, all priests, secular as well as religious, even the exempt, are bound to follow them in their respective churches.[2] No authority is given these Ordinaries to issue prescriptions for semipublic oratories of exempt religious.[3]

MISSIONS

In legislating concerning this function of her apostolate, the Church (cc. 1349–1351) enumerates three distinct types of missions, those namely to Catholics, to non-Catholics in general, and to pagans. The first two are conducted in territories already ruled by a properly constituted hierarchy, and are called internal missions; the last mentioned are established in other territories, generally still pagan, and are known as external or foreign missions.

I. INTERNAL MISSIONS

These missions consist in a popular and special manner of preaching the word of God for the purpose of moving the *faithful* to penance and more intensive Christian living, or non-Catholics to embrace the true faith. Local Ordinaries have authority with respect to the organization of this ministry; hence, exempt religious engaged in parish work must obey the prescriptions of the local Ordinary regulating the same. The organization of internal missions in nonparochial churches of exempt religious is not subject to the jurisdiction of the local Ordinary.

II. EXTERNAL MISSIONS

These missions are established in order to propagate and strengthen the faith in countries which are still pagan, and which have not yet a canonically constituted hierarchy.[4]

The Instruction of the Propaganda, issued in 1929, explains somewhat in

---

[1] Cf. S.C.EE.RR., Apr. 7, 1579, ap. Biz., p. 224; see Coronata, II, 927.

[2] Cf. Bened. XIV, Const., *Etsi minime*, Feb. 7, 1742, ap. *Fontes*, I, 324; see Melo, p. 113; Coronata, II, 927.

[3] Cf. Blat, III, 235.

[4] Cf. S.C.P.F., Instr., Dec. 8, 1929, ap. AAS, XXII, 111; see Bouscaren, I, can. 1350; *Per.*, XIX, pp. 255–265; Vromant, I, 4; Ayrinhac, *Administrative Legislation*, 194.

detail the legal principles which regulate foreign missions. As the dependence of missionaries belonging to exempt institutes on the Ordinaries or superiors of the missions is herein definitely determined, a brief summary of the Instruction is pertinent to our present matter.

1. The Church usually intrusts to religious or missionary societies the evangelization of definite territories.

2. The sole objective of an institute in this work is the propagation of the Kingdom of God.

3. The territory is not absolutely relinquished to the care of the institute. The Church keeps the principal part, that is the entire government of the mission, and expects from the institute the generous subsidy of apostolic workers and of means for the prosecution of the work.

4. The territory of the mission should in nowise be considered the property of the missionary institute. When the good of souls so demands, the Congregation of Propaganda can freely assign the mission to other institutes or put it under the jurisdiction of the native clergy.[5]

5. The Holy See appoints the real superior and governor, who rules the mission not in the name or by the authority of the institute, but in that of the Church itself.

6. In his government he is responsible to the Holy See and must fulfill her wishes not those of the superior of the institute (can. 1350).

7. The propagation of the faith in the territory belongs to and is controlled by him. He decides and ordains the course and methods to be followed. It is his business to establish mission stations, to open primary and higher schools, to provide hospitals, orphanages, dispensaries, and other works of Christian charity, and to build chapels and churches. He must determine the manner, the time, and the curriculum of the catechetical work, and judge of the sufficient knowledge and fitness of the catechists to be employed.

8. Without him, no one, whatever his authority, can establish, change, or discontinue any work in the mission. He controls the means and personnel of the mission. However, the ecclesiastical superior of the mission cannot force an institute to provide expenses and shoulder the debts for whatever work he chooses to undertake. Rather, if the mission superior plans to accomplish some work for whose execution neither necessary funds nor suitable workers are at hand, he should take the matter up with the superiors of the institute, or even according to circumstances have recourse to the S. C. of the Propaganda.

9. The mission superior has authority not only over missionaries in the strict sense, that is, those who are engaged in the preaching of the Gospel

---

[5] Cf. S.C.P.F., May 3, 1923, ap. AAS, XV, 370; Pius XI, Epist. Encycl., *Rerum Ecclesiae,* Feb. 27, 1926, ap. AAS, XVIII, 82; see Vromant, I, 43.

and the conversion of souls, but also over all priests who are otherwise engaged in apostolic labors in the mission, and over lay brothers who are engaged in missionary works.

10. There is, however, no objection to the establishing of special agreements between the ecclesiastical superior and the institute of men or sisters, by which their mutual rights are equitably specified. Such agreements, for their greater force and stability, are usually submitted to the S. C. of the Propaganda for approval.

11. Religious houses and provinces, even exempt ones, may be erected in mission territories, in accordance with the requirements of law. The Holy See welcomes such establishments.

12. The offices of the superior of the mission and the superior of a missionary institute are distinct and not in opposition to one another. The mission superior should occupy himself solely with mission affairs, the religious superior should be solicitous only for the religious discipline of his subjects. However, the latter should exercise vigilance over the missionary activities of religious.[6]

13. Mutual agreement, and trust, should characterize the actions of both superiors. Only in this way will they be able to reap the fullest fruits of their apostolate.

ARTICLE II. SEMINARIES

The general law states that the Bishop shall decide what is necessary and profitable for the proper administration, government, and progress of the diocesan seminary, and shall see to it that his prescriptions are faithfully observed. In using this authority he must at the same time abide by the particular provisions of the Holy See affecting the seminary (can. 1357).

Sometimes seminaries are intrusted to the care of religious institutes. The subjection of the religious to the Bishop in such cases varies with the different types of seminaries.

When the establishment which they are given charge of is *pontifical* in character, the religious are generally withdrawn from the authority of the local Ordinary and kept under the immediate jurisdiction of the Holy See alone.[7] The extent of this exemption is to be judged from the contents of the particular papal decrees and from the common exemptive right of the religious, if the latter belong to exempt institutes.

When *diocesan* seminaries are intrusted to exempt religious (or others), an agreement concerning their government and direction is generally entered into between the Bishop and the religious institute. If conditions

---

[6] Cf. *Per., loc. cit.,* p. 264.
[7] Examples are had in the *Acta* of Pius IX, Pars. I, Vol. I, pp. 473, 533; see also Lucidi, Vol. I, 123.

of this agreement derogate provisions of the Code or rights of the Bishop and of his successors, authorization of the Holy See is necessary,[8] for the validity of the same. In the event of approval by the Holy See, the agreement constitutes a particular law which cannot be derogated by either party.[9]

According to Ferreres, such pacts contain stipulations granting to the Superior-General the right to select the rector and professors, and to the religious the administration of the seminary, and make provisions preventing the present and future Bishops from arbitrarily rescinding any article of the agreement.[10]

However, the Bishop always retains the right and duty to make his canonical visitation, and the religious Ordinary has the same right of visitation that he possesses with respect to the other houses under his charge.[11]

Article III. Schools and Other Institutions

Because of false theories concerning the functions of Church and State in education, the Holy See has clearly defined the extent of her supernatural mission in this matter. Particularly pertinent to our present discussion is her declaration that the religious and moral training of youth is subject to her authority and inspection (can. 1381). This jurisdictional power, which is of divine origin, authorizes the Church to supervise religious and moral training in all public and private schools, whether these be elementary or secondary institutions, colleges or universities.[12]

Likewise, local Ordinaries are the custodians of the faith and morals of the Christians dwelling in their territories.

Institutions pertaining to exempt religious are often engaged in the religious and moral training of youth. Their schools, orphanages, hospitals, etc., are all occupied in the furtherance of this work. What is their juridic status in this matter?

I. BEFORE THE CODE

The relationship between schools of Regulars and local Ordinaries is clearly defined in the constitution, *Romanos Pontifices,* of Leo XIII, May 8, 1881. The Pontiff set down norms for two types of schools:

1. *Elementary or Primary Schools*

The religious and moral education of youth in a diocese belongs to the

---

[8] Cf. Ferreres, II, 358, bis; *Epit.,* II, 708; Coronata, II, 936.
[9] Cf. Ferreres, *loc. cit.*
[10] Cf. *Epit., loc. cit.*
[11] Cf. *Epit., loc. cit.;* Ferreres, *loc. cit.;* Coronata, II, 939.
[12] Cf. Pius IX, Syllabus, 45, 47: see also, Wernz, II, 68, 69, 72; Cavagnis, 56–63; De Meester, III, 1328; Coronata, II, 948.

office, or is the duty of the Bishop; hence, the primary and elementary schools are manifestly engaged in a work which is definitely diocesan in character. For this reason the Pontiff, in summarizing former decrees, stated that local Ordinaries have the right to make the canonical visitation of all such schools whether they be located in Regular or secular missions and parishes.[13]

2. Other Schools

He drew a distinction between these elementary parochial schools and the others conducted by Regulars. "The case," he declared, "is entirely different with respect to the other schools and colleges in which male religious, by the prescriptions of their order, occupy themselves with the education of Catholic youth. For in these institutions, both right reason and We ourselves demand that the privileges which have been granted by the Holy See retain their entire juridical force."

After the issuance of this Constitution, no one any longer questioned the exemption of these last-mentioned schools, even with regard to their moral and religious program.[14] A later decree of the Propaganda, January 18, 1886, confirmed both the exemption of these schools and their freedom from episcopal visitation.[15]

II. LAW OF THE CODE

1. Religious and moral education in the elementary parochial schools of exempt religious is, as formerly, subject to the jurisdiction of the local Ordinary.

2. Concerning other schools, canon 1382 states: local Ordinaries can, personally or through others, make the juridical visitation of *any* schools, oratories, asylums, orphanages, etc., for the purpose of inspecting whatever pertains to religious and moral education. None, except internal schools for members of exempt institutes, is immune from this visitation.[16] Hence, institutions of exempt religious, with the one exception mentioned, are subject to episcopal visitation in matters specified by canon 1382.

What is now to be said of the exemptive rights of the nonparochial schools of Regulars?

The provisions of the Constitution, *Romanos Pontifices,* are still in force. Canon 1382 contains no revocatory clause annulling the contrary rights of particular institutes; consequently the many institutes that, through priv-

---

[13] Cf. *Romanos Pontifices,* par. 19.
[14] Cf. *Per.,* XV, p. 57.
[15] Cf. *Coll.* P.F., 1651.
[16] Cf. Conc. Trid., XXII, de Ref. cap. 8; Bened. XIV, Const., *Ad Militantis,* par. 31, Mar. 30, 1742; S.C.EE.RR., Litt., May 14, 1872.

ilege, custom, or prescriptive right have enjoyed exemption and immunity from visitation in the matter under discussion, still retain that status.[17]

All schools and institutions engaged in the education of nonexempt persons are subject to the vigilance of the local Ordinary in matters which pertain to the teaching of religion, good morals, religious exercises, and the administration of the sacraments (cc. 1491; 1381, § 1).[18] Therefore, local Ordinaries must see to it that no dangerous or perversive teachings or practices are permitted in schools of their territories (can. 1381, § 2).[19]

To fulfill properly their duty they are empowered to approve teachers and textbooks of religion and to demand the removal of any teachers or books that are detrimental to the faith or morals of their subjects (can. 1381, § 3).

These provisions are chiefly concerned with the evident evils arising from non-Catholic education,[20] though they apply to all schools, even to those conducted by exempt religious.[21] However, in the case of the latter, it must be observed that local Ordinaries have the right of vigilance but not jurisdiction (can. 615).[22]

Even though local Ordinaries possess this right and can approve teachers and textbooks, it is clear, from reason itself, and from provisions in the rules of different religious institutes, that the selection of teachers and textbooks and the direction of religious courses and moral training are left to the Regulars maintaining the schools. This is manifest from the following statement of the Holy See:

"Quoad collegia et collegiorum scholas atque convictus in quibus religiosi viri secundum Ordinis sui praescripta juventuti instituendae operam dare solent, et recta ratio postulat, et S.S. vult firma atque integra privilegia Regularibus concessa manere, adeoque regimen eorum Institutorum, tum personarum in iis destinatio ad superiores Regulares spectat, juxta Societatis Constitutiones, et quatenus opus est, facto verbo cum SSmo . . . (SSmus annuit)."[23]

---

[17] (Cf. cc. 4, 6, 613.) (Cf. *Per.*, XV, pp. 59–61); Fanfani, 444; Prümmer, Q. 412; Blat, III, 408; Schäfer, 86; Melo, p. 157; Coronata, II, 950, 1031.

[18] Cf. Conc. Trid., sess. XXII, *de ref.*, cap. 8; Schäfer, 86; Melo, pp. 130, 156; *Epit.*, II, 815; Blat, III, 408; Ayrinhac, *Administrative Legislation*, 309; Coronata, II, 1031 states that the institutes of pontifical right spoken of in canon 1491, § 2, especially those belonging to Regulars, seem subject to the vigilance but not the canonical visitation of the local Ordinary.

[19] Cf. Conc. Trid., sess. XXV, *de ref.*, cap. 2; Pius IX, Encyc. Letter, *Cum non sine*, July 14, 1864; Leo XIII, Const., *Conditae a Christo*, par. 2, n. 10, Dec. 8, 1900.

[20] Cf. Augustine, VI, can. 1381.

[21] Cf. Schäfer, 485; Fanfani, 444; Coronata, II, 950.

[22] Cf. Leo XIII, *Romanos Pontifices*, pars. 19 and 20; S.C.P.F. Resp. Jan. 18, 1886; *Per.*, XV, pp. (57)–(61); Melo, p. 130.

[23] Cf. S.C.P.F., Resp. ad 4, Jan. 18, 1886; ap. *Coll. P.F.*, II, 1651; see *Per.*, XV, p. 58.

Article IV. Censorship and Prohibition of Books

I. CENSORSHIP

Previous censorship consists in the examination, judgment, and approval or rejection of writings intended for publication (can. 1384).

In what follows we shall treat of all cases in which the publications of exempt religious are subject to the jurisdiction of the local Ordinary, whether that jurisdiction implies censorship, permission, or mere supervision.[24]

A. *Preliminary Remarks*

The law contains general principles defining the extent to which exempt religious are dependent upon the local Ordinary in the matter of publications. Since the terms, "books" and "publish" (edere) are of frequent occurrence in this chapter of the Code, they merit special attention.

1. Book

Strictly speaking, a book is a volume of some bulk, of about 160 or more pages, containing a unified treatment of a subject.[25] Generally, except in cases of penal law, it is unnecessary to hold fast to this description; for in the present legislation, unless otherwise indicated, previous censorship is required not only for books but for newspapers, periodicals, and other writings (can. 1384), whether they be pamphlets, leaflets, etc., and whether they be printed or produced in other ways.[26]

It is to be noted that *printed sacred images,* with or without accompanying prayers, fall under the censorship of the Church (can. 1385, § 3).

2. Publish

A local Ordinary cannot arbitrarily force exempt religious to submit all their writings to previous censorship. Only works that are to be *published* (edita) must be previously examined and approved. The term "publish" is taken to mean: offered for public sale, or destined for the general public, or purchasable by the latter.[27]

At the present time manuscripts are not considered published works. The same may be said of printed matter that is reserved to private use or to a limited number of readers.[28] Under this classification should be listed courses of professors for their students, instructions of superiors for their religious, etc.

---

[24] Discussion of publications subject to the censorship of the Holy See (cf. cc. 1387; 1388, § 2; 1389; 1391) we omit as irrelevant.

[25] Cf. W.-V., IV, Vol. II, 710; Augustine, can. 1384; Ayrinhac, *Administrative Legislation,* 229.

[26] Cf. W.-V., IV, Vol. II, 710; Ayrinhac, *Administrative Legislation,* 229.

[27] Cf. W.-V., IV, Vol. II, 710; Coronata, II, 952; Augustine, VI, can. 1384.

[28] Cf. Coronata, *loc. cit.;* Epit., II, 722.

B. *Publications Subject to the Local Ordinary*

1. The following works are subject to the previous censorship of the local Ordinary:

a) Books of Sacred Scripture or annotations and commentaries on the same (can. 1385, § 1, 1°).

b) Books which treat of Holy Scripture, sacred theology, ecclesiastical history, canon law, natural theology, ethics, or any other religious or moral subject of this nature; books or pamphlets of prayers, of devotions, of moral, religious, ascetical, mystical doctrine and instructions, and of other matters of this kind, even though they may seem likely to foster devotion; in general, all writings which have a special bearing on religion or morality (can. 1385, § 1, 2°).

c) The publishing or printing of sacred images, with or without prayers attached to them, and no matter how reproduced, i.e., whether engraved, lithographed, photographed, etc.

Mortuary, ordination, anniversary, or any such commemorative cards bearing sacred pictures are not subject to this provision, for they are not edited in the sense already explained. It is probable, too, that medals are not envisaged by this law, for their production is not classified as printing properly so called.[29]

One is given a choice of local Ordinaries. Permission to publish the books and images specified in canon 1385, § 1, 1°, may be granted by the Ordinary of the place where the author lives, or where the writings and images are published, or where they are printed, in such a way, however, that if any of the said Ordinaries has denied approval, the author may not petition another without informing him of the previous refusal (can. 1385, § 1, 1°).

2. Books, collections, pamphlets, leaflets, etc., containing grants of indulgences may not be published without the *consent* of the local Ordinary (can. 1388, § 1).[30] The option of the Ordinary specified in canon 1385, § 1, seems to be accorded in the present instance.[31] Mortuary, ordination, or such like commemorative cards, even though they may contain prayers and a notice of the indulgences attached to them, are not included under this provision.[32]

3. In editing liturgical books or parts thereof, and litanies approved by the Holy See, *official acknowledgment* of their conformity with the approved editions should be obtained from the Ordinary of the place where

---

[29] Cf. *Epit.*, II, 725; Ayrinhac, *Administrative Legislation*, 236.

[30] Cf. Leo XIII, Const., *Officiorum ac munerum*, n. 17, Jan. 25, 1897.

[31] This opinion is held by: Prümmer, *Man. J. C.*, Q. 416; Ferreres, *Inst. Can.*, II, 385; Coronata, II, 956; Cocchi, VI, 62; Blat, *De Rebus*, 276. Vermeersch admits its probability, cf., *Epit.*, II, 726.

[32] Cf. Ayrinhac, *Administrative Legislation*, 234.

the works are printed or published (can. 1390). Though this law mentions only the Ordinaries of the place where the work is published or printed, authors maintain that such matters may also be submitted to the proper Ordinary, in accordance with the norm given in canon 1385, § 1, 2°.[33]

4. Translations of Holy Scripture into the vernacular may not be printed unless they have the approbation of the Apostolic See, or unless they are published under the *supervision* of the Bishops and contain annotations from the Fathers of the Church and learned Catholic writers (can. 1391). The term "Bishops" does not include the Vicar Capitular or the Vicar-General.[34]

5. Translations and new editions of approved works require a *new approbation* (can. 1392, § 1). This is true even when the new edition is identical with the one formerly approved.[35]

Articles taken from periodicals and published separately are not considered new editions, and hence need no new approbation (can. 1392, § 2). Compilations of such excerpts, though equal to a book in size, require no new approbation.[36]

6. Writing of a purely secular character requires the *previous permission* of the local Ordinary. Canon 1386, § 1, states that religious, without the permission of their higher superior and of the local Ordinary, are forbidden to publish books on secular subjects, to write for newspapers, magazines, or other periodicals, or to undertake their direction. Writings, therefore, of a strictly literary or scientific nature, are embraced by this law, no science or topic being excepted.[37] Occasional or brief communications and contributions do not seem to fall under this prohibition.[38]

"It is doubtful whether permission must be asked for the publication of a prospectus or of a circular in which the program of studies, the list of expenses, or other information of this sort is given."[39] In practice, since this particular point of legislation places restrictions on the free exercise of one's rights, it must be strictly interpreted (can. 19).

Previous permission demanded by this canon is different from previous censorship (can. 1385); it calls merely for the consent of the local Ordinary, while the latter requires a scientific examination and consent for publication.

Religious should first obtain permission of their major superior, i.e., of their provincial or general, before asking the consent of the local Ordinary (can. 1386, § 1).

---

[33] Cf. Coronata, II, 956, p. 326; Ferreres, *op. cit.*, II, 385; Prümmer, *loc. cit.*
[34] Cf. Coronata, II, 956.
[35] Cf. *Epit.*, II, 726.
[36] Cf. Ayrinhac, *Administrative Legislation*, 236.
[37] Cf. Augustine, VI, can. 1386; Coronata, II, 955.
[38] Cf. Pius X, *Sacrorum Antistitum*, Sept. 1, 1910; see, *Epit.*, II, 728; Ayrinhac, *Administrative Legislation*, 233; Augustine, *loc. cit.* Application of canon 1386 to exempt religious is discussed later, Chap. XVIII, Art. III, II, A, 3.
[39] Creusen, 316.

C. The "Imprimatur"

Permission to publish should be granted by the Ordinary in writing, and must be printed with his signature together with the date and place of concession at the beginning or end of the book, leaflet, or image (can. 1394, § 1).

Publications not subject to censorship, but merely requiring the previous permission of the local Ordinary do not bear the imprimatur.[40]

Authors should be shown due respect and consideration. If permission for publication has been denied, the reasons should generally be given the author upon demand. Only for a grave cause may a local Ordinary withhold such information (can. 1394, § 2).[41] This rule should especially be observed when the work in question can readily be corrected.[42]

An author whose work has been denied approval may submit it to one of the other Ordinaries mentioned in canon 1385, § 2, so long as he acquaints the other Ordinary of the previous refusal (cf. can. 1385, § 2). Furthermore, an author who has been denied approval is always permitted to seek the intervention of higher ecclesiastical superiors.

II. PROHIBITION OF BOOKS

In accordance with her divine mission to protect the faith and morals of her subjects, the Church has the authority to forbid the reading of any books she considers dangerous to the faithful. Prohibitions of the Holy See are binding for all her subjects (can. 1395).

Particular councils and local Ordinaries have similar authority over their own subjects (can. 1395). However, they have not this power over exempt religious (can. 615).[43]

Abbots of autonomous monasteries and supreme moderators of exempt clerical institutes may, with the assistance of their Chapter or consultors, forbid books to their subjects. A just cause must underlie such prohibitions (can. 1395, §3). Formerly, Bishops acting as delegates of the Holy See had some authority over Regulars;[44] in the law of the Code they are conceded no competency in this matter.[45]

When delay would be dangerous, other major superiors, v.g., Provincials, with the assistance of their consultors, may forbid books. In such cases they are obliged immediately to inform the Superior-General of their action (can. 1395, § 3). By virtue of their dominative power, all religious superiors can

---

[40] Cf. *Epit.*, II, 729; Ayrinhac, *Administrative Legislation*, 239.
[41] Cf. *Epit.*, II, 730; Augustine, VI, can. 1394.
[42] Cf. S. C. Indulg., Sept. 3, 1898: see, Ferreres, *Inst. Can.*, 387.
[43] Cf. *Epit.*, 713; Noldin, *De Praeceptis*, 704; Boudinhon, pp. 222, 223; De Meester, III, 1354; Melo, p. 70; Coronata, II, 960; W.-V., IV, Vol. II, 724.
[44] Cf. S. C. Ind., Aug. 24, 1864, ap. *Coll. P.F.*, 1261.
[45] Cf. Augustine, VI, can. 1395, and the authors just cited.

forbid the reading of certain books that might prove dangerous to their subjects.[46]

The classes of books forbidden by general law are enumerated in canon 1399; condemnations of particular books are contained in the decrees issued by the competent authorities specified in canon 1395.

Neither local nor religious Ordinaries are bound by the ecclesiastical prohibitions of books, though they must observe the precautions necessary in this matter (can. 1401).

For urgent reasons, these same Ordinaries may grant their subjects permission to read books forbidden either by law or by decree of the Apostolic See (can. 1402, § 1), but they can do this only in particular cases. This limiting clause does not mean that they can concede this faculty only for one specific book at a time; rather their power is to be understood as restricted to specifically *determined* books.[47]

When a general apostolic faculty has been granted to religious superiors for the benefit of their subjects, it should be communicated to the latter with discretion, and only for just and reasonable causes (can. 1402, § 2).

ARTICLE V. THE PROFESSION OF FAITH

The last three canons on the teaching office refer to the custody of the faith. They deal with the *profession of faith* which the Church, in her solicitude to guard against false doctrines, requires of certain specified persons.

Exempt religious, in the instances expressly stated by law, are obliged to make the profession of faith before the local Ordinary or his delegate. Express provisions (can. 1406, § 1, 7°) require this profession: of candidates for the subdiaconate before the reception of this order; of priests destined to preach or hear confessions before the concession of faculties; of pastors or priests receiving any kind of benefice to which the care of souls is attached.[48]

Those not having a legitimate excuse, who fail to comply with the provisions of canon 1406, should be given a warning and accorded a reasonable time to fulfill their obligation; after the expiration of the time, those who refuse to obey should be punished even with privation of their office, benefice, dignity, or function, and they forfeit in the meantime the right to any revenue derived therefrom (can. 2403).

---

[46] Cf. Coronata, II, 960; *Epit.*, II, 731; Augustine, VI, can. 1395.
[47] Cf. Boudinhon, pp. 196 ff.; Coronata, II, 965.
[48] Cf. Fanfani, *De Jure Religiosorum,* 123; Bondini, p. 133. Professors of philosophy, theology, and canon law teaching in institutions pertaining to exempt religious, must make this profession before their own superiors; see Fanfani, *loc. cit.*

OATH AGAINST MODERNISM

The Holy Office has declared that the prescriptions regarding the oath against Modernism contained respectively in the Constitution of Pius X, *Pascendi* (Sept. 8, 1907), and in the *"Motu proprio"* of the same Pontiff (Sept. 1, 1910) remain in full force, even after the Code, until the Holy See decrees otherwise.[49] In this connection, two points are worthy of note:

1. It is sufficient to pronounce this oath before the reception of the sub-diaconate. Religious are obliged to do this in the presence of the Ordinary conferring the sacred order.[50] An Ordinary may, however, delegate the religious superior to receive this oath.[1]

2. Religious destined to preach and hear confessions shall take this oath before the Ordinary who is to grant the faculties in question or before his delegate.[2]

---

[49] Cf. S. Off., Mar. 22, 1918, AAS, X, 136; Bouscaren, I, can. 6.
[50] Cf. S. C. Consist., Mar. 24, 1911, AAS, III, 25 and 181, ad 2.
[1] Cf. *Per.*, V, 272; Coronata, II, 970, nota 8.
[2] Cf. S. C. Consist., Dec. 17, 1910; see Coronata, II, 970, nota 9; *Epit.*, II, 740; *Per.*, V and VI.

CHAPTER XV

BENEFICES AND OTHER NONCOLLEGIATE ECCLESIASTICAL INSTITUTES

Benefices and other noncollegiate ecclesiastical institutes may pertain or be entrusted to exempt religious. The regulations, therefore, governing these juridical corporations, given in Part V of the Third Book of the Code, have a bearing on exemption. The purpose of the present chapter is to explain the measure or extent of exemption enjoyed by religious Orders and privileged congregations with respect to these corporations.

Article I. The Nature and Kinds of Benefices

According to the Code, a benefice is a juridical entity erected in perpetuity by a competent ecclesiastical authority, which entity consists of a sacred office and a right to acquire a portion of the revenues from the endowment attached to the office (can. 1409).[1]

Free but reliable contributions of the faithful, such as for the most part constitute the stable funds in parishes of the United States, are equivalent to the endowment mentioned in canon 1409 (cf. can. 1410). Since May 29, 1918, by virtue of the promulgation of the Code, such parts of dioceses in the United States whose limits have been designated by a decree of the local Ordinary and have assigned to them a particular rector for the care of souls, are to be considered and to be called parishes (cf. can. 216).[2]

Of the various kinds of benefices treated in the Code, it is important in our discussion to distinguish between the secular and the religious ones. Benefices are secular or religious, depending upon whether they pertain exclusively to secular or to religious clerics. In cases of doubt, those established outside of churches and houses of religious are presumed to be secular (can. 1411, 2°).

Article II. Union, Transfer, Division, Dismemberment, Conversion, and Suppression of Benefices

The modifications of benefices here specified comprise in reality any alterations affecting the rights, obligations, territory, location, and specific character of the benefice.[3]

---

[1] The juridical entity is the same as a noncollegiate moral person or a juridical institute; cf. W.-V., II, 141.

[2] Cf. S. C. Consist., Declar., Aug. 1, 1919, AAS, XI, 346; Bouscaren, I, can. 216; Per., X, p. 57.

[3] Cf. W.-V., II, 154; Coronata, II, 979.

1. The General Rule

Fundamental in this matter is the principle laid down in the Decretals of Gregory IX, namely: ecclesiastical benefices must be conferred without diminution of the same.[4] A similar rule is contained in canon 1440 of the Code. Since the modifications here considered nearly always necessitate the diminution of a benefice, they are normally forbidden by law. Any actions causing modifications in ecclesiastical offices are odious in character,[5] and practically always prove injurious to the person or religious institute holding the same.[6] It has been said that these changes in benefices are *normally* forbidden, for there are cases expressly defined in law in which specified modifications are permitted.[7]

From the basic principle just considered it follows that local Ordinaries are not competent to alter or modify religious benefices, especially those of exempt religious, except in the cases expressly defined in law. The force of this conclusion is beyond questioning in the light of canon 1422, which declares that the Apostolic See reserves to itself actions effecting: extinctive unions, suppression, or dismemberments implying a withdrawal of revenues without the erection of a new benefice; unions whether *equal* or *less principal* of a religious with a secular benefice, or vice versa; and any modification whatsoever which involves the transfer, division, or dismemberment of benefices pertaining to religious.[8]

Without an indult of the Apostolic See no parish can be united "pleno jure" to a moral person, in such a way namely, that the moral person becomes the pastor, according to the norm contained in canon 1423, § 2 (can. 452, § 1). Therefore, only the Holy See can unite a parish in the aforesaid manner to a religious community.

2. Particular Provisions

Though in general benefices belonging to exempt religious cannot be altered by local Ordinaries, their parochial benefices are, within the limits defined in law, subject to the jurisdiction of these Ordinaries.

(A) *Local Ordinaries Have a Limited Jurisdiction Over Parishes Incorporated With Houses Belonging to Exempt Religious*

This is clear from canon 1425, which states that if a parish is united *in temporal matters only* with the religious house, that is, if a "non-pleno jure" incorporation is established, the religious house acquires the right merely to

---

[4] Cf. Decret., Greg. IX, rubricae, tit. 12, lib. III; see, Reiff., on the cited Decret., III, 12, 2.
[5] Cf. W.-V., II, 154.
[6] Cf. Blat, III, 329.
[7] Cf. Coronata, II, 979.
[8] Cf. c. 12, X, *de constitutionibus*, I, 2; Bened. XIV, Const., *Ad Militantis,* par. 11, Mar. 30, 1742.

the revenues of the parish; the religious superior must present to the local Ordinary a priest of the secular clergy to be appointed as pastor, and must assign to the priest a reasonable portion of the revenue. If the incorporation is "pleno jure," it becomes a religious parish and the superior has the right to appoint a priest of his own institute to exercise the care of souls; the local Ordinary, however, has the right to examine and approve him and has the power of jurisdiction, correction, and visitation in all matters relative to the care of souls, according to the norm expressed in canon 631 (cf. can. 456).[9]

(B) Local Ordinaries May Divide and Dismember Religious Parishes

Canon 1427 states that local Ordinaries may for a just and canonical cause divide parishes of any kind by establishing a perpetual vicariate or a new parish, or by dismembering the territory of the parish; and they may do this even against the wishes of the pastor and without the consent of the people.

The prescription accords local Ordinaries this authority over all parishes, and, according to the common opinion of authors even over those united "pleno jure" to a religious house.[10] Leo XIII formerly enacted a similar law for religious parishes situated in mission territories.[11]

Dismemberments or divisions may only be made under the conditions stipulated in the law, namely, when there exists great difficulty for the people to attend their parish church, or when the faithful are so numerous that their spiritual welfare cannot be properly attended to even by the appointment of assistants to the pastor[12] (can. 1427, § 2).

Local Ordinaries are obliged to see that proper provision is made for the support of the new parish. If they cannot obtain funds elsewhere, they may employ a portion of the revenues of the old parish, so long as they leave a sufficient income to the latter (can. 1427, § 3). As the new parish may thus share in the goods of the old, so also it should normally share in the debts contracted by the latter. It is the duty of local Ordinaries to arrange an equitable distribution of these matters, in accordance with the relative importance of each parish and its debts and resources, with due regard to the will of founders and to acquired rights which may not permit the division of certain goods, and in conformity with the particular laws governing moral persons (cf. cc. 1427, § 3, 1500).

---

[9] Cf. above, Chap. X, Art. I, B.

[10] Cf. Augustine, VI, can. 1427; Coronata, II, 983; Blat, III, 334; Claeys Bouuaert-Simenon, 219; Ayrinhac, Administrative Legislation, 267; Epit., II, 757; Woywod, II, 1441: Vidal, however, seems to admit the contrary; cf. W.-V., II, 163.

[11] Cf. Leo XIII, Const., Romanos Pontifices, May 8, 1881.

[12] Cf. W.-V., II, 163; Coronata, II, 983.

The newly constituted parish, after the division of a religious parish, does not pertain to the religious (can. 1427, § 5).

Any division or dismemberment that has been made without a canonical reason is null and void. Only a devolutive recourse is permitted against the local Ordinary's decision to divide or dismember a parish (can. 1428).

(C) Conversion of Parishes

Local Ordinaries cannot convert religious parishes into secular, or secular into religious (can. 1430).

(D) Suppression of Parishes

The suppression of religious parishes, or benefices, is reserved to the Holy See (can. 1422).

ARTICLE III. CONFERRING OF BENEFICES

By virtue of a presumption of law, local Ordinaries have the right to confer vacant benefices within their territory (can. 1432, § 1).

Secular benefices must only be conferred on secular clerics, and religious only on the members of the institute to which the benefice pertains (can. 1442).

There are, nevertheless, cases in which secular parishes are conferred on religious. Canon 296, § 1, for example, presupposes that even Regulars may be assigned to such parishes, a practice which has been customary in mission fields and which is further confirmed by Apostolic provisions according Vicars and Prefects Apostolic the right, within defined limits, to constrain even exempt religious stationed in their territories to undertake the care of souls.[13]

In countries like the United States and England, secular parishes are frequently entrusted to religious.[14] When by virtue of an Apostolic Indult such assignments are made, it is customary for the Bishop to form an agreement with the religious institute involved, and to draw up special statutes determining mutual rights and obligations relative to parochial affairs.[15] It should be noted that such parishes do not belong to the religious but are merely *entrusted* to their care.[16]

ARTICLE IV. RIGHTS AND OBLIGATIONS OF BENEFICIARIES

A beneficiary enjoys all the temporal and spiritual rights attached to his benefice from the moment he has taken legitimate possession of the same (can. 1472).

---

[13] Cf. S.C.P.F., Decr., July 25, 1920, AAS, XII, 331, and Dec. 9, 1920, AAS, XIII, 17: see, W.-V., III, 414, nota 12; *Per.* X, 201 ff.; Konings, *Com. in Facultates Apost.*, p. 62 (1884).
[14] Cf. Conc. Pl. Balt. III, 86 f.; Syn. Westmor. II; Leo XIII, Const., *Romanos Pontifices.*
[15] Cf. W.-V., III, 414.
[16] Cf. Rota, Mar. 23, 1914, AAS, VI, 317.

When beneficiaries of a parish are religious (exempt or otherwise), their rights and obligations are governed by special provisions. Different norms apply to the beneficiary of a religious and the beneficiary of a secular parish.

1. Beneficiaries of a Religious Parish

a) When a parish is united "pleno jure" to a religious house, the house itself is the beneficiary. Yet the house is only the habitual, not the actual, pastor charged with the care of souls (cf. cc. 451, 452). The superior of the house must present one of his religious, as vicar, whom, if fit, the local Ordinary shall institute as pastor (can. 471, § 2).

The vicar has ordinary jurisdiction over the parish and exercises it independently of the religious house. Entire care of souls, together with all the rights and obligations of pastors, pertains to the vicar (can. 471).

With the exception of his observance of religious discipline the religious pastor or vicar is subject, in the same way as secular pastors, to the full jurisdiction, correction, and visitation of the local Ordinary.[17] The administration of the temporal goods of such parishes will be considered in the next chapter.[18]

b) When a parish is united "non-pleno jure" to a religious house, the house acquires the right to the revenues of the parish, after assigning a suitable portion to the pastor. The religious superior has the right to present a secular priest to the local Ordinary, the latter has the right to institute the priest as pastor. In all other matters, the church is governed in the same way as any secular parish (can. 1425).

2. Beneficiaries of Secular Parishes

There are general norms defining the rights and obligations of such beneficiaries, even though they be exempt religious.

a) They are subject to the jurisdiction, correction, and visitation of the local Ordinary with regard to all the spiritual and temporal affairs of the parish (cf. cc. 329, 335, 451, 456).

b) Parish goods are the property of the parish, as a moral person, and are to be administered by the pastor subject to the authority of the local Ordinary and conformably with the provisions of law (cf. cc. 1476 ff., 533, 630, 631).[19]

---

[17] Cf. above, Chap. X, Art. I, B.

[18] To the religious house, not to the pastor, pertains the custody of the Blessed Sacrament, the care of the church and the administration of its goods and pious legacies (can. 415, § 3, 1°, 3°). The religious superior must take care that sacred functions are carried out in accordance with the liturgical law (can. 415, § 3, 2°), and that they do not cause harm to the explanation of the catechism and Gospel to be given in parochial churches (can. 609, § 3); cf. Fanfani, *De Jure Parochorum*, 425.

[19] Cf. Conc. Trid., XXII, c. 9, *de ref.*; sess. XXIV, c. 3, *de ref.*; W.-V., IV, Vol. II, 770; Leurenius, *Forum Benefic.*, I, Q. 5; Schmalz., III, tit. 25, n. 3, 5.

N.B. Norms governing administration are treated more fully in the following chapter.

ARTICLE V. OTHER NONCOLLEGIATE ECCLESIASTICAL INSTITUTIONS

Besides benefices there exist other noncollegiate ecclesiastical institutions, such as hospitals, orphanages, and the like, destined for spiritual and temporal religious or charitable purposes (can. 1489).[20] Intervention by a competent superior of the Church is necessary in order that these establishments be ecclesiastical in the proper sense of the term. The Roman Pontiff, local Ordinaries (can. 1489) and Ordinaries of exempt religious (cf. cc. 497, 1208, 1550)[21] are such superiors. They can endow a noncollegiate institution with juridical personality, or give it simple approval, and can unite the same to a religious house (cc. 1491, § 2; 1493, § 3).[22]

Although local and religious Ordinaries may give the required approval, they have not arbitrary nor unrestricted authority in such matters, for they must conform to limitations provided for by law. Thus, local Ordinaries cannot erect juridical persons in religious Orders, provinces, or houses; religious Ordinaries cannot establish hospices, schools, orphanages, or like edifices separated from their religious house, without permission from the Ordinary of the place (cf. can. 497, § 3).

Since Ordinaries of exempt religious can juridically erect or approve certain noncollegiate institutions, and that exclusively,[23] they enjoy in such cases definite exemptive rights within the limits determined by law or by particular privileges they may possess.[24]

One founding a noncollegiate institution should describe in the charter its complete constitution, purpose, endowment, administration, and government; also the use to be made of its revenues, and the disposal of properties to be effected in case the establishment goes out of existence (can. 1490).

With regard to its administration, the rector of the foundation should proceed in accordance with the stipulations set down in the charter. He has the same obligations and enjoys the same rights as administrators of other ecclesiastical goods (can. 1489, § 3).

Foundations pertaining to exempt religious are withdrawn from the

---

[20] Hospitals, orphanages, and similar organizations, as schools and recreational centers (can. 1352), are pious or profane depending upon whether their charitable end bears a relationship to God, or is merely humane and philanthropic in character; cf. Wernz, III, 195; Coronata, II, 1024; *Epit.*, II, 812.

[21] Cf. Gillet, p. 247; Maroto, 461; Augustine, VI, p. 546.

[22] Pious institutions not authorized by an ecclesiastical authority are *lay*, and hence not affected by laws governing ecclesiastical organizations. Thus, the St. Vincent de Paul Society, founded by Ozanam, in 1833, without ecclesiastical intervention, is a lay organization; cf. S. C. Conc., Resolutio, Nov. 14, 1920, AAS, 1921, 135; *Per.*, X, 293.

[23] Cf. can. 1550.

[24] Cf. Gasparri, *De Euch.*, I, 560 ff.; Wernz, III, 200; Coronata, II, 1028.

jurisdiction of local Ordinaries in all spiritual and temporal matters which affect them and not the faithful in general (cc. 500, 615). However, if a foundation *separate from a religious house* has been endowed with juridical personality, it is subject to the local Ordinary's canonical visitation (can. 1491, § 1), unless it be endowed with a contrary privilege. The scope of the visitation must be restricted to the affairs under his jurisdiction, namely to those bearing upon the faith and morals of his subjects (cf. can. 1382).

Institutions which are united to houses of Regulars, with the exception of schools, etc. (cf. can. 1382), are wholly exempt from local Ordinaries' jurisdiction and visitation.[25] Nor would it seem that they are obliged to render the account exacted by canon 1492.[26] The Ordinary of the religious has the right and duty to make a visitation, and to exercise such vigilance as will guarantee the proper administration of the institution (cf. cc. 1515, 1550).

Without permission from the Apostolic See, these establishments cannot be suppressed or united to others, or converted to purposes other than those stipulated by the founder, unless the charter itself provides otherwise (can. 1494).

---

[25] Cf. Reiff., III, 36, 5–7; Coronata, II, 1031.

[26] Coronata, *loc. cit.;* see Canon 1525, cited by Gasparri as a basis for canon 1492, par. 1. It should be observed that this parallel provision, i.e., can. 1525, envisages only *pious places canonically erected,* and not institutions devoid of juridical personality which are united to religious houses.

CHAPTER XVI

ACQUISITION AND OWNERSHIP OF TEMPORAL GOODS

Temporal goods of both physical and moral persons pertaining to exempt religious institutes are withdrawn from the jurisdiction of local Ordinaries, except in the cases expressly defined in law (can. 615).[1] The extent of this exemption is determined: (1) by the general canonical regulations which establish the right of acquisition and ownership for religious, and those which permit a diminution of the right through taxation by local Ordinaries; (2) by regulations which govern the right of administration and the right of vigilance. The present chapter treats of the former regulations, the following chapter of the latter.

Worthy of notice is the fact that the capacity of individuals to own and acquire property is not dependent upon the authority of local Ordinaries, but is a right vindicated by common law.

Limitations of these rights in the case of individual religious is due to the nature of their vows: religious of simple vows have full rights; those of solemn vows, very limited ones (cf. cc. 580, 582).[2]

Problems involving exemption do not arise from these rights, but rather from those of *moral persons* pertaining to exempt religious institutes.

ARTICLE I. ACQUISITION AND OWNERSHIP BY MORAL PERSONS PERTAINING TO EXEMPT INSTITUTES

For an adequate treatment of the rights of such moral persons with respect to temporal goods, we shall consider first, their right to acquire, retain, and administer such goods; and secondly, the different ways in which they may acquire the same.

I. RIGHT TO ACQUIRE, RETAIN, AND ADMINISTER TEMPORAL GOODS

Moral persons of exempt religious institutes are vested with these rights and may exercise them independently of local Ordinaries. Their temporal affairs are exempt from the jurisdiction of local Ordinaries except in the

---

[1] Cf. above, Part III, Section III, introduction.

[2] Cf. Conc. Trid., Sess. XXV, *de regul.*, c. 2; Greg. XIII. Bulla, *Ascendente Domino,* May 25, 1584; Layman, *Theol. Mor.*, L. IV, tr. V, c. VII, nn. 3, 6.

cases expressly mentioned in law (cc. 500, 615). Besides this fundamental law regulating all matters pertaining to these religious, the positive prescriptions of the Code on temporal affairs puts the exemption of these persons in clearer outline.

By virtue of canon 1495, all properly constituted ecclesiastical moral persons possess the free, independent right to acquire, retain, and administer temporal goods in accordance with the ends proper to such persons.

The exercise of these property rights is subject to the supreme authority of the Roman Pontiff (can. 1499, § 2), who, as head of the Church, enjoys the power of eminent domain (altum dominium) over ecclesiastical goods, and has, therefore, the inherent sovereign authority to safeguard, defend, and control the administration of the same.[3] "The Code explicitly states, as the best canonists had taught for some time, that the title to ecclesiastical property is vested in the particular moral person that has legitimately acquired it under the supreme control of the Pope" (Ayrinhac, *Administrative Legislation*, 313).

Since the properly constituted juridical person is the proprietor of its goods, it follows that, under ordinary conditions, neither the Roman Pontiff, nor any other authority is competent arbitrarily to dispose of them.[4] No religious superior, not even a General, can licitly or validly dispose of properties belonging to a particular house or community, unless legitimately granted such power by the administrator of the goods or by approved rules or constitutions, or by the Holy See itself, given in rare circumstances.[5]

Institutes, provinces, and houses of exempt religious, being properly constituted juridical persons,[6] enjoy the property rights provided for in canon 1495, but, as stated, in accordance with the norms of the sacred canons.

Canon 531 supplies us with a definite norm, namely: religious institutes, their provinces, and houses[7] have full and inviolable property rights,

---

[3] Cf. *Collect. Lac.*, t. VI, col. 554: see, Bened., XIV, ep., *Cum Encyclicas*, May 24, 1754, *Fontes*, II, 428; d'Annibale, *Summula*, P. I, nn. 43 ff.; W.-V., IV, Vol. II, 741; Vromant, *De Bonis Eccl. Temp.*, 48; Coronata, II, 1039; Santamaria, IV, 344–345; *Epit.*, II, 721; Claeys Bouuaert-Simenon, III, 254; De Meester, III, 1449; Ayrinhac, *Administrative Legislation*, 313; Blat, L. III, part VI, 419; Woywod, II, 1489.

[4] Cf. W.-V., IV, Vol. II, 741; Prümmer, q. 443.

[5] Cf. Vromant, *De Bonis Eccl. Temp.*, 48; *Epit.*, II, 818; *Prümmer*, q. 443.

[6] Cf. can. 531, and can. 536, § 1, in which they are expressly termed moral persons; also, can. 1557, § 2, 2°: see Gillet, p. 241.

[7] Monasteries (cf. can. 1423) and monastic congregations (cf. can. 1557, § 2, 2°) are explicitly referred to as juridical persons, and are, therefore, endowed with property rights in accordance with canon 531; cf. Gillet, pp. 241, 242; Larraona, C.p.R., XII, p. 247, nota 446. Concerning the juridical capacity of Vice-provinces, Quasi-provinces, etc., see Larraona, C.p.R., XII, p. 248, and V, pp. 263–264, and nota 169.

unless these rights are denied or restricted by rules or constitutions.[8]

True inviolability results from the nature of such rights (cf. can. 1495), and from the fact that ecclesiastical properties, because destined for definite purposes, are sacred in character.[9]

The Church has constantly forbidden her ministers to usurp or alienate ecclesiastical goods, and when she does allow alienations, it is always for ecclesiastical purposes and in accordance with the strict provisions of law. Those who violate these prohibitions have always been liable to the severest penalties.[10]

Grave penalties of the Code against delinquents show that the Holy See has not lessened her solicitude for the protection of these rights. Canon 2346 decrees that if anyone either personally or through others, presumes to appropriate and usurp ecclesiastical property of any kind, movable or immovable, corporeal or incorporeal, or prevents either physical or moral ecclesiastical persons from receiving the fruits or income due to them, he becomes and remains excommunicated until full restoration has been made and the above-mentioned obstacle has been removed and he has obtained absolution from the Apostolic See; if the patron of a church or properties should commit these spoliations, he is by that very fact deprived of the right of patronage; a cleric, however, committing or consenting to these crimes, shall in addition be deprived of all benefices and rendered incapable of obtaining any others in the future, and shall be suspended from the exercise of his orders at the discretion of his Ordinary even after he has made full satisfaction and obtained absolution.

II. WAYS OF ACQUIRING TEMPORAL GOODS

Moral persons of exempt religious institutes enjoy independence and freedom from the jurisdiction of local Ordinaries with regard to the application of legitimate methods in the acquisition of property, for every moral person in the Church may acquire temporal goods by any just method which natural and positive law sanctions in the case of other persons (cf. cc. 1499, § 1, and 1488). Begging alms, as will be seen below, is the sole exception to this rule.

---

[8] The Council of Trent, Sess. XXV, *de regul.*, c. 3, granted all orders permission to possess property in common. Houses pertaining to Capuchins and Friars Minor do not partake of this privilege. The constitutions of some orders, as the Discalced Carmelites, and the Society of Jesus, allow but a restricted use of it; see Pius V, Const., *Cum indefessa*, July 7, 1572; Suarez, *De Statu Rel.*, tr. X, L. 4, cc. 7 ff.; Ciravegna, *De Soc. Jesu Paupertate*, c. I; Schmalz., L, III, t. 31, n. 12; Pell., I, III, 12; Arregui, *Annot. ad Epit. Inst. S.J.*, n. 2; Bied.-Führ., pp. 18 ff.; Larraona, C.p.R., XII, p. 251, nota 464; W.-V., III, nn. 25, 215; *Epit.*, I, 724.

[9] Cf. R. J., 51 in VI; W.-V., IV, Vol. II, 744.

[10] Cf. c. 5, X, *de rebus Eccl.*, III, 13; c. 1, *de rebus Eccl.*, III, 9, in VI; *de rebus Eccl.*, III, 4, in *Extravag. com.*; Pius IX, Const., *Apostolicae Sedis;* Conc. Trid., sess. XII, c. 11, *de ref.*

To understand the extent of this exemption, it will be useful to review briefly the various methods which are generally employed by moral persons of exempt institutes in acquiring property.

A. *Pious Foundations*

By a foundation is meant temporal goods given to a moral person in any manner with the obligation in perpetuity or for an extended period of time to use the annual revenue derived from the goods for the offering of Masses, or for the performance of other ecclesiastical functions, or works of piety and charity (can. 1544, § 1).

Exemptive rights over such foundations are explained in the following chapter.[11]

B. *Donations and Bequests*

Moral persons pertaining to exempt institutes may receive goods for pious causes from persons free to dispose of them. They may accept either direct donations or donations to become effective after the death of the donor (can. 1513).

All offerings must be applied to the purposes for which they were given, for justice requires that the known intention of the donor be exactly fulfilled (can. 1514). When the purpose of the gift is doubtful or unknown the goods are to be disposed of in accordance with the particular statutes or legitimate customs in force. Should these be wanting it appears that the recipient acquires the gift by a claim based on right.[12]

Major superiors of exempt clerical institutes are the executors of all donations and bequests made in favor of their own organizations (can. 1515).[13]

C. *Fiduciary Goods*

If an exempt religious receives *in trust* a donation or bequest for pious purposes the Code requires that he notify his religious Ordinary and give a detailed account of all the goods entrusted to him and of the obligations involved (can. 1516, § 1).[14]

In accordance with canon 1515, the religious Ordinary must see to it that the trustee makes safe investments of the goods and faithfully executes the will of the donor (can. 1516, § 2).

---

[11] Cf. Chap. XVII, Art. IV.

[12] Cf. Vromant, *De Bonis Eccl. Temp.*, 74; *Epit.*, II, 823; De Meester, II, 837; J. Brys, *J.P.*, 1930, pp. 201 ff.

[13] Cf. *Epit.*, II, 836; Woywod, II, 1508; Coronata, II, 1055; Prümmer, q. 448: Pejska, p. 64; Ayrinhac, *Administrative Legislation*, 341.

[14] Capuchins and Friars Minor are forbidden to act as trustees, cf. Coronata, II, 1056; Woywod, II, 1509.

However, the Code defines several cases in which a religious acting as trustee is subject to the authority and vigilance of the local Ordinary. These are contained in canon 1516, § 3, which states that a religious must notify the local Ordinary concerning the obligations and the nature of all fiduciary goods which have been committed to him for the benefit of churches of the place or diocese, in behalf of the faithful and pious causes in the place; and that the local Ordinary must demand that the goods be safely invested, and he must be vigilant concerning the execution of the intentions stipulated by the donor, in accordance with the norms set down in canon 1515.

Therefore, when a religious receives fiduciary property, by a gift "inter vivos," or by testament, in order to determine his dependence on the local Ordinary, it is necessary to know whether the gift was made for the benefit of his religious institute or of some pious cause which does not pertain to his institute. If the former is true, the local Ordinary has no right of jurisdiction or vigilance in the matter; if the latter, two distinct cases are possible. *First,* when the goods have been left in trust for a church of the place or diocese, or for the benefit of the faithful or pious causes in the place, the religious, even though exempt, is obliged: (*a*) to indicate to the local Ordinary the amount of property donated and the obligations involved; (*b*) to abide by his mandate concerning the investment of the funds and the execution of the donor's intention; and (*c*) to give an account of the manner in which he has fulfilled his duties in the matter (cf. cc. 1515, 1516). *Secondly,* when the goods have been left for pious causes in general, that is, in behalf of any person or place whatever, exempt religious receiving the trust fund seem to be subject to their religious Ordinary rather than the local Ordinary.[15]

Concerning the first case just mentioned, it should be noted that canon 1516, § 3, gives the local Ordinary authority over the religious with respect to goods he has received in trust for the benefit of *churches of the place or diocese.* This provision does not expressly accord the local Ordinary authority over trust funds which have been donated in behalf of *exempt churches* located in the place or diocese. Hence, in these matters exempt churches are withdrawn from his jurisdiction.[16]

Does the same rule apply to trust funds given to parochial churches which have been incorporated "pleno jure" with an exempt religious house?

It would seem that it does. For by the nature of such an incorporation the parish becomes a religious benefice and, as expressly declared in canon 1425, § 2, the religious pastor or vicar is subject to jurisdiction, correction, and visitation of the local Ordinary in those matters only which refer to

---

[15] Cf. Fanfani, *De Jure Rel.,* 176; Nebreda, C.p.R., VII, pp. 326, 327; Bondini, p. 141.
[16] Cf. Coronata, II, 1056; Augustine, VI, can. 1516.

the care of souls.[17] An analogy with canon 1550 which places pious foundations established in such churches under the exclusive authority of the religious superiors, seems to confirm this interpretation.

D. *Acquisitions Through the Industry of Subjects*

Whatever a religious has acquired by his own industry, or in respect of his institute, belongs to the institute (can. 580, § 2). Goods of this kind are: Mass stipends, remunerations for works undertaken, royalties from books, etc.

Parish work is a frequent source of revenue. Although parochial property is vested in the parish, as a moral person, a religious pastor is the usufructuary, and thereby has the right to the revenues of his benefice (can. 1472).[18] Where no *founded* benefice exists, as is generally the case in the United States and England,[19] a pastor has the right to share in the voluntary offerings of the faithful, or in the fees sanctioned by diocesan decrees or approved custom, which funds either separately or conjointly constitute the endowment of the benefice (cf. can. 1410). He has the right to the revenues and contributions which approved custom and legitimate taxation allot to him.[20] Such goods are for his maintenance, in accordance with canon 630, § 1, but like Mass stipends, become the property of his religious house.[21]

E. *Acquisition Through Prescriptive Right*

Goods can be obtained by prescription. This manner of acquisition must be carried out in accordance with the provisions of civil law and the prescription contained in canons 1509-1512.

F. *Alms*

Begging has constituted one of the chief methods employed by *mendicant* Orders to procure the sustentation of their members and the advancement of projects peculiar to their institutes.

In the past, difficulties have arisen between local Ordinaries and religious concerning this means of acquisition, and, at present, particular circumstances of time and place might occasion serious disputes.[22] In order to eliminate, as far as possible, such difficulties, and to assure moderation,

---

[17] Some authors, on the contrary, maintain that the expression "churches of the place or diocese" employed in canon 1516, § 3, embraces "pleno jure," incorporated parishes, cf. Coronata, II, 1056; Augustine, VI, can. 1516.
[18] Cf. W.-V., II, 771.
[19] Cf. Davis, *Moral and Pastoral Theology*, II, p. 251.
[20] Cf. Ayrinhac, *Const. of the Church*, 272.
[21] Cf. Creusen, 325.
[22] Cf. S. C. Rel., Decr., *De eleemosynis colligendis*, Nov. 21, 1908, AAS, I, 153.

Sacred Congregations[23] and the Code of Canon Law (cc. 621–624; 1503) have established special provisions governing alms-seeking.

The General Rule

In the matter of alms-seeking, Regulars in general, and all religious pertaining to congregations, are subject to the jurisdiction of local Ordinaries; *mendicants* are exempt from the same and possess the right to beg alms in all places where they have a canonically erected religious house.

To understand the full meaning and application of this rule, it is necessary to determine which Regulars are comprised by the term "mendicant," and what is meant by "begging," in the juridical sense of the word.

1. Regulars Comprised by the Term "Mendicant"

There are several types of mendicant Orders.

a) Mendicants, strictly so called. These are Regulars who by their Institute bear the name of mendicants, and are so in fact; i.e., those whose rules and constitutions forbid not only individual property, but also the holding of property in common. Under this classification are grouped the Friars Minor, Capuchins, Jesuits, and Discalced Carmelites.[24]

b) Mendicants in a proper but wide sense. These are Regulars who, though according to their primitive rule could have no goods or fixed revenues in common, are at present dispensed from this form of poverty. Examples of such mendicants are the Conventuals and Dominicans.[25]

c) Mendicants improperly so called. In this class are included all religious to whom the privileges of mendicants have been communicated, e.g., the Cistercians, Camaldolese, Theatines, and Canons of the Lateran.[26]

Only religious who are *mendicants in the strict sense* have the right to beg without permission from the Ordinary of the place. However, this freedom is limited to places in which the religious have a canonically erected house. In dioceses where they possess no such establishments, they need the written permission of the local Ordinary (can. 621).[27]

Local Ordinaries, especially those of adjoining dioceses, may not, without grave and urgent reasons, refuse or revoke this permission if the religious cannot possibly subsist on alms collected in the diocese alone in which they are living (can. 621, § 2).

[23] Cf. S.C.EE.RR., *Paren.*, June 18, 1574; *Senen.*, May 8, 1576; *Derthonen*, Sept. 9, 1587; *Aretina*, Jan. 21, 1593; Decr., *Singulari*, Mar. 27, 1896: S. C. Rel., Decr., Nov. 21, 1908, I, 8–13 and II, 9, 10.
[24] Cf. Conc. Trid., sess. XXV, *de reg.* c. 3; Pius V, Const., *Cum indefessae*, July 7, 1571; Suarez, *De statu rel.*, tr. X, L. 4, c. 7 ff.; Bied.-Führ., p. 18; W.-V., III, n. 25; Creusen, n. 319 ff.
[25] Cf. Cod. Com., Oct. 16, 1919, AAS, XI, 478; Vermeersch, *Per.*, X, 103.
[26] Cf. Piat, I, p. 30, II, p. 101; W.-V., III, n. 25.
[27] Cf. Cod. Com., Oct. 16, 1919, AAS, XI, 478; *Per.*, X, 103; J.P., 1923, 68.

2. Meaning of Alms-Seeking or Begging

The legislation under consideration governs alms-seeking in the canonical sense of the term, and not other methods of securing financial assistance. Alms-seeking, properly so called (i.e., "quaestuatio" in canons 621 ff., "stipem cogere" in canon 1503, or "eleemosynas colligere," in Conc. Balt. II, 95), is a personal and rather general endeavor to collect goods or money for charitable purposes.[28] Ordinarily, begging alms means collecting from house to house, and from persons other than the special benefactors of an individual religious or of a community.[29]

Hence, the alms-seeking provided for by general and particular laws is of a definite type and by no means embraces all modes of enlisting charitable aid. For this reason the following cases are not classified under alms-seeking, and hence are not governed by the laws controlling this activity:

a) Seeking aid of acquaintances;[30]

b) Asking aid of a *few* persons even though they be not acquaintances;[31]

c) Soliciting donations in a church, or from some society or organization;[32]

d) Making appeals at homes to which one has been invited;[33]

e) Requesting assistance of single benefactors or of groups of the same;[34]

f) Making written appeals for help, v.g., by circular letters.[35]

Though the last-mentioned case might seem debatable, it is certainly not alms-seeking in the canonical sense. That is clear from the Decree, *Singulari*,[36] which expressly declares that a superior, without the permission of the local Ordinary, may send letters petitioning financial assistance to anyone whatsoever. Also, conformably with the norm set down in canon 6, 3°, 4°, this matter is to be interpreted according to the provisions in force previous to the Code.[37] As a matter of fact, commentators of the Code[38] commonly hold this interpretation.

The manner of begging alms must conform with the instructions from the Apostolic See regulating this matter (can. 624).[39]

---

[28] Cf. Vromant, *De Bonis Eccl. Temp.*, 75; *Epit.*, I, 724; De Meester, II, 1037; Bastien, D. C. Can. 319; Fanfani, *De Jure Rel.*, 357; Schäfer, 428.

[29] Cf. Creusen, 319.

[30] Cf. *Epit.*, II, 823; Vromant, *De Bonis Eccl. Temp.*, 76.

[31] Cf. Prümmer, 257; Vromant, *loc. cit.*

[32] Cf. Vromant, *loc. cit.;* Schäfer, 428; Goyeneche, *De Rel.*, 86; Cappello, *Summa J.C.*, 625.

[33] Cf. Vromant, *loc. cit.*

[34] Cf. S.C.EE.RR., Decr., *Singulari*, n. IV; Goyeneche, *loc. cit.;* Schäfer, 428; Vromant, *loc. cit.;* Creusen, 319; *Epit.*, II, 823.

[35] Cf. Creusen, 319.

[36] Cf. S.C.EE.RR., Mar. 27, 1896, ap. Vermeersch, *De Rel.*, II, 200.

[37] Cf. W.-V., III, 410 f.; Vromant, *loc. cit.*

[38] Cf. Chelodi, J.P., 283; Prümmer, q. 248; *Epit.*, II, 823; W.-V., III, 408; Coronata, II, 1042; Cocchi, VI, 177, c.; Goyeneche, *De Rel.*, 87.

[39] Cf. S.C.EE.RR., Decr., *Singulari*, Mar. 27, 1896, n. 8; S.C., *De Rel.*, decr., Nov. 21, 1908, n. I, 8–13, II, 9, 10.

In the provisions of the Code, no mention is made of the permission needed for begging by Regulars who are not mendicants in the strict sense of the term. However, according to former practice and the common opinion of authors, these religious may not beg without the said permission. Though they have not the right from the Code to seek alms, they may enjoy privileges from the Holy See.[40] In this case, they would seem to require written permission from the Ordinary of the place where they propose to seek alms,[41] for by expressed provision of law (can. 621) only Regulars who are mendicants in name and in fact are said to have the right to beg without this authorization.

By virtue of canon 490, the rules on begging alms apply equally to religious women who are mendicants in the strict sense. Nuns are bound by the laws of cloister and hence will have to entrust the collection of alms to auxiliary sisters living outside the enclosure of the convent (cf. can. 693).[42] When occupied in collecting alms, religious women must observe the rules formulated by the Holy See in previous decrees on this matter.[43]

ARTICLE II. GOODS OF EXEMPT MORAL PERSONS AFFECTED BY TAXES AND CONTRIBUTIONS PRESCRIBED BY LOCAL ORDINARIES

Local Ordinaries are authorized to exact various contributions from clerics and ecclesiastical moral persons, but are obliged to confine these to the limits established by law.[44]

Must physical or moral persons pertaining to exempt institutes give the contributions and taxes demanded by local Ordinaries? No. The religious in question have no obligation to accede to such requests, except in the cases in which the law expressly subjects them to local Ordinaries (can. 615). We give here the few cases wherein the law accords local Ordinaries a qualified authority over exempt religious.

I. THE CATHEDRATICUM

The cathedraticum or synodaticum[45] (so called because it was usually offered at the diocesan synod) is a small annual tax levied, conformably with canon 1507, § 1, in token of respect and subjection to the episcopal see.[46]

By virtue of canon 1504, all churches and benefices subject to the juris-

---

[40] Cf. Schäfer, *De Rel.*, 429.

[41] Cf. Creusen, 319.

[42] Cf. Schäfer, 429; Fanfani, *De Jure Rel.*, 358; Vromant, *De Bonis*, etc., 79.

[43] Cf. Creusen, 321; *Epit.*, I, 724.

[44] Cf. cc. 1505–1507; Conc. Lat. III, can. 7; Conc. Trid. sess. XXIV, *de Ref.*, c. 3; c. 6, X, III, 39; Bened. XIV, *De Syn. Dioec.*, L. V, c. 6, n. 2.

[45] Cf. Bened. XIV, *De Syn. Dioec.*, L. V. cc. 6, 7; Aug. VI, can. 1504; Ayrinhac, *Administrative Legislation*, 325.

[46] Cf. S.C.C., *Resolutio*, Mar. 14, 1920, AAS, XII, 444.

diction of the Bishop must pay this tax.[47] Exempt churches and benefices which are withdrawn from episcopal authority remain free from the tax. On the contrary, secular parishes entrusted to exempt religious must give this contribution.[48]

The Code asserts the Bishop's absolute right to exact the cathedraticum from those subject to him, and prohibits any prescriptive claims to the contrary (can. 1509, 8°).[49]

(For a fuller explanation of the cathedraticum, consult the article of Claeys Bouuaert in *Nouvelle Revue Théologique*, 48 [1921], pp. 195 ff.)

II. EXTRAORDINARY SUBSIDIES

To meet special diocesan needs of an urgent nature, local Ordinaries may impose a moderate and extraordinary assessment on secular and religious beneficiaries. It is clear from canon 1505 that this subsidy must be a temporary, not a regular periodic one.[50] Nor is it levied, as the cathedraticum, on moral persons and benefices but on the beneficiaries themselves. Both seculars and religious are liable; but all exempt religious, except those in charge of secular benefices, are immune from these imposts.[1]

III. SEMINARY COLLECTIONS AND TAXES

In default of necessary funds, Bishops may exact contributions in support of their seminaries and the education of subjects for the sacred ministries. Canon 1355 declares that Bishops may order *pastors* and *rectors* of nonparochial churches, even though they be exempt, to make periodic collections in their churches for the benefit of the seminary. Hence, exempt religious pastors, whether of secular or religious parishes, are obliged to comply with the wish of the Bishop, as are rectors of exempt churches. It should be noted, however, that religious superiors governing churches which pertain to the community and in which the religious celebrate religious functions, are not rectors in the canonical sense of the term (cf. can. 479), and, therefore, are not affected by the prescription under discussion.[2]

Besides collections, the Bishop may impose contributions or taxes for the support of his seminary. In this event, the moral persons of exempt institutes are generally assessed. Present legislation is practically the same

---

[47] It is to be offered to Bishops, not to other local Ordinaries, therefore during a vacancy of the episcopal see, this tribute is discontinued; cf. S.C.C., Aug. 20, 1917, AAS, IX, 497–502; Coronata, II, 1043.
[48] Cf. *Epit.*, II, 625; Coronata, *loc. cit.*; Aug. VI, can. 1505.
[49] W.-V., IV, Vol. II, 840; Vromant, *op. cit.*, 89.
[50] Cf. Ayrinhac, *Administrative Legislation*, 328.
[1] Cf. Can. 615; also Reiff., III, 39, 26; W.-V., IV, Vol. II, 840; Coronata, II, 1043; Ayrinhac, *Administrative Legislation*, 328; *Epit.*, II, 826.
[2] Cf. Coronata, II, 936; Melo, p. 161.

as that in vogue since the Council of Trent.[3] Those subject to seminary taxes are enumerated in canon 1356.[4] They include the following:

1. All benefices, even those belonging to Regulars;

2. All parishes or quasi-parishes, whether they be incorporated with a religious house or merely entrusted to the care of religious (it should be noted that when appointing a pastor, the Bishop may not impose a tax for the seminary);[5]

3. Any religious house, even though exempt.

Two exceptions to this case are explicitly noted in canon 1356.

a) Houses supported solely from alms are exempt from seminary taxes. It seems certain that houses possessing negligible annual revenues fall under this exemption.[6] All houses of mendicants are freed from this tax. This opinion has been commonly held by authors prior to and after the promulgation of the Code.[7] Parishes pertaining to mendicants are bound to pay the seminary tax.[8] It is disputed whether or not houses of nuns having no benefices are subject to this law.[9]

b) Any house to which is attached a college (or community) of pupils or teachers for promoting the common welfare of the Church, is exempt from the aforesaid tax.

Hence, not only seminaries[10] but boarding and day schools belonging to religious enjoy this exemption. This tax exemption according to Augustine, "is verified in any Catholic college worthy of the name, which is open to all Catholics, without discrimination, for such institutions greatly promote the welfare of the Church at large" (Augustine, VI, can. 1356).[11] Blat classifies as bodies whose teaching actually promotes the common good of the Church, communities of writers publishing periodicals or reviews in explanation or defense of the Catholic faith, groups of priests engaged in missions, etc.[12]

4. Hospitals erected by ecclesiastical authority, confraternities canonically erected, and fabrics of churches provided they have their own revenues are subject to the seminary tax.

---

[3] Cf. Conc. Trid., sess. XXIII, c. 18; also Bened. XIII, Const., *Creditae Nobis*, Mar., 1726, together with the Instruction of the same year, ap. Ferraris, Bibl. v, *seminarium;* Barbosa, *Collect. Doct. ad Conc. Trid.,* sess. XXIII, c. 18; Blat, III, 245, 246.

[4] Claeys Bouuaert, N.R.T., 48 (1921), pp. 230–232.

[5] Cf. Cod. Com., Oct. 16, 1919, AAS, XI, 479.

[6] Cf. Coronata, II, 936.

[7] Cf. Ferraris, v, *seminarium,* 25; Barbosa, *De Off. et Potest. Episc.,* P. III, alleg. 77, nn. 14, ff.; and *Collect. Doct. ad Conc. Trid.,* sess. XXIII, c. 18, n. 30; W.-V., IV, Vol. II, 693; Coronata, II, 936; Cappello, *Summa J. C.,* II, 786.

[8] Cf. Ferraris, v, *seminarium,* 26; Augustine, VI, can. 1356; Coronata, II, 936; Melo, p. 161.

[9] Cf. Ferraris, v, *seminarium,* nn. 32, 146, 181; Augustine, VI, can. 1356; Coronata, II, 936.

[10] St. Pius V declared that novitiates and houses of study pertaining to religious are, like secular seminaries, exempt from taxes; cf. W.-V., IV, Vol. II, 693.

[11] Cf. *Epit.,* II, 690; Coronata, II, 936; Melo, p. 161; W.-V., IV, Vol. II, 693.

[12] Cf. Blat., III, 246.

Confraternities erected as moral persons in Regular churches, after the manner of an organic body, seem to be exempt from the seminary tax.[13] All customs contrary to the provisions of canon 1356, § 1, are reprobated, and all contrary privileges are abrogated.

The seminary tax must be general in character, that is to say, levied on all who are subject to it indiscriminately and according to the same quantity. It can be increased or decreased but the maximum rate must not exceed 5 per cent of the *net income* of the moral person. As the income of the seminary increases, the tax should be lowered (can. 1356, § 2). The income subject to this tax is only that which remains at the end of the year after all obligations and necessary expenses have been deducted. If the revenue of a moral person, v.g., a parish, is entirely made up of the offerings of the faithful, a third part of it is tax exempt (can. 1356, § 3). Moral persons mentioned in 1356, § 1, who have no revenue after the payment of their obligations and expenses are not liable to this taxation. Religious houses, therefore, may subtract from the taxable income the amount they are obliged to contribute to their own seminaries and colleges.[14]

IV. OTHER CONTRIBUTIONS

Common law forbids local Ordinaries to impose tributes other than those mentioned above. They have, however, the right to exact tributes on the occasion of the foundation of benefices and other ecclesiastical institutions and of the consecration of churches, provided the endowments of such places are sufficient to enable these churches or institutions to make the payments. Under no consideration may taxes be levied on stipends for either manual or fundation Masses (can. 1506).[15]

The tributes a local Ordinary can impose on the occasion of foundation and consecrations, mentioned in canon 1506, may not be exacted of places which have been withdrawn from his jurisdiction.[16]

From canons 1506, 500, and 615, it is manifest that local Ordinaries have no authority to constrain exempt religious to make contributions for pious or charitable causes, such as, clerical relief, the furtherance of Catholic education, the support of missions, the needs of the Bishop, etc.

In some countries, as in the United States, the Holy See tacitly permits Bishops to assess parochial revenues for their own proper support.[17] Though this practice involves a departure from the norm given in canon 1506, it has at least the negative approval of the Holy See.[18]

---

[13] Cf. S.C.EE.RR., Mar. 1, 1805; Biz., 404–407; Coronata, II, 936.
[14] Cf. Augustine, VI, can. 1356.
[15] Cf. Ayrinhac, *Administrative Legislation,* 204.
[16] Cf. Vromant, *op. cit.,* 98.
[17] Cf. Conc. Balt., II, 99.
[18] Cf. Wernz, III, 223; Ayrinhac, *Administrative Legislation,* 330.

CHAPTER XVII

ADMINISTRATION OF TEMPORAL GOODS

Administration is that care and management which is consonant with the nature and the proper end of temporal goods. It embraces acts which contribute to the conservation and amelioration of the substance, to the legitimate increase, preservation, and use of revenues; and acts which involve contractual obligations and alienations. The norms regulating these acts are found in the provisions of the Code governing ordinary and extraordinary administration (cf. cc. 532–534; 550; 630; 1495; 1519; 1530–1551, etc.).

ARTICLE I. ORDINARY ADMINISTRATION

Acts of ordinary administration are those which are considered regularly necessary for preserving the substance of property, securing its revenues and providing for normal needs and eventualities. Examples of this are: buying and selling in order to meet daily needs, operations necessary in order to obtain revenues from investments, collecting payments on debts, making short-time bank deposits, effecting expenditures necessary for the conservation of properties, investing funds, etc.[1] All acts which an administrator can *validly* perform by virtue of his office are considered acts of ordinary administration (cf. cc. 532, § 2; 1527, § 1).[2]

In the administration of their property, religious are exempt from the jurisdiction of the local Ordinary, for from its very nature and by positive law (cf. can. 532; 1495, § 2; 1519, § 1), the administration of property pertains to the owner, or, in the case of a benefice, to its titular (can. 1182).

Hence, property of physical and of moral persons pertaining to exempt institutes is administered in accordance with the norms contained in their constitutions and common law (cc. 532; 569), and, generally speaking, local Ordinaries have no authority over such matters except in the cases expressly mentioned in law.

I. THE ADMINISTRATION OF PROPERTY BELONGING TO INDIVIDUALS

Common law permits novices to retain the free administration of their property. However, on account of inconveniences which may result from

---

[1] Cf. W.-V., III, 223; McManus, *The Administration of Temporal Goods in Religious Institutes,* pp. 79, 93; Larraona, C.p.R., XII, 356; Coronata, II, 1067.
[2] Cf. W.-V., III, 222; McManus, *op. cit.,* p. 80.

the exercise of this right, particular constitutions may demand that they cede the same to another during the time of the novitiate.[3]

Before the profession of simple vows, whether temporary or perpetual, the novice must cede, for the whole period during which he will be bound by simple vows, the administration of his property to whomsoever he wishes, and dispose freely of its use and usufruct, except the constitutions determine otherwise. If the novice, because he possessed no property, omitted to make this cession, and if subsequently property comes into his possession, or if, after making the provision he becomes under whatever title the possessor of other property, he must make provision, according to the regulations just stated (can. 569, § 1), for the newly acquired property, even if he has already made simple profession (can. 569, §§ 1 and 2).

As regards this cession or disposition of property, the professed religious can modify the arrangement, not however of his own free choice except the constitutions allow it, but with the permission of the Superior-General, or, in the case of nuns, of the local Ordinary, as well as with that of the Regular superior, if the monastery be subject to Regulars; the modification, however, must not be made, at least for a notable part of the property, in favor of the institute; in the case of withdrawal from the institute, this cession and disposition ceases to have effect (can. 580, § 3).

II. THE ADMINISTRATION OF PROPERTY PERTAINING TO MORAL PERSONS

A. The General Rule

Since religious institutes, provinces, and houses normally own their goods and properties, they enjoy independence or immunity from the jurisdiction of local Ordinaries in the administration of the same[4] (cf. cc. 532, § 1; 1495, § 2). Ordinarily, moral persons cannot personally perform their administrative functions but must do so through superiors or officials. The latter are empowered to administer the temporal goods of the moral persons they represent. This power must be exercised in accordance with religious constitutions and the prescriptions of common law.[5]

B. The Administration of Parochial Goods

Administrative rights of religious who have charge of parishes are determined by common law.

1. A beneficiary is obliged to administer the goods of his benefice according to the norm of law (can. 1476, § 1). Further, a religious in charge of a parish, whether as pastor or vicar, is the administrator of alms or gifts collected or received for the benefit of parishioners, Catholic schools

---

[3] Cf. Creusen, 216.
[4] Cf. above, Chap. XVI.
[5] Cf. W.-V., III, 221.

or pious places connected with the parish. In the exercise of this function, he is always subject to the vigilance of his religious superior (can. 630, § 4).

2. The religious superior has the administration of alms which have been collected or received for the building, maintenance, restoration, and ornamentation of a parochial church which is owned by the religious community (can. 630, § 4).

3. If the parish church is not owned by a religious community, the local Ordinary has the administrative rights mentioned in n. 2 (cf. can, 630, § 4).[6]

N.B. The cases in which religious are obliged to give the local Ordinary an account of their administration will be dealt with in Article III of the present chapter.

C. Investments

The term "investment" may be used in a strict and a broad sense. In the strict sense, "to invest" signifies: to loan money upon securities of a more or less permanent nature; or to place it in business ventures or real estate; or to employ it in any legitimate manner whereby it can produce revenues. In the broad sense, it is taken to include short-time bank deposits. The latter type of investment remains, morally speaking, in the possession of its owner; its chief purpose is to place the funds in security. The small interests realized on these deposits do not constitute them investments in the strict sense.[7]

Canon 533, as will be seen, states the rule governing investments in general. It is practically certain that this norm refers only to investments strictly so called.[8]

THE AUTHORITY OF LOCAL ORDINARIES

1. Concerning Exempt Religious, Pertaining to Male Institutes

a) Regulars need no permission of local Ordinaries to invest their own funds. This is true even when the money to be invested has been donated or bequeathed to them for expenditure locally on divine worship or on works of charity.[9]

Religious belonging to exempt clerical congregations appear to enjoy this same exemption.[10]

---

[6] Concerning the dispute on this point, see Nebrada, C.p.R., VII, pp. 196–198.

[7] Cf. Vromant, Jus Missionarium, II, n. 176, p. 189; Larraona, C.p.R., XII, p. 438.

[8] This interpretation is given by: Vermeersch, Epit., I, 652; Nebreda, C.p.R., VII, p, 263; Coronata, I, 559; Raus, Inst. Jur. Can., p. 290; Vromant, Jus Missionarium, VI, 173, 176; Augustine, III, can. 533, p. 181; Cocchi, De Personis, 54; Prümmer, q. 194: the contrary is held by Oesterle, Prael. J. C., (1931), I, 277.

[9] Cf. W.-V., III, 225.

[10] At present this is the more common opinion; cf. Chelodi, Jus De Personis, 360; Bied.-Führ., 54; Schäfer, 197; Pejska, p. 64; Cappello, Summa J. C., II, 592; Larraona, C.p.R., XIII, pp. 24 ff.; Vidal maintains the contrary, cf. W.-V., III, 225.

b) All religious, even members of Regular institutes must obtain the local Ordinary's consent to invest money which has been given to a parish or a mission, or which has been given to them in behalf of a parish or mission (can. 533, § 1, 4°).

This provision applies only to that money which has been given for *a definite parish or mission*. Therefore, the administration and investment of money received by a religious for missions in general, or for missions of his institute, pertains to the religious, with due submission to his superiors. The same is true of donations made to a Regular pastor, in view of the fact that he is a member of a certain community or institute, for although the goods given him in behalf of the parish are acquired by the parish, *all other gifts* are acquired by him in the same manner as those acquired by other religious (can. 630, § 3).

In the case of a Regular parish, that is, one which is "pleno jure" incorporated with a religious house, the pastor or vicar seems subject to the religious superior alone, both with respect to foundations established in the church and with respect to every other kind of donation (cf. cc. 1550; 630, § 4, in fine). For churches merely entrusted to religious, the provisions of canons 630, § 3, and 533, § 1, 4°, must be observed.[11]

Sometimes it is difficult to determine whether a donation was made in the interest of a parish (or mission) or for the benefit of the religious. When the donor's will is not clear, various norms can be applied which afford an interpretative expression of that will and constitute legal presumptions, i.e., presumptions in which the law assumes the existence of the donor's intent until it is disproved by evidence (cf. can. 1826).[12] Positive circumstances of time, manner, persons, place, and the like, may clearly show that the donor wished to benefit a religious as such, or as his friend, or as the member of a particular institute. Unless there be proof to the contrary, this would seem to be the case with regard to gifts accorded a religious: (1) by parents, relatives, friends, or benefactors known to be particular admirers of a religious, his community, or his institute; (2) on some special occasion, v.g., on the feast day of a religious, in token of gratitude for personal kindness shown by the religious, or in reciprocation for some personal work of the religious.[13] Unless the contrary is proven, donations made to a church, even a church of religious, are presumed by law to be made in favor of the church itself (can. 1536, § 1), and hence become the property of this moral person.

---

[11] Cf. W.-V., III, 226, nota 15.

[12] Cf. norms contained in Const., *Romanos Pontifices,* par. 26, Leo XIII, and the allegations of the Conc. Westmon. II, ap. Collect. S. C. de P.F., II, 1552.

[13] Cf. W.-V., III, 226, and note (15); Creusen, 159; Vermeersch, Par. VI, Suppl. XVII; Vromant, *op. cit.,* 65 ff.; Schäfer, 197.

2. Concerning Nuns

Nuns do not enjoy the exemption had by Regulars or other privileged religious relative to their investments. They are generally subject to the local Ordinary.

a) Because of the dangers which are continually met with in this type of administration, the Code prescribes that the previous consent of the local Ordinary must be obtained by superiors of nuns for any investment of money; nay more, if the monastery of nuns be subject to a Regular superior, his consent also is necessary (can. 533, § 1, 1°). According to Creusen, there is no need of having recourse to the Bishop for investments which have no importance in proportion to the habitual expenses of the monastery, for example, to buy three or four bonds worth five or ten dollars each in a monastery which is fairly well off. Usually the Ordinary or his delegate will leave instructions sufficient to resolve particular cases of this kind.[14]

b) The Code makes special provisions concerning the supervision which local Ordinaries must have over the dowry of religious women. These have already been mentioned in Chapter VI, Article II, n. VII.[15]

Article II. Extraordinary Administration, or Alienation

Religious, like other property holders, have the right of disposing of their goods independently of local Ordinaries. Nevertheless, administrators of moral persons pertaining to religious possess only a restricted exercise of this faculty, for canon law does not favor alienations of church properties.

Alienation, in the ecclesiastical meaning, is any act effecting the transfer of ownership from one person to another, or causing the diminution of one's right in a thing (jus in re). Examples of this are: donations, loans, exchanges, mortgages, cessions of securities, long-term leases, admission of passive or cession of active servitudes that lessen the economic value of a thing, etc.[16] Purchases or payments of debts with money not stabilized as capital, borrowing money free of interest, repudiations of gifts, etc., do not fall under this classification.[17]

N.B. There is question here only of property which belongs to a moral person of exempt religious, for ecclesiastical property is that which pertains to a moral ecclesiastical person. Consequently, canons 534, 1530 ff., dealing with the alienation of property, do not apply to the personal property of religious; cf. Creusen, 162.

---

[14] Creusen, 161.

[15] Concerning the ways of administering a dowry, consult: Creusen, 186, and the same author in R.C.R., VI, pp. 74–76; Larraona, C.p.R., XII, pp. 436 f.

[16] Cf. W.-V., III, 219; Creusen, 156; Ayrinhac, *Administrative Legislation,* 359; Schäfer, 199.

[17] Cf. W.-V., *loc. cit.;* Schäfer, *loc. cit.;* Ayrinhac, *loc. cit.;* Prümmer, 451; *Epit.,* 1851.

Although superiors and officials of exempt institutes are independent of local Ordinaries in administrative acts involving alienations, they are bound by the canonical measures restricting such matters. Thus the Code (can. 534) demands that Apostolic authorization must be previously obtained for the alienation of precious objects, or other property the value of which exceeds the sum of thirty thousand francs or lire (at present about ten thousand dollars),[18] or to contract debts or obligations above that sum. To act otherwise will render the contract null and void. In other cases, the written permission of the superior, given according to the terms of the constitutions and with the consent of his Chapter or Council, manifested by secret voting, is requisite and sufficient.

"An Apostolic indult is required not only in the event of a single transaction exceeding the sum of six thousand dollars [gold: at present, approximately ten thousand dollars], but an Apostolic indult is necessary in every case where a coalescence of the debts or obligations of every kind and nature exceeds the said sum of six thousand dollars."[19]

All alienation requires: a grave motive; the appraising of the value by experts; the sale to the highest bidder; and the secure investment of the money acquired by the alienation (cf. cc. 1530, 1531).[20]

Administrators can effect an exchange of negotiable paper (stocks, bonds, and notes payable to bearer) for other investments at least equally safe and profitable. In such transactions, they must avoid every species of trade and speculation, and must obtain the consent of the major superior (can. 1539, § 2). Authorization of the Holy See is not required.

In the case of *nuns* wishing to alienate properties or to contract debts and obligations, the written *consent of the local Ordinary* also is necessary, as well as the consent of the Regular Superior, if the monastery of nuns be subject to Regulars (can. 534, § 1).

Of the requisite solemnities, only those demanding the consent of legitimate ecclesiastical superiors affect the validity of the act or contract. It seems correct to say that acts of alienation are invalid when made without the previous permission of the Regular superior.[21]

Superiors must beware not to allow the contracting of debts unless it be certain that the interest on them may be met from current revenue, and that within a reasonable time the capital may be paid off by means of a lawful sinking fund (can. 536, § 5).

Debts or obligations incurred by acts of ordinary administration, even though they exceed ten thousand dollars, are not included under the alienations forbidden by canon 534.

---

[18] Cf. Ellis, *Per.*, XXVII, pp. 348–353.
[19] Letter of Apost. Delegate to U. S. A., Nov. 13, 1936.
[20] Cf. Creusen, 162; W.-V., III, 227.
[21] Cf. W.-V., III, 227.

Violations of the provisions on alienations are punished according to the norms set down in canon 2347.[22]

Parties Responsible for Debts

Those responsible for debts contracted by an individual religious or by a moral person pertaining to an exempt institute are determined by canon 536. Difficulties on this point may arise in the case of exempt religious administrating diocesan or mission property.

It is clear that debts legitimately contracted by a Regular as administrator of a secular parish or mission are *incurred by the parish or mission itself*, for any corporate entity contracting debts or obligations is personally responsible for them. This is the principle enunciated in canons 536, § 1, and 1495.[23] It would be a violation of equity and justice to hold a Regular or other administrator, or his institute, responsible for such debts.

Article III. Vigilance Over Temporalities

Since superiors and officials have not the ownership but only the administration of properties belonging to the moral persons of their institutes, they are obliged to give an account of the fulfillment of their administrative functions. This principle applies to religious men and women vested with the office of administrator.[24]

Particular constitutions normally determine the persons to whom this account is to be rendered. Superiors of religious, generally Provincials, are obliged to make canonical visitations of the moral persons within their jurisdiction, and it is their duty to exact an account of the administration of the temporal goods pertaining to these corporate entities. Every five years the Superiors-General must give the Holy See an account of their entire institute (cf. can. 510).[25]

In the Code, supervision of this kind is called *vigilance* (cf. cc. 534; 535; 1519, etc.). It may be described as that right whereby superiors (generally Ordinaries) are entitled to exact an account, and to prescribe the mode or manner of administering temporalities.[26]

I. EXEMPTION FROM THE VIGILANCE OF LOCAL ORDINARIES

The juridical status of exempt religious with respect to local Ordinaries is definitely established by law. This is manifest from canon 1519, which declares that it is the duty of the local Ordinary to exercise careful vigi-

---

[22] Cf. Schäfer, 208; Creusen, 165.
[23] Cf. W.-V., IV, Vol. II, 741.
[24] Cf. Schäfer, 209.
[25] Cf. S. C. Rel., Decr., Mar. 8, 1922, AAS, XIV, 161; Bouscaren, I, can. 510; *Per.*, XI, 28; W.-V., III, 234.
[26] Cf. *Epit.*, II, 843; Cocchi, VI, 200; Fanfani, *De Jure Rel.*, 452; Nebreda, C.p.R., VII, pp. 118, 261 ff.

lance over the administration of all ecclesiastical goods in his territory, *with the exception of those which have been withdrawn from his jurisdiction.* Therefore, he has not this right of vigilance over temporalities of exempt male institutes, since, as has already been seen,[27] they have been withdrawn from his authority.

Further proof of this can be drawn from the particular exemptive privileges granted to each institute, from the provisions of canons 500 and 615, and from canon 344, § 2, which states that Bishops are entitled to make a canonical visitation of exempt religious only in the cases expressly defined in law.[28] No law expressly grants to local Ordinaries the right of vigilance over the temporal goods belonging to exempt institutes of men.

Although this exemption is indisputable, there are instances in which the administrative functions of religious men pertaining to exempt institutes do not enjoy such immunity. These are generally cases in which the religious are administrators of goods (v.g., parochial benefices) which are not entirely removed from the authority of the local Ordinary.

In what follows we shall endeavor to explain these cases, and, likewise, the cases in which nuns are subject to the same vigilance.

II. SUBJECTION OF EXEMPT RELIGIOUS TO THE VIGILANCE OF ORDINARIES

A. *Institutes of Men*

The following cases describe the extent of a local Ordinary's right to exercise vigilance over the administrative activities of exempt religious.

1. Religious Pastors of Secular Churches

Religious in charge of secular parishes are, like secular priests, subject to the entire jurisdiction, correction, and visitation of the local Ordinary in all matters connected with their parochial office (can. 631, § 1). They must submit an account of their administration of the temporalities to this Ordinary, for the benefice of which they have the care is *secular* in character and consequently remains subject to his jurisdiction. No custom contrary to this prescription is to be tolerated (can. 1519). Local Ordinaries have the right to impose measures that shall guarantee prudent administration, always, of course, in accordance with the provisions of common law (can. 1519, § 2).

Furthermore, since all legacies and foundations[29] presented to a secular

---

[27] Cf. above, Section III, preliminary notions.

[28] Cf. above, Chap. X, Art. I: see Reilly, *The Visitation of Religious*, p. 124.

[29] *Legacies*, or bequests, as opposed to foundations, include all goods which are left to a person or corporation, especially by testament (or in any other way), without the obligation to conserve them in a stable manner. *Foundations* are revenue-producing goods left to a person or corporation in any way whatever, with the obligation of conserving the capital and the right of enjoying the revenues derived therefrom. *Pious foundations* are a special kind of foundation, as will be seen in Article III, of this chapter.

parish for the benefit of the same, or to a religious in behalf of such a parish, become the property of that parish, the local Ordinary has a right to exact an account of their administration, safeguarding at the same time the provisions of canons 630, § 4, and 1550.[30] The two canons cited mention definite exemptive rights of religious with regard to the matter under consideration.

a) Canon 630, § 4, states that, notwithstanding his vow of poverty, a religious pastor or vicar may receive or collect alms offered in any manner for the benefit of parishioners, or for Catholic schools and pious places connected with the parish, and may undertake the administration of the same; and he may likewise distribute these alms according to his own prudent judgment and the intention of the donor, *under the vigilance, however, of his superior.*

This right of vigilance on the part of the superior does not entitle him to prohibit the collecting or accepting of such alms, nor to determine their distribution, v.g., for the benefit of his community, nor to undertake the administration of the same.[31]

To invest any of the funds in question, the pastor must, as already has been seen,[32] obtain the previous consent of the local Ordinary (in the case of secular benefices) (can. 533, § 3). He must, likewise, give the local Ordinary an account of these investments (cf. can. 631).[33]

Secondly, canon 630, § 4, declares that the right to receive, retain, and administer alms for the building, maintenance, repair, and ornamentation of the parochial church is vested in the superior, if the church pertains to the religious community; otherwise, in the local Ordinary.

It is to be remarked that even though a parochial benefice is united "pleno jure" to an exempt religious house and the parish becomes a religious parish, the church connected with the parish may remain a nonreligious church and thus pertain to the diocese, not to the religious. Although this procedure is not generally followed in acts of incorporation, it will be had if a Bishop incorporates the parish and at the same time excludes the church from the transaction.[34] In this case the Bishop has the administration of the funds in question,[35] but he may, with the consent of the religious superior, delegate this office to the religious pastor or vicar in charge of the church.[36] In the latter arrangement, the religious is obliged to give the local Ordinary an account of his administration.

---

[30] Cf. Cod. Com., July 25, 1926, IV, AAS, XVIII, 393.
[31] Cf. Coronata, I, 635, p. 825.
[32] Cf. above, Chap. XVII, Art. I, n. II, C.
[33] Cf. Coronata, I, 635, p. 825.
[34] Cf. Nebreda, C.p.R., VII, p. 263; Coronata, I, 635, p. 825, nota I; *Monit.*, XXXVIII, pp. 341 ff.
[35] Cf. Melo, p. 90, nota 1.
[36] Cf. Melo, p. 90; *Epit.*, I, 632; Coronata, I, 635, p. 825.

b) Canon 1550 states that the major superior has the exclusive power of jurisdiction, vigilance, etc., over *pious foundations* when these are established in churches, even in parish churches of exempt religious. The meaning of this is that the major superior, and not the local Ordinary or anyone else, is to supervise the administration of these gifts. This is true not only when the parish church is "pleno jure" but also when it is "non-pleno jure," incorporated with the religious house.[37]

Concerning supervision over secular ecclesiastical goods in general, it should be remembered that, besides local Ordinaries, religious superiors have the right to exercise vigilance over any of their subjects acting as administrators, and may institute whatever investigation they deem necessary (cf. can. 630, § 4). This is further borne out by the prescription of canon 631, § 2, which empowers them to enact opportune decrees and inflict penalities that have been merited by their subjects because of delinquencies in their parochial charge.[38] Should decisions of the local Ordinary and the religious Ordinary be incompatible, that of the former shall prevail (can. 631, § 2).

By virtue, therefore, of this right of vigilance, the religious superior may demand an account of the pastor's administration, and may correct the inordinate and imprudent acts of his subject.[39] To this end he may remove his subject from the office of pastor, and this even without the consent of the local Ordinary (cf. can. 454, § 5).

2. Religious Pastors or Vicars of Parishes Incorporated "Pleno Jure" With an Exempt Religious House

Local Ordinaries have the right to make a visitation which will include an investigation of both the pastor and the church. The visitation of the church must, however, be confined to those objects only which pertain to the service of the parish. A list of these is given in the constitution, *Firmandis,* of Benedict XIV.[40] Supervision over temporalities is not included in this list. Furthermore, canon 1425, § 2, declares that the local Ordinary has the power of jurisdiction and visitation over pastors of such parishes with respect to those matters which pertain to the *care of souls,* but does not mention that he has authority over temporalities.

The Code Commission was asked whether, in virtue of canons 631, § 3; 535, § 3, 2°; 533, § 1, 1°, 3°, and 4°, the local Ordinary has the right to exact an account of the administration of foundations and legacies to a religious

[37] Cf. Nebreda, C.p.R., VII, p. 329; see below, Art. IV of present chapter.
[38] Cf. Vromant, *De Bonis Eccl. Temp.,* 196, 243; W.-V., II, 415, 416; Schäfer, 501; Goyeneche, *De Rel.,* p. 183.
[39] Cf. W.-V., III, 416.
[40] Cf. Bened. XIV, Const., *Firmandis,* par. 7, Nov. 6, 1744; see above, Chap. X, Art. I; Reilly, *The Visitation of Religious,* p. 138.

parish such as is mentioned in canon 1425, § 2. The Commission replied in the affirmative, adding that its interpretation was in nowise prejudicial to canons 630, § 4, and 1550.[41]

This reply makes no express mention of parishes which are "pleno jure" incorporated with *exempt* houses, hence it should not be applied to the same. Likewise, canon 1550, cited by the Commission, expressly states that pious foundations established even in parish churches of exempt religious are exclusively subject to the major superiors of the religious. This norm governing pious foundations seems "a fortiori" true of legacies.

Hence we conclude, with Vidal, that the administration of the temporal goods pertaining to parish churches which are "pleno jure" incorporated with *exempt* religious houses, is subject to the jurisdiction and supervision of the major religious superiors and not that of local Ordinaries.[42]

3. Investments of Gifts to a Parish or Mission

The local Ordinary has the right to exact an account of investments of money given to any religious, even a Regular, when the money has been donated to a parish or mission or to the religious in behalf of the parish or mission.

This regulation is binding in all instances except the one just mentioned under "Number 2," namely, except the parish or mission in question is incorporated "pleno jure" with an exempt religious house. Donations of any kind to this type of parish are subject to the jurisdiction and supervision of the major superior.

4. Trust Funds for Diocesan Churches

The local Ordinary has the right to exact an account of all funds (properties or money) left in trust to a religious for the benefit of churches of the place or dioceses, in behalf of the faithful or pious causes of the dioceses (can. 1516). All other trust funds left to religious are under the supervision of their proper Ordinary (can. 1516, § 3). As stated above,[43] the local Ordinary has no jurisdiction or supervision over trust funds granted in favor of a church which is incorporated "pleno jure" with an exempt house.

5. Donations to Secular Churches

Donations given to *rectors* of secular churches for the benefit of such churches are under the supervision of local Ordinaries. Rectors are described in canon 479, § 1 (can. 485).[44]

---

[41] Cf. Cod. Com., July 25, 1926, IV: Bouscaren, I, can. 1425; *Per.*, XV, 172.
[42] Cf. W.-V., III, 226, nota 15, 235.
[43] Cf. present chapter, Art. I.
[44] Cf. Nebreda, C.p.R., VII, pp. 268–271.

B. *Temporalities Pertaining to Nuns*

Nuns do not enjoy the same immunity from the vigilance of local Ordinaries that is possessed by exempt religious of male institutes. This is manifest from canon 535, which contains the rules governing their administration of temporal goods, and from canon 550, § 2, which contains a specific prescription regulating the investment of dowries.

1. The General Provisions of Canon 535

a) For every monastery of nuns, even though exempt, the superioress must furnish an account of her administration once a year, or even oftener if the constitutions so prescribe it, to the local Ordinary, as well as to the Regular superior, if the monastery of nuns be subject to Regulars (can. 535, § 1, 1°).

The Code Commission declares that in the case of a monastery of nuns subject to a Regular superior, the account is to be given to the Regular superior, and also to the Ordinary of the place.[45]

b) If the Ordinary does not approve of the aforesaid account which has been furnished him, he may apply the necessary remedies, including even the removal from office, if the circumstances demand it, of the bursar and other administrators; but if the monastery be subject to a Regular superior, the Ordinary shall request him to see to it, and if the Regular superior fails to do so, then the Ordinary himself must deal with the case (can. 535, § 1, 2°).[46]

From this provision, it is plain that the local Ordinary may not immediately apply corrective measures in the case of nuns subject to Regulars. His authority is *conditional,* for it is only had when the Regular superior, after being warned of a defective administrative account, fails to remedy matters.[47]

Authority is not given the local Ordinary to dictate to the Regular superior the mode of correction to be used. So long as the latter's action has been productive of the desired result, it must be considered efficacious. Hence, although the local Ordinary may not agree with the Regular superior on the procedure the latter uses in correcting the nuns, he cannot charge that the superior is negligent in his duty.[48]

---

[45] Cf. Cod. Com., Reply, Nov. 24, 1920, AAS, XII, 575; see Bouscaren, I, can. 535; *Per.*, X, 249.

[46] What is said here of Regulars may be applied to superiors of clerical exempt congregations which have religious women subject to them, v.g., the Redemptorists, with respect to the religious women of their institute; see, *Epit.*, I, 610; Schäfer, 219.

[47] Cf. Larraona, C.p.R., XIV, p. 349.

[48] *Ibid.,*

2. The Regulation Concerning Dowries

From canons 549–551, it is clear that the legislator wishes every possible precaution to be taken in order to insure the proper administration and safe investment of dowries. For this reason he places upon the local Ordinary the duty of vigilance over such matters. The Ordinary is obliged carefully to inquire about the administration of dowries and to demand an account thereof, especially at the time of his annual visitation of nuns (can. 550, § 2). It should be remarked that the expression "especially at the time of his annual visitation" connotes that the Ordinary may exact such accounts at other times also. The Ordinary in question is the one who governs the place where the superioress (either the Mother-General or the Mother-Provincial) who has the care of the dowries habitually resides (cf. can. 550, § 1).[49]

Canon 550, § 1, accords the local Ordinary the right of vigilance only; it does not permit him to determine what specific investments are to be made, for this would be equivalent to the right of administration which is vested only in the superioress. He can, nevertheless, prevent nuns from making those investments which lack the safety required by law.[50]

ARTICLE IV. PIOUS FOUNDATIONS[1]

I. GENERAL NOTION

In the strict canonical meaning, pious foundations are temporal goods given in any way to a moral ecclesiastical person with an obligation, which is perpetual or of long duration, to employ the annual revenue thereof for the offering of Masses, or the fulfillment of specified ecclesiastical functions, or for the promotion of works of piety and charity (can. 1544).

From the wording of the canon, it is clear that this Title of the Code deals with *fiduciary* foundations, whereas, v.g., Titles XXV and XXVI are concerned with autonomous ones. A foundation is fiduciary if the goods destined for the designated pious purpose are given by the founder to some *moral* ecclesiastical entity which is *already endowed with juridical personality*. The foundation has not in itself juridical personality. The difference between fiduciary and autonomous foundations consists in this: for the former, the founder donates goods to a moral person already existing; for the latter, the founder donates goods which are then formally established

---

[49] Cf. Coronata, I, 577, n. 4°.
[50] *Ibid.*
[1] Although the laws concerning pious foundations are contained in a special Title of the Code (Title XXX of Book III, Part VI), we shall treat of them here under the administration of temporal goods. The truth is that the canons of the cited Title refer chiefly to acts which are administrative in character.

as a moral person through the intervention of a competent ecclesiastical superior.[2]

The goods of the pious foundation may be transferred to the moral person in any manner whatever, that is, by last will and testament or by acts "inter vivos."

After the foundation has been legitimately accepted, it has the force of a bilateral contract — "do ut facias" — between donor and recipient (can. 1544, § 2).

II. THE EXEMPTIVE STATUS OF PIOUS FOUNDATIONS

This status is determined by the nature of the foundation. If it is made to a moral person pertaining to an exempt institute, the foundation is withdrawn from the jurisdiction of local Ordinaries; otherwise it is subject to their jurisdiction.

FOUNDATIONS IN FAVOR OF MORAL PERSONS OF EXEMPT INSTITUTES

All goods, and consequently those of pious foundations pertaining to exempt institutes, their provinces, houses, and churches, are withdrawn from the jurisdiction and vigilance of local Ordinaries, and are subjected exclusively to the authority of the religious superiors (cc. 500; 615; 1550).[3]

Canon 1550 expressly declares that major superiors of exempt religious have exclusively the rights and obligations mentioned in canons 1545-1549. From the canons cited, it follows that, in the case of pious foundations made to moral persons of exempt religious, major superiors have exclusive authority in the following matters: they alone are empowered to issue prescriptions determining both the limits below which a pious foundation cannot be accepted, and the proper distribution of the income to be derived from the goods (can. 1545); their previous consent is required before a valid acceptance of the foundation can be had (can. 1546).[4]

Depositing of the endowments, pending investment, must be effected according to the directions of these superiors, and the investing of them must be done according to their specifications (can. 1547). An account must be given them of all the temporal and perpetual obligations connected with the foundations, of the fulfillment of the same, and of the stipends involved (can. 1549).

---

[2] Cf. W.-V., IV, Vol. II, 782, 783; De Meester, III, 1499; Coronata, II, 1079. It is to be noted, as Vidal remarks, that a fiduciary *foundation* differs from a fiduciary *donation,* for the former is a gift of the kind specified in can. 1544, to a *moral* person, while the latter consists of goods given in trust to a *physical* person; cf. W.-V., IV, Vol. II, 782, nota 97.

[3] Cf. above, Section III, preliminary notions.

[4] Cappello, *De Sacramentis,* I, 716, states that the acceptance of a foundation without the previous consent of the superior is *illicit* and rescindable.

Although the norm given in canon 1550 expressly mentions only churches of exempt religious, it has in reality an extension that is far reaching.

1. It comprises all exempt religious, lay and clerical,[5] whether they belong to Orders or to exempt congregations. Hence the canon applies to all exempt religious, without exception. If it referred only to clerical institutes, the term "Ordinary" would have been used in place of "major superiors."[6]

Are *investments* of these funds by religious of exempt *congregations* subject to the local Ordinary?

This point is disputed. Some authors maintain that, in virtue of canon 533, § 1, 3°, religious of exempt *congregations* require the previous consent of the local Ordinary in order to invest the funds of a foundation made to their moral persons or to alter such an investment, and that this administration of the foundation remains under the vigilance of the local Ordinary.[7] Others hold that, by virtue of canon 1550, pious foundations pertaining to exempt religious, whether of Orders or of congregations, are entirely withdrawn from the jurisdiction and vigilance of local Ordinaries.[8] The latter seems to be the correct interpretation. For canon 1550 declares that the matters in question are under the exclusive jurisdiction and vigilance of the major superiors of *exempt religious,* nor does it restrict this exemption to Regulars. Further, canon 533, § 1, 3°, does not expressly mention *exempt* religious, as is usually the case, v.g., in canon 512, when the legislator subjects them to local Ordinaries.[9] Unless this interpretation be accepted it is difficult to see how the provisions of canon 533, § 1, 3°, and canon 1550 are reconciliable.[10] According to Nebreda, a still more forceful argument justifying this interpretation may be drawn from the sources of canon 533, and especially from the Constitution, *Conditae a Christo,* [11] of Leo XIII.[12]

2. The provision of canon 1550 refers to foundations made in any church, even parochial, pertaining to exempt religious.

It embraces, therefore, all Regular or conventual churches and all parochial churches which are incorporated "pleno jure" or "non-pleno jure" with a religious house.

Hence, although the local Ordinary is entitled to make a canonical visitation of parochial churches pertaining to exempt religious,[13] he may not investigate or demand an account of their pious foundations.

---

[5] Cf. *Epit.,* II, 869.

[6] Cf. Miller, *Founded Masses,* p. 51.

[7] Cf. Chelodi, *Jus De Personis,* 260, and p. 433, nota 2; Claeys Bouuaert-Simenon, I, 632; Prümmer, qq., 194, 195; Fanfani, *De Jure Rel.,* 155.

[8] Cf. *Epit.,* I, 656; Blat, *De Personis* (1938), 259; Bied.-Führ., 54; W.-V., IV, Vol. II, 789; De Meester, II, 980; Woywod, II, 1541; Nebreda, C.p.R., VII, pp. 320 ff.

[9] Cf. *Epit.,* I, 656.

[10] Cf. Prümmer, q. 194.

[11] Cf. Leo XIII, Dec. 8, 1900.

[12] Cf. Nebreda, C.p.R., VII, pp. 321, 322.

[13] Cf. above, Chap. X, Art. I.

The one exception to this rule is Mass foundations pertaining to lay confraternities which are established in these exempt churches. Unless such confraternities have an express exemptive privilege, the administration of their temporal goods is subject to the local Ordinary, to whom they must render an account, annually, of the same (cf. can. 691).[14]

Since the aforesaid pious foundations are exempt, with far greater reason must it be maintained that foundations made to exempt oratories are withdrawn from the jurisdiction and vigilance of local Ordinaries, for these places enjoy in general a more extensive exemption than do churches, especially parish churches.

3. Although churches alone are mentioned in canon 1550, it is apparent, from the nature of exemption,[15] and from canons 500 and 615, that pious foundations given in favor of other moral persons pertaining to exempt religious are entirely withdrawn from the jurisdiction and vigilance of local Ordinaries.

FOUNDED MASSES

Pious foundations for Masses which have been made to moral persons pertaining to exempt religious, are, as has been seen, exempt from the jurisdiction and vigilance of local Ordinaries.

Hence, although exempt religious are bound by the decree of the local Ordinary or the diocesan custom fixing the manual Mass stipend (can. 831, § 2), they are exempt from any such authority in the case of *founded* Masses. Neither canon 831 nor canon 1545 accords local Ordinaries jurisdiction over founded Masses of exempt religious; rather, canon 1545, which must be understood according to the norm set down in canon 1550, when there is question of foundations to exempt religious, expressly declares that it is the exclusive right of major superiors to prescribe the minimum amount of endowment required for pious foundations of this type.[16]

---

[14] Cf. above, Chap. VIII, Art. III: see S.C.C., in *Nucerina Paganorum*, June 23, 1629; see also Gasparri, *De Sanctissima Eucharistia*, I, 566; Piat, II, pp. 59, 60; Beringer-Steinen, II, 171.
[15] Cf. above, Section III, preliminary notions.
[16] Cf. Miller, *Founded Masses*, p. 52.

PART IV

The Limitations of Exemption

INTRODUCTORY REMARK

The final part of this treatise is concerned with the restrictions affecting exemption. It views, as it were, the extension of exemption in a negative way, for the expression "limitations of exemption" is used here to mean those cases which form restrictions or exceptions to exemption; in other words, the cases in which local Ordinaries have jurisdiction over physical or moral persons, places, and things pertaining to exempt institutes.

Vermeersch[1] points out that limitations of exemption are not to be confused with *juridical conditions* whose fulfillment are necessary in order that exemption be enjoyed. The latter are prerequisites which must be verified before exemption can be had, the former are restrictions placed upon already existing exemptive rights. Examples of such prerequisite conditions are those expressed: in canon 616, § 1, which states that Regulars unlawfully absent from their houses do not enjoy the privilege of exemption; and, in canon 497, § 1, which declares that an edifice cannot be considered an exempt religious house unless it has been erected with the approval both of the Apostolic See and of the local Ordinary. Yet, although such cases are not in the strict sense exceptions to exemption, they may, we think, for practical purposes be classified as such, for they are instances in which exempt religious and the houses, etc., belonging to them are not withdrawn from the jurisdiction of local Ordinaries.

As the content of cases limiting exemption has already been explained in the foregoing chapters, we shall restrict the remaining two chapters to a discussion of the canonical norm regulating the limitations of exemption (Chap. XVIII), and to an enumeration of the limitations contained in law (Chap. XIX).

---

[1] Cf. *Epit.*, I, 775.

CHAPTER XVIII

THE NORM REGULATING THE LIMITATIONS OF EXEMPTION

Regulars, and other privileged religious (can. 500), together with their houses, etc., are *exempt* from the jurisdiction of local Ordinaries, *except in the cases expressly stated in law* (can. 615).

This is the rule which determines the limitations or exceptions to exemption. The precise meaning of the rule will be seen in the explanation of its different elements given in the following articles.

ARTICLE I. REGULARS AND PRIVILEGED RELIGIOUS ARE EXEMPT

From this it is not to be concluded that the cases expressed in law constitute the only instances in which exempt religious are subject to the jurisdiction of local Ordinaries. Apparently the terms of the norm of limitation must be accepted in their context (can. 18), that is, as referring to the specific kind of exemption envisaged by canon 615. As has been seen previously, especially in Chapters I and II, this exemption is *passive*.[1]

By virtue of such exemption the persons, places, and things pertaining to the exempt institute are withdrawn from the jurisdiction of local Ordinaries and placed under the authority of their own religious Ordinaries and the immediate jurisdiction of the Holy See. This immunity together with the jurisdiction accorded the religious superiors does not affect persons or things not belonging to the exempt institutes.

Hence, in evaluating the cases of limitations we should eliminate as not strictly bearing on exemption and consequently irrelevant, juridical prescriptions which treat of the relationship between exempt religious and persons or things not pertaining to their institute. Thus, for example, since *the care of the souls of the faithful* is not comprised under the passive exemption enjoyed by religious,[2] it follows that any jurisdiction which the local Ordinary has over exempt religious in this matter is not, strictly speaking, a limitation of their exemption.[3]

The importance of the aforesaid principle is clear. Only by virtue of it can some doubtful cases be correctly solved, for it often determines whether

---

[1] Cf. Bened. XIV, *De Syn. Dioec.,* II, XI, 2; Suarez, *De Censuris,* V, IV, 6; Petra, in C. 4, Calisti, III, t. 1, 6; Thesaurus, II, Episcopus, V, 1; Pignatelli, VII, VIII, 8 ff.; Geraldi, II, XXI, I, 825; Chokier, Q. 103; Fine, p. 707; Piat, II, p. 6; Vermeersch, *De Rel.,* I, 362; Bondini, pp. 6, 7; Melo, pp. 2, 3; Ojetti, *Com. in Cod. Excursus ad can. 14;* Chelodi, *Jus De Personis,* 281.
[2] Cf. Leo XIII, Const., *Romanos Pontifices,* par. 10, May 8, 1881.
[3] Cf. Vermeersch, *De Rel.,* I, 370.

a law should be interpreted as favoring the religious or the local Ordinary. When the solution of a doubtful case will affect exemption properly so called, *it must always be made in favor of the exempt religious.*[4] When the doubtful case involves matters which do not pertain to passive exemption and which by law are normally subject to the jurisdiction of local Ordinaries, it should be solved in favor of these Ordinaries, for restrictions of the free exercise of one's rights are to be strictly interpreted (cf. can. 19).

In view, therefore, of the *passive* nature of the exemption enjoyed by Regulars and other privileged religious, we are forced to differ with Vermeersch,[5] concerning the following cases which he lists as limitations or exceptions to exemption:

A. *Canon 1338,* § 2

This prescription contains two provisions: the first is not a limitation of exemption; the second is.

In order to preach to nonexempt persons, exempt religious require the faculty from the Ordinary of the place where the sermon is to be delivered. This is not a limitation of exemption, because, with the exception of the cases provided for in canon 514, exemption does not confer on its possessor jurisdiction over nonexempt persons.

On the contrary, the obligation of Regulars to obtain this faculty when they are to preach to nuns who are subject to them, is a true limitation of their exemption.

B. *Canons 874, 875*

By virtue of their exemption, religious are not entitled to hear the confessions of nonexempt persons, excepting in the cases provided for in canon 514; hence, their dependence on the local Ordinary in this respect is not a limitation of their exemption.

The necessity of obtaining faculties from the local Ordinary in order to confess nuns and their novices when these are subject to exempt religious (cf. can. 876), is a true limitation of exemption.

C. *Canon 1385*

The provisions of this canon concerning previous censorship of books, etc., by local Ordinaries refer to the teaching office of the Church relative to nonexempt persons. As seen already (Chap. I, n. 2; and Sect. III, Prelim. Notions), the exemption of religious does not withdraw them from the

---

[4] Cf. above, Chap. II, Art. I, n. II. This favorable interpretation must be employed: because exemption is a pontifical right benefiting the Holy See and religion in general; see, Chokier. Q. 4; and Melo, p. 34: and because it is a remunerative privilege given in token of gratitude, or, as a reward for labors borne by the religious; see, AAS, XXV, 245; *Per.,* XXII, 98–101. It is the common teaching of authors that these types of privileges must be interpreted broadly.

[5] Cf. *Epit.,* I, 775.

jurisdiction of local Ordinaries in matters which pertain to the faith and morals of the faithful in general.

D. *Canon 1505*

By virtue of this law, the local Ordinary may, under the specified circumstances, exact a subsidy from either secular or religious beneficiaries. However, he has the power only over beneficiaries who receive the revenue of a secular or nonexempt benefice. Since such benefices are not withdrawn from the local Ordinary's jurisdiction, his authority to make the stated exaction is not a limitation of exemption.

The local Ordinary has no authority to exact this subsidy from the beneficiary of an exempt religious benefice.[6]

E. *Canon 1516*

This canon states that the local Ordinary has authority with regard to the investment of fiduciary donations made to churches of the place or diocese, and has the right of vigilance over the administration of these goods.

As seen above,[7] this provision does not affect exempt churches of places or dioceses.

F. *Canon 533, § 1, 4°, and § 2*

The provisions herein contained require the consent of the local Ordinary with regard to the investing, or change of investment, of gifts made to a parish or mission or to a religious in behalf of a parish or mission.

When the parish is secular its subjection in this respect is not a limitation of exemption (cf. can. 1519); when a parish is incorporated "pleno jure" with a religious house, the law does not subject it to the jurisdiction of the local Ordinary.[8]

ARTICLE II. REGULARS AND PRIVILEGED RELIGIOUS ARE EXEMPT, EXCEPT IN THE CASES . . .

From these words it is clear that the legislator has not promulgated a multiplicity of norms which determine in a positive fashion the matter in which religious are withdrawn from the jurisdiction of local Ordinaries. He has declared, rather, that the religious in question have *general* exemption, and that this is limited only in the cases which are expressly stated in law. This legislation is the same as the discipline in force prior to the Code.

---

[6] Cf. c. 6, X, *De censibus,* etc., III, 39; c. 16, X, *De offic. jud. ord.,* I, 31; Schmalz., *loc. cit.,* nn. 53 ff.; Wernz, III, 224; *Epit.,* II, 826; Coronata, II, 1043; W.-V., IV, Vol. II, 840; Reiff., *loc. cit.,* III, 39, nn. 26–28.
[7] Cf. Chap. XVI, Art. II, n. II, C.
[8] Cf. W.-V., III, 226, and nota 15.

BEFORE THE CODE

That the exemption enjoyed by Regular and other privileged institutes was *general* in character is clear from pontifical documents.

The Bull of Sixtus IV, *Regimini Universalis Ecclesiae,* commonly called *Mare Magnum,* states: "In order that diocesan and other Ordinaries . . . may not presume, contrary to the ordination of our Predecessor, to claim any jurisdiction or authority whatever over persons or places pertaining to the Friars Preachers, we strictly forbid that anyone promulgate in any manner, either specifically or generally, without the commission and authority of the Holy See, any sentence of excommunication, suspension, or interdict, or exercise any rights of pre-eminence, authority, or jurisdiction . . . over the persons and places pertaining to the said Order of Preachers, because they possess *full* exemptive rights."[9]

The constitution, *Licet* (par. 3) of Paul III, concerning the Society of Jesus, declares: "We liberate and exempt this Society and all its members, persons, and whatever goods it possesses from all authority, jurisdiction, and correction of Ordinaries, and we place . . . this said Society under our protection and under that of the aforesaid (Apostolic) See."[10]

Leo XIII in his constitution, *Romanos Pontifices,* says: "Regulars who live in the missions are exempt from the jurisdiction of the local Ordinary in the same way as Regulars dwelling within the cloister except in those cases expressly mentioned in law, and generally in matters pertaining to the care of souls and the administration of the sacraments."[11]

The immense care and diligence which the Holy See has always employed to specify exactly the cases in which local Ordinaries have jurisdiction over exempt religious, is sufficient to show that the aforesaid See held that the exemption in question is general and has only those limitations which are expressly defined in law. Hence it is, as Leo XIII stated, that houses of Regulars are looked upon "as certain specified territories withdrawn, as it were, from the dioceses."[12] Therefore, in exercising jurisdiction over exempt religious a local Ordinary should bear in mind that such persons together with their houses, persons, and things, pertain, as it were, to a territory beyond the limits of his jurisdiction, and that consequently he has power over them only in those cases expressly stated in law.[13]

It should be remarked that pontifical documents show that this same

[9] Cf. Sixtus IV, Bull, *Regimini Universalis Ecclesiae,* par. 9, Aug. 31, 1474; the same Bull was issued in favor of the Friars Minor: see, *Don. Rerum Regul. Prax.,* tr. 13, q. 8; Delbene c. 12, dub. I, sect. III, nn. 14, 15, 16; Lezana, *Summa Quaest. Regul.,* Tom. III, *In Mare Magnum FF. Minorum,* pp. 43 ff.

[10] Cf. Paul III, Const., *Licet,* Oct. 18, 1549; see Inst. S.J., I, Comp. privilegiorum, 211.

[11] Cf. Leo XIII, Const., *Romanos Pontifices,* par. 10, May 8, 1881.

[12] Cf. Leo XIII, Const., *Romanos Pontifices,* par. 7, May 8, 1881.

[13] Cf. Vermeersch, *De Rel.,* II, Suppl. VII; Delbene, c. XII, dub. I, sect. II, 13.

general exemption is enjoyed by exempt congregations, such as the Passionists and Redemptorists.[14]

Ample testimony to the possession of this general exemption by exempt religious may be found in the works of authors treating of this matter.[15]

The following are illustrations:

"Tales Religiosi (exempti) prorsus sunt exempti a jurisdictione Episcoporum. . . . ergo et a legibus eorum in his omnibus quae per sacros canones non sunt excepta."[16]

"Exceptis casibus a jure expressis, nullis praeceptis et constitutionibus Episcopi tenentur Religiosi, si exempti sunt a jurisdictione Episcoporum, qualiter iam fere omnes exempti sunt."[17]

"In dictis monasteriis Regularium, Episcopus sedere non potest pro tribunali nec exercere in ipsis aliquem actum jurisdictionis praeter illos qui expresse et in specie ipsi conceduntur."[18]

IN THE CODE

Canons 500 and 615 contain the common law which shows in clear terms that the exemption of Regulars and other privileged religious is *general*.

Exemption of this sort noticeably restricts the number of cases which may be classed as exceptions. For by its nature, general exemption establishes a legal *presumption* in virtue of which doubtful cases must be interpreted in favor of the exempt religious.[19]

ARTICLE III. EXPRESS CASES OF LIMITATIONS

With the exception of a few liturgical laws, the Code contains all the limitations affecting exemption. It retains, too, the same norm as was formerly in force for determining these limitations, namely, exempt religious are subject to the jurisdiction of the local Ordinary in those cases only which are *expressly* stated in law (cf. cc. 500 and 615).

To determine with accuracy the extent of limitations, we shall endeavor to explain: the meaning of this norm, and its application to the exemption commonly enjoyed by religious and to the special exemptive concessions made to particular institutes.

---

[14] Cf. Rescript, Sept. 21, 1771, ap. ASS, I, p. 97; Pius VI, Const., *Sacrosanctum,* Aug. 21, 1789; Pius VII, Br., *Qui sicut,* Jan. 9, 1807; S.C.EE.RR., Sept. 16, 1864.

[15] Cf. Vermeersch, *De Rel.,* II, Suppl., VII.

[16] Suarez, *De Legibus,* L. IV, c. 20, n. 5.

[17] Leurenius, *Forum Eccl.,* L. I, q. 113.

[18] Delbene, c. XII, dub. I, sect. II, n. 13; see also, Pirhing, L. V, t. 33, nn. 49 ff.; Reiff., L. I, t. 31, n. 89; Schmalz., L. III, t. 33, n. 252; St. Alphonsus, *De Priv.,* 78; De Angelis, L. III, t. 36, pp. 196–197; Santi-Leitner, L. III, t. 36, n. 13; Piat, N.R.T., t. 31, pp. 576 ff.; Wernz, III, 701; Fine, pp. 709–711; Vermeersch, *De Rel.,* I, 365–367.

[19] Cf. Santi-Leitner, L. III, t. 36, n. 13; Vermeersch, *De Rel.,* II, Suppl. VII, I, 365, *De Prohib. et Cens. Libr.,* 64; Suarez, *De Legibus,* VIII, c. 27; Piat, II, p. 7; Melo, p. 9; Larraona, C.p.R., VI, 184.

I. THE MEANING OF THE WORDS "EXPRESS CASES"

The term "expressed" has various significations in law. This can be seen from its usage both before the promulgation of the Code and in the Code itself.

BEFORE THE CODE

To treat this matter summarily, we offer several of the legal significations which Barbosa[20] has collected from various sources. The term "express" may mean:

whatever is signified by the words employed (Ax. 8);

whatever is contained in or can be inferred from the words employed (Ax. 5, 6);

whatever can be drawn from the nature of the terms employed, or what is contained in the general meaning of the terms (Ax. 7);

whatever is virtually contained in the terms, that is, whatever is naturally contained in them, or is a necessary antecedent of the matter treated (Ax. 12);

whatever can be deduced from similar reasoning, etc.

IN THE CODE

The term "expressed" is frequently used in the Code. Consult, v.g., Book I, cc. 2; 4; 5; 6, 1°; 11; 12; 16; 20; 22; 27, § 2; 30; 31; 33, § 2; 36; 40; 42; 46; 48, § 2; 49; 61; 66, § 2; 83, etc.

From a perusal of these canons and the commentaries on them it is readily seen that the term "expressed" often has different meanings in different canons. Its signification, too, in a single canon, is sometimes a matter of controversy.[21]

In general it may be said that terms of law can contain or manifest the lawmaker's intention either *explicitly* or *implicitly*. His intention is *explicit* when it is actually and distinctly, or verbally expressed in the law. His intention is implicit when it is contained in the terms he employs: as an effect in its cause or a conclusion in its premises,[22] or as a part of something is contained in the whole, or as a species in a genus, or as a condition *sine qua non*, that is, whose existence must be admitted in order that a canon or group of canons have a juridical meaning.[23]

---

[20] Barbosa, Tract., *de axiomatibus juris usufrequentioribus Axioma 89*, sub. v, expressum.

[21] For example, there is a diversity of opinion concerning its use in canon 11. Michiels (*Normae Generales*, I, pp. 275 ff.) maintains that "express" in this prescription signifies what is both explicitly and implicitly manifested: Van Hove (*Com. Lov. I*, Tom. II, 161) on the contrary denies that the term "express" or its equivalent includes what is implicitly contained in a law.

[22] Cf. *Epit.*, I, 76.

[23] Cf. Michiels, *Normae Generales*, Vol. I, p. 103.

IN CANON 615

Whether or not the term "expressed" is accepted in general, as meaning an explicit or implicit manifestation of the legislator's intention, in canon 615 it must be taken to mean that cases of limitation to exemption are expressed in an *explicit manner*.

The following reasons warrant this interpretation.

1. Both as a privilege and a law, exemption must be interpreted broadly;[24] hence its norm of limitation must be interpreted strictly. Therefore, "cases expressly stated in law" means in the strict sense cases *verbally* or *explicitly* manifested by law.[25]

When a general law of this favorable type is enacted, any restrictions, exceptions, or limitations of the rights it grants, must be so manifested as to leave no doubt concerning the legislator's intention. If his intention with regard to limitations be doubtful, one must follow his *certain intention* expressed in the general provision. Only *explicitly expressed* limitations can exclude such doubts. Hence, the authority of local Ordinaries over exempt religious may not be extended beyond the cases explicitly expressed in law.[26]

2. This interpretation of the term "express" is that actually employed by Leo XIII in his Constitution, *Romanos Pontifices,* par. 10. He states that Regulars are exempt from the jurisdiction of local Ordinaries, except in the cases expressed "by name," or verbally, in law ("praeterquam in casibus a jure *nominatim expressis"*).

3. The general norm for interpretation, expressed in canon 19, confirms our conclusion.

Limitations of exemption restrict the free exercise of the exempt religious' immunity from the jurisdictional power of local Ordinaries. Any law restricting the free exercise of rights must be strictly interpreted (can. 19). Hence, the norm of limitations, namely, "cases expressly stated in law," signifies only cases explicitly expressed in law.[27]

One cannot, therefore, argue that a case forms an exception to exemption by reasoning from analogy or similitude with cases definitely expressed by law.[28] For such supplemental juridical norms, as provided for in canon 20, may be used only when either general or particular legislative prescriptions covering certain matters *have not been expressed* in law. Canon 615 states that all cases of limitation to exemption must be expressed in law. Hence,

---

[24] Cf. above, Chap. II, Art. III.
[25] Cf. Delbene, C. XIV, d. XIV, nn. 1–6.
[26] Cf. Delbene, C. XIV, dub. XIV, nn. 9, 10.
[27] Cf. Goyeneche, *De Religiosis,* 83, n. IV.
[28] Coronata, I, 623, seems to draw such an inference.

any inferential method employed to prove a limitation to exemption is invalid.

II. APPLICATION OF THE NORM OF LIMITATION

From the meaning of "expressed cases," just explained, it is clear that exemption is limited only in the cases explicitly expressed in law.

Cases expressly stated in law may limit the general exemption acknowledged by canons 500 and 615, or the exemptive rights contained in special grants. In what follows we shall consider express cases of limitation relative to each type of exemption.

A. *Express Limitations Relative to the General Exemption Enjoyed by Regulars and Others*

The Code does not employ uniform terminology in designating the express limitations to general exemption. As a result, it will be seen that although these cases are always explicitly expressed in law, they are not manifested with the same degree of clarity.

1. In practically all cases, terms are used which place the matter of limitation beyond dispute, for the legislator expressely declares that *exempt* persons, places, things, or *Regulars,* or *nuns* are subject to the jurisdiction or vigilance of the local Ordinary. Thus: *exempt persons* or *places* or *things* are designated in canons, 106, 6°; 337, § 1; 496, §§ 1, 3, 4; 512, § 2, 2°, 3°; 552, § 1; 612; 792; 804, § 3; 831, § 3; 874, § 1; 1261, § 2; 1274, § 1; 1293; 1334; 1336; 1343, § 1; 1345; 1356, § 1; 1382; 1579, § 3; 2269, § 2; 2412: *Regulars* are expressly mentioned in canons 295, § 2; 621; 919, § 1; 964, 1°; 1155, § 1; 1169, § 5; 1199, § 2; 1291, § 1; and *nuns* are expressly mentioned in canons 512, § 2, 1°; 533, § 1; 535, § 1, 1°; 603, § 1; 1338, § 2.

2. In several laws, as has been said, the expressed limitations lack the clarity of the cases just cited. Examples of these less explicit restrictions are found in canons 965 and 1162, § 4.

a) Canon 965, taken in conjunction with canons 956, 957, 959, and 964, expressly subjects exempt religious to the diocesan Bishop in the matter of sacred orders.

b) Canon 1162, when explained together with canon 497, expressly requires that exempt religious must obtain the previous consent of the local Ordinary in order to build a church in a definite locality.

3. Cases are sometimes said to be limitations to exemption which in reality do not seem to be explicitly expressed in law.

It would seem that canon 1386 is an instance of this. The canon, which is distinct from those on previous censorship, forbids religious to edit books on secular subjects, or to write in newspapers, magazines, or periodicals, or to assume the direction of the same, without the permission of the local

Ordinary. The general term "religious" is employed, which does not of itself expressly signify "exempt religious."

Although some authors[29] classify this as a limitation of exemption, neither the words nor the context of the law (the law does not refer to matters of faith or morals) seem expressly to include exempt religious. Furthermore, according to the discipline in force prior to the promulgation of the Code, Regulars were exempt in the matter under discussion.[30] Therefore, conformably with canon 6, 4°, it appears that the former interpretation should be followed.

B. *Express Limitations Relative to Special Exemptive Privileges*

Besides general exemption, Regulars and other religious enjoy *special exemptive privileges* which have been obtained by direct concession, communication, custom, or prescription (can. 63).

To determine whether these are abrogated by a limiting expression contained in a law, it is necessary to observe the precise nature of the expression employed.

Two types of limiting expressions are used. The first, which we shall call *generic,* limits general exemption, as we have just seen. It states that local Ordinaries have jurisdiction in certain matters over *even exempt* religious (etiam exemptos) or *Regulars* (Regulares) or *nuns* (moniales) (cf. v.g., cc. 612; 919; 603). The second type, which we shall term *specific,* declares that local Ordinaries have jurisdiction in certain cases even over exempt, *notwithstanding special privileges to the contrary,* or *notwithstanding privileges and customs to the contrary,* etc. (cf. v.g. cc. 876, § 1; 1356, § 1).

Apparently the efficacy of each type of limiting expression is different. Hence, their relationship to special exemptive privileges will be considered separately.

1. Generic Limiting Expressions Relative to Special Exemptive Privileges

Any special exemptive privilege of an exempt institute[31] will of its very nature constitute a right of immunity from the jurisdiction of local Ordinaries, which is over and above those rights established by the general exemption of canons 615 and 500. It follows, therefore, that a privilege of this kind is directly opposed to some express provision of law which restricts the common exemption.

---

[29] Cf. Coronata, II, 955; W.-V., IV, Vol. II, 715; Bondini, pp. 132, 133; Toso, L. II, part. II, can. 615; *Epit.,* I, 775.

[30] Cf. Vermeersch, *De Rel.,* I, 371; Genicot, *Theol. Mor.,* I, 460; Bondini, p. 133; W.-V., IV, Vol. II, 715, nota 35.

[31] It should be noted that we are not concerned in this discussion with rights or privileges possessed by private individuals pertaining to such institutes, but with those had for the benefit of a community or institute as a whole.

Yet the *generic* limiting expression does not abrogate or nullify the specific exemptive privilege opposed to it.

This is true in general of special exemptive privileges obtained either before or after the promulgation of the Code.

Concerning such privileges or rights acquired before the Code, canon 4 states: Acquired rights, and also privileges and indults which up till the present have been granted to physical or moral persons by the Apostolic See, if they are still in use and have not been revoked, remain in their entirety, unless they have been *expressly revoked* by the canons of the Code. Hence, exemptive privileges of the kind herein specified are not revoked by the fact that they are opposed to the legislation of the Code. To effect their cessation, a law of the Code must contain a *specific* abrogatory expression, such as "notwithstanding any privilege to the contrary."[32] Exemptive customs, however, which had been in force at the time of the promulgation of the Code, even though they were immemorial, must be corrected as corruptions of law, if they are expressly *reprobated* by the canons themselves; others which are centenary and immemorial, may be tolerated if Ordinaries, by reason of circumstances of places and persons, judge that they cannot be prudently abolished; the rest are to be considered as suppressed, unless the Code expressly provides otherwise (can. 5).

Special exemptive privileges acquired in any legitimate manner, after the promulgation of the Code, are not limited by contrary canonical provisions (cf. can. 63). Every communication of privileges between religious institutes is henceforth excluded (can. 613).

Proof of the existence of such privileges is required.

Since these privileges are opposed to the express generic limitations of the Code, unless they be notorious, their *existence* must be proven, for derogations of law are odious. Until proof is given, the local Ordinary may exercise that jurisdiction over exempt religious which the Code expressly accords him.[33]

To show the original document or an authentic copy of the same is enough to prove the existence of a privilege. Copies of a privilege found in books of the religious institute, or in its proper Bullarium, should be accepted as sufficient evidence.[34]

Once the existence of a privilege has been established, local Ordinaries may not interefere with or obstruct the free exercise thereof.

The contents of such privileges are subject to broad interpretation. This follows from the fact that exemptive privileges are granted in perpetuity, not for the benefit of individuals but for that of the entire institute (cf.

---

[32] Cf. Cicognani, *Canon Law,* Can. 4 (p. 479).
[33] Concerning the necessity of this proof, cf. Schmalz., V., 33, n. 227, f.; Piat, II, p. 7; ASS, I, p. 97.
[34] Cf. Van Hove, *Com. Lov.,* I, Tom. V, *"De Privilegiis,"* 54.

can. 50). In canonical science privileges of this type are considered equivalent to laws.[35]

2. Specific Limiting Expressions Relative to Special Exemptive Privileges

As stated above, under B, specific limiting expressions occur in law. We shall explain the efficacy of such expressions, and the cases actually contained in the Code.

(A) *The Efficacy of Such Limiting Expressions*

Special exemptive privileges are not revoked unless particular mention of them is made in a law or act of the legislator (cf. cc. 71, 61).[36] Such privileges, as stated above, can be obtained by custom, indult, or acquired right. Each has its own peculiar juridical efficacy and consequently can be revoked only by a clause making specific reference to it. For this reason the Code contains a variety of revocatory expressions, such as: "reprobata qualibet contraria consuetudine et abrogato quolibet contrario privilegio" (can. 1356); "revocata qualibet contraria particulari lege seu privilegio" (can. 876, § 1); "revocato quolibet contrario privilegio" (can. 964, 1°); "revocato quolibet indulto Superioribus concesso" (can. 964, 4°).

Clauses abrogating or derogating *privileges* (cf., v.g., cc. 876, § 1; 2269, § 2) affect those privileges only which have been accorded by a special indult of a superior, for this strict meaning of the term should be applied since limitations to exemption are odious. Hence, clauses of this kind do not affect exemptive privileges obtained through particular law,[37] custom,[38] acquired right,[39] nor those whose revocation is effected only when special mention is made of them.

Clauses derogating *customs* do not affect privileges acquired through custom, those *reprobating* customs (cf. can. 1356) annul such privileges.[40]

To abolish *acquired rights* gained through prescription abrogatory clauses must specifically mention them.

(B) *Cases Limiting Special Exemptive Privileges*

The following cases that limit special exemptive privileges are found in the Code.

---

[35] Cf. Van Hove., *loc. cit.*

[36] Cf. c. 1, *De Constitutionibus*, I, 2 in VI; Mayr, V, 33, n. 160; Suarez, *De Leg. L.*, VIII, c. 39, n. 2; Piat, II, p. 139.

[37] Cf. Michiels, *Normae Generales*, II, p. 393; Van Hove, *Com. Lov.*, I, Tom. V, *De Privil.*, 222.

[38] Cf. Suarez, *De Leg.*, L. VIII, c. 7, n. 15; Wernz, I, 160, II, c.; Michiels, *loc. cit.*; Van Hove, *loc. cit.*

[39] Cf. Van Hove, *loc. cit.*

[40] Cf. Van Hove, *Com. Lov.*, I, Tom. V, 225.

Canon 544, § 2

Male aspirants of *any* institute must furnish testimonial letters from the Ordinary of the place of birth and from the Ordinary of whatever other place in which, after completing their fourteenth year, they have lived for more than a year, morally continuous, *notwithstanding any privilege to the contrary.*

Canon 876, § 1

With the exception of the cases specified in canons 239, § 1, 1°; 522; 523, all priests both secular and religious of whatever grade or office, require a special faculty validly and licitly to hear the confessions of religious women and their novices, *all particular laws or privileges contrary to this prescription being revoked.*

Canon 964, 4°

Every indult accorded superiors to issue to professed of temporary vows dimissorial letters for major orders *is revoked.*

Canon 964, 1°

A governing abbot of Regulars, even though he be not an abbot "nullius," may confer tonsure and minor orders on those who are his subjects by reason of at least simple profession, provided the abbot be a priest and have lawfully received the abbatial blessing. Outside these limits, ordinations conferred by him are invalid, unless the abbot possesses episcopal character, *and all contrary privileges are hereby revoked.*

Canon 1356, § 1

Liable for the seminary tax are all benefices, even those of Regulars, all parishes and quasi-parishes, hospitals erected by ecclesiastical authority, canonically erected sodalities, churches which have their own revenue, and all religious houses even though exempt, unless the religious live solely on alms or have attached to their house a college for pupils or teachers for the purpose of promoting the common welfare of the Church, *all customs contrary to this provision being reprobated* and *all contrary privileges being abrogated.*

CHAPTER XIX

EXPRESS CASES OF LIMITATIONS STATED IN LAW

In the preceding chapter, we endeavored to explain the precise meaning of the norm of limitations; now, by way of conclusion, we offer a list of these express cases.

The arrangement and enumeration of the cases is that formulated by Vermeersch[1] and adoped by other Canonists of note.[2] Several of the cases enumerated by Vermeersch, however, are excluded from the list because, as has been stated in Chapter XVIII, Article I, they are not, strictly speaking, limitations or exceptions to the exemption under consideration.

With respect to this enumeration, it should be remembered that individual institutes enjoy special exemptive privileges which free them from some of the limitations expressed in law.

All cases of limitation, with the exception of a few liturgical cases which will be pointed out, are expressly stated in the canons of the Code.

LIST OF LIMITATIONS

A. Things a local Ordinary can do with relation to exempt religious:

  1. In the churches of exempt religious:

    preach (can. 1343, § 1);

    exercise pontificals (can. 337, § 1);

    administer the sacrament of confirmation (can. 792).

  2. Make a canonical visitation:

    of their churches and public oratories to enforce any special statutes he has enacted concerning divine worship (can. 1261, § 2);

    of their schools (with the exception of those for professed students of the institute), oratories, recreational centers, etc., concerning matters pertaining to religious and moral instruction (can. 1382).[3]

B. Things to be left in the hands of the local Ordinary:

  1. The consecration (not the benediction) of sacred places (can. 1155), bells (can. 1169, § 5), and immovable altars (can. 1199, § 2);

---

[1] Cf. *Epit.*, I, 775.

[2] Cf. W.-V., III, 404; Schäfer, 97.

[3] Cf. AAS, XXII, 49. Canon 1382 contains no revocatory clause. Hence, secondary schools, colleges, and universities conducted by Regulars are not subject to this visitation (cf. above, Chap. XIV, Art. III).

2. Judgments in cases pertaining to the Holy Office (cc. 501, § 2; 1555);
    settlement of controversies between physical or moral persons of different religious institutes (can. 1579, § 3);
    settlement in urgent cases of controversy concerning collegiate precedence (can. 106, 6°).
3. Examination of postulants or sisters before the novitiate and before the profession of both temporary and perpetual vows (can. 552).

C. Things exempt religious must do at the command of the local Ordinary:

1. Recite prayers ordered from a motive of public utility, without prejudice to the privileges and constitutions of each institute (can. 612);
2. Recite collects (or orationes imperatas) prescribed for Mass, and name the Bishop in the canon of the Mass (Liturgical law);
3. Celebrate prescribed sacred solemnities (can. 612);[4]
4. Observe prescriptions concerning the ringing of bells for a public cause, without prejudice to the privileges and constitutions of each institute (can. 612);
5. Give catechetical instruction to the faithful especially in churches of their institute (can. 1334);
6. Give a brief explanation of the Gospel or of Christian doctrine on feast days (can. 1345);
7. Observe prescriptions concerning divine worship (can. 1261);
8. Participate in public processions, according to the provision of cc. 1291, 1292;
9. Observe regulations regarding manual Mass stipends (can. 831);[5]
10. Contribute the seminary tax, unless they live solely by alms, or conduct educational institutions for the common good (can. 1356, § 1);
11. Observe regulations regarding the admission of visiting priests to celebrate Mass in their churches, according to the prescription of can. 804, § 3;
12. Attend diocesan conferences, if the religious has the care of souls, i.e., if he be a pastor or, according to can. 476, § 6 a priest taking his place and helping him in the entire parochial ministry, and others with confessional faculties from the local Ordinary, if no conferences are held in their religious house (can. 131);[6]
13. Major superiors, if invited, must attend Provincial Councils (can. 286, § 4);
14. Observe local interdicts inflicted by the Bishop (can. 2269);

---

[4] Cf. *Per.*, XXI, pp. 38*–43*.
[5] Exempt are not bound by norms of the Bishop regulating founded Masses, cf. can. 1550.
[6] Cod. Com., Feb. 12, 1935, AAS, XXVIII, 92.

D. Things exempt religious cannot do without the intervention or consent of the local Ordinary:

1. Erect a religious house; convert to other uses a house already erected, except the alteration be of such a nature that, without prejudice to the provisions of the foundation, it affects only the internal regime and the religious discipline; build and open an edifice separated from the religious house (can. 497);[7]

2. Erect a church or public oratory in a certain specified place (can. 1162, § 4, and can. 497);

3. Hear confessions of religious women or their novices (can. 876);

4. Preach to nuns subject to them (can. 1338, § 2);

5. Reserve the Blessed Sacrament in the principal oratory of a religious house (can. 1265);

6. Expose the Blessed Sacrament in a monstrance or give Benediction of the Blessed Sacrament exposed in a monstrance (can. 1274, § 1);[8]

7. Place, or cause to be placed, in churches or sacred places unusual images (can. 1279, § 1);

8. Conduct unapproved exercises of piety, including prayers, in churches or public oratories (can. 1259, § 1);

9. Designate the rector of a church not attached to a convent (can. 480, § 2);

10. Divulge new indulgences granted to a church, which have not been promulgated in Rome (can. 919, § 1);[9]

11. Receive holy orders if their own superiors are not competent to ordain (cc. 956–959, 964);

12. Establish pious associations among the faithful (cc. 686, §§ 2–4; 703, § 2);[10] prescribe the uniform which members of pious associations are to wear at sacred functions, or make a change in the uniform (cc. 713, § 2; 714); appoint a member of the secular clergy chaplain or moderator of an association erected in the church of an exempt institute (can. 698).

13. Conduct public processions outside the church, except during the octave of Corpus Christi (can. 1291, § 2);

14. Make the profession of faith (and the abjuration of modernism) as confessors, preachers, and beneficiaries (can. 1406, § 1, 7°);

15. Beg alms, unless they belong to mendicant orders (cc. 621, 622).[11]

As has been explained in Articles I and II of Chapter XVIII, the follow-

---

[7] Cf. AAS, XIV, 554, n. 2.
[8] Cf. Cod. Com., Mar. 6, 1927, III, AAS, 161; *Per.*, XVI, p. 60; E.R., 76, 610.
[9] Cf. S. Poen., Decree, Feb. 22, 1929, AAS, XXI, 200; *Per.*, XVIII, 135.
[10] Cf. AAS, XIII, 135.
[11] Cf. Cod. Com., Oct. 16, 1919, n. 10, AAS, XI, 478; *Per.*, X, 103.

ing canons listed by Vermeersch are not, strictly speaking, limitations of exemption: cc. 1338, § 2; 874; 875; 1385; 1505; 1516; 533, § 1, 4° and § 2; 1386. In practically all these cases exempt religious are subject to the jurisdiction of the local Ordinary but in matters which do not, properly speaking, pertain to the *passive exemption* enjoyed by the religious.

We have also excluded canon 609, § 3, from the list of limitations. The canon contains two provisions, neither of which subjects exempt religious to the *jurisdictional* authority of the local Ordinary.

The legislator declares: *(a)* that superiors should be on guard lest the celebration of divine offices in their own churches be a hindrance to the catechetical instruction or the explanation of the Gospel given in the parochial church. In this no reference is made to jurisdictional power of local Ordinaries. He further states: *(b)* that it pertains to the local Ordinary to decide whether any such hindrance exists. By this right, according to Vermeersch himself,[12] the Ordinary has no repressive power over the rights of the exempt religious or their churches. Therefore, although the religious should abide by his decision, they are not subject to his jurisdictional power.

---

[12] Cf. *Epit.*, I, 697.

GENERAL INDEX

ABBOT,
governing, blessing of, 71; power to confer orders, 71; privilege of pontificating, 71
ABBOT primate,
judicial power of, 38
jurisdiction of, 30
ABBOT or prelate "nullius,"
jurisdiction of, 4
ACCOUNT to be given,
by nuns, of administration, 263; of administration of property, 74
of administration of parish, 260
of administration of temporal goods, 258
of funds left in trust for church of place or diocese, 262
of parish investments, 262
of pious foundations, 265
of pious foundations of confraternities, 267
to Holy See about state of institute, 79
to local Ordinary, of temporal goods of associations, 86
ACQUISITION and ownership,
authority of Roman Pontiff over rights of, 241
by industry of religious, 245
by moral persons of religious institutes, 240–248
by pastor, as usufructuary, 245
rights of institutes, provinces, houses, 241 f.
rights of moral persons, 240–242
usurpation or alienation of rights of, 242
ways of acquiring temporal goods, 242–248
ADMINISTRATION of temporal goods,
by nuns, defective account of, 263
extraordinary, 256–258
laws on, 252–267
meaning of expression, 252
ordinary, 252–256; after profession, 253; before profession, 253; exemption of religious in, 252; investments, 254–256; meaning of, 252; of alms for building, maintenance, restoration, of religious parish, 254; of moral persons, 253–256; of parishes, 253 f.; of property of individuals, 252 f.
AGGREGATION of associations, for participation in indulgences, 83
ALIENATIONS,
by nuns, 74, 257
canonical measures on, 257
contrary to law, punishable, 258
debts or obligations not included under, 257

meaning of term, 256
of burial places, 149
requiring apostolic indult, 257
ALMS-SEEKING, see Begging
ALTAR, of parish subject to visitation, 121
ALTARS,
canonical provisions on, 144–147
change of title of, 146
dedication of, 145 f.
erection of, 144
exemption of, 144
faculties for consecration of, by local Ordinaries in the United States, 198
fixed and portable, 145
loss of consecration, 145
privilege of portable, 146 f.
privileged, 181
reconsecration of, 145 f.
APOSTATES from religion,
excommunication of, 31
funeral services of, 150
unlawfully absent from house, 50
ARCHCONFRATERNITIES, privileges of, 11
ARCHCONFRATERNITIES and Primary Unions,
aggregation to, 92
meaning of terms, 91
ASSOCIATIONS of the faithful,
attitude of Holy See on, 81
cessation of, 88 f.
constituted after manner of an organic body, 84
convocation of meetings, 87
dismissal of members of, 86
erection of, 82–84
funds not to be diverted, 86
general norms regarding, 82–89
government of, 85
internal government of, 86–88
meaning of, 81 f.
moderators and chaplains of, 87 f.
moral persons, 82
particular kinds, 89–92
status of exempt religious regarding, 81–92
statutes of, emendation in, 85; examination and approval of local Ordinary, 84 f.
suppression of, 88 f.
temporal goods of, 85 f.
AUGUSTINIANS,
how classified, 65
privilege of exemption, 8
privilege regarding Holy Orders, 186

INDEX OF CANONS